COMMUNITY DISORDER
and
POLICING

Conflict Management in Action

COMMUNITY DISORDERS and POLICING

Conflict Management in Action

EDITED BY
TONY F MARSHALL
ON BEHALF OF
THE FORUM FOR INITIATIVES IN REPARATION AND MEDIATION
(NOW MEDIATION, UK)

WHITING & BIRCH
LONDON
MCMXCII

© The Forum for Initiatives in Reparation and Mediation

All rights reserved. No reproduction, copy or transmission of this publication may be made without written permission from the publishers.

Published by Whiting & Birch Ltd, PO Box 872, London SE23 3HL.
United Kingdom
London 1992

British Library Cataloguing in Publication Data
A CIP catalogue record is available from the British Library

ISBN 1 871177 25 1 (casebound)
ISBN 1 871177 26 X (limp)

All royalties from this publication are contributed to the Forum for Initiatives in Reparation and Mediation, which is a registered charity (no. 297204). FIRM is a voluntary organisation whose members are involved in mediation or conflict resolution training, or are interested in promoting constructive conflict management. FIRM provides up-to-date information about conflict resolution, assists and advises groups wishing to start new mediation initiatives, promotes the use of non-confrontational and non-violent techniques, and attempts to influence social policy generally in the direction of creative problem-solving and conciliation. FIRM is located in Bristol, England. Tel: 0272 241234.

Printed in the United Kingdom by Short Run Press, Exeter

ACKNOWLEDGEMENTS

I am grateful for the opportunity provided by FIRM for compiling this collection on their behalf. Although it was my own initiative, and the overall contents, shape and conclusions are all my own responsibility, I have received encouragement and support from all those in FIRM who saw that these things needed to be said. So much is heard from those who denigrate certain ethnic or poor communities as fomentors of trouble, or from those who blame the police and other officials for all our ills, that it seemed to be not only timely but urgent to publish the voices of those who are actively working for better relations and improved social conditions, and who are in touch with the complexity of real situations, where everyone is, if truth be told, at a loss and no-one entirely to be blamed. FIRM, in its promotion of skilled mediation and conflict resolution, is the appropriate body to represent that less shrill, moderate voice that maintains our common responsibility and the need to proceed without rancour, through active understanding and cooperative endeavour.

I am also grateful to all the contributors to this collection, who have spent time and effort getting their ideas into shape, despite being busy with more practical things. I am especially grateful that their efforts were so well composed that I have, as editor, had a very easy ride. I would also like to thank Sean Creighton for sending me the Consultative Group report used for Chapter 4, and Nigel Yeo, of Management Training and Development, Metropolitan Police, Hendon, who helped with three of the papers in Section III. Our thanks, too, to the American Academy of Political and Social Science, the Society of Professionals in Dispute Resolution, and the Mennonite Conciliation Service for allowing us to reproduce Chapters 11, 13 and 14 respectively.

More generally, I have benefited enormously from many discussions on this topic with Ian Beckett, Jonathan Gosling and Tim Newburn. But most of all I would like to give credit to all those who are working in the field to develop the effectiveness and public acceptance of the techniques of non-violence and conflict resolution, for it is through their practical efforts that this volume has been possible. I hope their reward will be that, through these writings, their work will become better known and understood and that they will receive the support and encouragement that is their due.

TONY F MARSHALL
March 1992

CONTENTS

Acknowledgements	v
Preface	ix
Introduction	xi

Section I: Theory — 1
1. Theories of Violence and Principles of Conflict Management
 (Tony F. Marshall) — 3
2. Conflict Theories, Government Policies and the Urban Riots of the Early 1980s
 (Sir Christopher Leeds) — 25

Section II: The Community View — 39
3. Taking a Stand for Non-Violence
 (Jim Murtagh) — 43
4. The Brixton Disorders of 1985
 (Community/Police Consultative Group for Lambeth) — 53
5. Conflict Within the Community: An Opportunity
 (Greta Brooks) — 73
6. Policing the Poor: Conciliation or Confrontation?
 (Yvonne Craig) — 77

Section III: The Police Response — 87
7. Brixton SW9: Post-Conflict Policing
 (Commander Alec Marnoch) — 93
8. The Notting Hill Carnival: An Exercise in Conflict Resolution
 (Commander Larry Roach) — 101
9. Crowd Control: Are There Alternatives to Violence?
 (Sally Sadler) — 107
10. Conflict Management in the Police: A Policing Strategy for Public Order
 (Chief Supt. Ian Beckett) — 129

Section IV: The Mediators - United States — 141
11. The Citizens' Role in Justice
 (Raymond Shonholtz) — 145

12. Police-community Mediation in the United States: The Department of Justice Community Relations Service *(Tim Newburn)*	*159*
13. Triggering Incidents for Racial Conflict *(Wallace Warfield)*	*169*
14. Creating Space for Dialogue *(Ron Claassen)*	*175*
15. Negotiating and Mediating in Stressful Situations *(Maria R Volpe & Robert J Louden)*	*183*

Section V: The Mediators - Great Britain *191*

16. Letting Young People Have Their Say *(David Ward)*	*195*
17. Conflict, Change and the Police: Experiences in the Borough of Newham *(Pauline Obee)*	*209*
18. Learning From the Community: Facilitated Police-Community Workshops at the Local Level *(Robin Oakley)*	*217*
19. Managing Aggressive Behaviour: A Workshop *(Pat Sawyer)*	*229*

Section VI: Opening the Door (*Tony F Marshall*) *237*

20. The Analysis of Social Conflict	*239*
21. Crisis Intervention	*249*
22. Post-Crisis Intervention and Prevention	*263*
23. Conclusions	*291*
Notes on the Contributors	*299*
Index	*303*

PREFACE

Community policing is a vague phrase that has become a vogue one. Inside police circles, it is too often seen as a soft option, a cul de sac in which officers near retirement are parked, with a small budget and a great deal of lip service. Even as it grows fashionable in police circles to restore 'good relations with the community' and put more bobbies back on the beat, many sceptics on both sides of the thin blue line ask what these officers are expected to do that is different from walking the beat and talking to people, as any decent copper has always done. They ask what effect will community policing have on the issues that dominate the headlines regularly - rising crime figures, drug abuse, and the regular outbreaks of public disorder.

This book addresses those questions in a serious, broad-ranging and pragmatic way. It takes the idea of community and policing on to a plane where the two can actually meet, and help one another. That is the first hurdle, for community policemen themselves often find themselves losing the trust of their colleagues the more they gain the trust of the community.

In reality, their interests should be complementary, not antithetical. Quite apart from their dominant role in crime prevention and the maintenance of law and order, the public also provide the necessary information on the vast majority of cases which lead to prosecutions and convictions. This flies in the face of police mythology, both inside the force, where community policing is not seen as 'real coppering' and in the mythology of police fiction, in which detectives brilliantly deduce who dunnit in appropriately heroic or anti-heroic style. That clearups are only a small proportion of the estimated total crimes only reinforces the limitation on the police role in fighting crime.

Conventional policing is equally inadequate to the task of conflict resolution - ranging from domestic to full scale public order problems. The police in their fire fighting mode are singularly inappropriate agents of peace and understanding. The community itself needs to play the leading role in dealing with conflicts, but understanding police officers, acting in a thoughtful, considered way can promote non-violent solutions or at least accommodations between conflicting parties. It is clearly in the interests of all parties that they should do so.

Classical policing is about conflict resolution. Old-style bobbies walked slowly to a fight, hoping it would end before they arrived. But fights prevented are less the stuff of canteen sagas than fights stopped or won. Since the arrival of personal radios and patrol cars, macho officers rush into neighbouring areas in hopes of joining in. The late John Duke, Chief Constable of Hampshire used to call it the 'honeypot syndrome' and made it a disciplinary offence.

So too with riots, where adrenalin surges through the veins of everyone on the scene, including those officers sent to quell the disturbance. The longer they are kept pent up in vans before moving in to 'knock heads together' the more often they unwittingly make it worse before making it better.

We and they need to pay due respect for the cunning, skill and courage needed to mediate and defuse conflict situations long before they reach boiling point. This respect must be part of the new ethos of the police if real change is to be achieved in the canteen culture, where hard policing still holds sway against the soft.

This involves a wider grasp of community dynamics. There is no such thing as a single homogeneous community. Community relations officers in inner city areas like Islington have to deal with as many as eighty different language groups, not to mention the differences in politics, religion, and sexual orientation. Each interest group can either be a source of support or disturbance, depending on how they see themselves in relation to the rest.

The so-called black community, for example, in the Brixton riots described by Alec Marnoch, was actually deeply divided between themselves, both between generations, and in relation to the law-abiding and the minority of less law-abiding youth. They were more united by their mistrust of the police than by a sense of common interest.

Within Afro-Caribbean and Asian communities, the differences can be many and intense. The uneven history and recent success of the Notting Hill Carnival where so many groups come together under intense conditions for three days is a prime example: crude policing can escalate small problems into big ones, while discreet policing aimed at conflict resolution can promote an atmosphere of tolerance in a potentially volatile situation.

Ultimately, conflict resolution is a long term matter, in which notions of equity, fairness, and community justice must be developed by all the groups involved. The police role in promoting community justice requires them to see law and order in a new perspective, not just as a lull in which the radio is quiet, but as a consummation devoutly to be wished.

This book should play a key role in articulating the principles which underpin community justice. The commitment of MEDIATION UK to constructive conflict resolution is a needed antidote to the cries for punishment emanating from Fleet Street, Parliament, and parts of the Home Office over the last decade.

Now the all too evident failures of the criminal justice system to achieve law and order through punishment make the principles of conflict resolution described in the book most timely. The new Criminal Justice Act promotes the idea of justice in the community. It is part of a number of growing efforts to take the pressure off the police and prisons to do the impossible. This book should become a handbook to all those who wish to seize the opportunity it provides to make the rhetoric a reality.

ROGER GRAEF
London, March 1992

INTRODUCTION

This is not an academic book. Although it uses insights from what can loosely be termed "conflict resolution theory", or "CR" as it has come to be called for short, that theory has itself arisen out of practice rather than armchair speculation. The informing belief behind this book is that progress in social policies will only come from a free interchange between theoretical development and practical experience. The former needs to remain open to the complexity and "messiness" of the real world, not retreating to ivory towers for the sake of an academic "purity" that may be aesthetically neat but is ultimately sterile. At the same time, the latter needs to proceed by reflection and self-criticism, itself avoiding the corresponding danger of ossification and inflexible adherence to "rules" of operation. Good practice must have a sound philosophy, just as good philosophy must be demonstrable in effective practice.

Some of the contributors to this book are "academics", but all have had practical involvement in putting their ideas into effect. The majority of the contributors, however, are social activists, CR practitioners, or other professionals involved in grass-roots pioneering work. That they share certain concerns and certain visions, that each is very much concerned to reflect on that experience and re-examine those visions, is the link that puts all the writers on a par, whether they are writing from the point of view of the police, a local community, or some other stance.

All the contributions to this book are tentative. They are the working through of ideas, experiences and practices that are new and experimental. They do not represent a completed project - a set of "ten easy steps" to the eradication of violence and public disorder. They do represent, however, a conception of where social policy needs to be headed in the next decades. They represent a trend that is inevitable if we are ever as a society to be in control of our destiny - or, rather, in control of how we are to progress towards whatever destiny may be in store - and not to be bulldozed under the wheels of history in some disaster that we can only watch and not guide. It is not sufficient to say that we are, after all, only animals with instincts and passions, and that therefore our history can only be a matter of "territorial imperatives" and the acting out of aggressions. We know that this is not inevitable, that most, if not all, of us, given the proper social conditions for generating self-respect, can act with higher motives and more rationality than that. The ideas behind CR - collaboration, openness, creativity - are necessary to our survival as a species. They are both rational as a basis for social organisation and fitted as an evolutionary principle. Their application to all areas of social policy thinking is crucial if we are to prove that we can live like human beings. There is hope at present in the evidence, from across the world, that people are no longer dominated ideologically by traditions that deny them their rights. In that same yearning for freedom (which can only be relative not absolute) there are, unfortunately, also the seeds of future conflicts. The test is whether that conflict can be handled in such a way as to lead to better forms of government, community and citizenship, or whether it will be allowed to destroy the very hopes that inspired it and lead to another generation of dictatorships and repressions.

The history of the world is a history of conflict, and this will always be so. It has also been a history of violence, but this need not always be so. This book is about the possibility of a non-violent future.

I am passing, however, well beyond the boundaries of the book, which focuses on one specific area of application of CR principles, albeit a crucial one - the field of public disorder, whether it is manifested in a multitude of individual quarrels that threaten to disrupt some communities, or in confrontations between major social groups, such as different racial groups or between, say, young people and the police. As the statutory agency given the main role in keeping order - from crisis intervention in domestic fights to the control of demonstrations and riots - the police are central to any consideration of social policy in this area. In their attempts at keeping the peace they inevitably become parties to the conflict themselves. How they react to these terrible pressures and how others react to their behaviour is crucial to the natural history of conflict-riven communities, particularly in our inner cities, and ultimately to the evolution of our whole society. While the police have a central role to play, they cannot be saddled with the whole responsibility, which lies much more with the rest of us. One agency can only police a dominant morality, can only have the power to control the marginal deviants. If we as citizens act as a whole in a violent, a confrontational, an intolerant, a discriminatory way, then there is nothing any number of police, however well trained, however purely motivated, can do to prevent a violent, confrontational, intolerant and discriminatory society. Nothing, that is, to prevent the conflagration when it comes, somewhere, sometime. If there is one simple message from this book as a whole it is this: that we can only achieve peace in our communities, and the eradication of fear, by working together -

Introduction

citizens, police and policy-makers - affirming and encouraging each other to act according to civilised principles. Fear makes us act irrationally. Fear makes us violent. We can only work against violence by ensuring that others do not fear us. Their violence is our responsibility.

❦

As editor I have applied a light touch. Each contributor has been allowed to convey their own message in the style and manner with which they most felt at ease. The cohesion of the volume as a whole comes from the selection of contributors - all of which were known to share a belief in the fundamental principles of CR, whether or not they see themselves as advocates of these and whether or not they have even conceived themselves to be part of any such movement. I have, however, tried to bring out the commonalities in introductory and linking passages, while a final concluding section tries to draw out what has been learned so far, list some of the criticisms, and generate an outline for future progress. Much of this last section will no doubt be overturned by further experience, but the intention of this book is to ensure that we do at least gain such further experience by stimulating others to follow the leads provided here - wherever they will go.

The plan of the book is simple. The first section deals with the basic ideas. The second provides some views, from community residents (in Manchester and London), of violence and public disorder, and of the police reactions to these that they have witnessed. These views are critical but they are not destructive: they are attempts to understand what happened in a rational way, without preconceptions and without applying blame. The third section provides an account of some recent police policies in London that attempt to deal with problems encountered in the past in a more constructive way. It also provides a picture of police methods in other European countries.

The next two sections are written from the point of view of the uninvolved "neutral" - mediators, trainers, academics etc. The first five contributions are about developments in the United States, where CR and mediation are more institutionalised than they are as yet in this country. The next four chapters all deal with British initiatives, both in the form of mediation and training for handling conflict. The concluding section attempts to draw together some of the lessons from all the contributions and point some ways forward, but the views expressed are my own and are not necessarily to be attributed to FIRM (now Mediation UK) or the other authors.

The boundaries between the sections are not rigid, but they do serve to encapsulate the basic theory that views that are traditionally seen as opposed (at least in our inner-city trouble-spots) - the police and the community - can be synthesised into a system where the one works with the other cooperatively - albeit assertively and critically - for ends which benefit all.

TONY F MARSHALL

SECTION I:

THEORY

In Chapter I we look at theories of violence. Despite the large number of distinct ideas represented in the academic literature on the causes of violent behavour, virtually all of them agree on the importance of individual and social reactions to aggression. Whatever other contributory factors there might be, the many empirical studies have clearly shown that a major cause of violence actually manifesting itself, rather than remaining latent, is the way societies behave towards individuals or groups that are showing aggressive tendencies. In practical terms, the theories converge on the need to manage violence in a rational manner and to employ techniques for de-escalating its intensity.

This is not, however, a simple prescription for peace. Just as individuals are biologically programmed to react to threats to their survival with a rush of adrenalin and instinctive "flight" or "fight" responses (see also Chapter 19), so societies are also prone, although for different reasons, to react with threats to order and stability by analogous non-rational impulses either to isolate and ignore (cf. imprisonment of violent offenders) or to hit out and destroy. The theory of "constructive conflict resolution" integrates what we know about the way violence develops into a coherent theory of immediate practical import on how to control and manage such violence in the most effective way. It leads to the definition of a series of skills that may be learned and applied by anyone who may at some time be faced with making a decision in the face of a threat of aggression - and that is, literally, anyone. The rest of the book is a working through of these ideas in the light of real grounded experience.

Chapter 2 examines the ideas that have been put forward for the cause of the race-related riots that occurred in the sixties in America and in the early eighties in Britain, with a particular focus on the latter. Again the theory of conflict resolution is found to provide the fullest explanation of such disorders (as distinct from explanations of the community frustrations underlying them, the major responsibility for which Chris Leeds ascribes to government policies), and this is borne out by more pragmatic discussions of similar disorders in

Britain and America in chapters 4, 5, 7, 12 and 13. The conclusions of the study of riots are therefore in complete alignment with those of Chapter 1 on the study of violence generally, individual and social. In particular, Chris Leeds makes the telling distinction between "negative" and "positive" peace - between bottling up frustrations (by the use of overwhelming force to quell their outward manifestations, for instance) and a realistic attempt to deal not only with the violence but also with the underlying reasons for it. The first leaves the situation ripe to explode (at many times the original magnitude) at some later - unpredictable - time; the second is a rational approach to restoring positive relationships and eliminating the need for aggression.

Chapter One

Theories of Violence and the Principles of Conflict Management

TONY F MARSHALL

Introduction

VIOLENCE, LIKE sex, is one of those phenomena to which we tend to react in an instinctive knee-jerk way. Yet, whether it is interpersonal violence or a social problem of community disorder, it is just such a response which is not only most likely to be ineffective but even encourages the problem to continue and to escalate. Violence feeds on irrationality. It is one of the principles of conflict management theory (as will be seen in the third section of this chapter) that problems of conflict must be approached in a rational frame of mind. Violence can only be tackled if it is also understood, understood not only in others but also in ourselves. For the way we habitually respond to violence is itself a reflection of the violence we carry with us as our biological inheritance. When the murder of a police officer or a young child is greeted with fervent calls for capital punishment, "a life for a life", one can see this violence on the surface. It is a well-honed response underscored by millennia of evolution as a successful strategy for physical survival in a dog-eat-dog world, but when it is turned within the species it becomes self-destructive in a way to which the human animal seems uniquely prone. And we pride ourselves on being the "brains" of the outfit, the rational self-conscious pinnacle of development! We have discovered much with which to exploit and even devastate the world about us, but we have discovered precious little about ourselves. Or if we have discovered anything, we do not seem to be putting it into practice.

In the next section of this chapter I will seek to outline what we have achieved in trying to come to an understanding of violence, so that the problem can be approached in a systematic, analytical way. Of course, understanding the violence is not enough; we also need to understand how best to deal with it, and that will be the subject of the remaining sections of the paper, and indeed of the whole book itself.

For the purpose of this paper, "violence" is defined as:

(a) a human act
(b) causing injury or discomfort to, or coercing behaviour by,
(c) another person
(d) with the intention of so doing
(e) in circumstances where such an act is held to be illegitimate.

This cumbersome definition is necessary in order to make clear that the following are excluded: attacks by animals or of diseases; mere "show" of violence or empty threats; harm to animals, property or the environment; accidents or negligence (eg traffic fatalities); and acts of war or acts by agents of the state necessary to the survival of the nation or maintenance of order within (including chastisement of children by parents or teachers). All these have at some time been treated as problems of violence, but need to be separated from the central topics considered here because of their distinct nature. The first three elements of the definition are more or less objective: the fourth must be inferred, but "intention" is used here in the widest possible sense to include not only conscious purpose but also internal urges; the fifth element depends entirely on the perspective of particular social groups, which vitiates any attempt to obtain total agreement on what constitutes violence (ie illegitimate). Actions by agents of the state, such as the police, that are acceptable to some groups, may be seen as excessively violent by others, or their right to use coercion at all questioned by those who do not recognise the legitimacy of state intervention in the events in question (eg demonstrations, strikes). Most of the works examined here implicitly assume a definition of legitimacy grounded in the dominant social norms, but this cannot be accepted as a proper solution in that it provides no way of seeing, say, the actions of authoritarian governments or police-states as abuses of power. There is no ultimate solution short of allowing all possible views on legitimacy equal status. Nevertheless, harmful acts do not become "violent" until they are seen as illegitimate in the eyes of someone.

Despite the elaborate definition, the violence considered here is far from unitary, ranging from psychopathic assaults to fights, hooliganism, wife battering, child-abuse, rape, robbery, terrorism, police brutality, and so on. It is not to be expected that one theory will explain such diverse phenomena (cf. Tutt, 1976).

No attempt is made in this paper to describe the various types of violence, except insofar as these relate to the theories under review, nor to present empirical evidence on the incidence of violence and its change over time. It should, however, be noted that there is no unequivocal evidence that present times are more or less violent than any other. Many writers have referred to the "normality" of violence as a feature of social history that seems to recur in all eras and all societies. (Cf. Campbell, 1976; Robottom, 1976; Pearson, 1983; Newson & Newson, 1976; Tilly, 1979; and Brown, 1975.)

Theories of Violence

Instrumental

The bulk of theory is dedicated to those influences, internal or external, that lead people (unreasoningly, it is assumed) into violence. Perhaps the most under-studied aspect of violence, within the social sciences at least, is of its deliberate use as an instrument for the attainment of personal or social ends, for instance by terrorists or organised criminals. Such rational- economic uses of violence have been the subject of political philosophy rather than sociology or psychology. One particularly thinks of certain Marxist philosophers such as Sorel (1908), who advocated violence as the only feasible means of achieving social change, or Sartre (1960), for whom violence is the only truly liberating means of self-expression.

Both Marx (1976) and Frank (1976) have independently put forward the theory that "trouble" may be caused by those with grievances or personal needs in order to bring the attention of others to their plight and hence to engage their cooperation in its solution. To be effective the violence must be sufficient to make others react but sufficiently limited ("restrained loss of control" - Marx) not to alienate their sympathy. Normally observers respond in an equally restrained and solicitous way and restore peace, but an inappropriate over-aggressive response may escalate the violence beyond that which either party desires.

French and Raven (1959) and Tedeschi (1983) point out that aggression is in fact often effective in competition for scarce rewards. Clutterbuck (1980) also describes the exploitation of general grievances by political activists like the IRA or the National Front. Empirical research by Gurr (1979), however, concludes that the use of force is only successful for those purposes which command extensive popular support, and that otherwise terror is counter- productive, and Rubenstein (1988) argues that, although at times it may appear that violence is successful in getting the voice of disadvantaged groups heard and achieving needed reforms, successes tend to be short-run and cosmetic, limited to the advancement of a few leaders rather than the group as a whole. Violence, then, is seldom an efficacious method of resolving grievances, except insofar as powerful groups are ready to make concessions that do not threaten the political hierarchy. In any case, the use of violence raises the emotional temper of a conflict, so that any short-term gains have to be weighed against the longer term loss of trust and desires for later revenge likely to stored up for later expression. Violence, at most, can lead to the repression of a problem, never to a solution.

Biological

Tournier (1978) has developed a philosophy of aggression as a natural force which is both normal and healthy, if used constructively. He argues that persons in authority have more resources for the use of force, but that such recourse calls forth violent reactions in others, so that with authority or power goes an obligation of restraint in the interests of social order. Even in the interests of justice, the use of force should be kept to the minimum. Ethologists have shown, even if aggression is a genetic trait, that it is called forth largely by other external factors (see Craig, 1928). Eliciting factors, according to Marler (1976) are primarily (a) proximity of a competitor, (b) lack of relationship to a competitor ("stranger"), and (c) aggressive behaviour on the part of the competitor. Marler particularly develops the potential of the second of these as a means of preventing violence - ie enhancing familiarity. This would be achieved by promoting social and community ties between individuals or groups likely to come into contact or competition.

A particularly fruitful observation of ethologists is of the frequency among animals of the use of
as a means of avoiding or de-escalating harmful encounters (see Marler 1976, and Fox, 1982). Going even further, de Waal's (1989) studies of non-human primates lead him to argue that strong and effective instincts for peacemaking have evolved in close association with competitive and aggressive behaviours, at least among social animals. Fights within the group are followed by reconciliation - among chimpanzees literally by "kissing and making up" - and chimpanzee females will sometimes act as mediators, leading reluctant combatants to reconciliation. Social anthropologists, most notably Max Gluckman (1963), have also shown similar mechanisms of ritualised aggression in long established stable human societies, and mediation has a length of tradition and a breadth of universality in the same circumstances that has been well documented (eg Gulliver, 1977). Recently British sociologists have found similar mechanisms operating in our own society that lessen the injurious impact of what may on the surface - or to outsiders - seem very threatening indeed. Mungham (1977) has observed this in relation to pub and club scuffles and among youth gangs in inner city areas. He observes that while public violence of this kind seems a big problem, its effects are usually very limited. The invisibility and seeming harmony of private domestic life may obscure a problem of family violence that may be far less restrained for that very reason (eg child abuse). Marsh et al (1977) have made similar observations in relation to football hooliganism, which the researchers view as

Social Psychological Theories

THE FRUSTRATION HYPOTHESIS

Based on early writings of Freud, Dollard et al (1939) developed the very influential theory that the experience of frustration causes an emotional reaction (anger) which predisposes the individual to aggression, although the expression of this in concrete action may be inhibited by situational features. A more recent exponent of this theory is Berkowitz (1962), who has elaborated the psychological factors which affect tolerance of frustration (from genetic features to family relationships) and whether the consequent aggressiveness is acted out (such as past reinforcement of aggressive and other behaviour, and internalisation of moral standards). Empirical research has seemed to show that "perceived intentionality" of the agent of frustration, rather than the degree of frustration itself, elicits aggression. In other words, if one blames someone else for one's predicament one is more likely to act aggressively than if one blames oneself or regards the situation as unavoidable. This argument forms the basis of Ferguson and Rule's (1983) "attribution theory". More recently, in response to many demonstrations of the salience of social factors in explaining violence, Berkowitz (1982) has argued that the frustration/aggression theory fits individual acts of violence rather than those committed in a group context. Even so, the theory has, despite a certain apparent plausibility, been criticised for the basic ambiguity of the concept of "frustration", which tends to be defined in terms of whether it results in aggression and therefore makes for a circular argument, and also because other emotional reactions to frustration seem to be equally likely, such as fear leading to avoidance reactions.

SOCIAL LEARNING THEORY

Another influential social psychological theory is that of Bandura (1973). He argues that individuals learn response patterns through socialisation, are stimulated by social forces to enact them, and receive positive or negative reinforcement according to social norms. Thus some social situations will be conducive to repressing aggression and others will encourage it. Experiences may alter over time, so that it is a dynamic theory. It is of particular interest that Bandura's theory leads to completely opposite predictions to those on the basis of Lorenz's in relation to catharsis: for Bandura, the regular channelling of aggression into specific activities would positively reinforce such a response and encourage its expression more generally. One social observation which seems to support Bandura in this respect is the problem of post-war adjustment to normal social life among soldiers habituated to living with violence, a problem which has been particularly marked among American Vietnam veterans, who were specifically trained to act and react with extreme aggression. Another supporting piece of evidence is the tendency for abused children when grown up to abuse their own families, or indeed for any kind of physical punishment on a systematic basic to tend to legitimise violence in the eyes of the sufferers (Maurer, 1974). On the basis of this theory, Goldstein (1983) advocates "prosocial" teaching. ".....techniques and materials exist ...... for teaching the following: moral reasoning abilities to typical school children, self-control and reflectiveness to impulsive children, and constructive problem-solving methods to disruptive pre-adolescents. They are also being employed to teach aggressive adolescents the means for resisting peer group pressure and for responding constructively to failure. In addition, prosocial teaching techniques can be used to help develop parenting skills among child-abusing parents, to foster communication skills among argumentative couples, to promote negotiation and other conflict- management behaviours among adult prisoners and to nurture family dispute resolution skills among police and so on". (More on these activities will be learned in the course of subsequent chapters of this book.)

INTERACTION PROCESSES

The preceding theories have taken the aggressor as the subject of study. A major step forward was taken, however, in the fifties, when Marvin Wolfgang, an American criminologist, wrote a seminal paper (1957) that focused as much on the victim as on the offender. Very often empirical studies of murder and assault have discovered that the victim and offender already know one another, frequently quite intimately, that there was in many cases a history of conflict and aggression by both parties, and that the victim sometimes directly precipitated or evoked the offender's wrath. To understand such violence it was not sufficient to look at the offender. As Toch (1969) wrote subsequently "To understand violence it is necessary to focus on the chain of interactions between aggressor and victim, on the sequence that begins when two people encounter each other - and which ends when one harms, or even destroys, the other."

This is especially so for violence within the family. As Straus (1973) showed, domestic violence is a product not of individual pathology, but of the way in which family members react to each other, by escalating or suppressing expressions of violence. But this approach is relevant to many more situations besides the family - Curtis, in 1974, found that by far the most common cause of murder or serious assault in the United States was minor altercations between acquaintances or neighbours (around a third of all such offences). Comparisons with other countries, admittedly on the basis of somewhat dubious data, led him to put forward the hypothesis that minor disputes lead to murder in urbanised Western societies more often than they do elsewhere. For some reason it seems that our society is less well adapted to the settlement of petty quarrels before they escalate to criminal violence. Observations of pub violence in this country also led Marsh (1980) to stress the importance of how the landlord interacts with drunken or troublesome customers for whether the incipient trouble develops into violence or not. This perspective has led Howells (1976) to advocate social skills instruction for violent offenders to enable them to handle conflict without escalating it. Imprisonment, he argues, only enhances their problems by isolating them from the experience of normal relations with others.

The same ideas can be applied to group disorders: insensitive management may lead to unnecessary violence. Lea and Young (1984) have argued that the natural basis for policing, as they term it "consensus policing", is a good relationship with the local community, whereby information, help and understanding pass both ways. In some inner city areas, however, this relationship has broken down and the police come to rely on a different style of policing that Lea and Young denominate as "military". This style is based on confrontation and distrust, which leads police-community relations into a "vicious circle" of increasing distance, alienation and misunderstanding. In such circumstances incipient disorder may more easily escalate into overt violence. The Scarman Report (1982) seems to confirm this view as far as one of the causes of the Brixton riots is concerned, and a paper by Paul Cooper (1985) notes that at the time of the 1981 Toxteth riots, the local police were stressing policing by "coercion" rather than "consent". Others have also been of the opinion that actions by the police have been implicated in the escalation (as against the instigation) of violence in the case of the miners' strike, recent "Stonehenge" clashes with hippy convoys and the Hillfields football stadium disaster in Sheffield.

SELF-ESTEEM THEORIES

A special sub-set of "interaction process" theories emphasise the role that self-esteem may play in promoting escalation of conflict. In 1965, Short and Strodtbeck described violence among American youth gangs as arising from perceived threats to their self-esteem. Toch (1969) took this idea further by arguing that such violence may not only arise simply in defence against a threat but that some individuals ("self-image promoters") may precipitate violence in order to demonstrate their power and enhance their self-esteem. (Also see Lofland, 1969.) The problem may occur even beyond gangs in more everyday encounters:

> Interpersonal conflict is inherent in social life. Open expression of disagreement and animosity are often interpreted as attacks on self that call forth a similar response from the person attacked and thereby produce an aggressive encounter ...... persons may retaliate in order to maintain a favourable situational identity when they perceive they are being attacked. (Felson, 1978)

Such behaviour is not particularly "rational", as Berkowitz (1978) has pointed out, being mediated by emotions such as anger, and is therefore not necessarily effective in raising other people's respect, but the subjective nature of self-esteem is such that an individual may feel that it is being preserved by the very act of defending it. This approach has been applied to football hooliganism by Murray (1977), who argues that it is not just a matter of a few violent individuals, but that any coercive action of rival supporters, or even by the police or officials, may give rise to the feeling that "honour" needs to be defended across the whole group of fans identifying with a particular team. He goes on to stress, therefore, the importance in crowd management of avoiding such apparent threats.

Sociological Theories

Social reaction

Interaction theories stress that violence is a characteristic of the way in which conflict is managed. Some theories have particularly focused upon the reactions of others to incipient deviance. The interruption of what is and what is not acceptable behaviour, of where the limit lies past which repression is felt necessary, is necessarily subjective and a matter of changing social mores. For instance, Banks (1962) has presented evidence that the apparent increase in violence offending since the war is due to convictions for more minor offences than hitherto, which she attributes to increasing social sensitivity to, and intolerance of, aggressive behaviour. Thus more (and more minor) offences are reported to the police and more are prosecuted, without there necessarily being any increase in the absolute incidence of violence (or even in association with an actual decrease in incidence). The irony is that if the reaction is out of proportion to the real threat the response may encourage escalation and actually cause violence.

Labelling

A large literature has developed on the basis of the "social reaction" perspective, especially in terms of the variables that affect whether or not specific behaviour becomes "labelled" as deviant or criminal or unacceptable. This perspective has informed several studies of violent behaviour, most notably Cohen (1972) on the Mods and Rockers phenomenon, Hall et al (1978) on the mugging scare, and Marsh et al (1977) on football hooliganism. All these studies have demonstrated how the mass media can exaggerate a minor or limited problem out of all proportion to its real seriousness, and help to create the greater disorder which it sought to avoid, by giving it notoriety and "glamour". Nevertheless, none of these authors see labelling theory as an adequate explanation on its own. As Harrington (1976) states, the mass media role is "one of amplification rather that causal", and the problem usually does exist in some form before achieving publicity (see, eg Robins and Cohen, 1978, with respect to football hooliganism, or Scull, 1972, with respect to the spread of hard drugs in Britain.)

MASS MEDIA

The mass media have been implicated in other ways, too, in the encouragement of violence. Mary Whitehouse (1985), writing in *The Guardian* after the Brussels tragedy, blamed mass media portrayal of violence and obscenity for inuring the public to such excesses and making some individuals more prone to indulge themselves. Predictably, subsequent letters in reply have pointed out the flaws in this argument - that violence is far older than the mass media (and was probably far nastier too) and that the same objections could be made to other violent images, such as the crucifixion. An audience may be stimulated, revolted or sobered in response to portrayals of violence, and research has had great difficulty in establishing the preponderance of one or other reaction, or the conditions under which one is more or less likely. Recent summaries of the literature on the effects of television conclude that any adverse effect is limited to particular conditions (very young children only, who have not yet learnt to discriminate between contexts and have not internalised social inhibitions, in Geen, 1983; and those already disposed to be violent anyway, in Murdock, 1982). More important effects of the mass media may be indirect ones. Murdock points out that media exaggeration of violence is more likely to have a grave impact on the levels of fear among the vulnerable, such as the elderly, and cause them to lead more restricted life-styles than they would otherwise do. The labelling studies mentioned above also indicate that the way a problem is represented by the press or television may affect the level and style of response by the authorities, and thus help towards exaggeration of the perceived threat, mismanagement and escalation of conflict. Halloran (1978) makes many of these points, as well as the fact that the portrayal of affluent lifestyles and commercial advertising stresses materialistic values and heightens the frustration of poorer groups within society (see Anomie below).

CULTURAL THEORIES

While the mass media play a role in promoting and transmitting modern "culture", every society (and sub-group) has much more deeply seated norms and expectations that tend to be quite resilient to change in the short-term. Such mores may reflect upon the legitimacy of violence and therefore affect its likelihood of occurrence in a particular society. Much American criminology, for instance, has been concerned with the perception that the southern states of the USA are more inclined to violence than the northern ones. A feature of our own social norms (and of most other societies, too) that has occasioned a great deal of theoretical writing is the discrepancy between expectations of male and female behaviour, the former being expected to be more extravert, directive, and aggressive than the latter. It is certainly true that in most types of violence men are implicated much more than are women. This may be because of differences in opportunity as well as difference in inclination or socialisation, but in either case the difference lies ultimately in discrepant sex-roles. More directly, much feminist literature implicates men in deliberate coercive subordination of women and systematic violence against wives in order to maintain their dominant status in society (see, eg Dobash and Dobash, 1979). Such arguments tend to fail to explain variations in the use of violence among men. Nevertheless, it is true that, to a lesser extent now perhaps than at earlier times, the husband is assumed to have some "proprietorial" claim over his wife and that chastisement by the husband is still accepted in many circles. Domestic violence, too, despite its prevalence, has traditionally received much less publicity than types of violence of which men are generally the victim. The evidence of several attitude surveys is that women are very much more likely to perceive their social world as hostile and threatening than are men.

Discrepant sex-roles are not only harmful to women. They may also cause anxiety to men, especially in a world of changing social conditions and attitudes, to which earlier emphases on "masculinity" are less well adapted. Talcott Parsons (1947) has formulated the theory that boys grow up in Western society in mother-dominated homes (the fathers being away at work, in contrast to peasant society) at a time when they are internalising sex roles and identifying with parents. The dominance of a female role-model occasions tensions and ambiguities for male children, and they tend to act out the resulting anxieties in exaggerated "masculine" behaviour in order to "prove" their sexual identity. Erikson (1959) describes the period from adolescence to full manhood as a particularly difficult one of "identity crisis" and points out that such problems are worked out and controlled in primitive societies by means of "initiation ceremonies" that firmly establish one's status as male and as adult, rituals which Western society lacks. It is certainly true that adolescence in our society is a time of particularly high rates of violent offending, although only among a small proportion of all lads. E Wilson (1983) sees the problem as explaining a good deal of violence against women, and suggests reforms in child-rearing practice that would break down rigid sex-roles that are dysfunctional for both sexes. The fact that law-enforcement bodies are very much male-dominated, and given that they are trained to use force, has led Toch (1976) to argue that such agencies tend to have an exaggerated "machismo" culture themselves which may make them over-react at times to apparent challenges to their authority, especially from young males.

Many of the forces thought to lead to violence strike unevenly across society. Social groups whose members share an above average degree of frustration, of deprivation, or of discrimination, may develop their own culture which rejects many of the values in the surrounding culture, just as they feel rejected themselves by the wider society. Such groups, according to Wolfgang and Ferracuti (1967), among many others, tend to reinforce aggressive tendencies towards the dominant culture or its representatives and to develop their own internal status system based on the groups' own distinct values, which may include rebelliousness and illegality. Although the youthful members of a subculture are most likely to be implicated in actual violent behaviour (see Cohen, 1955), the values with which they operate are usually seen as permeating the whole of their community, which seems to be universally envisaged as an "inner city", "lower working class" or "poverty" community. Thus Oscar Lewis (1961), based on studies in Latin America and later in New York, described a "culture of poverty", with a stress on immediate gratification, machismo and fatalism, which appear to be more or less direct adaptations to the uncertainties of future survival. Such a culture, Lewis believes, is a fertile soil for violence. Based on studies in American cities, W B Miller (1966) elucidated six "focal concerns" of lower working class culture, some of them overlapping with features described by Lewis: concern with getting into, and keeping out of, trouble; toughness; out-smarting others; excitement; belief in fate; and a concern for personal autonomy. Studies of lower working class British communities demonstrate similar value systems, and some work on football hooliganism (Williams et al, 1984) directly implicates a subcultural explanation, the sport being a more or less incidental context in which such life-styles can be played out. As the authors say: "fighting is one of the few sources of excitement, meaning and status available to males from this section of society".

Anomie

Whether or not communities in socially deprived areas develop an antagonistic culture, there are many sociological studies that affirm that members of a society denied the expected rewards of belonging, or denied full access to opportunity for advance, are more likely to resort to law-breaking, including violence, whether with expressive or instrumental purposes. The classical French sociologist Emile Durkheim (1952) first formulated the theory of "anomie" to express the condition of finding oneself in a powerless position, without appropriate standards for action, without purpose, that may arise from diverse conditions, including rapid social change or, as developed by the American sociologist Robert Merton (1957), finding oneself denied access to legitimate means of "getting on" because of barriers of race or class. The condition of "anomie" is assumed to be an intolerable one for the individual who may resort to a diversity of rebellious or bizarre behaviours, including suicide, the original subject of Durkheim's theory, and crime (see Powell, 1966). Such a condition has been identified in relation to hooliganism:

> .... what is reflected in hooliganism is the experience of marginality and worthlessness among young, particularly lower working class men in an advanced industrial society. In a singing community of his peers he comes alive and discovers a sense of membership which is denied him elsewhere .... (Pearson, 1976)

and in relation to the 1981 riots:

> Rioting may come to signify an attempt to gain symbolic control over areas and lives in which people feel they have lost mastery. It can become a reply to the experience of oneself as an object moved around by external forces. Violence has been a frequent resort of those who are denied a substantial identity in the world; it is a vehicle for prowess, assertiveness and a new set of standards for gauging character" (Rock, 1981).

According to "anomie" theory loss of commitment to society results in a lack of commitment to that society's norms of behaviour. Lack of investment in relationships with others gives no reason to accommodate one's own behaviour to them. Burgess (1979) attributes much child abuse to such a lack of "parental investment" in a child for whatever reason - the child may be retarded or difficult, it may be a step-child, or one of a large family. Where primary social bonds are weak, informal social control is correspondingly attenuated - the basis for Hirschi's (1969) influential "social control" theory. For these reasons, Toch (1976) argues that a criminal justice system which "makes war" on offenders, rejects them and isolates them, only reinforces their need to be violent. Although punishment may be necessary, one should also build in mechanisms for reconciliation and reconstructing social participation, not simply counter violence with violence (Marshall, 1989).

There are numerous reasons why groups or individuals may come to feel alienated from the general society. One of the major ones is discrimination on the basis of race, ethnicity or religion. In a large international comparative survey of political violence, Hibbs (1973) found that the most powerful predictor of such violence was the degree of social differentiation between ethnic groups. Where this was combined with political separatism, there was a particularly high likelihood of violence. Other studies with similar conclusions include Sears and McConahay (1973) (Watts riots in Los Angeles), Budge and O'Leary (1973) (Northern Ireland), Blau (1977) and Blau and Blau (1982). The eighties riots in Britain had similar racial overtones.

"Modernisation" is another variable often invoked to explain anomie, especially rising rates of violence and disorder across the world. Social changes during the century may have been accelerating at such a rate as to outrun human adaptability. Modernisation in developing countries is often implicated in the violence commonly witnessed there. "Urbanisation", with concomitant conditions of anonymity and overcrowding, is also frequently thought to favour violence, although empirical studies of historical development usually show a rise of violence in the early phases of urbanisation only, followed by a decline as cities become more stable and established.

Other factors cited as leading to anomie include widespread unemployment and the aftermath of war (".... war is the single most obvious correlate of all the great historical waves of crime in England and the United States", Gurr, 1979. See also Archer & Gartner, 1976; Einstadter, 1978.) A final factor which may be of more general impact, however, concerns the behaviour of crowds. In the classic text on "The Crowd", Gustave Le Bon (1972) argued that the individual was insulated from usual social norms and inhibitions by immersion in a crowd, which tended to act as a single organism with a collective mind of its own. It is generally considered nowadays that Le Bon overemphasised the homogeneity and integration of crowds, but more recent studies have confirmed many of his arguments. One of the more notable works is Turner and Killian's "Collective Behaviour" (1957). Being one of a crowd tends to produce an intensification of feelings, a sense of anonymity and power, and an impression of overwhelming universal unanimity. Such a state favours more extreme behaviour (although, it is found, still within limits), a lowering of inhibitions, spontaneity and excitement. Crowds, Turner and Killian hold, develop norms of behaviour through interaction, often under the influence of a few leading members. Such norms are powerful and facilitate the suspension of inhibitions by giving confidence that disorder is controlled and within certain limits. What may appear to be chaos to an outsider may be understandable and not at all anarchic to the crowd member. Nevertheless, group behaviour is associated with greater risk-taking, a lack of guilt or shame feelings, and inhibition of normal pity or compassion for the individual. Crowd behaviour can get out of hand and often does, while no-one is really able to control it beyond the early stages. Given today's "mass society" when large gatherings are increasingly frequent, crowd dynamics are probably worthy of fuller study.

Implications for Policy

After burrowing through such a complex mix of theories, is any light to be glimpsed at the end of the tunnel? Somewhat surprisingly there are some convergences across the different theoretical approaches which may provide some hope for planning a way forward.

Violent impulses are part of human nature. Conflict is a necessary concomitant of individuals living together. No-one proposes that such problems can be eliminated completely. What most writers are tending to say, however, is that they can be managed more effectively. This emerges from almost every theoretical viewpoint. What all these different perspectives are converging upon is the necessity of taking measures that avoid the exaggeration and escalation of trouble and provide means for reconciliation between persons in conflict with one another or with society. In particular, authorities with responsibility for order need to learn skills for the management of crowd and group disorder. They need to be able to distinguish shows of aggression and symbolic violence from really dangerous behaviour and to react appropriately, with sensitivity to the needs and feelings of those involved and without treating them as if an enemy or as animals. Agents of order naturally react to violence like any other person, but they should be trained to contain their anger and to counter aggression with control rather than further aggression.

A "war on crime" only produces an enemy with no alternatives but to fight back. Firmness coupled with fairness are better controllers than anger. Nor should one forget the message of Elias (1978) - that "civilisation" may be the most potent force for the control of animal instinct that has yet been witnessed. Society moves on. It is not possible to return to previous conditions of civility. Present-day society must be able to adapt to freedoms of thought and choice that did not exist in the past. Nevertheless, it should be possible to work towards a civilisation of the future that can cope with these new conditions. There are already signs of a "return to community", but not the old community which would now be found unacceptably oppressive. The movement is expressed in advances (particularly in America) towards "community mediation" and "conciliation" within the context of civil and criminal justice. The new "reparation projects" (Marshall & Merry, 1990) are founded on the philosophy of "reconciliation" between an offender and, in the first instance, the victim, but more broadly, too, the community. New moves to improve police-community liaison are also part of this movement to break down the distance between the people and the agencies that serve them. Even in the context of public disorder, Waddington et al (1989) reinforce this approach, based on empirical study, when they criticise Smelser's ideas: "His prescriptions for avoiding disorder seem to us more likely to cause it: (a)Prevent communication in general, so that beliefs cannot be disseminated. (b)Prevent interaction between leaders and followers, so that mobilisation is difficult. (c)Refrain from taking a conditional attitude towards violence by bluffing or vacillating in the use of the ultimate weapons of force. (d)Refrain from entering the issues and controversies that move the crowd; remain impartial, `and fixed on the principle of maintaining law and order." There is much in succeeding chapters of this book to reinforce their criticisms.

Building barriers may succeed in the short term but, like the walls of Jericho, they may come tumbling down eventually on those that built them. To build bridges may be a better theme for the development of policy to cope with violence.

Theory of Conflict Management

While this paper has focused on theories about the causes of violence, some of those causes are deep-rooted and will not be capable of eradication. Insofar as violence arises from within the individual, it may be difficult to distinguish such antisocial drives (aggressiveness) from more desirable ones (ambition, activism). The difference may lie largely in the social circumstances and how aggression is managed by others. Insofar as violence arises from social conditions, governments need to be concerned with eliminating, as far as is in their power, discrimination, poverty, alienation and so on - but they should be concerned with these whether or not they are criminogenic. Any policies in these areas, moreover, will only yield fruit in the fullness of time, while violence is with us now. In the last section the case was made for sensitive conflict management as a major, direct and relatively quick method of both limiting violence and preventing further trouble.

Conflict management theory is not new, although its widespread adoption and detailed formulation is very recent. Its origins can be found in orthodox organisational management theory, in the writings of Mary Parker Follett (1942), in social anthropological accounts of how different communities handled violence and crime (synthesised, for instance, in Hamnett, 1977), and in evolving practice in international mediation, which particularly informed the writings of Curle (1986), Fisher & Ury (1981) and Kriesberg (1973), which are now seminal.

Conflict resolution theory attempts to formulate principles for resolving conflicts in socially reconstitutive and constructive ways, avoiding aggression and escalation into violence. The main principles - now well established in all contexts from neighbour disputes to international aggression, from divorce settlement to the management of corporations, are as follows.

1. The need to be open about conflict. Instinctive reactions to conflict, reinforced by the dominant culture, are generally "flight" or "fight". In the first case the problem is ignored or, in the unwillingness to act directly, it is suppressed or escape sought by physically moving location (eg moving house to escape a dispute with a neighbour, or school truancy to avoid a problem with a fellow pupil or teacher).
In the second case, although the problem is acted upon, it is in a way that exaggerates and escalates it, by setting out to "beat" the person seen as the cause of it (the "opponent"). Very often the fight response suppresses the reality of the conflict as much as the flight one, by oversimplifying it in black/white terms.
Both responses tend to be ineffective - flight because it does nothing to change the problem at all, and fight because it destroys personal relationships and reduces the number of potential solutions to the one where "winner takes all", leaving the "loser" with a grudge that may surface later in even worse conflict or general uncooperativeness. Avoidance is sometimes the simplest and least costly option, but is not always possible, while suppression may lead to brooding resentment that erupts eventually in a violent over-reaction. Constructive conflict resolution is based on being open about the fact that conflict exists and attempting to approach it realistically and rationally.
2. The need for all parties to participate in resolution. The law takes conflict out of the hands of parties. Other people take all the decisions. Without the intimate knowledge of their social situations and feelings that only the parties themselves can have, such "third party" decisions are typically imperfect. They are also likely to be restricted to stereotyped forms - such as the "sentences" available to a criminal court. The parties are less likely to feel personally committed to a third party decision - especially those who see themselves as "losers". (Often both parties see themselves as losers after a court battle - especially in something like a divorce case.) Independent decisions also concentrate on the material aspects in dispute, and fail to deal with parties' emotions. The decision can seem a very good one from a bystander's perspective, but be rejected by the parties because they are still upset or did not feel involved in it.
Resolution can therefore be more successful, and exploit a wider

range of options, if all relevant parties are involved throughout. Not only would they retain some control, be able to express their needs and feelings, and have recourse to information unavailable to "outsiders", they would also benefit from the experience of working more or less directly with the other party, breaking down stereotypes and providing a basis for improved relationships. Mediation is an example of a process that provides for such participation. The third party is not there to make decisions but to help the parties communicate effectively and to collaborate.

3. Conflict is a shared problem. The typical view of conflict consisting of two "opponents" at opposite poles, each of whom can only "win" if the other "loses", tends to lead to a battle where, at best, each may win a bit, but both lose a lot more. A more productive paradigm comes from seeing conflict as a shared problem, which neither can resolve without cooperation of the other. If conflict can be seen in this way, parties can be saved the necessity of expending resources on attacking or denigrating each other. Working together on what becomes a shared problem-solving exercise, they create both solutions and a modus vivendi.

4. Constructive conflict resolution requires certain skills. The skills involved in shared problem-solving are part of normal social skills, but extra experience or training may be needed for people to maintain them through an emotional confrontation. Particularly obstructive emotions or insufficiently developed communication skills or unawareness of alternatives to adversarial methods may mean that the assistance of a skilled intermediary is desirable.

Skills of direct negotiation include active listening (attention divorced from personal prejudices or preconceptions of the other party), affirmation (ability to obtain the cooperation of the other party by using a positive approach and avoiding "put-downs"), assertiveness (ability to identify and represent to others one's own interests, needs, views and feelings clearly and accurately), self-confidence (avoiding defensive attitudes and reluctance to communicate), recognising and dealing with emotions as well as material issues, and creativity (avoiding thinking "in a rut" or position-taking, and keeping an open mind about what a settlement might look like)

These principles inform a variety of new approaches to social problems that habitually involve violence and confrontation. As a society we deal with criminal offenders, for instance, in a way which is basically combative. Ideas of restorative justice are being developed (see, eg, FIRM 1989) on the basis of conflict resolution principles, allowing for the active participation of both offender and victim in the resolution process (criminal justice), affirming both the offender's responsibility while at the same time offering him/her a real opportunity for social re-acceptance, dealing with the victim's material and emotional needs, and seeking creative forms of resolution to the misbehaviour (viewed as a problem shared by offender, victim and society) that re-establish relationships between all three.

Some of the most destructive conflicts are those between divorcing couples, especially parents. Divorce conciliation schemes all over the country are trying to settle child custody and access, and even property division, by voluntary cooperative agreements through mediation. Other conflicts within families and between relatives are also ideally suited for mediation, because everyone normally wants to find a solution. In domestic conflict of this sort emotions usually run very high, which is why an outside mediator may be useful in helping people see their way through the problems. Emotions may still run high even when disputants are not closely related. Neighbour conflicts can lead to violence if left unresolved, although the mediator's job may involve persuading one party that there really is a problem which they have failed to recognise. Community mediation schemes (or neighbourhood justice centres) are now in operation in the United States, Canada, Norway, Australia, United Kingdom, Ireland, and many third world countries like the Philippines, for resolving such disputes. (See Marshall, 1985, Chapter 4.)

All organisations contain conflicts within them. If they get out of hand or are suppressed and ignored they may seriously decrease the efficiency of the organisation. In America there is a growing profession of "institutional ombudsman", whose job is to receive complaints from members of the organisation or its clients and attempt to resolve them by bringing the people involved together in mediation. Other conflict resolution specialists are involved in training for the members of organisations, of which a particularly important branch is training in schools, helping pupils, staff and parents resolve conflicts between and among themselves. The involvement of children is seen as especially crucial, for they thereby receive ideas and skills that provide a basis for operating in a democratic society for the rest of their lives. A democracy, as Ray Shonholtz argues in Chapter 11, can be seen as cooperative conflict resolution writ large and depends on the same principles of openness, participation and cooperation, etc.

Many conflicts range beyond individuals. Race conflict, gender conflict, cultural differences, environmental and planning problems, police/community relations, prison riots, public disorders all reflect conflicts among groups, often more than two groups at once. ACAS (the Advisory, Conciliation and Arbitration Service) has already built a highly successful process for facilitating the resolution of such problems in the industrial relations arena. The process can be complex, demanding and time-consuming, but the end-product is worthwhile because of the serious implications of allowing such conflicts to continue until violence or social disruption occurs. Much pioneering work in the area of police/community relations has also been carried out by the Community Relations Service of the United States (see Chapters 12 & 13). Other practitioners have been developing training both for potential victims (eg women's groups, social workers - see Chapter 18) on how to handle and prevent violence on the part of others, and for potentially violent persons themselves on how to understand, manage and contain their own aggression (such as the work of the American Alternatives to Violence Project, AVP, with prisoners incarcerated for violence offences). The latter is not repressive or negative, unlike say medical treatment, but seeks out the positive potential in individuals through enlightenment and the development of alternative behaviour through constructive social skills.

In sum, the approach increases options rather than shutting them down. As Mark Twain once said "When the only tool you have is a hammer, every problem looks like a nail."

References

ARCHER, D and GARTNER, R (1976) "Violent acts and violent times: a comparative approach to postwar homicide rates". American Sociological Review, 41, 937-965

BANDURA, A (1973) Aggression: a social learning analysis. Prentice-Hall

BANKS, C (1962) "Violence". Howard Journal, 11,13-25

BERKOWITZ, L (1962) Aggression: a social psychological analysis. McGraw-Hill

(1978) "Is criminal violence normative behaviour? Hostile and instrumental aggression in violent incidents". Journal of Research in Crime and Delinquency, 15,148-161

(1982) "Violence and rule-following behaviour" in P Marsh and A Campbell (Eds) Aggression and Violence. Blackwell.

BLAU, JR and BLAU, PM (1982) "The Cost of inequality: metropolitan structure and violent crime." American Sociological Review, 47, 114-129

BLAU, PM (1977) Inequality and Heterogeneity. Free Press

BROWN, RM (1975) Strain of Violence: historical studies of American violence and vigilantism. Oxford University Press

BUDGE, I and O'LEARY, C (1973) Belfast: approach to crisis. Macmillan

BURGESS, A (1962) A Clockwork Orange. Penguin

BURGESS, RL (1979) "Family violence: some implications from evolutionary biology". Paper presented at annual meeting of American Society of Criminology Philadelphia, USA

CAMPBELL, C (1976) "Perspectives of violence" in N Tutt (Ed)Violence, HMSO

CLUTTERBUCK, R (1980) Britain in Agony: the growth of political violence. Penguin

COHEN, AK (1955) Delinquent Boys: the culture of the gang. Routledge
COHEN, S (1972) Folk Devils and Moral Panics. McGibbon and Kee
COOPER, P (1985) "Competing explanations of the Merseyside riots of 1981" British Journal of Criminology, 25,60-69
CRAIG, W (1928) "Why do animals fight?" International Journal of Ethics 31,264-278
CURLE, A (1986) In the Middle. Berg
CURTIS, LA (1974) Criminal Violence. Lexington
DE WAAL, F (1989) Peacemaking among Primates. Harvard University Press
DOBASH, RE and R (1979) Violence against Wives. Free Press
DOLLARD, J et al (1939) Frustration and Aggression. Yale
DURKHEIM, E (1952) Suicide. Routledge
EINSTADTER, WJ (1978) "Robbery - outlawry on the US frontier, 1863-1890" in J A Inciardi and A E Pottieger (Eds) Violent Crime: historical and contemporary issues. Sage
ELIAS, N (1978) The Civilizing Process: the history of manners. Urizen
ERIKSON, E (1959) Identity and the Life Cycle. International University Press
FELSON, RB (1978) "Aggression as impression management". Social Psychology, 41,205-213
FERGUSON, TJ and RULE, BG (1983) "An attributional perspective on anger and aggression" in R G Green and E I Donnerstein (Eds) Aggression: theoretical and empirical reviews. Academic Press
FIRM (Forum for Initiatives in Reparation & Mediation) (1989) Repairing the Damage. Beaconsfield: FIRM
FISHER, R and URY, W (1981) Getting to Yes. Houghton Mifflin
FOLLETT, MP (1942) Dynamic Administration: the collected papers of Mary Parker Follett. (Ed.HC Metcalf & L Urwick.) New York: Harper.
FOX, R (1982) "The Violent imagination" in P Marsh and A Campbell (Eds). Aggression and Violence. Blackwell
FRANK, AW (1976) "Making scenes in public: symbolic violence and social order". Theory and Society 3, 395-416
FRENCH, JRP and RAVEN, BH (1959) "The bases of social power" in D Cartwright (Ed). Studies in Social Power. Ann Arbor: Institute for Social Research
GEEN, RG (1983) "Aggression and Television Violence" in R G Geen and E J Donnerstein (Eds) Aggression: theoretical and empirical reviews. Academic Press
GLUCKMAN, M (1963) Order and Rebellion in Tribal Africa. Cohen and West
GOLDSTEIN, AP (1983) "Needed : a war on aggression" National Forum, LXIII, 4, 14-15
GULLIVER, PH (1977) "On mediators" in I Hamnett (Ed) Social Anthropology & Law. Academic Press
GURR, TR (1979) "On the history of violent crime in Europe and America" in H D Graham and T R Gurr (Eds) ibid.
HALL, S et al (1978) Policing the Crisis. Macmillan
HALLORAN, JD (1978) "Studying violence and the media: a sociological approach" in C Winick (Ed) Deviance and Mass Media. Sage

HAMNETT, I (1977) Social Anthropology & Law. London: Academic Press
HARRINGTON, J (1976) "Violence in groups" in N Tutt (Ed) Violence, HMSO
HIBBS, DA (1973) Mass Political Violence: a cross-national causal analysis. Wiley
HIRSCHI, T (1969) Causes of Delinquency. University of California
HOWELLS, K (1976) "Interpersonal aggression". International Journal of Criminology and Penology, 4, 319-330
KRIESBERG, L (1973) The Sociology of Social Conflicts. Prentice Hall
LEA, J and YOUNG, J (1984) What is to be done about law and order? Penguin
LE BON, G (1972) The Crowd. Unwin
LEWIS, O (1961) The Children of Sanchez. Random House
LOFLAND, J (1969) Deviance and Identity. Prentice-Hall
LORD JUSTICE SCARMAN (1982) The Scarman Report. Penguin
LORENZ, K (1966) On Aggression. Harcourt, Brace and World
MARLER, P (1976) "On animal aggression: the roles of strangeness and familiarity. American Psychologist March, 239-246
MARSH, P (1980) "Violence at the pub". New Society. 12 June
MARSH, P, ROSSER, E and HARRE, R (1977) Rules of Disorder. Routledge
MARSHALL, TF (1985) Alternatives to Criminal Courts. Aldershot: Gower (1989) "Punishment in the dustbin" Paper delivered at British Criminology Conference, Bristol, July.
MARSHALL, TF and MERRY, S (1990) Crime and Accountability. London: HMSO
MARX, E (1976) The Social Context of Violent Behaviour. Routledge
MAURER, A (1974) Corporal punishment. American Psychologist, August, 614-626.
MERTON, AK (1957) Social Theory and Social Structure. Free Press
MILLER, WB (1966) "Violent crimes in city gangs" Annals of the American Academy of Political and Social Science, 364
MUNGHAM, G (1977) "The sociology of violence". New Society 13 October
MURDOCK, G (1982) "Mass communication and social violence: a critical review of recent research trends" in P Marsh and A Campbell (Eds) Aggression and Violence. Blackwell
MURRAY, C (1977) "The soccer hooligans' honour system". New Society, 6 October
NEWSON, J and NEWSON, E (1976) Seven Years Old in the Home Environment. Allen and Unwin
PARSONS, T (1947) "Certain primary sources and patterns of aggression in the social structure of the Western world". Psychiatry, 10, 167-181
PEARSON, G (1976) "In defence of hooliganism: social theory and violence" in N Tutt (Ed) Violence. HMSO
_____ (1983) Hooligan: a history of respectable fears. Macmillan
POWELL, EH (1966) "Crime as a function of anomie". Journal of Criminal Law, Criminology and Police Science, 57, 161-171
ROBINS, D and COHEN, P (1978) Knuckle Sandwich. Penguin
ROBOTTOM, J (1976) "A history of violence" in N Tutt (Ed) Violence, HMSO
ROCK, P (1981) "Rioting". London Review of Books, September, 17-30
RUBENSTEIN, RE (1988) Group Violence in America. Working Paper 2.

Center for Conflict Analysis and Resolution, George Mason University, Virginia, US.

SARTRE, J-P (1960) Critique de la Raison Dialectique. Gallimard

SCULL, A (1972) "Social control and the amplification of deviance" in J Douglas and R Scott (Eds) Theoretical Perspectives on Deviance. Basic Books

SEARS, DO and McCONAHAY, JB (1973) The Politics of Violence: the new urban blacks and the Watts riot. Houghton Mifflin.

SHORT, JF and STRODTBECK, F (1965) Group Process and Gang Delinquency. University of Chicago

SOREL, G (1908) Reflections on Violence. Peter Smith

STRAUS, MA (1973) "A general systems theory approach to a theory of violence between family members". Social Science Information 12, 105-125

TEDESCHI, JT (1983) "Social influence theory and aggression" in R G Green and E I Donnerstein (Eds) Aggression: theoretical and empirical reviews. Academic Press

TILLY, C (1979) "Collective violence in European perspective" in H D Graham and T R Gurr (Eds) Violence in America. Sage

TOCH, H (1969) Violent Men. Penguin

_____ (1976) Peacekeeping: police, prisons and violence. Lexington

TOURNIER, P (1978) The Violence Inside. SCM Press

TURNER, RH and KILLIAN, LM (1957) Collective Behaviour. Prentice-Hall

TUTT, N (1976) "Introduction" to Violence, HMSO

WADDINGTON, D, JONES, K, & CRITCHER, C (1989) Flashpoints: studies in public disorder. London: Routledge

WHITEHOUSE, M (1985) "Obscenity that fuelled the Brussels brutality" The Guardian, 10 June

WILLIAMS, J, DUNNING, E and MURPHY, P (1984) Hooligans Abroad. Routledge

WILSON, E (1983) What is to be done about violence against women? Penguin

WOLFGANG, ME (1957) "Victim-precipitated criminal homicide" Journal of Criminal Law, Criminology and Police Science, 48, 1-11

WOLFGANG, ME and FERRACUTI, F (1967) The Subculture of Violence: towards an integrated theory in criminology. Tavistock

Chapter Two

Conflict Theories, Government Policies and the Urban Riots of the Early 1980s.

SIR CHRISTOPHER LEEDS

Introduction and Comparison between the British and American Riots

THIS PAPER looks at the urban riots which took place in mainland Britain during the period 1980-85, the role of the police, and the extent to which the Conservative government policies since 1979 were contributing factors. Further, certain conflict theories are discussed which are relevant to the causes, progress, management and prevention of this form of civil disorder. Conflict theorists agree that the outbreak of physical violence within a community is an indication that something is wrong within the political or social system. However, they differ in the same way as the ordinary public and politicians as to what are perceived as the causes and remedies. This aspect is developed in greater detail later.

The right-wing view tended to regard the urban riots during the early 1980s as irresponsible criminal behaviour, the culprits being those directly involved in the disorders, who should be punished accordingly. In contrast the left-wing would argue that police tactics, government policies, and racial disadvantage were important factors, and that despair can drive people directly to collective violence, hooliganism or to individual acts of crime.

In reality the actual riots appeared largely to be a form of collective protest, a signal that society had failed to provide properly for the needs of some of its members. However, some of those involved were not particularly deprived nor did they harbour strong grievances, but merely took advantage of the disturbances by committing straightforward criminal acts, theft and vandalism.

Riots on such a scale had never happened before either in Britain or in Europe. They took place in certain deprived inner city areas where the non-whites of Afro-Caribbean or Asian origin constituted an important part and sometimes the majority of the population. The following summarises the time and place of the five most important riots.

COMMUNITY DISORDERS AND POLICING

1. **St. Paul's** district, Bristol, 2 April 1980.
2. **Brixton**, Borough of Lambeth, South London, 10-12 April 1981.
3. **Toxteth**, Liverpool (July 3-6) and **Southall**, West London, 3 July 1981.
   These riots spread like a chain reaction to over thirty British cities or towns. Whilst the period of July 10-12 experienced the most intensive period of rioting, battles between police and youths continued spasmodically into August.
4. **Handsworth**, Birmingham 9-10 September 1985. This led to mini-riots elsewhere such as Brixton, 28 September.
5. **Tottenham**, Borough of Haringay, North London, October 1985.

In many respects the urban riots resembled the American riots of the late sixties, which occurred in the United States, in Watts, Los Angeles (1965) and in some 23 cities during 1967, notably Detroit and Newark. In terms of their origins, the Kerner Commission (Kerner, 1968) listed in order of importance - police practices, unemployment and housing. These issues were those most frequently cited in relation to the British riots. Moreover, a typical American riot started as a result of a fairly minor or routine police action which developed into a confrontation between the police and the community. The riot continued with widespread looting, arson and attacks on the police. The British riots followed a similar pattern.

Neither the American nor the British riots were the result of political agitation, organised meetings or demonstrations. In both cases the disturbances occurred in urban centres, deprived partly as a result of government policies. The rapid spread of the riots in the United States in July 1967 and in Britain during July 1981 provided strong evidence that media reporting constituted an important element in stimulating "copycat violence". (Field & Southgate 1982:6)

While the American riots were basically race riots - blacks rioting against the police - the rioters in Britain were of mixed ethnic composition (Afro-Caribbean, Asian and white). Southall, near London Heathrow airport, proved to be the exception, being inhabited entirely by Sikhs. Unlike the other riots, these Asians were provoked into rioting by the racist behaviour of white skinheads, who had entered the area in coaches, proclaiming that they were on a "Paki-bash". Another aspect of the British riots, unlike the American ones, lay in the involvement of younger age groups (10-15), while the focal age group tended to be the 16-19 year olds, single and unemployed. During the Detroit riots of 1967, 83% of male rioters involved had jobs, and over half were members of the United Auto Workers trades union. (Hodgson, 1981)

After the St. Paul's riots, Mr David Lane, then chairman of the Commission for Racial Equality said:

> There's been too much apathy. As a nation we haven't done enough to get to the root of the sort of problems that boiled over last night. It must make it clear that it could happen elsewhere. (Chesshyre & Brock, 1980)

Historical Background and National Identity

Successive governments after 1945 failed to appreciate the importance of creating a form of national identity with which both the native inhabitants, the English, Scots, Welsh and Irish, could identify as well as all past or recent immigrants. In fact the authorities and others, particularly the English, tended to comfort themselves with two illusions based more on hope rather than reality. First they believed the country had a stable political system and a homogeneous tolerant population. Second, tension or racial conflict would not occur following the concentration of immigrants from the West Indies (Afro-Caribbeans), India and Pakistan (Asians) in large urban centres.

With reference to the first point, it is certain that the government has tolerated a substantial degree of cultural diversity among the four nationalities of the United Kingdom. One of the reasons has been described as follows:

> To have tried to make the United Kingdom into an English nation would have required Anglicizing Scots, Welsh and Ulstermen - a difficult task given the resistance of English people to assimilating others as well as resistance from those to be assimilated. Alternatively, making a common British nation would involve an even more difficult task, 'denationalizing' English people in order to make them Britons. (Rose 1982:10-11)

Bonds of "Britishness" weakened from the late 1950s as a result of the decline of both Britain's power and influence worldwide and of its economy. Nationalist parties demanded greater freedom for the Scots and Welsh, while civil disorder in Northern Ireland from 1969 symbolised the clash of allegiances felt by many on the periphery of the United Kingdom, far from the strongholds of the centre based on London and the Home Counties.

There is no space in this paper to go into all the varied meanings which have been ascribed to "English" and "British", terms which have sometimes been used interchangeably, but Richard Rose (1982) has explored this problem in detail. Certainly cohesive and unifying tendencies exist in Britain, but some of the groupiness and tribalism of the British based on class, region, community or club tends to be ethnocentric and inward-looking, and barely conducive to the promoting of harmonious relations with others of different origins, religions or cultures. As an editorial in *The Observer* put it on the 28 April 1982, "the British tend to see coloured immigrants as interlopers that they have difficulty in seeing as either English or British".

John Osmond (1988) has linked together the two problems of internal national identity among the British inhabitants and that of integrating recent immigrants into the British society. He points out that Britain lacks a written constitution with a clearly established code of human rights, and consequently the absence of a formal constitutional structure in which conflicts such as those that occurred in the inner cities in the early 1980s could be regulated. The black communities can be compared "with the projection within the United Kingdom of separate Ulster, Scots and Welsh identities, as well as the regionalist stirrings in the English North".

If certain inhabitants had difficulty in reconciling their national allegiances with loyalty to the overall national identity of the United Kingdom, no wonder newcomers had difficulty in discovering with what they should be identifying. In fact the existence of a degree of open hostility and racism by the British made it even more difficult for recent immigrants to feel really at home. Various Afro-Caribbeans interviewed in Handsworth in the early 1980s said that immigrants from the West Indies after 1945 had been led to believe that England was a friendly, hospitable place. In practice, because of their colour, blacks led a limited life since they were not acceptable in many places, or met abuse and mistrust. (Ratcliffe 1981:24.)

As mentioned earlier, political leaders assumed that "race" would never pose a problem or at least tried to convince themselves of this fact. "Race" became a taboo subject with any public discussion discouraged. Scholars looked at "race" as something likely to cause a problem in Africa rather than in Britain. Early warning signs of racial ill-feeling in Notting Hill, London (1958) and Nottingham were largely written off as local aberrations, and their importance minimised by MPs, the mass media and the Churches.

In April 1968 Mr Enoch Powell warned the public about the likelihood of violence developing as a consequence of coloured settlement in Britain, and the creation of ghettoes in the main cities. Using particularly vivid, colourful language he declared:

> As I look ahead, I am filled with foreboding. Like the Romans,
> I seem to see the River Tiber foaming with much blood.

Although Powell received much support from ordinary workers, the authorities and the left-wing tended to regard his speech as racist and "alarmist". His warning went unheeded, and the Conservative leader, Edward Heath, dismissed him from the Shadow Cabinet.

The British government did not attempt to force newcomers to assimilate with the host community but tried from the late 1940s to encourage immigrants to integrate voluntarily. From the late 1950s the government abandoned this in favour of creating a multi-ethnic, multi-cultural or non-racial society. The general objective was to enable newcomers to keep their own identity and language based on their origins, while encouraging them to adapt to the lifestyle and culture of the country of adoption as far as this was necessary in terms of education of children, basic requirements of social interaction, employment and trade. Legislative measures were taken to discourage racism and racial disadvantage, namely the Race Relations Acts of 1965, 1968 and 1976.

During the early 1970s Britain experienced both mounting rates of inflation and unemployment. Apart from legal measures taken to discourage racism, the government took few other measures to create a real multi-cultural society. Yet other observers argued from time to time, as Powell had done in 1968, that the combination of urban decay, high unemployment, unsatisfactory race relations, and clumsy police handling of a situation could lead to a replay in Britain of the American riot experiences of the late 1960s. Efforts to promote race relations were not helped by the activities of the National Front, an extreme right-wing political party which, after its creation in 1967, organised a number of provocative anti-black marches. It had as one of its slogans "Ain't no black in the Union Jack".

In 1974 two researchers (Butler & Stokes, 1974) concluded that strong and overwhelming hostile attitudes towards coloured immigrants were quite general in Britain, particularly among unskilled manual workers, based on competition for housing and jobs, plus the deterioration of health and living standards they thought immigrants brought about.

Policing and the Riots

Virtually all the riots started when the police stopped to question or to arrest blacks suspected of having committed a crime. The impact on ethnic minorities of a new style of "hard" policing, clumsy police techniques and a breakdown in police-community relations were all identified as immediate causes of the riots. (Kettle & Hodges, 1982.)

Usual police methods in town and country have been called consensus policing. The police kept a low profile, and active cooperation existed between the public and the police. By and large crime rates were low and the public helped provide the police with information so that the latter could identify specific offenders. In large urban areas the equivalent of consensus policing has been community policing, a practice achieving reasonable success from

1977 in Handsworth, Birmingham. The local police chief made police officers get out of their patrol cars and go back "on the beat" so that they would be closer to the public. It also involved the building up of a network of community leaders with whom the police could discuss problems.

The public has traditionally held a good image of the police, who remained normally unarmed in contrast to most police forces in the world. The prolonged civil disturbances in Northern Ireland since 1969 and occasional violent confrontations with trade unionists in the 1970s, notably at Grunwick in 1977, led to the police adopting stronger tactics so as to more effectively defend themselves and to crush any disorders. Crime rates continued to rise from the 1970s, and statistics showed that most crime occurred in the deprived decaying urban areas of Britain's major cities.

The blacks suffered from a structure of racial disadvantage which confined them to low pay jobs, while the rise in long-term unemployment from the late 1970s particularly affected this sector of the population. Peter Walker, Secretary of State for Agriculture, pointed out in a letter to the Prime Minister published in *The Times* (8 July 1981) that high unemployment among teenagers, black or white, "has always meant a massive increase in crime." However, much of the petty theft was often committed by the very young between 10 and 15 years old.

Gradually police-community relations deteriorated in certain areas as the police started to adopt hard vigorous methods of fire-brigade policing to combat crime. The police ceased to patrol the streets, so becoming less accessible to the public, and started to use "blanket" tactics. This involved numerous policemen descending from cars and vans to "stop and search" potential suspects on the street or in social centres. Ethnic minorities, especially young blacks, began to feel that they were being unduly harassed and that the police were often racially prejudiced. A two-way marginalisation process started, whereby the community ceased being a helpful source of information to the police, while the police increasingly distanced itself from the public. Both sides began to develop negative images of each other. Ethnic groups saw the police increasingly as a threat, as the enemy, the nickname "pigs" first being used in the late 1970s. Likewise the police began to feel that it was only dealing with the "slag", some 5-10% of the population. The young particularly objected to the "sus" law, whereby a person could be arrested solely on the grounds that the police suspected him/her of intent to commit a crime.

The process by which relations between the police and local communities deteriorated in a number of urban centres from the late 1970s reflected the way Johan Galtung (1966) and others have argued that a conflict intensifies. Given a situation of latent conflict, the perception of the parties involved becomes over-simplistic, and they display negative attitudes towards one another, expressed in terms of mutual distrust, lack of respect, etc. Lastly this becomes reflected in their increasingly uncooperative and aggressive behaviour. The groups become polarised, each side thinking it is right and the aggrieved innocent party, and that the other side is in the wrong. In such a deteriorating situation it only needs a "spark" or minor incident to make the latent conflict manifest.

Handsworth, Birmingham, had a tradition of good police-community relations, and police tactics from 1977 to 1985 generally had the approval of the residents of the area. However a change in police leadership in April 1985 led to a clamp-down on certain activities previously tolerated, such as the use of cannabis by black youths. The police had obtained evidence that hard drugs were also being traded and, following public demand for action, decided to intervene. The new tactics increased the tension between the young and the police. In July 1985 two serious disturbances went unreported in the media. Consequently the context within which the riot occurred on 9 September was one of deteriorating youth-police relations. The buying and selling of cannabis represented the sole form of livelihood for many of the young black community. *The Guardian* (11 October 1985) quoted one of them as saying:

If we can't sell our weed then we is going to do armed robbery."

The Conservative Approach to Violence, Aggression and the Urban Riots

Traditional groups of theories relevant to violence have been variously named as the order or harmony perspective, functionalism, consensus or systems theory. Certain sociologists, such as Emile Durkheim and Talcott Parsons, argue that each part of society performs a function and that society tends towards consensus and cooperative behaviour. This approach, widely accepted regarding race relations, especially in the United States, is largely associated with a political conservatism which favours the status quo, or at most with a cautious type of liberalism favouring minor changes. (Farley 1982: 65). Social violence was largely seen as a pathological phenomenon.

Basically those inclined to the right-wing in politics have a pessimistic view regarding human nature. Aggression is a basic and natural instinct, and self-control has to be exercised, otherwise people's instincts will get them into trouble (Storr, 1968; Eysenck, 1957). People of this school of thought tend to blame the offenders or culprits directly involved in disorder or crime, and talk about lack of self-discipline and parental control, and the need for harsh punishments as deterrents.

To a large extent this approach characterised the reaction of the

Conservative government to the urban riots. During a television interview on April 13 1981 the Prime Minister, Mrs Thatcher, rejected the view that unemployment had been a primary cause of the Brixton riots, stressing that the government had given substantial funds to Lambeth for housing and other projects during 1980. (Keesing's Contemporary Archive 1981:31078.)

After the Toxteth riots in 1981 the right-wing of the Conservative party blamed the black community and demanded stronger immigration controls against non-whites. Both the government and the police avoided discussing the causes, which might have been embarrassing for them. Instead they concentrated on the damage which resulted. The Home Secretary, Douglas Hurd, described the Handsworth riots in 1985 as crime, not as outbreaks of social disorder. How absurd to think that the rioters could have been driven by despair, he said, since over £20 million had been spent on the area over the past four years as part of the government urban aid programme. (*The Times*, 12 September, 1985). Norman Tebbitt (1985), another Conservative minister, blamed "wickedness" as the prime cause of the Tottenham riots. *The Observer* (13 October 1988) called this a "cosy notion" since it absolved the government from doing little more than lock up the offenders, most of them black. Tebbitt also blamed in part the growing permissiveness in Britain since the late 1960s which had encouraged too much freedom and less discipline. Judges often gave soft sentences for crimes and this encouraged criminal offenders to continue committing crime. He also argued that violent programmes on the television encouraged "copycat violence" and suggested that there should be less glorification of criminals and violence in the mass media.

Various aspects of the riots justified or at least gave credence to the right-wing views which interpreted the disturbances as "criminal" and "wicked". Arson, murder, damage to property and looting had taken place which had led to the death of an Asian during the Handsworth riot and a policeman during the Tottenham riot, and numerous police injuries. An undoubted criminal element existed throughout most of the riots, especially among those white youths who joined the riots purely for personal gain rather than to express grievances. The riots which started in early July 1981 in Liverpool and Southall (West London) gradually spread to the rest of the country. The Home Secretary pointed out that the country was experiencing criminal hooliganism from people motivated by simple greed and that agitators had moved around from one area to another. (Keesing's Contemporary Archives 1981:31079.) Secondly, unemployment did not especially explain the active involvement of the very young aged between 10-15, although they might be discontented by the conditions in which they lived and by police harassment. However it could be argued that lack of parental control, or inability of parents to control their young explains why much petty crime is committed today by this age group. If they lead dull lives, involvement in a riot is exciting, and a means of filling a void in their empty lives. As *New Society* observed (25 October 1984):

Danger is fun - especially if you are young, fit and not exposed to too much of it for too long.

Lastly Lord Scarman (1981) in his Report reinforced the conservative or right-wing view that in a democracy, whatever the extenuating circumstances, riots contravene the law. He defined a riot as "a tumultuous disturbance of the peace by three or more persons assembled together with an intent mutually to assist one another by force, if necessary." (p.42)

The Liberal and Radical Approaches to Violence, Aggression and the Urban Riots

The consensual theory had a difficult time in explaining the race riots of the late 1960s in the USA. As a consequence the conflict perspective underwent a revival.

It is important to stress that many differences exist among the theorists of the conflict school, which originated partly out of the ideas of Karl Marx, and were developed by modern sociologists such as C Wright Mills and Ralf Dahrendorf. Conflict is built into society since wealth and power are distributed unequally, and therefore different groups have conflicting, opposing or divergent interests. Conflict is desirable or functional since this makes change possible, which may result in a more equitable distribution of wealth and power. (Cf, Farley 1982:65-7; Boulding 1978:10.)

Most liberal thinkers tend to favour peaceful change to bring about reforms while some agree with the radical approach. The latter suggests that where powerless people are acutely oppressed or exploited unjustly by governments, organisations or individuals, in other words suffering from structural violence, they have the right to rebel. The actual term "structural violence" was first used by the Norwegian academic Johan Galtung. Arguably this idea has something in common with the contract theory of John Locke (1690) which Thomas Jefferson used as a justification for the Declaration of Independence in 1776. An extension of this is the view that collective violence is justified under certain conditions, being part of the process "by which competing interest groups maintain power, gain power or lose power." (Feagin & Hahn, 1973) Collective (social) or spontaneous violence in the form of riots should not be treated merely as a form of rampant criminality since they are symptomatic of grievances and a plea for political change. (Joshua et al, 1983; Field & Southgate 1982:2; Coser 1970). Regarding the riots in the British cities in the early 1980s, nearly half of the young unemployed interviewed in one opinion poll justified the use of violence to bring about political change. (*The Sunday Times*, 6 September 1981.)

Conflict theorists would generally agree with the school of thought which argues that aggression is not necessarily an innate instinct but that violence often results from learning, experience and need (Montagu, 1968). Some people live in very deprived conditions, suffering from poverty, unemployment or racism. They feel marginalised, left out of mainstream life. They may live under very repressive authoritarian regimes, or in a society where the normal democratic processes do not respond quickly enough to the legitimate concerns of a community. Usually they cannot fight back directly at the presumed cause of their discontent, alienation or frustration, whether a government or absentee landlord. As a result their dissatisfaction or sense of injustice may find an outlet in crime or a form of civil disorder such as rioting. A scapegoat may be found as an alternative target for anger - called displacement aggression - whether inanimate things such as property or other people. Studies in the United States found that mobs of poor American whites, aggrieved by their low economic and social position, vented their feelings by attacks on Black Americans. (Dollard et al, 1939) The left-wing, principally the Labour Party, tended to blame Thatcherism or Conservative policies for much of the growth in poverty and violence in various forms (hooliganism, urban riots, mugging) since 1979.

First, a number of incidents occurred in which the Thatcher government did not seem to be acting fairly. When 44 young dancers died in a Dublin discotheque in February 1981, the Prime Minister sent a message of condolence to her Irish colleague. A month earlier 13 black youngsters died in a fire in South-East London but no government official sent a message of sympathy to the bereaved relatives.

Secondly, the government made no effort to amend Section II of the Local Government Act (1966) which the last Labour government intended doing if it had not lost the 1979 election. The Act provided government help to local authorities to meet the needs of recent Commonwealth immigrants whose language and customs differed from those of the rest of the community. This provision needed amending so that it would apply to people born in the UK who faced problems of racial disadvantage.

In his Report on the Brixton riots Lord Scarman (1981) referred to the existence of "racial disadvantage" as a fact of current British life and also to widespread racial discrimination (p.135). He pointed out that, regarding unemployment and social opportunities, "practices may be adopted by public bodies as well as by private individuals which are unwittingly discriminating against black people" and that this should be swiftly put right. (p.11)

Thirdly, Mrs Thatcher's policies of curbs in public spending were blamed as part cause of Britain's economic recession 1979-1981 and the steep rise in unemployment. This hit the ethnic minorities and the young hardest. Among them unemployment increased faster than among the general population. Unemployment among members of ethnic minorities tended to be of longer duration than that among the white population, caused by racial discrimination, the problem of language and the lack of skills. In addition, the black population is much younger than the white population. In early 1981 unemployment in the area of Brixton Employment Office stood at 13% but ethnic minority unemployment in the area was 25%. Over the years to February 1981 total unemployment increased by nearly 66% compared to 82% among ethnic minorities (Scarman, 1981). All the older people - white and black - blamed unemployment as a key cause of the riots.

The three wards affected by the Handsworth riots in 1985, according to the 1981 census, had more than twice the national average of single-parent families. In 1985 Handsworth had an average unemployment rate of 36% compared to 20% in Birmingham generally. Among Handsworth's under-24 youth the jobless rate had reached 50%. Whereas one school-leaver in five among white and Asians eventually found work, among black school-leavers the figure was 1 in 20.

While the government continued to give money for urban renewal this was less than the cuts in government grants to local authorities. Consequently the local authorities had to reduce spending for education and public housing. To provide a specific instance, the government spending on Urban Aid for Liverpool doubled between 1980-81 and 1983-84 from 6 million to 12 million, yet during the same period Liverpool's housing subsidies fell by £13 million, and its rate support grant by £23m. Other cities had similar experiences (Osmond 1988: 207).

Various forms of welfare, social security, family and unemployment benefits were reduced from 1979, making life in the 1980s harder and tougher for the less well-off sections of the community. By 1981 social expenditure as a proportion of the GNP was less than the average for OECD countries and the lowest of the EEC countries. This particularly affected the sick and disabled, pensioners, the low paid, sole parents and the unemployed, who were within the low income poverty category (Townsend, 1987).

The government spent money on encouraging people to start businesses and also on Youth Training Schemes. However, whites had a greater chance of getting employment than blacks. Often many of the jobs created by new businesses starting up in large cities tended to be taken up by skilled people who commuted from the country. Lastly, the non-whites were particularly affected by government economies and privatisation programmes which led to a reduction in public sector employment and consequently in the opportunities for unskilled jobs.

Conflict Resolution and Management

The two approaches to law and order, violence and crime, held by the right-wing and the left-wing respectively, have already been described. Both can be linked with the views regarding negative and positive peace developed by conflict theorists. In other words, the classic right-wing approach is to keep the peace internally and externally by means of a strong police force and armed forces, supported by a substantial stock of weapons. Often unresolved problems persist, such as fear of unemployment, poverty, crime and racism. Such latent conflict situations can erupt into open violence (manifest conflict) as in the case of the urban riots already described.

The right-wing answer to violence tends to be resort to heavier punishments, and more spending on arms, punitive or deterrent measures. This was reflected in the Police and Criminal Evidence Act (1984) for England and Wales, which gave the police greater powers, and the measures taken by the government in June 1986 to provide the police with more powerful weaponry. While it can be argued that this is necessary, especially in the short-term, Kinsey et al (1986) have pointed out it only intensifies and gives a "further twist to the vicious circle of police-public alienation." (p.4) In other words, repressive measures only provoke greater violence and crime by those who think it is a means of getting even with society.

People from very deprived backgrounds may redirect their frustrations and anger against minorities, or express their anger in the form of vandalism or criminal acts. If so, only when the original source of fear and tension is removed will the redirected conflict behaviour cease, along with the search for scapegoats (displacement aggression). One view is that "working-class racism in the inner city is, at least in part, a product of the socio-economic decline of such areas" (Miles & Phizaclea 1979:23).

The left-wing solution for violence and crime is normally to try and make basic reforms and changes in the law so as to create a society which is fairer and more just. In other ways attempts are made to remove the causes of violence, focusing on "preventive medicine" rather than on "curative medicine", so as to achieve a situation of positive peace.

A *Guardian* editorial (25 August 1984) argued that as long as extreme poverty exists then "any type of policing" can only make a limited impact on crime. This echoes the final remarks of Lord Scarman in his report on the riots (November 1981): "Good policing will be of no avail unless we also tackle and eliminate basic flaws in our society." He quoted from President Johnson's address in the United States upon the need to change conditions that breed despair and violence such as ignorance, discrimination, slums, poverty, disease, unemployment. (See *The Economist*, 15 May 1982.)

Conflict Theories, Government Policies and Urban Riots of the Early 80s

Since the mid-1980s there have been no serious outbreaks of urban violence. The government has not been spending vast sums on improving the housing and education of the inhabitants of the very poor urban centres or on improving the work opportunities of the very poor. However, unemployment has dropped since 1986 as the economy has continued to expand, and certain developments have taken place since 1985 which are helping to diminish the gap between two Britains - white and black.

Lord Scarman suggested in 1986 that efforts should be made to create a black Middle Class. If non-whites in greater numbers achieved positions of authority and influence, this would improve their capacity to work peacefully for the legitimate needs and grievances of their communities. Certainly since 1981 a number of organisations have come into existence to help non-whites in this way. Following the 1987 General Election, the first ever group of black MPs achieved election to the House of Commons.

Secondly, more efforts have been made to study conflict management techniques so that effective measures can be taken to deal with grievances before conflicts escalate to the stage of manifest violence. In his original proposals in 1981 Lord Scarman suggested greater liaison between local organisations, including the police. Recently, a number of local authorities, in London and elsewhere, have begun to set up bodies to provide mediation and conciliation services to resolve neighbourhood conflicts peacefully. In addition, more people, including teachers and police officials, are becoming convinced of the value of training to help them deal directly with disputes by negotiation rather than by confrontation.

Successful negotiation between two sides is helped if each party is willing to abandon hostile polarised images of the other and "tunnel vision" (ie perceiving the conflict in terms of the "goodies" and "baddies"). Instead each side might start to appreciate the viewpoint of the other and, rather than viewing the conflict in terms of winners and losers, see the problem as one which might be resolved to the benefit of all. Trade-off arrangements might be envisaged, so that concessions by one side in one area might be matched by concessions from the other side in another. Some evidence exists that improved police-community relations in areas where they were previously poor has been the result of this attempt to work towards common shared goals. In this connection the following *Times* editorial (26 November, 1981) is apt:

> The quality, and ultimately the safety, of society depends on black and white citizens working consciously to live in toleration together.

References

BOULDING, K (1978) Stable Peace. Austin & London: University of Texas Press

BUTLER, D & STOKES, D (1974) Political Change in Britain. London: Macmillan

CHESSHYRE, C and BROCK, G (1980) "The Revolt of Britain's lost tribe". The Observer, 6 April.

COSER, LA (1970) "Some social functions of violence". In R Hartogs and E Artzt (Eds) Violence: Causes and Solutions. New York: Dell Publishing Co.

DOLLARD, J et al (1939) Frustration and Aggression. Yale University Press

EYSENCK, HJ (1957) Sense and Nonsense in Psychology. Harmondsworth: Penguin

FARLEY, JE (1982) Majority - Minority Relations. Englewood Cliffs, N J: Prentice-Hall, Inc.

FEAGIN, JR & HAHN, H (1973) The Politics of Violence in American Cities.

FIELD, S & SOUTHGATE, P (1982) Public Disorder: a review of research and study in one inner city area. Home Office Research Study No.72, London HMSO

GALTUNG, J (1966) "International relations and international conflicts: a sociological approach." Transactions of the 6th World Congress of Sociology, 121-161

HODGSON, G (1981) "Beware the easy explanations." The Times, 8 July

JOSHUA, H, BOOTH & WALLACE (1983) To Ride the Storm.

KERNER, O et al (1968) Report of the National Advisory Commission on Civil Disorders. Washington: US. Government Printing Office

KETTLE, M & HODGES, L (1982) Uprising - the Police, the People and the Riots in Britain's Cities. London: Pan Books

KINSEY, R, LEA, J & YOUNG, J (1986) Losing the Fight Against Crime. Oxford: Basil Blackwell

LORD JUSTICE SCARMAN (1981) The Brixton Disorders 10-12 April 1981. Report of an Inquiry by the Rt Hon The Lord Scarman, OBE Cmmd. No.8427. London: HMSO

(1986) "Injustice in the Cities". New Society, 14 February

MILES, R and PHIZACLEA, A (Eds) (1979) Racism and Political Action in Britain. London: Routledge & Kegan Paul

MONTAGU, MFA (Ed) (1968) Man and Aggression. London: Galaxy Paperback, OUP

OSMOND, J (1988) The Divided Kingdom. London: Constable

RATCLIFFE, PT (1981) Racism and Reaction - a profile of Handsworth. London: Routledge & Kegan Paul

ROSE, R (1982) Understanding the United Kingdom. London: Longman

STORR, A (1968) Human Aggression. London: Allen Lane/Penguin Press

TEBBITT, N (1985) "My cure for our sick society". Daily Express, 15 November

TOWNSEND, P (1987) "Welfare State in Contemporary Britain." Talk to the Politics Association, University of Bristol, 25 September

SECTION II:

THE COMMUNITY VIEW

This section is wholly written from the perspective of people who have been resident, and actively involved, in areas where violence and public disorder have occurred. No other contributions can match such "insider" accounts for their vivid portrayal of how such problems appear at first hand, and this is especially true of the first of these chapters (Chapter 3) by Jim Murtagh. Like the other authors in this section, however, Jim Murtagh does not only write from the perspective of the local resident, but also from the perspective of one who is trying to understand the reality of what is going on, to stand back and avoid stereotypical preconceptions, and to find a "better way" through the tangle of emotions, fears, misunderstandings and power-strivings he sees around him. They write, then, from the perspective of both insiders and outsiders, in the belief, in line with the first principle of conflict resolution - openness to perception of the true reality of the conflicts in which one is involved - that a rational response can only derive from a dispassionate (and sympathetic) analysis. This attitude does not prevent any of these writers expressing quite strong opinions about the circumstances they have observed - but it does ensure that there is no precipitate ascription of blame to any particular group or party. To a large extent the picture one gains is of individuals - whether community activists, uninvolved residents, police, officials or other intervenors - quite at sea in the complexity of the social situations in which they find themselves, assailed by strong emotions - their own and others', striving to do "right" but not being at all clear about what that "right" might be. Apart from a few deviant individuals in each group, no-one wants violence or believes it will do any good, but, nevertheless, violence is what so often occurs.

Each of the writers strives after some sort of resolution of this conundrum. In Jim Murtagh's case it is through the efforts of individuals who firmly adhere to a belief in the avoidance of violence at all cost and who risk being the victims of it by trying to act directly, by rational argument and appeals for calm, on those who manifest aggressive tendencies. To do this is no easy thing - as Jim readily admits in his honest disclosures of how he feels in such a situation and the realisation of his own limitations as a single individual in a crowd of strangers. The fact that he could even try is due to the training he had already received in the techniques of avoiding aggression in oneself, to the ability he amply demonstrates of controlling instinctive impulses in the face of threat and fear and maintaining a dispassionate, calm and rational attitude. He himself provides non-violence training for others, especially for men who wish to assert control over their own tendencies to dominate women, physically or otherwise. The effect of such training is not to suppress natural instincts, but to release powers and potentials that lie unrealised within most of us, particularly the power to control the conduct of our own lives and to be able to resist the flood-tides of emotion that carry us in directions we later regret. By understanding such emotions they can be harnessed to constructive undertakings which are consciously selected. We shall return to these ideas in Sections IV and V.

Jim Murtagh describes an incipient riot, involving Muslims and the police, in the centre of Manchester. The remaining writers all hail from inner city areas of London. Brixton - scene of the worst of the early 1980s riots - is the subject of both Chapters 4 and 5. Chapter 4 is extracted from a report (submitted to the Metropolitan Police District [MPD], the force that patrols London, and the Home Office, the government department responsible for policing, criminal justice and public order generally, as well as race relations) compiled by the Community/Police Consultative Group for the borough of Lambeth in which Brixton lies. The report deals with the riots that ensued after the police shooting of an innocent black resident, Mrs. Cherry Groce, in 1985. It uses a variety of evidence from reliable witnesses to present a picture of how the disorders arose and how they might have been prevented, focussing particularly on the role of the police, as the only agency geared up to intervention in threatening crisis situations of this kind. As the police were also held to be the immediate cause of the crisis, their role was made doubly difficult, but (as is pointed out in Chapters 12 and 13) this is by no means an unusual circumstance triggering such riots.

The Community/Police Consultative Group was itself set up as a response to earlier riots in 1981. That its existence did not prevent a repetition in 1985 perhaps shows that those who had criticised it as being a superficial measure with no real power were to some extent justified. In Chapter 7, however, Commander Marnoch of the MPD argues that its existence enabled the police to get the disorders more quickly under control and prevented a much more serious situation. Certainly, although the Consultative Group is not perfectly representative of all the communities in the Borough, it is a group of very active and very concerned local people, who take their job of encouraging a style of policing responsive to the needs of all the communities making up the area (which is ethnically very mixed) extremely seriously. The extracts from their report that make up Chapter 4 show a capacity for being both dispassionate in assessing the realities of the conflict and fervent in their advocacy of improvements in policing where their analysis showed that this had been lacking in foresight, effectiveness or empathy. It does not constitute an attack upon the police force (it explicitly recognises problems of under-resourcing and inadequate information at their disposal, and does not view the police mistakes as stemming from improper motives, except in the case of a few individuals) and recognises the corresponding responsibility of the community for itself preparing to control its own disorders, but it does not, either, seek to whitewash the police operation, being critical of certain deficiencies in management. It also recognises the responsibility of the country as a whole (reinforcing Chris Leeds' message) for allowing an area of poverty, disempowerment and disillusion to persist in the midst of general affluence. No-one is accused of ill will, but everyone shares responsibility and those who are most responsible must be those who have the greater power and resources to change matters for the better.

Chapter 5 takes the form of some reflections on the Brixton situation from a slightly later time (1989), by one of the members of the Consultative Group, Greta Brooks. But Greta is not just a member of this body, but, like many of the other contributors to this book, an extraordinary individual in her own right, as anyone who has met her will know. Even in those years that among others would have constituted a time of "retirement", Greta has manifested abundant vigour in many directions, not least almost single-handedly steering through its years of gestation a community-based neighbourhood mediation project for the resolution of local conflicts that has now officially been launched as a fully-fledged service. Although the birth of such an innovative and unfamiliar scheme is dependent on the cooperation and sympathy of a great many local people and particularly of those who make up its management committee, as Greta would be the first to point out, it was her energy, commitment and plain hard work that saw it through. As such, she is committed to the idea of constructive conflict resolution in all its forms, whether it be for neighbour disputes, complaints against the police (for which she also, unfortunately without success, advocated a mediation facility) or police training and policies for managing incipient public disorder. In this short paper Greta draws the conclusion, from her experiences generally, that conflict is not something to be feared or hated, but should be viewed as an opportunity - an opportunity for all of us to re-examine the myths we hold about one another, to extricate ourselves from the mess in which we have suddenly found ourselves by default, and to reconstruct our relationships on a basis of tolerance, understanding, respect and genuine humanity. If we regard conflict in this positive light, then we shall be empowered to begin to resolve it constructively and successfully.

The final chapter of this section is by another person who has regarded chronological seniority as an excuse for redoubling her efforts in aid of the community good. Although being advanced in years is not a general characteristic of the writers in this collection, or of mediators, both Greta and Yvonne Craig, the writer of Chapter 6, should remind us that long experience of life's vicissitudes is a very good background for the attitudes and skills of being an effective mediator. While some may narrow their visions and stick even harder to their prejudices, the majority come to a more mature dispassionate understanding with increasing age which, physical abilities permitting, makes older people, as a group, the greatest under-used resource in this country. While other countries, especially in the third world or Japan (from which we also stand to learn many other things - including the use of mediation as a standard social process for healing conflicts), see their elders as a valued source of wisdom and considered advice, we tend to push them aside as persons whose useful life is over - a waste, a travesty and a huge injustice.

Yvonne Craig calls on her knowledge of two contrasting inner city areas of London - Bermondsey, a docklands area, after the wartime Blitz, and Tottenham, where she is now a magistrate, and which has seen race-related disorder and police/community confrontation in recent years, most notably on Broadwater Farm. She concentrates on drawing general comparisons between Bermondsey, as an area where the community and police used to work together, and "Babylon", a composite picture of present inner London areas characterised by high proportions of black and Asian cultures, high crime, social disadvantage and poor police-community relations. ("Babylon" is derived from Afro-Caribbean jargon for a state of repression.) Like other writers in this volume, Yvonne paints a picture of relative deprivation coupled with feelings of injustice as providing the conditions for the breakdown in support for the police and the growth of desperation manifested in spasmodic social unrest and general violence. (Cf. Chapters 12 and 13.) Like those other writers, too, she sees one remedy emerging from concurrent initiatives on the part of both the police and the local communities, although she considers changes in the social and economic infrastructure to be paramount (cf. Chapter 2).

Chapter Three

Taking a Stand for Non-Violence

JIM MURTAGH

July 13th 1989, Rusholme, Manchester

I GUESS it was about 11pm. I was cycling home from Moss Side to Levenshulme. When I came to the main road (Oxford/Wilmslow Road) which runs south from the City Centre, I saw that the whole of the road was blocked off and what seemed like several police riot vans were parked nearby. I was a bit puzzled by who or what was blocking the road and concerned about the presence of riot vans. I decided to try and see what was going on and stopped and asked the first people I came to. They told me that nothing was happening, it was just a celebration. This didn't quite fit with the presence of riot vans so I remained puzzled. Three other people came up and asked me the same question, "What was going on?" I didn't know but we had a nice chat anyhow during which we tried to work out what the police (especially riot police) were doing there. They then left. I, however, was still curious to know more and still concerned about the presence of the police, thinking that didn't bode well.

As I walked on, I vaguely took in the number of police. I reckon there were three riot vans as well as three ordinary police vans. A few officers were directing traffic and a couple of senior officers were engaged in conversation. This was all at the south end of the road. Later on I was to discover that many of the shops and restaurants on both sides of the road had a couple of officers standing outside them. At the far (north) end there were also more traffic police, a couple of riot vans and maybe a couple of ordinary vans. (These are not necessarily accurate recollections - I never actually counted.) Meanwhile, I guess there was a crowd of a few hundred. The road and pavements were densely filled for a distance of some 50 yards (at a guess).

As I made my way through the crowd, wheeling my bike as I went, I noticed a van playing loud music, parked at the side of the road. So there did seem to be some sort of celebration. At this stage I just thought that some high spirited people had taken over the road and that was why the police were there. Meanwhile, as I emerged from the throng, something told me to turn round and as

43

I did so I noticed someone walking a few yards behind me. I turned back and carried on walking. A few paces later I turned round again. This time I made a mental note that both times he'd hesitated and slowed down when I turned round. So, although I turned back and continued on my way, I more consciously decided to turn round a few paces later. This time he hesitated, stopped, turned round and walked off. I was fairly sure he had something in his hand which I guessed might have been a knife. The 'feel' of it was that he'd intended to take my bag by cutting the straps. This was a bit disconcerting to say the least.

Tension in the Air

I then walked round for a bit still trying to puzzle out what was going on. On the one hand there was music and celebrating, on the other hand there seemed to be tension in the air and even in some respects an intimidating atmosphere. For example, someone would point at a car and a whole group of people would surround it and jeer. It seemed to me that the drivers were in a hurry to get away. In another incident, a youngish white male was trying to talk to a police officer and both of them were immediately surrounded by a large group of black youths who seemed pretty angry. (The crowd was predominantly young, Asian and male.) I guess the police officer advised him to leave and he did so fairly sharpish. It was all very puzzling and made me feel on edge not least because I felt if the police decided to try and clear the road, it was potentially a very explosive situation.

Ironically enough, I'd just about concluded despite my uneasy feelings, that it was OK to leave when I saw most of the crowd were moving towards me. (I was standing on the pavement, holding my bike, towards the North end of Oxford Road at the time.) I assume that the police had chosen that moment to order them to leave. I've no idea why the decision was taken at this point in time. Anyway, as the crowd moved north, they approached two police officers who were in the middle of the road facing them. I guess that like me the officers could see that they looked pretty angry and so they decided that discretion was the better part of valour, turned round and started walking towards the safety of the police vans on the north side. At this, the crowd began jeering them and making monkey/gorilla noises (and actions) at them. At the same time, a few plastic cartons were thrown, followed by a drinks can. (I think it was more or less empty.) The latter hit one of the officers on the head and spilled what was left of its contents down his shirt. Many people laughed and cheered.

Arrest

At this the two officers angrily turned round to confront the crowd. But, suddenly, whilst all eyes focused on them, two other officers swooped out of nowhere, grabbed someone in a headlock and dragged him off. I'd no idea if he'd thrown anything and I'd find it difficult to believe that they did. (Not that, in my opinion, their action would have been acceptable even if he had.) Whilst these two were still dragging this person towards the police vans, the other two were still standing facing the crowd. In that instant it seemed to dawn on people that they could vent their anger at this arrest on these two other officers, who found themselves facing a huge surge of people striding purposefully towards them.

There was a very brief attempt to deal with this by relying on their authority as police officers, before they abandoned this tactic and turned to seek the safety of the police vans. Fear and consternation was written all over their faces and a brisk walk turned into a run as the crowd converged on them and sought to cut them off. It seemed they'd left it too late. They were not going to make it. I'd seen this situation before. I felt if people caught those police officers, they were feeling so angry and so intent on revenge that their intention was to cause them harm. Consequently, I was frightened for the consequences in terms of escalation of the violence, especially as, out of the corner of my eye, I saw riot police beginning to disembark from their vans to rush to the scene. It was at this point, almost without thinking about it, that I decided to walk into the road and place myself and the bike between the onrushing crowd and the two police officers.

The Surprise Factor

I've often thought of what I would do if I found myself in just such a situation. I know I feel I ought to do something because I'd feel terrible if I stood by and watched people getting hurt. It was because I thought that violence might erupt that I'd stayed in the first place and now here it was staring me in the face. I had to do something and the only thing I've ever thought of doing is to place myself between the two. What surprised me and still surprises me was how calm I felt, especially considering the situation. I've felt much more frightened intervening in cases of an individual man's violence to a woman. I still don't understand why this was so. I didn't feel I would get hurt and I felt confident it would have some effect.

Nevertheless, I was still scared, but in some circumstances, the adrenalin that was surging round seems to produce this exterior calm that hides the inner turbulence provoked by fear and anxiety or worrying about people being hurt; not wanting to feel guilty for not doing anything; not wanting to feel a coward; and fear, huge fear of violence. Actually, in retrospect, I think my mind must have blanked out the risks to myself because it feels like I was acting on 'automatic pilot', on impulse. Very little, if any, conscious decision making went into my actions. It was a very unusual feeling.

So, I walked across the width of the road, facing the people coming towards me and asked them to "calm down", "Please, calm down, or somebody will get hurt." "Please calm down." By the time I reached the far side of the road, the whole crowd had more or less stopped and the two police officers had reached safety. Meanwhile, a few of the police officers who had rushed to rescue their colleagues had just about reached me, so I turned my attention to them, asking that they, too, calm down. At this point, the full-scale confrontation that I had feared seemed to have been averted.

In so far as this was due to my action, my guess would be that this was because of the surprise factor. People just seemed bewildered; couldn't make out who I was or what was going on - judging from the looks on people's faces - which proved to be sufficient to defuse the situation. No-one from either the crowd or the police threatened me. This despite the fact that saying "calm down" to people who are angry isn't particularly a pacifying thing to say. (As I mentioned, I wasn't thinking about what I said, it just came out.) I think I was gentle, calm, non-threatening and assertive and that together with the surprise factor seemed to be enough.

My Back Tyre is Slashed

Meanwhile, I think a riot van had appeared and was trying to drive through the crowd and so clear a path through it. It approached from the south and so the crowd's focus shifted from the north where I was to the south. Consequently, I crossed back across the road to the pavement and then walked along the pavement until I reached a point opposite the riot van. As I was walking, someone, presumably not happy with what I'd done, told me to fuck off. I ignored him. As the van drove through, people were shouting at the police inside, banging on the sides and back and spitting at it (and particularly trying to spit through the open windows). A few police officers on foot were trying to clear a path for it. I moved into the road towards the van whilst I pondered what to do about this situation. Then something caught my attention behind me; my bike felt different. I turned round in time to see a few hands withdrawing from my back wheel, which was now flat. They were grinning. I assumed that this was another indication that people were not happy with what I'd done. I just looked at them as if to say, "Well, that will help us all a great deal won't it?" At the time I thought they'd just released the valve but I later discovered they'd slashed the tyre and so punctured the inner tube. I turned back to what was happening with the riot van.

Dangerous and Provocative

It had made its way through the crowd, turned round and was on its way back, having had no noticeable effect in clearing the road but a considerable amount in winding people up. Suddenly the driver, presumably, and not surprisingly, cheesed off with all the spitting and banging decided to reverse straight back into the crowd. Fortunately, everyone managed to move out of the way and no-one was hurt. He was lucky; it could have been entirely different. I was really annoyed with his behaviour and without any hesitation went straight up to the van and said to him "My friend that was an extremely dangerous thing to do and very provocative. The best thing you can do is leave the area." Amazingly, he listened without saying a word, but no doubt he was taken by surprise as well. At this point, an officer on foot came up and said "could you move away from the van please." I turned to him and said, "My friend, I've something very important to say to the driver." However, it was too late. The driver had taken the opportunity to move off and my path was blocked by the police officer in front of me. However, I was relieved to see that the van had driven off to rejoin the other vans at the south end of Oxford Road.

Celebrating Ramadan

With the disappearance of the van, the situation seemed to calm down a little once again. I began to make my way to the pavement whence I intended to return to the north side to check what was happening there. As I did so three young men turned to me and one of them said something about the need to get my bike off the road. I was puzzled and asked him was he telling me the police had said no vehicles allowed. "Yes" he said. As I continued in the direction of the pavement, I was fairly sure I heard him say something like "Or you'll get beaten up." This made me angry so I turned round and asked him what he'd said. I think he said something about it being in my own interest to get off the road. The fact that I was going anyway together with my confusion as to what he'd said made me leave it there.

In retrospect, I think what he'd been saying was that I better get off the road or they (he and others in the crowd) would beat me up. It wasn't until later that I heard from someone who'd been listening to the radio that night, that a group of white youths had tried to break up the Muslim celebrations in Rusholme. (They were celebrating Eid, the Muslim equivalent of Christmas.) This probably explains at least some of the hostility towards me in what I assume was predominantly a Muslim crowd. Interestingly though, immediately after this altercation, another young man came up to me. He was very friendly and explained that he'd come from Burnley for the celebrations which happen every year at the start and end of Ramadan, the same as Eid. He thought most people were there for the same reason and only a few were interested in "causing trouble". He made no mention of white youths having attacked the celebrations, so at the time I was still completely in the dark as to what had happened before I arrived. I appreciated him talking with me like that and found it reassuring. We wished each other well and took our leave.

Flash of Panic

Almost immediately, a new incident developed at the north end. All I remember is two police officers arresting somebody. What happened just before that, I either did not see or cannot remember. His arrest provoked another angry response from people who started rushing towards the scene, intent, I guess, on intervening to stop the arrest. Police started pouring out from a riot van near by and charged at a section of the crowd nearest the arrest. The last I remember is people in that area running away down a side street being chased by riot police. My attention was then distracted elsewhere. Meanwhile I saw the two officers dragging the arrested man to a wall, holding him against it whilst one of them smashed him in the face with his forearm. Again, hardly thinking of the consequences, I stepped into the road and made for this incident, intent on trying to stop those police officers from what they were doing.

To do this I had to cross the whole width of the road as this was happening on the side furthest away from me. At the same time, more riot police were running towards this area from their vans at the north end. I was in the middle; the crowd to my right, the police to my left. For the first time I felt more frightened of the police than I did of the crowd. Here they were truncheons drawn, charging straight towards me. A sudden flash of panic struck me as I thought there was a real possibility of me being beaten by the police. Two or three times it flashed into my head that I might need to sit down as a way of saving the situation. However, it never came to this. For some reason, despite the flash of panic I kept on walking and turned my attention to the oncoming police. "Please calm down", "Calm down", is all I can remember saying to them. My memory is a bit vague at this point but I think some half dozen, maybe more, officers stopped in their tracks - no doubt very puzzled and surprised, judging from the looks on their faces. This was enough to allow people from the crowd in my area to leave unharmed.

Threatened With Arrest

Meanwhile one of the officers was blocking my route to the incident that had sparked off the latest escalation. (I think he was there for that purpose.) He turned to me and told me to go home; that I was being silly. I just said firmly no I'm not going home and no, I'm not being silly. (I didn't feel this was a particularly constructive thing to say, so I didn't feel very good about it. I wanted to explain what I was

Taking a Stand for Non-Violence

trying to do and what I'd seen the two officers doing but I couldn't think of the words fast enough.) I was also annoyed because I knew violence was still going on all around me and I was being delayed. The conversation then became disjointed but basically I think he was threatening to arrest me. I didn't want to get caught up in discussing this with him and began to say so. I think he thought I was going to say I didn't want to be arrested and so he began to say "No, I don't suppose you do" and then turned away. I began to tell him that wasn't what I meant but by then he'd already turned away. So, seeing out of the corner of my eye conflict continuing to my left and completely forgetting the original reason for being there, I hurried away to see what I could do.

The Officer in Charge

I arrived to see a group of about 15 facing one police officer and one of the group was really angry with him, shouting like mad. Again, I was scared that the officer might be harmed, so I appealed for calm. Someone immediately shouted at me why didn't I say that to him, he was the one who'd hit somebody. So, I turned to the police officer and said if he'd hit somebody he should apologise to them. He just stared blankly at me. Something then caught my attention and when I turned back, someone else was shouting at him. I think more officers then came over to try and break up the group. Again I found myself facing this same police officer and this time said to him something like, "My friend, for some reason your presence here seems to be inflaming people; will you please leave the area - I think that's the best thing you can do." Again, not too much thought went into what I said - it's just what came out at the time.

I think at this point someone whom I took to be the officer in overall charge appeared on the scene, on foot, accompanied by only one other officer. As far as I could see they were both unarmed. I'd guess that by this time, a third or maybe a half of the original crowd had been forced by the police onto the pavement. However he was immediately surrounded by what was still a sizeable group of people. People were very angry with him. "Why have you broken up our celebrations?", I heard someone say. (Though that was the only bit of the dialogue I heard.) After a while and to my surprise, I found myself feeling a certain amount of admiration for him. It was only afterwards that I realised why.

Contrast

He showed considerable courage in continuing the dialogue with people even though he spent at least half an hour surrounded by as many as 100 people with only one other person there supporting him.

During that time, his behaviour was the most non-violent of any police officer I saw that evening. Despite people's hostility and considerable anger towards him, he was not harmed and my guess is his courage (as well as his position of power) had a lot to do with it.

Yet this behaviour didn't seem to fit with the fact that presumably he had ordered the road to be cleared in the first place. He presumably ordered the riot van to clear the road and ordered the riot police to charge. I couldn't make sense of the contrast. His unarmed presence was, in my opinion, the single, most effective thing he could have done to defuse the situation. His presence focused most of the anger towards him and as he willingly engaged in dialogue and as he wasn't being violent to them (at that point), it was difficult for people to be violent to him. Consequently, it seemed to me to be fairly effective in defusing the situation. (Though I've no idea whether what he was saying was constructive or not, I felt reasonably good about the way he was saying it.) It confirmed for me what potentially could be achieved by a group committed to non-violence in such situations.

Shaken up

Meanwhile, as I left the road for the pavement again, someone else, presumably not happy with what I'd done told me to fuck off. I ignored him. In front of me I saw a young man holding his arm. I asked him if he was hurt and he said he was. He'd been hit a glancing blow by a police truncheon. He was shaken up by it, particularly by how badly hurt he might have been if it had caught him full in the face or on his shoulder or head. I asked him if he'd seen who'd done it. (I intended to challenge the officer about it if he'd known who it was, but he didn't.) I tried to commiserate and agreed the police violence was out of order. He was talking to his two friends and saying there was more of them than police and if everyone acted together, they could easily beat them. I said, "Please, don't use violence. If you want to challenge what they're doing then sit in the road or something." I think they were a bit taken aback by this, but we took a friendly enough leave of each other.

Fear

Shortly after this, fear just hit me as if I'd walked smack into a brick wall. All my limbs, particularly my legs, just turned into jelly and I just wanted to leave. I didn't want to have to intervene any more, although I could have forced myself if necessary. As I said, the action of the senior police officer had diffused the situation quite a bit (perhaps this was why the fear hit me at this point when I was no longer so 'needed') and I was suddenly left clueless as to what to do next. Any active course of action as opposed to passively standing and watching seemed too daunting. Yet I felt unhappy about this as the situation was still charged. (A couple of missiles were thrown at the police during this period, though no-one was hit.) So I stood and watched what was happening with the senior officer. Whilst doing so, something again made me turn round. This time I saw, no more than a couple of yards away, a young lad (14/15) who was definitely shielding something in his hand and this time I was fairly sure it was a knife. Again, I felt his target was my bag (or possibly the bike) not me personally. I thought about saying something but as I couldn't be sure, I contented myself with looking at him in such a way that he would know I knew what he'd intended to do.

A Police Officer is Hit by a Missile

It wasn't too long after this, even though I wasn't completely convinced that things would calm down, that I decided I was too scared to be able to do anything more constructive and decided to leave. Just before I did so, the officer accompanying the senior officer was hit in the head by a missile. I didn't see what was thrown or who threw it. I think he was a bit shocked and concussed by it (it's difficult to say how hurt he was) and was led away to the nearest police van by the senior officer, who commendably kept his cool. A few of the older members of the Muslim community lost their tempers at this point and began shouting at the others. The incident seemed to have a bit of a sobering effect, particularly as the police did not react to it with more violence of their own, which was both very wise and very commendable. I then took this opportunity to leave.

More Threats Against Me

Thirty yards down the road, I found someone with a bike pump. It was then that I discovered that my tyre had been slashed, not let down. Ah well, a three mile walk home to Levenshulme. Just as I set off two drunken men came up to me and one of them started talking as we walked along. There was an underlying aggression to what he was saying that made me feel uncomfortable and I was trying to humour him when I didn't really want to talk with him at all. I just wanted to be left to recover in peace. He fairly quickly got round to asking me if I'd got any money in my bag to which I told him no - which was true. This was after he'd asked me for some money saying he needed it for a fare to Leeds.

He then went on to ask me if I had any money on me. I told him I had. "How much?" he asked. I told him that was irrelevant as I wasn't going to give him any. What money I had I needed for myself - not strictly true but I couldn't think fast enough to explain the whole truth and his voice and manner was becoming more menacing all the time. He responded, "Listen, mate, there's a fucking riot going on back there so don't tell me it's not fucking relevant. How much have you got?" (or something like that). This was a very clear threat. At first, I'd thought he was asking for money as a homeless/drunk person. However, it was now obvious that he was demanding money under threat of violence. I felt angry, sad, sickened and very frightened.

Choice

I had a choice to make - give in to the threats and hand over the money or refuse and take the consequences. Again, more on impulse and fuelled by the anger at being threatened, I looked straight at him and repeated that it was irrelevant how much money I had and, without hesitating, just carried on walking. To my intense relief, he was obviously taken by surprise and stood still, muttering something about the cops being around. (Two traffic police on motorbikes were only about 30 - 50 yards away from us, though they hadn't been watching what was going on. Being honest, their presence was also a factor in my decision.) He then turned left and that was the end of that. My first and, I hope, last time, that I've been threatened with violence for money.

I felt sick because for me this incident epitomised the destructiveness and futility of violence. He might well have felt better (and certainly more powerful) if he'd beaten me up and taken my money but that wouldn't have changed his situation at all. He'd have just passed on part of his oppression to me and I would have become another victim. The social system, meanwhile, that produces all these victims, continued to survive intact. Having said this, I understand how years and years of oppression, feeling powerless, ground down and alienated produces very strong feelings of pent-up anger, frustration and hate. Normally these are repressed but a violent conflict like the one we'd just experienced allows them to come out. Unless this energy is used in constructive non-violent ways to challenge and change their situation for the better, it can only come out in violent and destructive ways, either against oneself or others.

I arrived home at about 1.30am without further incident. This was about 2-2½ hours after I first arrived on the scene in Oxford Road.

This paper was previously published as part of the Whose World? *Newsletter, No 57, July 1989.*

Chapter Four

The Brixton Disorders of 1985

COMMUNITY/POLICE CONSULTATIVE GROUP FOR LAMBETH, JULY 1986

[The Brixton riots in 1985 followed upon the shooting by a police officer of a black woman, Mrs Cherry Groce. The Community/ Police Consultative Group for Lambeth, the London borough containing the district of Brixton, had been formed after earlier riots in 1981. The following account is adapted from their July 1986 report on the 1985 disturbance and their recommendations for action by police, the Home Office & the local community. - Ed]

Introduction

THIS REPORT is not an attempt at a full account of the Brixton disturbances of September 28th and 29th 1985; still less is it a full study of the causes, either immediate or long-term. It is concerned with the lessons that might be learnt from the experiences of those two days, especially those that can be reduced to practical recommendations. In the nature of things, most of these recommendations are addressed to the police, but we have also given careful consideration to the contribution of the community and we have offered a few suggestions of a practical nature to the Home Office.

There are some issues which we do not cover, however. The circumstances of the shooting of Mrs Groce are still sub-judice. Matters to do with the police conduct of search and entry have been considered by the Group in a separate report.

To some extent, our recommendations are bound to overlap with those of the police force's own post-mortems; but we believe that the prevention of riots and their successful policing are so important that a certain duplication is no bad thing.

We hope that such of our criticisms as we direct towards the police will be accepted in the same forthright but constructive spirit as that in which we put them; and that it will be recognised that the objective of our criticisms is the more effective maintenance of law and order, which we all desire - for which public trust in the police is such a vital ingredient.

Prevention and Precaution

At 11am, on September 28th 1985, Scotland Yard issued the following statement: "At 7am armed officers went to 22 Normandy Road, with a warrant to search the premises. While they were there, a black woman in the house was accidentally shot by a police officer. She was immediately taken to St Thomas' Hospital, in Waterloo, where she is 'seriously ill'. We deeply regret the tragic accident and an investigation into the circumstances has been set up immediately".

It was right to issue a statement, but we believe its issue did not fully meet the needs of the situation. The statement cannot have been easy to word, but its terms seemed to some people almost to suggest that the question of serious blame was already disposed of; and it should have included an explanation that, if the facts established by the investigation justified it, the officer who had shot Mrs Groce would be charged and criminal proceedings would follow.

We also believe that, in addition to the formal statement issued to the media, a formal apology should have been made to the Groce family by a senior officer. (The family later stated that none was made to them.) An explanation of what had happened, of the terms of the apology and of the necessary legal procedures before the officer concerned could be suspended, or arrested or charged should the facts justify doing so, should also have been given to the friends and neighbours who gathered outside the Groce residence, by an appropriate officer, to allay tension in the earlier part of the morning, before it had a chance to mount dangerously.

Further, it could perhaps have been arranged for an official hospital statement on Mrs Groce's condition to have been relayed to the crowd in Normandy Road, as early as possible, rather than leaving it to the members of the Groce family to do so. As the Groce family later made several statements deploring a violent response to the shooting, it ought also to have been possible to have arranged, perhaps through community representatives, the issue of a statement from the family when anger was clearly mounting amidst rumours of Mrs Groce's death. The media, for their part, should have acted to facilitate and support such moves, rather than concentrating on speculation as to possible disorder in a way that must certainly have drawn trouble-makers to Brixton.

No community representatives were alerted by the police during the entire morning of the 28th. Although efforts were made to contact the Chairman of the Consultative Group during the morning, these were curiously ineffective, given that he was at home till at least 11am and subsequently in Brixton Recreation Centre, three minutes' walk from Brixton Police Station, at a youth conference, as his wife, who was in all day, could have told the police. He reckons that if he had been at Normandy Road, where he knew several of the by-standers as well as the Groce family, he might well have been able to prevent the build-up of an angry crowd, especially if other youth leaders and the like had been alerted to accompany him when the crowd was predominantly of local people, not outsiders.

No alert was issued to relevant home beat officers on duty, nor were any off duty summoned to their posts during the morning of the 28th when, even without knowing of a gathering crowd, ordinary members of the public who had heard the news of the shooting clearly saw the risk of a riot.

No alert was given to community groups or to shop-keepers at any time during the day or even after violence had begun (although two officers returning to Brixton Station from Brixton Hill informed a few shops on their own initiative at about 6 pm).

The Initial Phase of the Disorders

The apparent lack of contingency plans and of pre-set lists of actions to be taken when serious risk of disorder arises may have another explanation, a mistaken optimism about the likelihood of disorder that would also account for the deficiency of reserves once disorder had broken out.

The violence, which rapidly developed into full riot, began with the throwing of missiles at around 5.40pm, at least half an hour after the crowd from Normandy Road had arrived outside Brixton Police Station (and more than an hour after a clear warning of likely violence had been given to the Chief Superintendent in command of Brixton Division).

There was sufficient apprehension of trouble in the first half of the morning for reserves immediately to be put on stand-by and in the afternoon for operations rooms to be opened at Brixton and Scotland Yard, so the lack of men at 5.30pm is the more surprising, disorder being more, not less, likely to occur after outsiders had had time to arrive with dusk impending. Moreover, if reinforcement units had been summoned even as late as 5.30pm, nearly an hour would still have been available for DSU vans to arrive in time to join the action against the besieging rioters at about 6.20p n.

It was the lack of manpower combined with the need to relieve the siege on Brixton Station that forced the police to apply tactics of dispersal to the riots outside the station, causing them to move in three directions, north and south along Brixton Road and NW up Stockwell Road. In none of these directions were the police numerous enough at first to prevent cars being overturned and set on fire and shops being broken into and also in some cases being set on fire. Furthermore the police could not respond to a much wider spread of incidents of looting and attacks on people and premises. Between about 6.30pm and 9.30pm normal public order had broken down over a wide area of Lambeth.

Little if any of this violence, fear and loss of property need have occurred if there had been adequate manpower to subdue the besiegers of Brixton Station and prevent sections of them spreading the riot elsewhere.

It was put to the Commissioner, Sir Kenneth Newman, by Christopher Elliott in an interview in *The Sunday Telegraph* (October 6, 1985) that he had earlier said that if there were to be an outbreak of disorder on London's streets "it would be contained in 30 minutes". Sir Kenneth Newman replied that the police had been "very concerned that they made maximum use of community leaders to defuse tension. From the time the incident occurred they were busy informing local leaders and invoking their assistance". This is difficult to square with the tardiness of the police in contacting the Chairman of the Consultative Group; but in any event the efforts to reduce tension that were made had proved abortive by about 4pm, as the police were informed shortly afterwards.

Sir Kenneth Newman continued his reply by saying that "police were actually accompanied by community leaders on the steps of Brixton Police Station talking to the demonstrators to defuse the situation". The implication is that these "community leaders" had been asked by the police to come to their assistance.

In fact one of them, the Rev Ervine Smith, was a member of the Panel of Lay Visitors to Police Stations (and a minister in the Clapham area of Lambeth) who was there, not at the request of the police, or even with their prior knowledge, but in order to rendezvous with other Lay Visitors and make a visit to the cells, just in case there had been arrests in connection with Normandy Road demonstrators and in case such a visit might possibly help to reduce the tension. (Actually, no arrests had been made.) The other person at the Station entrance was Mr Hector Watson, formerly representative of the West Indian Ex-Servicemen's Association on the Community/Police Consultative Group.

Neither man was particularly suited by his local connections to make an impact on the crowd, which was now in a state of highly aggressive excitement, but they bravely made the attempt.

With all respect to Sir Kenneth Newman, the efforts to persuade the crowd at Normandy Road or outside the Station not to resort to violent action were in no way a justification for the delay in assembling sufficient police to enable the initial outburst of disorder to be "contained within 30 minutes". To put forward such a justification is only to undermine the concept of "community policing" which Sir Kenneth Newman has done so much to promote but which (on the evidence of letters to *The Job*, the London police newspaper) many officers appear to distrust, because they mistakenly suppose that it means holding back from a proper enforcement of the law in "sensitive" areas. (What it does mean is policing in such a manner as to elicit maximum public support in combating crime).

It has always been admitted by the police that dispersing the besiegers of Brixton Station had detrimental effects which could have been avoided if more men had been available. We do not claim the expertise to suggest what would have been the best tactics to employ against the besiegers or generally how to deal with a rioting crowd so that all its members could either be arrested or be dispersed without causing any further disorder. The police will obviously have such questions under continuous scrutiny. We do, however, suggest that the psychology of crowd behaviour is taken account of. People get caught up in the excitement of a crowd and may be induced by the collective mood of the crowd to do things which they would not otherwise be motivated to do. (Elias Canetti, author of "Crowds and Power" has described how as a young man he became infected with crowd fever and joined in an attack on a public building and its burning, quite contrary to his normal inclinations as a reflective, intelligent student). It would seem desirable whenever possible to apply tactics which deflate rather than stimulate crowd fever.

We wish officers to be given adequate means to defend themselves against injury and to be able to take all due measures against rioters, but we believe that the use of plastic bullets, when officers or members of the public are not themselves being fired on, would only tend to encourage rioters to resort to guns. There is no lack of illegally-held guns in Brixton and we do not believe rioters would be restrained by recognising a distinction between plastic bullets and conventional firearms.

The community relationship in policing, and conciliation as an essential element of it, is also relevant to any possible recourse to plastic bullets or other potentially fatal weapons to maintain law and order. Police need adequate protection in situations of violent disorder, but plastic bullets are an indiscriminate weapon (as the attempted euphemism "baton rounds" indicates) and they can cause serious injury and death. The ultimate use of a gun against an armed criminal is a balanced response. But the use of an indiscriminate weapon of potential death against aggrieved local rioters who tomorrow may be a section of the local community with whom relationships must be resumed must surely negate community policing. The events of last September support this connection. The Group meeting two days after the disorders was a bitter representation of unappeased community resentment at the shooting of Mrs Groce. But in the event there was no violence and the ability to make a public verbal assault on the police and on the Group released tension and helped to an early return to more normal community policing. Had plastic bullets been used and led to death or injury resentment would no doubt have doubled and any public meeting of the Group would have been at risk. It is a wrong sequence of thought to ignore apology/explanation, to maintain an internal complaints system, to reject public inquiry, to leave conciliation unexplored and yet to legitimise plastic bullets which might well, as they have in Ulster, create or at least signal a gulf between police and local community which subsequent local policing is unable to bridge. While a sense of powerlessness and alienation no doubt underlay the Brixton disorders of 1981 and 1985, the trigger in each case was grievance, justified or otherwise, over particular police actions. The use of "baton rounds" would institutionalise that sense of grievance and so make escalating conflict a way of life.

When the riot started outside Brixton Station at about 5.40 pm, in addition to quelling it as soon as possible, the police should immediately have taken other steps. Apart from sending out an alert of actual disorder to shops, services and residents' groups, urgent action should have been taken to set up appropriate cordons.

It is very strange that the Yard Traffic Control was not asked to set up a cordon until 6.40pm, according to the Marnoch Report (p.7) - an hour after the start of the riot. It then took a further hour and a half to complete the cordon.

A cordon was of considerable importance for a twofold reason. Firstly, members of the public were continuing to enter the area affected by disorder unaware of the dangers. We have no figures of the number of people injured or put in fear of their lives or of vehicles lost or damaged for lack of a prompt cordon. Certainly there were cases of people being dragged from their cars at knife-point and sometimes then beaten up. Secondly, of course, a cordon reduces the number of would-be rioters, looters and other criminals who can enter the area affected, or at least means that they arrive later or perhaps without vehicles in which to remove loot.

It is noteworthy that none of the senior officers of L District who dealt with the Brixton disorders of 1981 remained to meet the problems of the present occasion. The Policy Studies Institute (PSI) has stressed the disadvantages in general terms of transferring officers approximately every two years. They are particularly acute in the context of an area like Lambeth. Knowledge of the community here is especially important and it is sad to see how often it happens that just as officers gain familiarity and understanding of the scene they are moved somewhere else. Rapidity of transfer in all ranks must also be a factor in the short police memory-span as to resentments that build up over incidents of friction with the police, especially given the time-lag on the resolution of complaints against the police.

Shortcomings of Policing in the Later Phases of the Disorders

A lack of proper briefing and the purposeful control that should go with it adversely affected the policing of the second phase of the disorders of the 28th starting at about 10pm, by which time the major violence had been brought under control or had subsided and police manpower became plentiful. Sporadic looting continued and bricks were being thrown at police vehicles, but the police should have been

The Brixton Disorders of 1985

in command of the situation, able to deploy in an organised fashion so as to reassure the public in areas which had suffered violence and to protect shops against further looting.

What appears to have happened was rather different. Police vans were driven at speed up and down the main streets, apparently somewhat randomly and without visiting at least some of the areas where they would have brought reassurance. Meanwhile quite large numbers of the public had gone on foot towards the centre of Brixton. It is not clear whether a significant proportion of these were merely going to observe or whether almost all were demonstrating their hostility to the police. Some people were throwing bricks at passing police vans. Many seem to have been trading abuse with police on foot. Most of them, at least, were not behaving in a manner helpful to the restoration of calm. Equally, however, they were not rioting in the full sense of the term: concerted attacks on the police, the overturning of cars and setting fire to shops had ceased.

These crowds, we are reliably informed, were given conflicting instructions by the police and subsequently subjected to considerable violence while being hemmed in, pushed back, dispersed or arrested. It was not always clear what the police wished of the crowd and the evidence of excessive force is compelling (see Appendix).

It was during the second phase that the great majority of arrests were made - perhaps almost all of them. Caution should therefore be exercised in drawing any conclusions about the earlier, more serious phase of the riots from the make-up of those arrested (Lambeth residents and outsiders; blacks and whites etc).

During this phase at least one locality, which for an hour and more before 10pm had been getting no response to emergency calls although a number of houses had been attacked, besieged or broken into, still received no public response. Equally, many shopkeepers were unable to obtain assistance during this phase. The 999 system must be improved to cope with the demand during disorders.

The question arises whether a large proportion of the officers in action during this phase (perhaps all of them from outside Lambeth) were not more interested in forceful confrontation with antagonistic crowds than in the other aspects of policing that the circumstances demanded.

This hypothesis is consistent with the expressions of enjoyment on the part of policemen recorded by some observers. It is also consistent with similar statements recorded in the PSI Study commissioned by Sir David McNee ("Police and People in London", 1983). One constable cited there said "That Grunwick dispute, I liked that one best of all. It was such a fair, clean fight". Another, from a different Division, said of the Southall disturbances: "We went wanging down there, jumped out of the van and just started fighting. It was a great day out, fighting the Pakis .... I thoroughly enjoyed myself". (Vol IV, p88)

It is unfortunately clear that obscene and racialist abuse was uttered by many police officers during the disorders, and not just when they were under extreme pressure (the Appendix gives examples). This behaviour was strikingly at variance with the injunctions of the Commissioner's handbook, The Principles of Policing and Guidance for Professional Behaviour (1985), which specifies that "it is a duty ..... to treat every person of whatever social position, race or creed, with courtesy and understanding" and also that "it is a duty to show both resolution and restraint if faced with violent resistance".

The PSI identified the problem of racialism and bad language as part of a falsely "macho" self-image among many officers, which is unfortunately also prevalent in the sections of society from which many officers are recruited. It can only be overcome by strenuous effort by supervising officers and by yet further improvements in the training system.

The beating of shields by officers when they are under the greatest pressure is certainly preferable to the shouting of obscene, racist abuse, and may be required to maintain their morale, sadly remote though it is from normal policing behaviour.

Tale of Two Estates

It is noteworthy, though not so far much noticed, that in some places close to the seat of disturbance "neighbourhood policing" continued through the height of the riot, with beneficial results to all concerned, while in others it ceased (perhaps at least in part, unavoidably) to the detriment of the public and of the maintenance of law and order. In particular, we are aware of one estate close to the centre of Brixton with a high crime record where home beat officers were on duty (perhaps on their own initiative, perhaps on pre-arranged weekend shifts), where liaison was maintained with the Tenants' Association, old people reassured, young people discouraged from heading towards the disorders and where there was not so much as a broken window in the way of trouble. Furthermore the police dealing with the adjacent rioting maintained a cordon in front of the estate, thus protecting it while at the same time no doubt avoiding the more difficult and confused situation for themselves which would have arisen if the rioters had moved from the street onto the estate.

By contrast, another large estate, also adjacent to the disorders, was less lucky. Home beat officers were apparently absent throughout, and the police who were contending with rioters nearby made forays of pursuit onto the estate and in doing so, we are reliably informed, assaulted innocent residents, including women. Apparently all other exit routes from the street were blocked, so that instead of being cordoned off from the estate, rioters were forced onto it. Crime by rioters moving through the estate seems to have been limited to damage and looting suffered by one shop. Observers consider it might have been much worse and indeed that the estate could have become a riot-ground, bearing in mind the design of the blocks.

On the Sunday, the proceeds of looting were to be seen on the staircases of the estate, showing that the looters concerned were not residents. There were, however, still no local police to be seen. Admittedly they would not have been made welcome by many on the estate after the incidents of misdirected force by other police the previous day - which unfortunately, we are credibly informed, were repeated on this day, presumably again as a spill-over of the further smaller-scale disorders that took place nearby. (Examples reported of unwarranted abuse and violence by police are given in the Appendix).

We do not venture specific judgements on the experiences of the two estates. Differences in circumstances may account for much. On one, stretched manpower may have made impossible the kind of deployment senior officers would have desired and we recognise that, similarly, the pressure on officers and the viciousness of attacks on them may have been such that loss of temper and a degree of indiscriminate violence were excusable. We believe the contrast should be carefully pondered, however. We also believe that it shows that "community policing" - working with local people as closely as possible in order the better to maintain law and order - has a real application even during a riot. In the heat of violent struggle of course the police are right to use whatever force is necessary to overcome the violence: "the gloves have to come off". Away from the heat of violence the warrior attitude implied by such a phrase, should if humanly possible be set aside in favour the normal policeman's care for the boundaries which should be set to his use of force, for the difference between citizens acting criminally and those not doing so and for the proper way of addressing either sort of person. A "gloves off" approach which disregards these boundaries and distinctions is not merely a failure to practice "community policing"; it happens to be unlawful.

Initiators and Participants in Disorders

A few cautious points should be made on the questions of who initiated the disorders and what elements were involved subsequently. After the riots quite a lot was made of outside agitators with political motives. We know that there were such people; but it must be recognised that a riot can only occur if a crowd builds up and becomes so angry as to explode into violence. The most that agitators can do is by false rumours and rhetoric to fan the anger and augment the crowd. On this occasion the anger about the shooting of Mrs Groce was genuine and widespread, irrespective of the activities of agitators (though heightened certainly by rumours of her death). The existence of outside agitators (who may or may not have thrown the first petrol bombs) cannot provide an alibi for failing to address the other factors behind the disorders.

Many overlapping elements can be discerned among those who took part in the disorders, including those who were drawn in by the contagion of excitement or because it was fun and those both from close at hand or outside who engaged in opportunistic looting and other crime. There were blacks and whites; there were those who wished to attack the police and those, perhaps few in number, who, from the evidence of Victim Support and elsewhere, were racially motivated to attack whites; there is also the possibility that some attacks on Asian shops were by white racialists. It is impossible to quantify the different elements. (57% of those arrested were recorded by the police as black and 39% as white; 50% gave Brixton Division addresses. These figures may be misleading, however, for reasons given above.)

Underlying Causes of Disorders

This report has mainly concentrated on rather practical questions, but that does not mean that we do not recognise the importance of the larger issues of the possible underlying causes of the disorders. Two major possible candidates, about which we feel bound to say something, are unemployment and community-police antagonism.

Government Ministers have stressed that the riots at Brixton and elsewhere were due to "wickedness". We agree that, though it is right that there should be anger at incidents like the shooting of Mrs Groce, it is wrong for this anger to take the form of violence and all the more wrong the more ferocious and indiscriminate that violence becomes. We can all play some part in sustaining moral pressure against the resort to violence and to that extent talk of wickedness is justified. But it is not the end of the matter. To point the finger in condemnation, even to try to generate moral pressure, is not likely to reduce the likelihood of further riots to any substantial degree. The economic and social background to the riots has to be addressed, regardless of whether this is regarded as a matter of securing social justice or merely as one of hard-headed prudence. (We offer no opinion as to which reason for taking action is the more valid, as we wish to stay outside political controversy.)

Certainly it is untrue to say that the higher the unemployment rate of a community the greater the likelihood of a riot, just as the general crime rate is not simply proportional to the unemployment rate. Equally, however, as Ministers admit, there is obviously some link. Recent British riots have all occurred in high unemployment, run-down inner-city areas. And a relationship between unemployment and general crime (which is easier to quantify than for riots) was, for instance, clearly established by the all-party House of Lords Select Committee on Unemployment in their Report of May 1982. Correlations between arrest and unemployment rates in London Police Divisions have been established by Home Office Studies. In Brixton itself there is a striking parallel between the figures for youth unemployment and those for violent crime. By far the most substantial reversal in the generally upward trend in the numbers of unemployed peoples aged 16 to 19 between 1979 and 1985 was a 39% fall between January and April 1983. This was paralleled by far the most substantial reduction both for violent crime in general and for robberies in Brixton during the same six years - almost 40% over the first six months of 1983 compared with the first six months of the previous year.

The other underlying factor to be considered is the possibility that police conduct over the preceding months and years had engendered a high degree of antagonism and alienation among some sections of the community, particularly the young and particularly black people.

The first point that needs to be made is that Lambeth is not an easy area to police. As well as its high crime rate, it is subject to the tensions of "inner city" problems and the complexities of a population with large ethnic minorities. The second point that must be made is that in the years after the Scarman Inquiry - at which police conduct was much criticised - there was widespread agreement that police conduct improved. Officers attending the Consultative Group, admittedly almost all of senior rank, have almost all seemed to be working hard for a better relationship with the whole community. The Panel of Lay Visitors to Police Stations (empowered to enter the cell wings of the five Lambeth stations at any time) have established to their satisfaction that ill-treatment of suspects is at least not widespread, though from time to time they have felt a degree of concern arising from a very small number of complaints from the 3% sample of prisoners spoken to.

On the other hand has to be set the PSI Report of 1983 commissioned and accepted by the Metropolitan Police and based on the evidence of researchers sitting alongside the police for two years and in a hostel for young black people for several months, as well as on a big survey of Londoners' experience of policing. Since the fieldwork took place in 1980-82, there have been significant reforms within the Metropolitan Police, specifically in terms of training, and more generally in terms of "community policing", strongly promoted by the Commissioner, Sir Kenneth Newman... It is improbable, however, that all the ills identified by the PSI have disappeared in the succeeding three years, a supposition confirmed by fair-minded observers with their ears close to the ground in Brixton (as well as by the experience in the disorders themselves, recorded in this report).

The PSI found that, on average, police officers themselves believed that 5% of their number were often rude and that 5% used more force than necessary. Out of the hundred arrests witnessed by the researchers they considered excessive force was used in eight cases. They also found that "racialist language and racial prejudice were prominent and corrosive" in the force, though the degree of tension when in contact with black people was much less than might have been inferred from this or from media accounts; and the relationship with black people was found to be better in areas of high concentration like Brixton than elsewhere. Over half those aged 15-24 of West Indian parental origin believed that the police were guilty of excessive force in making arrests, of intimidation in questioning and of violence in police stations, but it has to be added that this group assessed police behaviour more critically than white people. Many young black people, the researchers found, were predisposed to be hostile to the police out of a sense of "struggling against sharply adverse economic circumstances" and the institutions of a predominantly white society, "justified to the extent that unemployment among young back people was about 50% and that "all the evidence suggests" that racial discrimination, especially in job recruitment, "continues at a high level".

Antagonism between police and black people is to some extent a vicious circle. It would certainly be wrong to put all the blame on the police. The situation is not improved by those who foment attitudes of total hostility to the police. We feel bound to mention the Greater London Council video film produced last summer and designed for distribution in youth clubs and schools. Even if all its individual criticisms were justified, its tone of unremitting hostility and its refusal to concede any good motives to the police must have an unhelpful effect. Its final words, "communities must rebel", for all that they were uttered only as part of a song, were virtually an invitation to disorder.

By contrast, the Lambeth Community/Police Consultative Group seeks to make its criticisms balanced and constructive and always to keep open a dialogue with the police. In this report we have naturally dealt with those aspects of policing which we believe could have been handled better, though we also draw lessons from some good aspects of policing and we recognise that in some respects we may be ignorant of effective and admirable action, especially in the moments of greatest violence. We also know of exemplary behaviour to set against poor behaviour elsewhere. One reason for criticising the latter is indeed because it detracts from the admirable behaviour and lowers the reputation of the force as a whole.

The Need for Public Inquiry into Disorders

Healing Community Rifts

The Government and the community are all in the same law and order trap. In any democratic society government itself, including law and order, can only be with consent. As wealth, jobs and opportunity have left and continue to leave some inner cities and to be seen concentrated in fewer and fewer hands, government, including policing, in these stranded areas commands less trust and less consent. If it is not to be simply oppressive, consent has to be won back. Real steps to win back this consent should begin and be seen to begin. Public inquiry and debate is an important part of this process.

A consultative group can do useful work when the problems involving the consent of the community in policing and police methods are potentially bridgeable by realistic local investigation and exchange. There were also disorders in Handsworth, Toxteth and Tottenham. The police cannot take the full burden of inner city ills. Unless the depth of the problems - not just the immediate response to incidents - which founded last autumn's disturbances are openly recognised and grappled with, the healing of the deep community rifts is a bridge too far. It is the belief of the Consultative Group, argued unsuccessfully with the Home Secretary at a meeting on 1 October 1985 and in subsequent letters, that there should have been public inquiry into three matters relating to the Brixton Disorders, but which are also relevant to past and future incidents which are followed by disorders: the incident; the police management of the aftermath of the incident and subsequent disorder; and the situation of young people.

The Need for Conciliation

There is a strong case for a much firmer grasp by the Home Secretary and the police of the whole concept of conciliation. There are inner city areas, whose main characteristics of deprivation have been described comprehensively in the Scarman Report, "Faith in the City" and elsewhere, where there is no early prospect of substantial improvement in the *quality of life*. In these areas, including much of Lambeth, deprived minority groups at odds with society may not readily accept a concept of community policing which implies a partnership or at least a relationship of trust between them and the police. To create and sustain such a partnership the actions of the police have to be as open as possible to public scrutiny, and where they come in question prompt and open answers to restore confidence are essential. While the work of this and other consultative groups has contributed to this public scrutiny, serious gaps remain as earlier sections of this report have indicated.

The Scarman Report referred briefly to a possible conciliation procedure, and John Alderson's Lawson Lecture has developed the theme, including the suggestion of a possible Peace Commission. The Scarman recommendations (paras 7. 24-26) were not taken up. With five years further experience since Scarman, and drawing on industrial experience such as that of ACAS, Mr Alderson offers a wider perspective of the place of expert conciliation in the peacekeeping process. The scope of conciliation is well worth examination.

Genuine and open processes of conciliation in the widest sense should be an essential part of community policing. If community policing is to be credible, it has to maintain its credibility despite the necessary changes of police role from neighbourliness to the assertion of authority and the maintenance of the peace when disorder threatens. Credibility cannot easily be maintained if the police action appears to cover injustice or oppression. Thus the inadequate response to the wrongful shooting of Mrs Groce left tension derived from a sense of outrage which grew, exploded and was exploited.

The Contribution of the Community

As described above, the Chairman of the Consultative Group was prompt to act as soon as he learnt of the shooting of Mrs Groce; other members, not themselves in a position to act, took steps to alert him. The Panel of Lay Visitors to Police Stations went into action on the mere possibility of arrests taking place. Two other community representatives went to Brixton Station before violence erupted. Yet others might perhaps have helped to stave off disorder. But we do not know of any who were alerted to the turn of events and who failed to come.

Within the community, word of potential trouble was passed around, but not on a systematic basis, there being a lack of phone lists for the purpose. Telephone tree alert systems have since been instituted, but these need to be further extended and interlinked.

During disorders there is little community representatives can do unless the police maintain contact and listen to them; but they should be available as far as practicable to guide and assist the police in coping with disorder effectively and properly (while using their influence to discourage any misconduct).

People not infrequently get stranded during riots, unable to get home because they are on the wrong side of belts of violence or police lines. If practicable, refuges should be available both for immediate safety and, where necessary, for overnight accommodation. There is an obvious problem of such refuges being vulnerable to spillover of disorder or to police incursions in pursuit of suspects. To reduce this risk, entry should probably be limited to young children, women and the old, though this too might raise problems.

Community bodies ought also to take steps of a wider nature to facilitate cooperation at times of difficulty, to counteract any rifts between sections of the community that might open up and to work generally for a united and harmonious society. A start could be by links of a social kind.

The growth of violent and antagonistic attitudes has been a bad feature of recent years. We believe that it is the duty of everyone, but especially of those whose work or position gives them influence, to work against the resort to violence and in favour of neighbourliness and public spirit.

It is clear that education must play a role in helping to create a more peaceful society. This is not a matter for specific recommendation from us but for positive effort by teachers, school governors and educationalists. To help improve relations between police and young people, police representatives should be welcomed in schools. Barring entry in no way serves as a deterrent to any misconduct on the part of officers; it only exacerbates mutual misunderstanding and antagonism.

People in the media, advertising and the arts - the essence of whose work is to influence others - share with the more obvious category of politicians the responsibility to work for a less violent society, as well as for greater justice, the diminution of prejudice and whatever other particular objectives they believe in. Along with the rest of us, they ought to set their influence to reverse all the existing tendencies favouring harsh, aggressive, antagonistic or selfishly grabbing attitudes, not just by promoting goodwill but by helping to sustain the sense of discipline and the moral pressure against wrongdoing which are the main defences against all kinds of violence in society.

APPENDIX TO CHAPTER FOUR

Note: This is a selection from the evidence on which the Working Party based such findings as might otherwise seem to lack substantiation, especially on points critical of the police. The extracts show what witnesses saw of particular incidents or situations. They are not intended to give a rounded impression of the entire disturbances, nor to show the behaviour of rioters except as relevant to the situations described. It should be noted that there is independent evidence, relating to certain other times and places, of the police conducting themselves properly and well.

The personal witnesses are all either known and trusted by members of the Group's Working Party that prepared the original draft of this report except the two marked *, who are vouched for indirectly, two who spoke at a Consultative Group meeting and one who responded to the Group's invitation to submit evidence but who wished to remain anonymous (+).

Round brackets ( ) are used for words of passages summarised editorially.

As night fell, police screeched around the streets in white vans. Occasionally they would form up to a posse and quickly break up any forming group. Roaming gangs were clearly waiting for trouble to start. The crowd dispersed rapidly but left a white woman, Miss Sarah Hodgson, aged 22, lying on the pavement bleeding profusely from a wound in the back of the head. A friend, Mr Michael Barett, said she had been drinking outside the pub, was tripped by a policeman as she ran away and was "hit twice with truncheons while on the ground and trodden on". In Acre Lane a policeman at the head of one detachment lost his temper with a man who had been shouting at him and hit him in the face with his riot shield. When the man retaliated other policemen hit the man repeatedly with truncheons while the crowd shouted "bastards". He and another man were bundled into the back of a police van.

The Times, 30 September 1985

8.45: A terrace of shops north of the White Horse pub is systematically looted. Fires break out in the debris. A gang of up to 600 youths pour down Brixton Road and into the side streets with their looted goods. "There hasn't been a policeman here for an hour and a half", says one eye-witness.

Observer, 29 September 1985

As the riot slowly began to wind down the police presence became perceptibly heavier. Mr Tom Minney, a photographer, said that at about 9pm police advanced from Coldharbour Lane into Brixton Road, beating their riot shields and yelling. Mr Minney said: "I was standing quietly on the corner when a policeman walked up to me and without a word hit me on the shoulder and over the head". Mr Tom McGovern, a young black man, said he had been sitting on a wall in a side street when a group of officers began kicking him without warning.

David Rose, *The Guardian*, 30 September 1985

On Brixton Road at 9.30pm people of all ages, from children to pensioners, were milling around, gazing at shattered shop fronts and looted window

The Brixton Disorders of 1985

displays ... As the night wore on the tension grew ... People grunted in unison to rile the police, and threw stones .... (At or before midnight) youths pulled scarves down over their faces. Suddenly, the police moved in to disperse the crowd, charging into Brixton Road. I saw several people hit by truncheons. In Acre Lane, a man was lying on his back, splayed through a smashed glass window, which had already been broken. I saw an exultant policeman waving his truncheon and shield above his head as though in triumph. The police charged along Acre Lane, vans driving ahead so that people were effectively trapped between squads. Officers aggressively chased people, hitting out with truncheons and shouting at them to move off. Three officers, truncheons raised, ran up to four of us walking along. One of them shoved his shield into my back and said: "You fucking bitch". (Later, in Branksome Road) a few officers, wielding truncheons and shields, charged up the road. This time I tried to run out of the way but stopped when an officer came after me. Shoving me into a doorway, he pushed a truncheon under my chin and fingered my right breast. When I said I was not doing anything, he said "What are you doing on the streets then, love? Go home".

Celia Locks, Sub Editor and local resident,
***The Guardian*, 30 September 1985**

We left at about 9.30 to 9.45pm and walked up Brixton Road, (towards the Town Hall), going into side streets when the police told us to. There was a massive police presence. Practically no rioters were visible. Most people were observers. A lot of the police were without their numbers. A lot of their epaulettes were undone so that you could not read the numbers. We got to opposite the Ritzy. The police presence was too great for people to be looting. We got in a group of ten to fifteen people. There were other groups. All were multi-racial - lefties, Rastas, black girls .... (When the police charged) I was pulled up by a neck hold. I got a truncheon in my stomach. I didn't resist or at any time offer any violence. In the van taking me to the station the police were shouting "Niggers" and one said "Doesn't time fly when you're having fun". My arresting officer remarked "There's nothing like a bit of coon-bashing". He had been in the force 17 years.

What was being said over the van radio was chaotic. I had to direct the driver to Kennington station. At the station the arresting officer explained to the officer taking details: "I asked him to f... off three times". There were 12 people in my cell. The police didn't answer the bell. We wanted the flap in the door opened because the temperature was so high. That was from 12.40pm till 10am.

Black young man, local resident

In Atlantic Road, on our way to the centre of Brixton, we saw a policeman who adopted a warrior stance in the middle of the road and shouted to a black youth a little distance away "Come on then!" - "Nigger". Only after that did we shout at them. Lefties were taking the micky out of the police. Occasionally bricks were thrown at passing police vans. At the centre of Brixton, when police were laughing at a crying woman who said she was Cherry Groce's sister, I said "Don't you have any conscience?" and one of the officers turned round to me and said: "Nigger-loving slag". We had

first been told to go one way, then we were told to go in the reverse direction. When the police advanced out of Coldharbour Lane there was panic in the crowd caught among the flower tubs opposite the Ritzy. An officer said, "Get the bitch over the barrier". I was pulled over the barrier, being hauled by the hair and dropped on my chin. I was unconscious perhaps for a few seconds. My arm was forced behind my back till I heard a crick noise. A knee was put in my back. I was told "Get up, bitch" and stubbed with a truncheon three times at the back of my spine as I entered the van without making any attempt to resist. Handcuffs were put on so tightly that my hand went almost black. White girl who was with the above young man
(A youth had thrown a brick in the direction of the police, was surrounded by officers and had no chance of escape). At this point I was shocked to see a police officer club the man three to four or maybe more times in a way that seemed to me unnecessary in the circumstances. The officer began hitting this man before he did anything else, either grabbing or anything. I was not able to get his number because none of the officers had their numbers displayed ... (I) had until this incident wanted to support the police as much as possible.

+ Resident of SW2

A green coach full of overalled police was waiting for an hour. I asked a senior officer why they were wearing no numbers. I was told to clear off. A member of the public at Consultative Group meeting of 15 October * Police arrested one brick-throwing youth, but instead of dragging him away he was beaten about the head with their riot shields. Reporter Stewart Morris was struck twice by police batons, while reporter Lesley Johnson was dragged several yards by one officer during one charge by the riot squads. Both had identified themselves as South London Press staff, but were told to "Get off the streets and go home".

***South London Press**, 1 October 1985*

The police attitude seemed to be that anyone who was on the street that night was a criminal ... A young man and woman ...had clearly come out to see what was happening ... a group of police came over to the young couple and kicked and thumped the man. This act was completely unprovoked. We shouted down to them and when they realised they were being watched they moved away.

* Church member resident in a flat overlooking the south end of Brixton Road

(I became aware that there had been trouble as I walked home from Clapham North Station.) People were gathered in groups... There was a strong presence of policemen wearing dark 'riot' suits which lacked identification numbers at the top of the arm ... (At about 12.10am) a black youth came running into Acre Lane from the direction of Coldharbour Lane .... Six or seven policemen ... moved towards him and outside the almshouses proceeded to hem him in close to the wall whereupon they set about him with their batons. At the time the amount of force used seemed excessive to secure an arrest. While the attack was going on one or two policemen emerged from the white van at the corner of Trinity Gardens and Acre Lane and joined in the attack. After a short time the police let the black man go and he continued up Acre Lane clearly limping. **Paul Wilce, local resident**

(At an Angell Town Estate tenants' meeting) residents claimed that police had moved through blocks of flats systematically breaking glass in their front doors. They say that this happened early on Sunday after the rioting had died away. Resident Janet Morris said: 'A policeman called me a black bastard. They smashed the glass in my door. They kept shouting "Nigger go home" ... Other tenants told similar stories.

Observer, **6 October 1985**

Kids of 12 and 13 were walking along, saw looting and got involved. There was a shout "Police coming". The police entered the shop, found one white kid. They took him in their van. Then he was thrown out - covered in blood, which he had not been beforehand. (Bystanders gave him first aid and took him to hospital.) The owner of the shop who was guarding it was told to get off the street by the police, who then hit him. The police shouted "Nigger lover" at white girls and were also saying "F... off home before you get hurt" ... One person who was asking if the petrol station was open was told aggressively to get back. He bridled. He was then beaten to the ground by the police. I intervened, but got a truncheon blow aimed at me for my pains ... When the crowd was pushed off Coldharbour Lane through Moorlands Estate a woman resident who came to her gate inside her fence was hit by police and her bloke, when he came out to ask what was going on was told something like "Get in there or we'll take you to the van and you won't be recognised when you get out" - and he was a youth leader ... On the Sunday a kid coming along Somerleyton Road was told by police "If you don't go back, you nigger, they'll have to scrape you up off the ground".

Youth Club Leader

On Sunday in Stockwell Avenue I saw a group of children, aged about 10-12 years standing in the corner of Bellefields Roads and Stockwell Avenue. Suddenly a police transit van drove the wrong way up a one way street (Bellefields Road) very fast indeed, braked hard by the children - policemen shot out and ran towards the children. Most of them scattered, one boy ran down Stockwell Avenue ... with two policemen in riot gear ... chasing him as fast as they could run. They caught him at the corner of Gately Road and lifted him bodily into the van at the first corner ... The whole thing was over in a minute or two, and the atmosphere felt very threatening ... I felt afraid, not of the children, but of the policemen. As far as I could see the children were not doing anything, apart from standing in a group watching what was going on that morning... In Brixton Road there were 4 police vans going along Pulross Road against the one way system; police were in high spirits - laughing and joking.

* Church member, local resident

Chapter Five

Conflict within the Community: An Opportunity

GRETA BROOKS

THIS IS a book on the management of conflict, public order and policing. My experience in these spheres is as an inner city dweller, working to further good relations between the police and the community, in all its variety. Therefore, so far as policing is concerned, I am used to conflict in the street, in the home, in the police station. I have no experience of public order set pieces like pickets and demonstrations. The public order problem situation I work to prevent is the disorder which can spring up, apparently spontaneously, from a commonplace confrontation between local officers and the people they police.

Conflict is not something I relish but I have come to see that when I am confronted by it, I am being given an opportunity, if I have the imagination and wit to recognise it. I appreciated this fully in the aftermath of the Brixton Disorders of April 1981. In March 1981 the Brixton Council of Churches were asking the police, community groups and Lambeth Borough Council to create a forum at least to begin talking to each other, in the hope that relationships could be improved. Others were working along the same lines. But no-one had heard us clearly enough to do anything. After Lord Scarman's Report on the Disorders was published in November of that year, the police, some community groups and the Council were called to a meeting at the Home Office, chaired by the Home Secretary. Resources were suddenly available. We had an opportunity. I think we grasped it and laid sound foundations. Although there were further disorders in Brixton in 1985 (see the last chapter), there was not the same inevitability about them. With better communication and a pinch of luck these particular disorders might never have happened.

That is the dramatic side of conflict. Within a community, conflict more frequently settles into miserable routine, destroying the joy of living, producing fear and sowing the seeds of violence and depression. If the two sides to a dispute, quarrel, or row, can only glimpse a new vision, namely that what they have is not a dispute but a common problem which they can tackle together, then they may find the opportunity in the conflict. They can begin to experience a fresh way of looking at their lives as they are, with the hope of once more being in control of them.

The very job that society requires them to do, predetermines that police officers will come into conflict with individuals in the community. In addition to that, they have a peculiar situation: they get a bad press at the drop of a hat but have few opportunities to defend themselves one to one. I would like to suggest to them that each time they find themselves in a conflict, they are being given just such an opportunity.

Where relationships are not good, myths thrive. They are believed by many who have no experience of the situations from which the myths arise. Each myth will continue to be accepted as true, until it is effectively challenged. If, when conflict occurs, a police officer reacts as a myth foretells, the opportunity has been lost. If the officer has a large basketful of options for approaching conflict situations and uses them, the opportunity to change perceptions may be grasped. Therefore I prize the training that teaches an officer to be confident without being arrogant, assertive without being aggressive, so that, without fear of losing control of the situation, every last chance to communicate effectively is seized; and I never tire of stressing the importance to good relationships of effective communication within the police service itself and outwards with the people they serve.

I think the idea was already in the pipeline before the Brixton Disorders, but it turned out to be shortly after the Disorders that a new course entitled "Human Awareness" was introduced into the Recruitment Training Scheme at the Metropolitan Police College at Hendon. That course and its development, now called "Policing Skills", concentrates considerable time on the art of communicating. Until it is felt to be justified to use resources to give full training in *conflict management* to, not just a few, but the majority of police officers, I would suggest that it is within Policing Skills Courses or Professional Development Programmes that officers are going to find the best tools to turn conflict situations into opportunities to win the community to their side. Within the skills they can readily acquire, I would count listening skills the most important. Once they can convince the disaffected that they have heard them, the victory is within sight.

In Britain, year by year, we ask more and more of our police. Within a hierarchical structure they take full responsibility under the law for their own actions. They are expected to switch from that autonomy to become the equivalent of a squad of disciplined soldiers in riot gear ready, in extremis, to control disorder with armoured cars and baton rounds. For the sake of police officers as much as the community, I would like to see resources poured into experiments involving concepts such as "Neighbourhood Policing" (see Chapter

10), with enough sergeants to manage the transition and foster the right atmosphere, and the community in parallel learning to turn its own conflicts into opportunities. That way we would have a chance of dealing with conflict within the community before frustration erupts into violence; that way we might sustain hope even where the quality of life is so poor as to raise the whole question of a just society.

Chapter Six

Policing the Poor: Conciliation or Confrontation?
A preliminary comparative study of policing poor white and black communities

YVONNE CRAIG

> *When we 'ear a copper cum*
> *We nah get justice inna dis ya Babylon*
> *We 'it 'im on 'is head 'n run*
> *We seek ah justice outta Babylon*
> *We are the Bermondsey Boys!*

Traditional English rhyme in *British Black English* (Sutcliffe, 1982:77)

> Within working class communities the police acted as mediators in their community conflicts ... it is to be hoped that they can continue this tradition, difficult though this makes the job of policing. (Vick, 1985 quoted in Thackrah, 1985:161)

"MASS URBAN devastation scenarios", as Jacobs calls them, have been common to both Bermondsey and Haringey (1988:142). Although Britain has a long history of public disorder its poor communities have generally been policed by their own constables with understanding and moderation. The people and their problems have traditionally been policed in conciliatory rather than confrontational ways. However, poor Afro-Caribbeans, called black people in this paper, complain about police prejudice and provocation in the ghettoes where they live. Their perspective is contrasted with that of poor white people in post-war bomb-blitzed Bermondsey, and references are made to relevant academic literature and personal social accounts of the areas concerned. It is suggested that a contemporary professional challenge for the police in a multicultural society is to retrieve and revise their positive social identity and that developing their conflict resolution skills is an urgent task.

Bermondsey Bobbies

Street by street, the police negotiated a complex, shifting largely unspoken 'contract'. (Reiner, 1985:60).

Living in a slum, slopping out in a backyard toilet three flights down, and washing in the Public Baths I established a shared social solidarity among Bermondsey neighbours in those 'good old days' when the Bricklayers' Boys and the Elephant Gang were fighting with razor blades and vitriol. Thirty years later, the Metropolitan Commissioner of Police, Sir Kenneth Newman, used the term 'symbolic location' to describe such areas of multiple deprivation where people struggle to find their social identity in depressive and oppressive environments (quoted in Ward, 1986:62-3). Paul Harrison's contemporaneous description in "Inside the Inner Cities" shows young people as "hectored, lectured, labelled and sometimes arrested. The child acquires a negative image of the police - and the police acquire a negative image of him" (1983:316). Bermondsey and Babylon represent critical social differences.

In post-war Bermondsey the police were popularly perceived by young and old as being brave in the Blitz, protective of the public in bridling local bully-boys, and co-operative in common complicity with the dockland black market. Chatting on the streets, working in youth clubs and friendly visiting to families in distress were welcome signs to a Cockney community that it was being cared for by its Cockney police. Community policing was actually experienced in Bermondsey long before its advocacy by Alderson (1984:8).

Mitchell observes that "the role of peace officer can be carried out only ... where there exists a high level of social cohesion" (1976:159). In Bermondsey social incorporation was a physical reality: families lived in and out of each other's homes in back-to-back bombed buildings bordering breweries, tanneries and pickle factories whose prevalent pungent smells prepared them for their collective annual hop-picking holiday. They had been congratulated for their wartime inner-city courage; they were confident about employment in dockwork shortly to be regulated for their benefit; and it was only the alcoholic celebrations of Irish single men which fostered police prejudice. This had consensual approval from the respectable Irish Catholics, early but assimilated immigrants to Bermondsey.

This split between the respectable and unrespectable members of an ethnic group parallels that which Hall describes as sub-cultural clashes amongst West Indian immigrants who eventually displaced the Irish poor (1978:155). Another narrative link between the two ethnic groups as products of colonial imperialism is provided by Fraser's classic study, "Children in Conflict", which derives from Marx's maxim that the Irish are seen as 'white niggers' and the

Policing the Poor: Conciliation or Confrontation?

psychological view that "every culture ... needs an outcaste group ... and to perceive it as inferior" (1973:118). Although Fraser's concern was with racial prejudice in Northern Ireland, his analysis of how social identity and discrimination are constructed fits experiential differences in Bermondsey and Babylon. The Cockneys enjoyed their historic and high folk-status, survived their poverty with pride and were policed with the bias of favour. The Caribbeans, feeling themselves labelled as a ghetto under-class, were trapped in that "increasing consciousness of kind, in which a minority group, unable to expand outwards, turns back on itself ... in a search for group identity" (Fraser, 1973:132). As Fraser says, this is "the most constant and reliable sign of impending revolt" and in Babylon it attracted, and was provoked by police prejudice (1973:131).

The Bermondsey police as friends and counsellors, mediators on the streets, protectors of public order and peacekeepers had a positive social identity which was lost to increasing numbers of young unemployed black people, and the white remnant who migrated to the new slums as rebuilt Bermondsey became gentrified and too expensive for its own people. They suffered what Richardson and Lambert have called 'dissimilation' (as opposed to assimilation), and the poor Irish element who had themselves discriminated against black labour in the docks before the closure, found themselves sharing West Indian enclaves and police surveillance (1986:51). The social identity of the police was transformed from that of 'friends' to 'foes and fixers' (Craig & Boulton, 1989:1).

The academic cataloguing of this social change has been extensive with regard to Afro-Caribbean relationships with the police.[1] The Irish voice their complaints periodically in *The Irish Post*, and, on their behalf, the Police Monitoring and Research Group has produced a critical study, "Policing the Irish Community" (1988). Personal experience suggests that poor older, single or unemployed Irish people occupy a substantial place in Tottenham tenements, although neither the 1981 nor the projected 1991 Census includes this group, who perceive the omission as prejudicial: the discrimination against them in housing and employment will remain undisclosed (*The Irish Post*, 25 November 1989).

Before focusing on Tottenham tenement life it is worth pointing to two particular social facets of the relationship between the poor and the police. The first concerns a community's conception of relative deprivation which Benyon & Solomos (1987) have shown to be a critical factor at the roots of urban unrest. In post-war Bermondsey people had no television sets from which to receive powerful visual imprints of the polarisation between the poor and the rich. The films featured good cops preventing bad guys from hurting nice folk who sometimes had problem kids, portraying what Hall et al have called "the dramatised symbolic reassertion of social values" (1978:64).

Bermondsey people felt secure in their social identity, protected by their police and by the thought that they enjoyed 'better breakfasts than the nobs'. Conversely, thirty years later, Tottenham people have an insecure social identity (Brown, 1989:2); they feel provoked by the police (Dunhill, 1989:125); their small screens assail them continuously with violent images which either kindle and fan fires of social rage, or vaccinate them against the dangers of uprisings.

A sense of injustice is the second aspect of alienation. In considering the idea of social injustice it is necessary to distinguish the constant awareness, which poor people have had throughout history, of hierarchical power and social control from the differing ways in which they have tolerated it. Bermondsey people traditionally and good-humouredly licensed and supported the police in their peacekeeping and crime prevention duties: there was a sense of public proprietorship of their police, and their local Labour MP was vigilant on the community's behalf. He championed individual cases of social injustice, and won a great social victory in the new docks employment scheme. Tottenham poor people had contrary experiences of social injustice, especially black people crowded in its tenements, considered next in more detail.

Tottenham Task Force

> It's as if the police wanted a riot, so many people witnessed the brutality of the officers (*The Voice*, 8 August 1989).

At the time when they were first built people pleaded to be housed there. Anecdotally, when a social worker in the area, I remember giving my carpet to a new resident, unaware that it might be subjected to petrol-bomb spillage a decade later. Subsequently retired but transposed to the local Justices' Bench, I saw the relationship of poor people with the police from a sadly stretched perspective. This had to accommodate two critically contrasting social accounts of mutual rising hostility which marked the demise of consensual policing and the rise of confrontational policing. This has been recorded and analysed by many police writers.[2] It has also been subject to an intensive critique by sociologists, criminologists and lawyers.[3]

All writers agree, despite their different explanations, that policing in recent years has been tarnished by racial discrimination, and in court cases it has been evidenced by the number of acquittals of charges against black defendants. Scraton chronicles the controversy about the current Merseyside overuse of the 1986 Public Order Act "to arrest, detain and charge well-known members of the black community with 'violent disorder'. A 90% acquittal rate suggests a use of this most serious charge to regulate community opposition to police policies and practices" (1989:15). Scraton's allegations match those of Tottenham's first black MP, Bernie Grant, who has claimed that some local junior police officers are "out of control ... fitting up innocent people ... to settle old scores", resulting in him having 40 current cases to place before the Police Complaints Authority (*Race & Immigration*, 1989:227).

Grant's identification of some junior police as racially prejudiced and provocative in their relationships with black people is confirmed by the police authorities, their critics and their consumers. Its incidence is hard to control for many reasons, chief amongst them being the social identity problems which young officers themselves have, the discretionary observance of the codes which should govern their practice, and current multiethnic pressures which incite confrontational rather than conciliatory responses.

The macho image of police canteen culture is reassuring to raw recruits tackling the frightening and degrading tasks which policing involves, and it is this which appears to attract career rewards. Success is thought to be bought at the price of improperly inflated arrest rates resulting from the misuse of 'stop and search' powers, which, when resisted as they often are by black youths, lead to multiple charges. It is this growing hostility, marked by deliberately offensive, or even unintentional, disrespect shown to officers of the law, which provides a more natural if insufficient explanation of differential policing. In addition the police are aware of counterculture political pressures to which even Rex admits: "it may even be the case that there are those in the black political leadership who do not want change in policing policy because confrontation is what they most need to advance their kinds of political causes" (1988:124).

However since the riots there has been a determined police initiative to change policies and practices, exemplified in The Principles of Policing and Guidance for Professional Behaviour: "It is a duty to show compassionate respect for the dignity of the individual and to treat every person of whatever social position, race or creed with courtesy and understanding" (Newman, 1985). More recently, the present Metropolitan Commissioner, Sir Peter Imbert, has released to the press details of his Statement of Common Purpose for the 1990s which uses 'non-discriminatory policing' as a key concept (*The Independent*, 27 November 1989). Unofficial police gossip comments that it is in media offices rather than police stations where new policy directives appear to be first discussed, and this bears out the contention that it is the transformation of police principles and values into constabulary practice which presents the primary and inadequately addressed problem.

Nevertheless in returning to the specific instance of policing in Tottenham, it is noteworthy that in Broadwater Farm Revisited, Lord Gifford's second inquiry into the October 1985 riots, or disturbances as he euphemistically calls them, he congratulates the local police who "have genuinely tried to tackle the issues raised in the inquiry's first report" (1989:25). He also identifies an emerging issue noted by many community activists regarding the "real danger that senior community spokespeople may cease to be genuinely representative but will rather be seen to represent particular power groups on the estate" (Gifford, 1989:110). It is admitted that there is a low level of democracy, with only 8% of the residents representing the highest number of those attending Tenants' Association meetings. The reasons for this are suggested, and even more persuasively argued, in Thomas's White Bolts, Black Locks (1986:38-65). Gifford does however point to one important innovation, which is that the Broadwater Farm Junior School head has developed a new educational project called "Co-operation" (1989:116). This is in line with widespread school programmes pioneered in and supported by poor black and white communities in the USA, where co-operative problem-solving approaches are taught in order to help the young reconstrue and recycle their aggression (Kestner, 1988). The training resembles that which an increasing number of police forces in Britain are including in their own educational programmes, the purpose of which is to foster good community policing. The fact that Gifford himself advocates "co-operative policing" should disarm conspiracy theorists who mistakenly view conflict management as a danger rather than remedy for poor white and black communities.

Conciliatory Constables

> Helping people to get away from the siege mentality and assisting them in talking things over with their neighbours ... points to conflict resolution (Sir Peter Imbert, *The Independent* 4 Nov 1989).

Jefferson et al observe that "like representation, participation is universally seen to be an essential component of a democracy on grounds which emphasise the rights of citizens to be involved in the decision-making processes which affect their lives" (1988:102). Reference is made to Rustin's belief that "face-to- face deliberative decision, after due discussion, is the proper socialist definition of democracy" (1984:14). Alternative dispute resolution or mediation aims to empower ordinary people, particularly the poor and the ethnically disadvantaged, amongst whom it has an ethical mandate to share its skills, to help people manage their conflicts so that they avoid criminalisation. There are increasing reported instances of this happening in poor black and white communities: Farrer, in his article on "The Politics of Black Youth Workers in Leeds", describes their conciliatory pragmatic approach to preventing further disorder after a riot incident (1988:114); Bootham of the Society of Black Lawyers reported that at the 1989 Notting Hill Carnival "two other lawyers and I were constantly trying to mediate between angry people trying to get home, and police stopping them" (*The Guardian*, 30 August 1989). These informal and individual non-confrontational strategies reflect only minimally the major collective initiatives being projected in the many community mediation services which are developing in poor white and black communities and which are described elsewhere in detail (Marshall, 1985; FIRM, 1989; and other chapters of this book).

The social skills of negotiating in conflict are regarded as a proud acquisition by the black youths who use them and, hypothetically, might be considered as an updated version of the traditional Bermondsey people's confidence that they could manage their own cops. In Babylon police sympathetic identification with and accountability to its local black communities is still in its infancy, although Gifford notes that Tottenham now gives its police special training "for co-operative policing in a multi-ethnic society" (1989:25). This was used spectacularly in mounting the Operation Kingfisher drugs seizure, over which local community leaders were earlier consulted, and then invited to do their own 'policing of the police' during the event. Although the required social protest by indignant residents was orchestrated by some black activists, a subsequent march to the police station to commemorate the death of Cynthia Jarrett in the 1985 riots "turned a bitter memory into a carnival ... in which there were no arrests" (*Caribbean Times*, 13-19 October 1989). The demonstration might be interpreted as public proof of the fact that stereotyping black people as violent in their response to perceived police provocation may be becoming as outdated as it is unconstructive.

Peacereapers

> I will, to the best of my powers, cause the peace to be kept and preserved.... (Police Oath)

The folk-history of 300 years of slavery, followed by 30 years doing the mother country's lowliest jobs with the worst housing, has developed cultural experiences and expectations among black residents which suggest to them that professed police policy changes may be merely cosmetic. Racialism is entrenched here, as it is in the world generally. Nevertheless the present police resolve to practice non-discriminatory policing is welcomed, especially as it will take much forbearance for young officers not to behave towards black youths (as the latter will surely, on some occasions, behave towards them) with anger, rudeness and challenge. Crime has to be prevented and stopped vigorously, of course, but with firmness and fairness, rather than with verbal and physical abuse.

The Police Foundation has itself set a model, described in its report Neighbourhood Policing, which was based on the work of a senior officer involved in conflict management training and supportive of community mediation services. In this it is argued that "the police should provide a positive model of pro-social helping behaviour" on the beat. "Attitude change is seen as a means of changing behaviour of patrol officers, their managers" and, as it goes on to say, thus the responses of local citizens and their community organisations (1989:2,23). If this sounds suspiciously like social engineering, it should be stressed that conciliation is effective only when it involves genuine participation and power-sharing. Weatheritt suggests that the police are "unlikely to dominate in forums designed for dialogue" although she agrees that "the mechanics of community policing need to be made visible ...". She argues that it is about "encouraging the development of the preventive and non-conflictual aspects of policing" (Weatheritt 1988:174). However, Layton-Henry warns that although "the police are visible mediators ... if (they) lose the confidence of part of the community then the authority and legitimacy of the state is eroded as well" (1984:109). Tragically this has been happening in Tottenham where poor black people complain that they are neither protected against racial harassment nor from crime. In return the police argue, with justification, that they themselves are discriminated against and harassed by aggressive black youths, and plagued by drugdealers operating in a community that has been unable to police itself.

In conclusion it can be seen that Chessyre's dictum that "an unstable community needs stable policing" might be directed towards Tottenham and its constables (1989:135). Bermondsey was a stable society despite its poverty and deprivation immediately after the war, and its police enjoyed a positive identity as friends of the people which made possible the always difficult and dangerous work of preventing crime and preserving public order. There is evidence from Sir Peter Imbert's already quoted 1990 Statement that he is determined to see that areas like Tottenham also enjoy stable policing, although the socio-economic reasons for it being an unstable community may still be inadequately addressed. If the police are to have what he has called their 'user-friendly' stations transformed into places where the police, as friends, provide what is now to be called 'service', then, in Tottenham at least, it will come about when confrontation is replaced by conciliation and hostility by co-operation (but see note 4). Meanwhile the police must face up to and resolve all abuses of police power which are being exposed by the press and the Crown Prosecution Service. Until this is accomplished, the fears and suspicions that prevent real co-operation and willing participation will not be allayed. The retrieval, restoration and enhanced development of the social identity of our police as being the best in the

Policing the Poor: Conciliation or Confrontation?

world is of critical current concern to the nation, and especially for its poor black and white communities.

Notes

1. Cashmore, 1981; Gordon, 1985; Miles, 1989; Rex, 1988; Sivanandan, 1988; Thomas, 1986; Tompson, 1988.
2. Alderson, 1984; Banton, 1964; Mark, 1978; Oliver, 1987; Pike, 1985; Waddington, 1988.
3. To name but a few: Cain, 1973; Cowell, 1982; Emsley, 1987; Jefferson & Grimshaw, 1984; Lambert, 1970; Lea & Young, 1984; Morgan & Smith, 1989; Quinney, 1977; Reiner, 1985; Richardson & Lambert, 1986; Taylor, 1981.
4. It should be recorded that Tottenham was the first Metropolitan Police area to respond to community demands by setting up a Domestic Violence Unit in 1988 based on multi-agency co-operation.

Bibliography

ALDERSON, J (1984) *Law and Disorder*. Hamish Hamilton.
BANTON, M (1964) *The Policeman in the Community*. Tavistock.
BENYON, J (1987) *The Roots of Urban Unrest*. Pergamon.
BROWN, P (1989) *Black and Blue: The Ethnic Minorities and the Police*. Unpublished paper, CSPO, University of Leicester.
CAIN, M (1973) *Society and the Policeman's Role*. RKP.
CASHMORE, E (1981) After the Rastas. *New Community,* X, 2, 173-179.
CHESSYRE, R (1989) *The Force: Inside the Police*. Sidgwick & Jackson.
COWELL, D, JONES, T and YOUNG, J (1982) *Policing the Riots*. Junction.
CRAIG, Y and BOULTON, S (1989) *Friends, Foes or Fixers?* Unpublished paper, CSPO, University of Leicester.
DUNHILL, C (1989) *The Boys in Blue*. Virago.
EMSLEY, C (1987) *Crime and Society in England*. Longman.
FARRER, M (1988) The politics of black youth workers in Leeds. *Critical Social Policy,* 23, Autumn.
FIRM (1989) *Directory of Mediation Projects and Conflict Resolution Services*. Beaconsfield: Forum for Initiatives in Reparation and Mediation.
FRASER, M (1973) *Children in Conflict*. Penguin.
GIFFORD, L (1989) *Broadwater Farm Revisited*. Karia Press.
GORDON, P (1985) *Policing Immigration*. Pluto.
HALL, S, CRITCHER, C, JEFFERSON, T, CLARKE, J and ROBERTS, B (1978) *Policing the Crisis*. Macmillan.
HARRISON, P (1983) *Inside the Inner City*. Pelican.
JACOBS, B (1988) *Racism in Britain*. Christopher Helm.
JEFFERSON, T and GRIMSHAW, R (1984) *Controlling the Constable*. Muller.
JEFFERSON, T, McLAUGHLIN, E and ROBERTSON, L (1988) Monitoring the monitors. *Contemporary Crises*, XII, 2, 91-104.
KESTNER, P (1988) *Education and Mediation*. American Bar Association.
LAMBER,T J (1970) *Crime, Police and Race Relations*. OUP.

LAYTON-HENR,Y Z (1984) *The Politics of Race in Britain*. Allen & Unwin.
LEA, J and YOUNG, J (1984) *What Is to Be Done about Law and Order?* Pergamon.
MARK, R (1978) *In the Office of Constable*. Collins.
MARSHALL, T (1985) *Alternatives to Criminal Courts*. Gower.
MILES, R (1989) *Racism*. RKP.
MORGAN, R and SMITH, D (1989) *Coming to Terms with Policing*. RKP.
NEWMAN, K (1985) *The Principles of Policing and Guidance for Professional Behaviour*. Metropolitan Police.
OLIVER, I (1987) *Police, Government and Accountability*. Macmillan.
PIKE, M (1985) *The Principles of Policing*. Macmillan.
POLICE FOUNDATION (1989) *Neighbourhood Policing*. Police Foundation.
POLICE MONITORING & RESEARCH GROUP (1988) *Policing the Irish Community*. London Strategic Policy Unit.
QUINNEY, R (1977) *Class, State and Crime*. Longman.
RACE IMMIGRATION BULLETIN (1989) No.227 July/August. Runnymede Trust.
REINER, R (1985) *The Politics of the Police* Harvester.
REX, J (1988) T*he Ghetto and the Underclass*. Avebury.
RICHARDSON, J and LAMBERT, J (1986) *The Sociology of Race*. Causeway.
RUSTIN, M (1984) Opening the future. *New Socialist,* Oct.11-15, 14-15.
SCRATON, P (1989) The law unto themselves. *New Statesman & Society.* 28 July, 15.
SIVANANDAN, A (1988) Left, right and Burnage. *Race and Class*, XXX, 1, 71-73.
SUTCLIFFE, D (1982) *British Black English*. Blackwell.
TAYLOR, I (1981) Policing and police. *New Socialist,* 2, 42-45.
THOMAS, D (1986) *White Bolts, Black Locks*. Allen & Unwin.
TOMPSON, K (1988) *Under Seige*. Penguin.
VICK, C (1985) An introduction to aspects of public order and the police, in Thackrah, J (Ed.) *Contemporary Policing*. Sphere.
WADDINGTON, P (1988) Cosmetics of public disorder. *Policing*, IV, 2, 116-129.
WARD, T (1986) *Inquest*. Inquest.
WEATHERITT, M (1988) Community policing, in Greene, J and Mastrofski, S (Eds.) *Community Policing*. Praeger.

SECTION III:

THE POLICE RESPONSE

The first two chapters in this section deal with particular inner-city areas of London where public disorder has been prevalent. Both are written by senior police officers of the Metropolitan force, who were responsible for developing the policies they describe. Chapter 7 deals with Brixton, which was also the subject of Chapter 4 from the perspective of the Community/Police Consultative Group. This paper covers the shift in policing policies since the early eighties riots, including the setting up of the Consultative Group and police training. This shift has been informed by many of the ideas contained in the theory of conflict resolution, and it is no coincidence that a number of senior Metropolitan police officers during the eighties attended courses on conflict resolution at City University run by Chris Mitchell, now professor at George Mason University in America. Chris's main specialisation was in international mediation, but he was a leader in the field of teaching domestic conflict resolution in this country as well. In the early days of the development of mediation skills and awareness in Britain, most people gained their knowledge through Chris Mitchell's courses.

Commander Marnoch's list of elements of policing he considers essential is strongly in line with conflict resolution theory. The identity of police and community objectives, the need for real consultation, operationalisation of objectives, avoiding defensiveness and over-sensitivity to criticism, asserting one's own views, being prepared for setbacks, and internal teamwork and confidence-building within the police force - all these can be re-stated in terms of concepts such as communication, collaboration, participation, problem-solving, the need for self-confidence, assertiveness, trust, and so on. Moving from here to results on the ground, of course, is the difficulty. While many senior police officers have imbibed these ideas, they have had little impact as yet on constables at street level. Genuine attempts to set up collaborative links with the community have been made, but they have encountered obstacles, mostly predictable. Police forces in Britain, and especially that in London, have come in for a great deal of criticism and blame in recent years, so it is not easy for officers to avoid that defensiveness that Alec Marnoch refers to, and which is a stumbling-block to open communication and trust-building. The "negative mode" of the Consultative Group in its early days was also to be expected - conciliation always requires a period of "ventilation" to express feelings, and to lower the pitch of emotions and general tension to the point where rational discussion can begin. It is a pity that the Group when set up did not have the services of a skilled facilitator who might have helped the parties to resolve these kinds of problem and begin to build trust. Although all this is happening, it has been slow and uncertain, and the degree of involvement of different parties is still very uneven.

Alec Marnoch also refers to "neighbourhood policing" (a system developed, in fact, by Ian Beckett, author of Chapter 10, when he was a Chief Inspector), pioneered in Brixton and three other divisions of the MPD. The system focuses around the need for increasing interaction between police and the public on a day-to-day basis (ie increasing contacts in more positive, less threatening, contexts than the investigation of specific crimes). Decreasing the emphasis on crime as the main reason for police contact with residents is in line with public demands, which have been calculated (by Ian Beckett) to be related to non-crime services in 75% of all public-initiated contacts. In inner city areas where crime rates are highest, the proportion of time spent by the police on non-crime services is likely to be at its lowest if deliberate efforts are not made to rectify the balance. (Such effort, of course, is a matter of resources as well as policy.) "Neighbourhood policing" involves the allocation of major responsibility for particular small geographical areas to specified groups of officers, who thereby become familiar to, and with, residents of those areas. Each of these sectors also has its "working party", which is a public forum for residents to raise policing issues and discuss them with police officers, mostly at constable level. All policy development and implementation, along with public consultation, involves not only administrative police grades but also those constables who patrol the streets and have the front-line contacts with local people. Although ostensibly such a policy involves a decreased emphasis on crime-fighting, it probably does more to decrease levels of crime by being strongly related to crime-prevention, an active stance compared to the reactive one of responding to crimes already committed.

Chapter 8 deals with Notting Hill, scene of the first of the British "race riots" of modern times, and of the annual Afro-Caribbean carnival which has international renown, but tends also to be a focus for trouble. Commander Roach deals with the application of a rational problem-solving approach to policing the carnival, and the

Introduction to Section III

steps taken to try to avoid the escalation of violence while maintaining the control on behaviour that the community generally expects of the police. The use of "stewards" from the community itself to assist with crowd control is an interesting feature which crops up also in one of the American examples in Chapter 12. While the previous chapter is orientated more towards reconstruction of relationships after disorder, Roach is dealing primarily with the prevention of disorder before matters get entirely out of hand.

It is difficult to be sure of the degree of success of these policies in practice. Since their introduction, there have been no major breakdowns of social order in association with the Notting Hill carnival, nor have the events been trouble-free, however. The limitations of a high-level top-down approach show up here. Commitment from the top is essential, but steps to ensure commitment at other levels are equally crucial. Negotiations about the planning of the carnivals between the community organising committee and high-ranking police officers may proceed relatively successfully, but is either party able to deliver on its promises? Kraybill (1990) has described how the current negotiations between the South African government and the African National Congress leadership are complicated by the fact that neither party is uniform in its views. The real negotiations, according to Kraybill, are carried on within each party, within the ANC and within the government, attempting to reconcile factions which may be further apart at times than the ANC and the Government as a whole. This is a feature of all inter-group conflicts, and Notting Hill is no exception here. It has often been difficult for the organising committee to deliver on the agreed number of community stewards, forcing the police to exert a greater numerical presence than either side wished. Similarly there are differences between police officers and among groups of officers, particularly between the non-local Police Support Groups and local forces.

Chapter 9 consists of extracts from the survey carried out by Sally Sadler, for the Quaker Council for European Affairs, of methods of crowd control and preparations for managing public conflict, as these are manifested across Europe. This provides a useful overview of the various techniques in use. Like the other writers she stresses the need to reduce mutual aggression by training in self-awareness and non-provocative communication, avoidance of technical aids that tend to escalate the level of violence, and by familiarising both sides to one another's views, interests and needs. A particularly interesting example is a provincial West German police training programme which deals with problem-solving, communication, understanding "the other side", coping with stress, controlled verbalisation, and active listening. Such features appear, too, in training programmes described in Chapter 10, and Sections IV and V of this book. It is important, too, that the finger of indictment is not pointed only at the police - indeed that it is not pointed at all, for accusation and blame only increases defensiveness and antagonism. So Sally refers not only to police training, but also the need to inculcate similar skills and outlook among community groups and demonstrators. She particularly bemoans the decision by two Quaker chapters in Britain not to provide non-violence training for local police, although such training was something they had experience in and which the police had requested. It is as important that community groups reach out to, and involve, the police as that the police reach out to the community.

Sally Sadler also raises the issue of "intermediaries" - unaligned groups that can negotiate with both sides in a dispute and facilitate communication when direct links have broken down. In the examples she provides from mainland Europe, the mediating body was a police union - seen as appropriately neutral in conflict between police and trades union demonstrators. In Europe there is no statutory or recognised body set up to establish credibility and skill as a neutral third party in public disputes (as ACAS, the Advisory, Conciliation and Arbitration Service, exists for industrial disputes in Britain), so that the provision of mediation is haphazard and ad hoc. In the next section we shall learn about one such body in America - the Community Relations Service - which has had much success in helping resolve police/community conflicts where there has been a racial issue. We shall also see in both sections IV and V other ways in which individual mediators or mediation projects can be of assistance. When conflict has reached the level of violence, a direct gesture of reconciliation by one side will usually be misinterpreted as either a "trick" or a sign of weakness, both tending to achieve the opposite of what was intended. A neutral third party can facilitate reconciliation without incurring the same degree of suspicion, and may be the only means of breaking a deadlock. One of the problems with the post-riot police response in areas like Brixton has been that every move they make - however reasonable - is liable to be regarded with suspicion by the local community, including, in the case of Lambeth, the formally elected local authority councillors. This has meant that reconciliation has been a slow and difficult process.

The final chapter in this section is written by Chief Superintendent Ian Beckett, who was one of those members of the Metropolitan Police who attended Professor Mitchell's courses at City University. The article clearly shows the influence of conflict resolution principles. Ian himself had direct experience of police work in the inner city during periods of violent disorder, and the lessons learnt then have had a lasting impact, reinforcing the academic ideas he has since received, and providing the impetus for trying to put them into practical effect both in police training and in on-the-street policing methods.

Introduction to Section III

Ian Beckett provides a systematic view of the theories behind the several innovations introduced by the police in London. He sees public disorder in a dynamic way, as a process with distinguishable stages, with corresponding stages in the police response. In normal circumstances the primary orientation would be preventative - employing community mediation services and so on to resolve isolated outbreaks of trouble. In a high tension (pre-riot) situation, 'conflict-reduction' (or de-escalation of the temper of relationships) would be the dominant aim, employing joint police and community action. In the event of a riot, the police can only be concerned with the management of the disorder itself, containing it, preventing damage to persons or property; the time is not ripe for trying to resolve the underlying problem. Even though the police response must be graduated to such stages, Beckett still asserts that the same principles of conflict resolution apply throughout, merely adapted to the different contingencies and intentions, although as the degree of disorder increases, police options for resolution decrease. As applied to policing, Beckett sees these principles being operated through what he calls a "contact strategy", with the emphasis on maintaining intergroup links and communication. At the "normal" policing level he sees such a strategy reflected in the various types of "partnership" policing, whether the particular rubric is community policing, team policing, neighbourhood policing or zonal policing. All of these approaches stress prevention, flexibility, and community involvement. As conflict grows, so, Beckett argues, the police action must be moved in gear with the degree of antagonism shown by the disorderly elements - corresponding in mood but not exceeding it, so as not to be responsible for escalation. One might argue that there are problems in this - that the police are in danger of losing control of their own actions, which are determined precisely by the initiatives taken by other groups. It is possible to argue that in some circumstances the police should be prepared to show more restraint than others, not to respond in the same measure to increases of aggression among others, in an active attempt to de-escalate. This is not to debate the whole approach, but merely to demonstrate that the application of conflict resolution principles is no straightforward matter in practical circumstances (as, I think, Jim Murtagh shows in Chapter 3).

There is a possibility that Beckett may be misunderstood on a few points. His perspective is, quite openly and appropriately, that of the police officer. His definition of a riot is purely in criminal legal terms: it has to involve general looting or an attack upon the police. In lay eyes, a riot may not have quite the same connotations. This could lead to misunderstandings. When the police see a change from one "stage" of conflict to another, community members may not see it in the same way, seeing the situation as either more or less severe. This could lead to conflict over changes in police operations that are seen as unwarranted or charges of inaction when intervention seems called for but does not occur. Conveying such perceptions between the police and the various community groups is no easy matter to sustain in the heat of conflict, and one can see some of the results in the 1985 Lambeth case in Chapter 4.

The police perspective comes through, too, in Beckett's assertion that riots are always "started" by "juveniles" and "older malcontents, criminals and activists". He is, of course, only too aware of the general causes of disorder in community-wide grievances. What he is saying is that active participation in the criminal aspects of a riot is limited to groups that are generally more inclined to break the law in any circumstances, and who take advantage of the riot situation to indulge such inclinations. It is inevitable that the police, whose job in the face of disorder is to identify and control risks to person or property, in other words to seek out crime, perceive these groups above all others. Again, however, this partial - although completely reasonable - perspective can lead to misunderstandings with the local community. It so easily leads to a dismissal of disorders as due merely to a small number of antisocial characters, and it is important that the police are careful not to publicise such a view, which discredits and trivialises the very real underlying grievances of the whole local community. Of course, the conflict need not become so violent, if such opportunists were not seeking to exploit it, but elimination of the outbreak of such self-seeking crime is not equivalent to the resolution of the basic conflict. This is why it is so important that the relatively brief but fierce - and as Beckett says, very tiring - phase of fire-fighting - the restoration of some semblance of order, is not seen as the end of the police responsibility. As Beckett says, it is crucial to go on from there to the "post-riot" phase of policing concerned with re-establishing relationships and tackling the precipitating grievances.

References

KRAYBILL, R (1990) Director's circle. *Conciliation Quarterly* (Mennonite Conciliation Service), Summer, 11-14.

Chapter Seven

Brixton SW9: Post-Conflict Policing

COMMANDER ALEC MARNOCH, METROPOLITAN POLICE

IN 1981 in Brixton, South London, we witnessed some of the worst rioting in mainland Britain this century. Although there were no fatalities several hundred police officers and members of the public were injured. Vast damage was wrought on local property, but of particular concern was evidence of a rift which had developed between some sections of that community and its police.

I feel it is inappropriate to dissect the particular circumstances of that disorder here. Nevertheless it is vital to consider the immediate social and economic conditions in any discussion of subsequent actions taken by the police and the community. The social and economic circumstances of that time serve to emphasise the considerable challenge facing police and community alike in the aftermath of disorder, also providing a constant reminder of the potential for further disorder. Lord Scarman highlighted the very serious crime problem which if neglected would overwhelm any efforts we might make to prevent large-scale disorder. Indeed crime generally, particularly when directed against people, has been described as a form of ongoing disorder or 'slow riot'.

> The dilemma facing the Police Commanders in Brixton is as simple to state as it was and remains difficult to resolve, how to cope with a rising level of crime - and particularly of street robbery (mugging) while retaining the confidence of all sectors of the community, especially the ethnic minority groups. (Scarman, 1981, 8.14)

Some commentators have described the Brixton of the early 1980s as a classic combination of inner city decay and deprivation. This I believe to be an oversimplification of the complex pressures to be faced by local residents (and it is regrettable that some of the features remain today). Two factors crucial to the quality of life experienced by Brixton residents were the twin evils of unemployment and poor/ inadequate housing - nestling in a depressive environment. In the early 1980s employment prospects for youths in Lambeth were extremely poor. As many as 75% of black youths had no job and indeed little prospect of getting one.

In spite of attempts to improve local housing conditions one in ten dwellings were still classed as overcrowded and one in five as substandard. Local authority initiatives to create new housing stock, demolishing many of the houses that remained after the war, have not resulted in the imagined utopia. It has been generally accepted now that the new high rise blocks can bring pressures and indeed squalor (albeit of a different kind to the old slums) for residents. Above all, these massive estates can create a sense of isolation and anonymity, destroying the better features of old established communities such as mutual help and a sense of ownership. The new estates inadvertently promoted the rule of the vandal and the burglar. The cyclical pattern evolves and, with features of deprivation developing, so this in turn promotes a spiral to further decline. Inevitably shops and small local businesses close in the face of shrinking markets.

Furthermore the census of 1981 revealed the shrinking population, a decline of 20% in the preceding 10 years - this fall being most accentuated in the working age group. Social stresses added to bad housing and unemployment; problems of public behaviour; disillusionment; disorientation; decay; crime and ever-present propensity for further disorder.

I believe that one of the key problems threatening public tranquillity in areas such as Lambeth is that of attitude. This can mean either the attitude of the police to the public or vice versa; poor attitude on either side can result in a challenge to the legitimate authority of the police. Undoubtedly it was the perception of many black youths in the early 1980s that the police were biased against them—reflecting their conviction that society's laws were racist (chiefly relating to the use of cannabis) and their frustration at being unable to achieve a high standard of living in a very materialistic society.

It must be less than honest to deny that the attitude of some of my police colleagues, beleaguered and working sometimes in appalling conditions, contributed to friction within this volatile situation. Nevertheless there were those elements within Lambeth prepared, if not to say eager, to make capital out of any 'incident' fuelling rumour and division with their sometimes gross stereotyping of police for their own political ends.

We recognise, never more so than now (eg. the current PLUS programme [Scotland Yard's drive to improve police relations with the public, run by the author.-Ed.]), that the adoption of the right attitude by police is paramount in seeking to serve the public. How we serve members of the public, whether we are courteous, caring and professional, is surely the key to securing the support and co-operation of the community. If we 'get it right' those everpresent dissenting elements will be isolated and without support in any endeavours to display their frustrations by way of disorder. By 'getting it right' we can reduce tensions and encourage many to assist police in the fight against crime. We recognised that it was imperative to harness the co-operation of the community in Brixton in the early 1980s; that police could not function in a vacuum.

What was needed in the policing experience of Lambeth in the early 1980s was a combination of sensitivity to the local people and problems, diligence, patience, hard work and a respectful attitude to the public–a combination that is little short of superhuman when related to the individual. In the absence of such I was convinced that the alternative lay in ensuring that those who represented the Metropolitan Police in Lambeth should be well trained and carefully selected. For that reason I decided to enhance the training programme for my officers with particular emphasis on understanding the local community and an awareness of the importance of projecting the right attitude.

One of my early initiatives in Lambeth was the development of a district (ie Lambeth-wide) training unit which in addition to normal on-the-job training was used to develop 'policing skills', with the emphasis on the involvement of the local community. It provided training for probationers, senior constables and detectives - some elements were introduced locally to obviate the need to travel in North London as well as providing a more Lambeth-based flavour. At the same time the Force was structuring a proper induction course for new recruits, after their basic Hendon Police College training. Ten weeks on the 'street duty course' taught them not only local geography and community characteristics but introduced them to operational policing in a guided situation. Not only had the six months training programme recommended by Lord Scarman been achieved, it was exceeded. In addition, experienced constables and senior officers received training in community orientated issues. In short no one serving in the police in Brixton could fail to realise the importance of and commitment to the 'maintenance of public tranquillity'. This is not to say that it is a course that should be adopted at the expense of crime prevention and the detection of offenders - that would be an abrogation of our duty and lead ultimately to the very situation we desired to avoid. The events of April 1981 served as a warning as to what could happen and what disorder could mean - September 1985 was in fact to demonstrate what a proactive stance by police and public could achieve, in how quickly normality was restored after the shock of the Saturday disorders.

So far most of the factors I have mentioned have been police orientated and therefore within our capacity to change. Community participation in what I have described was valuable but not essential - the elements to which I shall now turn would have been impossible without the goodwill of the majority and the tremendous commitment of a minority. Earlier I discussed the importance of attitudes on the part of the police and the public. How we treated each other dictated how fruitful the relationship between the police and the public would be.

The steps we had taken to improve police attitudes by way of training would never have succeeded had we not seen a parallel willingness on the part of a majority of the opinion formers within the community.

The Community/Police Consultative Group for Lambeth was and is the most overt and positive demonstration of that willingness. It was the direct result of one of Lord Scarman's recommendations, but when formally inaugurated in March 1982 it lacked the backing of law that it was to receive from Section 106, Police and Criminal Evidence Act 1984 - indeed it was to become the prototype for such statutory bodies.

It was agreed that the group should meet twice a month at Lambeth Town Hall; all its meetings were to be open to public and press, there being no provision for closed sessions. Indeed the open nature of its deliberations went further still in that any concerned member of the public was allowed to address the group. This happened on several occasions when an incident on the streets had sparked off feelings that, had they not been vented and responded to at group meetings, might have festered until the tension became violence. I was content to put myself on offer to these feelings at the outset rather than allowing them to grow and reflect more aggressively on my officers on the street. The group consisted (as of right) of police, local and GLC councillors, and Members of Parliament, plus a multitude of local community organisations - many of whom had attended the then Home Secretary, Lord Whitelaw's inaugural meeting; but equally there were significant contributions to be made by those who joined the group after they saw how effective it was.

The group set itself the following aims:- To work towards a substantial improvement in relations between the community and the police, in particular the black communities. - To work for the better prevention of crime. - To work for the maintenance of a peaceful community in Lambeth. - To work for a statutory provision to govern the consultative arrangements.

The relationship between the group and the police was recognised at an early stage as crucial to the degree that the one could help the other - accordingly their terms of reference were declared to be:- "The Police Commander will consult the Consultative Group on general matters of policy relating to policing and operations in Lambeth but it is recognised that, in the exercise of his professional responsibility, the final decisions rest with the Commander."

It was accepted that the Commander might not always be able to discuss operational matters in advance - although he was encouraged so to do and the Group reserved the right to discuss matters retrospectively if the situation arose where he could not.

Brixton SW9: Post-Conflict Policing

It must be said in those early days a great deal of time was spent in a somewhat 'negative mode'. The alleged failings of the police were constantly highlighted, cynicism and mistrust abounded. As the members learnt more about the police and the problems of the area, the standard of discussion gradually rose, although there remained many who would criticise the police given half the chance. It was a valuable lesson for us that the public would be supportive once they understood the constraints under which the police had to work. Two issues raised by my predecessor Commander Fairbairn did much to concentrate the minds of the Group members; firstly when he submitted a paper on the policing problems of the area (especially the crime) and secondly when he made a presentation to the Group on the on-going problem of Railton Road (seat of much of the 1981 disorder) and honestly revealed the indications that it was being somewhat turbulent again. An almost unprecedented degree of co-operation between the Group, police and the local council secured the eviction of some of the persons and clubs that were at the hub of the criminal activity there.

The group went on to consider many new policing initiatives, police training, search warrants, racial incidents, lay visitors to Police Stations - sponsoring the first scheme in London; the Police and Criminal Evidence Bill; and a number of ad hoc local issues. One interesting area of research was in the field of crime prevention where a sub-group undertook an extensive study of an estate in Brixton, attempting to draw out crime prevention recommendations that could be acted upon by the various social agencies involved - not simply the police.

Undoubtedly one of the principal reasons for the success of the Group was its open nature - both in terms of its willingness to be addressed by any person concerned enough to bring a problem before it and the enthusiasm with which it greeted new members, provided their bona fides and goodwill were established. The group was a formidable vehicle for facilitating communication between the police and the public in the course of its regular bi-monthly meetings or, at times of particular tension, at ad hoc meetings (on Railton Road for instance), that I and my senior colleagues found particularly valuable. Such meetings provided an opportunity to set the record straight or concede genuine criticism gracefully, to admit our mistakes and commit ourselves to remedial measures.

While the Consultative Group was to remain the primary medium of consultation it was not, of course, the only one and it is incumbent on police to maintain contact with all sections of the community. For instance I maintained a professionally close working relationship with the senior members of Lambeth Borough Council throughout my period as Commander even after they had adopted the local Labour Party policy of boycotting consultative groups. I attended various tenants association meetings, arranged for two public open

Police Days on Clapham Common and Brockwell Park–bringing police and public closer together. I actively encouraged all my officers to follow my example and they were willing to get fully involved themselves.

I have hinted here several times at some of the elements that I consider essential to reduce conflict after it has happened and prevent it happening again - they are not really difficult to grasp or particularly radical now, although perhaps they were more so then. (a) You need to know where you want to go - what your objectives are. (b) These must be the same as those of the community as a whole. (c) The purpose of 'consultation' must be seen by Police as a two-way exercise between members of the same community - not 'us' telling 'them'! It must be true consultation. (d) You need to know how you intend to go about attaining these objectives on behalf of the whole community. (e) You must not be too upset by criticism or become unnecessarily defensive. (f) You must be prepared to wrest the initiative from those who would oppose you (in other words stand up and be counted). (g) You must be prepared for setbacks and opposition. (h) You need a good team if you are tackling problems on the Brixton scale - some of those I had working for me I inherited, some I chose - all I valued.

The team issue leads me to consider the final element of the analysis to which I have referred; that is the attitudes of the senior police officers to their colleagues on the streets. I believe that nowadays it is generally accepted that the management style within an organisation such as the police will be reflected in the manner by which the operational officers 'manage' the public. If the police organisation treats its members in an adult, respectful, reasonable way then this will be passed on. I endeavoured to make plain to my colleagues that my policing policy revolved around: (i) an effective uniform presence; (ii) a professional, directed plain clothes deployment; (iii) the provision and use of good management information/intelligence; (iv) community involvement; and above all a higher profile style of personal leadership, personal commitment, personal accountability and personal courage - leaving your head above the parapet all the time.

Equally all officers had to be made to feel that they were part of the process - sometimes part of one element more than the others - but ultimately that the success or failure of policing in Lambeth owed much to their individual efforts. An incident of thoughtlessness or carelessness on the part of the crew of a Police Support Unit could undo weeks of work by community-minded officers. Therefore officers from outside Brixton were used on the streets as little as possible. At the same time all officers had to be made to feel their due importance as members of the team and that, provided they were reasonable in their behaviour, they would get my full support–if they weren't, then watch out!

The very special circumstances which exist following major disorder require a higher profile style of police leadership than many officers may feel happy with, as well as much work behind the scenes. All I can say is, it does require that kind of public accountability; it is a price that has to be paid before the police can become less obvious again. On the other hand there would have been no success had not both voluntary and professional, formal and informal, political and non-political, members of the community been prepared to stand up and be counted as being on the side of public tranquillity.

It is tempting to finish with a battery of statistics to show our success or to dwell at length on how even the brief hiccup represented by the disorders of September 1985 showed this by the way they dissipated so rapidly, with little residual ill-will towards the police. I shall rather close this consideration with a brief explanation of a system of policing that would be equally appropriate to the prevention of a riot, but was in fact introduced to Brixton after the riot, and remained after all the main police characters had left the Lambeth stage.

I am talking about the Neighbourhood Policing Project for which Brixton was a pilot site from 1984. The underlying theme of this Project is service to the public and encouraging officers to identify with their areas and areas with their officers (often referred to as geographic responsibility). This leads to a partnership and consultation at varying levels of formality and with various media, the end result of which is the alignment of the supply of police resources with that demand. It also embraces the concept of the community taking responsibility for policing itself - with Neighbourhood Watch the manifestation of public action.

Neighbourhood Policing is held together by a consultative approach to management, whereby all officers see themselves as having the opportunity to make a worthwhile contribution and being provided with the information so to do. Within the project the specially trained permanent beat officers are crucial - they must carry the banner of community-based policing - both within the community and within the police organisation. The Neighbourhood Policing Project was to embody much of what we were doing in Brixton in a post-disorder situation and place it in a theoretical context fitted to all policing environments.

I said in an article in 1984 "The Police are hopeful, we are determined and, dare I say it, we are able but we must not be complacent as we approach the future in Lambeth. One thing of which I am certain, we cannot afford to fail and the public themselves are beginning to realise this." I am only too glad that they made that realisation and grateful for the efforts so many good people made towards the goal of 'policing Lambeth by co-operation'.

Reference

SCARMAN (1981) *The Brixton Disorders 10-12 April 1981*. London: HMSO. Cmmd. 8427.

Chapter Eight

The Notting Hill Carnival: An Exercise in Conflict Resolution

COMMANDER LARRY ROACH, METROPOLITAN POLICE

THE NOTTING Hill Carnival is widely recognised as the largest street festival in Europe. At its peak on the Summer Bank Holiday Monday it can involve as many as three quarters of a million people concentrated into a small area around All Saints Road and Ladbrooke Grove in an otherwise residential district of Inner London. Whilst the Carnival has its own special history and characteristics, as well as a symbolic place in the folk lore of London and its black community, the policing of it cannot be isolated from its environment, from the needs and problems of the community of the area in which it takes place. Consequently the policing style and arrangements adopted for the Carnival must take account of the day to day requirements of the local community.

There may seem to be a certain paradox in finding that an event which had been born out of a community's desire for harmony and unity after the tensions and disorders of the later 1950s should have attained a certain notoriety as an occasion that could not pass without some sort of public disorder. But the spirit of the Carnival from its earliest Caribbean origins has always contained an element of resistance (even defiance of authority). On occasions that strand has surfaced in outbreaks of disorder and riot. Perhaps the worst instance occurred in 1976 when the scale and ferocity of the violence was such as to cause a re-evaluation of the police handling of disorder and the introduction of the now all too familiar 'riot' shield, use of which has become a regular feature of police training. Indeed the opinion was expressed then and subsequently that, in the light of years like 1976, the Carnival should not be allowed to take place at all, or alternatively should be removed from the streets to some 'sterile' area such as a large sports complex or a public park.

In the preparations for the Carnival, therefore, both police and community representatives have to acknowledge the possibility of further violent outbreaks - a possibility which itself breeds a tension that is often all but palpable on the day. At the same time everyone involved is only too well aware that for a minority, whose influence is out of all proportion to their numbers, the Carnival represents an opportunity to pursue selfish and totally criminal ends - to use the scale and density of the event as a cover for crime, particularly thefts from the person and drug dealing. In the course of the 1987 Carnival there were, for example, 1,161 instances of crime reported to the police - of which nearly 400 involved theft from the person or robbery: what the popular press will insist on calling 'mugging'. In the same year two people lost their lives - one at the hands of a robbery gang.

The public disorder and criminal aspect of the Carnival form the link to the day to day policing of the inner city area in which it takes place. Notting Hill is one of the dozen or so Divisions of the Metropolitan Police District that present themselves statistically as being at the forefront of areas requiring efforts by police to tackle street crime and combat the activities of drug dealers, who have historically found Notting Hill and especially its central All Saints Road conducive to their operations.

My most recent involvement with this complex of problems began on my appointment in March 1987 as Commander (Operations) for West London, when I was given a special responsibility for the Carnival by the equally newly appointed Deputy Assistant Commissioner (DAC) for the Area, Paul Condon. Our first decision was to recognise that any attempt to remove the Carnival from the streets, or to allow it to degenerate into regular riot, would be tantamount to an admission that it was impossible for Londoners and their police to achieve the goal of maintaining public order and safety while allowing the majority to go about their lawful and traditional celebration. We therefore concluded that the task for the police and the community was to ensure that the Carnival took place without undue danger to the local people or the visiting revellers - either from violent disorder or criminal activity. The theme of 'safety for the public' accordingly became the central plank upon which the policing of the Carnival was built.

It was the link between the arrangements for the Carnival and the policing of Notting Hill Division for the remaining 363 days of the year which was the key to the decision to seek to create a popular consensus on which the police strategy to reduce crime and conflict at the Carnival was developed. That approach is, of course, fully within the true tradition of policing in this country - 'policing by consent'. But any 'consent' the community affords to its police under that tradition must always be freely and knowingly given. It must therefore come from the police working with the community to establish what goals that community seeks to achieve and what policing measures that community is actively prepared to support in order to attain those

The Notting Hill Carnival: An Exercise in Conflict Prevention

agreed goals. We therefore began with a wide ranging consultation with all sections of the Notting Hill communities about both the present problem of the Carnival and its future.

The term often used in police circles for this kind of exercise is 'community involvement', in many ways a misleading concept, for it implies that this is a style and a type of policing which is distinguishable from other, perhaps more forceful, methods. In truth all policing is community based. So that what we were contemplating in the development of a police strategy for the Carnival was an intense effort on the part of police genuinely to work with community representatives and other opinion makers to establish what the goals of the community are for the event and what might be the most effective contribution by the police to their realisation. It was fortunate, but perhaps no accident, that Notting Hill Division was one of the pilot sites for the Neighbourhood Policing Project (see previous chapter) within the Metropolis, for that experience provided a base on which the whole approach to policing the Carnival could be built, giving both police and the community some confidence in the processes of consensus building and developing a recognition within the community that they have a responsibility to involve themselves in keeping peace in their area.

The crucial forum in this respect, where police and the community leaders meet on a regular formalised basis to discuss such policing issues as the Neighbourhood Policing Project, is the local consultative group - born out of the Scarman report and given force of law by S.106 Police and Criminal Evidence Act 1984. That group played a vital role in forming the consensus of community support for the police strategy for the 1987 Carnival.

The group regularly meets with its local senior police officers to discuss the problems of the area and to participate in the establishment of policing priorities. On occasions senior officers from the Area attend, that is, from the next tier of management within the Metropolitan Police District, headed by a Deputy Assistant Commissioner who enjoys considerable autonomy in operational matters. This provided an opportunity and a forum for Mr Condon and I, as Area officers, to link the normal policing of Notting Hill with our responsibility for, and command of, the policing of the Carnival in consultation with the community. It is, of course, not sufficient for the police to assume that a group such as this, vitally important though it is, will represent the totality of opinion within the community and a considerable amount of time and effort was therefore also committed by officers, right up to the highest level, to liaison with other community bodies such as a residents association, tenants associations, commercial interest groups and a whole range of representative voluntary and statutory bodies. Particularly important elements in that wider consultation were elected representatives of local government and, perhaps most important of all, the organising Carnival and Arts Committee.

The broad effort to establish a consensus approach to the general policing of both the area and the Carnival by the identification of what the community goals were and the alignment of policing policies to secure these goals, served also to isolate those elements within the community opposed to those goals. In simple terms these elements in Notting Hill were the drug traffickers and the various criminal elements associated with that trade. Once these elements had been isolated from the wider community any action by police to deal with the problems they create - provided it is reasonable and professionally executed - would become the action of the community; for by reaching a consensus the police were not acting alone but by, for and with the active support of the majority of the community.

The concept of the identification of police goals with those of the community has to run hand in hand with effective participative management within the police themselves in order that the whole organisation knows what is being done and why, and is able to understand the potential fruits of success. It is a truism of policing that every officer has the potential to make or mar an operation or policy and has therefore something to contribute to the whole. But to make a positive contribution he or she must know what the strategy is - not only know but understand and identify with it. In the same way every significant group within a community must be 'on board' if a widely based strategy is to succeed. In that two-pronged effort the media both locally and nationally can be extremely useful, but they must be kept apprised of what is happening in a proactive sense if they are to be of assistance. It is not sufficient for police to restrict their dealings with the media to the aftermath of any initiative. The media must be treated responsibly and openly and told as much of the truth as possible - even if they choose not to make use of all that they are given. If nothing else, at least the ground work of understanding will have been laid, so that police explanation of an incident of interest to the media will carry far more weight.

The crucial factors, then, that were seen as the background to preventing crime in the normal situation and preventing the crime and disorder at the Carnival, were the identification of commonly agreed goals between the police and the community, the establishment of police policies accordingly, the commitment of the whole police organisation to these goals and the proactive involvement of the media. However, it is recognised that even this may not prove to be enough and, thoroughly as these elements were pursued by the police and the people of Notting Hill, it was incumbent on police to prepare for the 'best laid plans' to come adrift - which meant the development of effective, simple and practical contingency plans to deal with crime and disorder either at the Carnival or before the event. Indeed to fail to make such preparations would surely have been regarded as a serious dereliction of our duty to our people. This we did and, in so doing, built up confidence both within and outside the police organisation that we were capable of doing what we had to do in support of the community goals.

The first goal identified by the consensus between police and the community was the elimination of hard drugs dealing from both the Carnival and the Notting Hill area. That objective was realised by the execution of Operation Trident in All Saints Road in which 15 major dealers and a large number of their associates were arrested and removed from the streets with the minimum of fuss. The subsequent absence of any complaints about the strong cordons placed on the streets for a significant period after the operation demonstrated to us how effective policing measures could be when they are taken to eradicate those elements opposing the community's goals. The support for the strategy adopted by police was unanimous. We took care to ensure that we were seen as acting on behalf of the community with professionalism and restraint and followed our action by supporting an intense multi-agency commitment to the area to prevent the vacuum we had created being filled by other criminals - in this the local beat officers and crime prevention officers played a full and vital part.

The second set of community goals, the creation of a safe and peaceful Carnival, did not proceed so smoothly, for 1987 saw the testing of our contingency plans for disorder. At 9 pm on the second day a serious outbreak of rioting did occur - arguably there had not been sufficient time for our preventative strategy to develop fully. However, the effective and efficient police response - based on specially created predetermined contingency plans which did not rely on traditional methods of control and communication - ensured that although there were 5 'seats' of simultaneous disorder amongst a crowd of some quarter of a million people, rioting was quelled in little more than half an hour and the entire area cleared shortly afterwards. In community terms the important facts were that no member of the public and no police officer was seriously injured and no property damaged in the process.

The programme to realise the second community goal was continued into the preparations for the 1988 Carnival which became another step in the on-going process outlined in this paper. The most significant change resulting from the experience of 1987 was that it was considered necessary to draw those elements with a special and direct interest in the Carnival, the Carnival Arts Committee, the British Association of Sound Systems, the Local Authorities and various ad hoc carnival organisations into a more formal multi-agency body which took on the specific task of securing a successful carnival with public safety paramount in everyone's mind. These bodies joined in what came to be called the Carnival Support Group and they were then actively encouraged to involve themselves in supporting the management of the Carnival by the provision of stewards, the adoption of a pre-determined route for the floats, the control of street traders and sound systems and in organising a programmed and orderly closure to the revelry. Bitter experience had taught us all the dangers of leaving groups of young people aimlessly 'milling' around the Carnival area when effectively all was over. In the event some of those organisations and agencies did not fulfil their early promise - for instance far fewer stewards were forthcoming than had been promised (although those who were there were good) and it fell to police to make good the shortfall. But the importance of the Carnival Support Group was that the police were seen to be acting to make the Carnival safe and crime-free manifestly with the consent of the majority of Carnival supporters, a perception reinforced as before by steps taken well in advance to inform the public and the media of developments in the Carnival preparations.

There was no disorder in the 1988 Carnival worthy of the name but on this occasion the contingency plans to deal with crime were needed and tested to the limit. These were based principally on the use of arrest squads of specially trained officers working under the direction of a computer-supported Intelligence and Information Cell, who made arrests in the most dangerous of circumstances in a confident professional manner - without any impediment or significant opposition because they were perceived as acting in the best interests of the Carnival and the wider community. As a result, more arrests were effected in 1988 than ever before, while the organisation of the Carnival, as negotiated between police and the Carnival organisers with the help of the Carnival Support Group, resulted in a reduction in the number of offences reported over the Carnival period to 193 compared with the 1,161 the year before. In addition there were a minimal number of injuries to the public - none of which were particularly serious.

The 1988 Notting Hill Carnival was an excellent example of conflict prevention - not simply because it was well commanded and professionally policed: nor because we had the commitment of our whole organisation and effective contingency plans (important as all these elements were); but because the police priority of public safety was consistent with the goals of the community itself - a goal that the public not only subscribed to but was prepared to support actively.

Chapter Nine

Crowd Control:
Are There Alternatives to Violence?

SALLY SADLER

The Scope of the Study

MUCH OF the information in this study was obtained from public and police authorities in the 21 Member States of the Council of Europe, largely by means of questionnaires, the first of which were sent in September 1983. Ministries of the Interior, Police Federations or Trade Unions in countries where these exist, as well as organisers of demonstrations, responded generously with helpful information. In addition, special visits were paid to the Netherlands, Great Britain, and the Federal Republic of Germany, to visit police training colleges, police headquarters, police trade unions, demonstration organisers, bodies which monitor police behaviour, and community leaders from areas of high social tension.

The Police and Crowd Control

Overall Trends

What trends have characterised the way crowd control has been handled in Europe over the last ten years? Have technical aids, such as shields, water cannons, and even plastic bullets been used to a greater or lesser extent? Have police forces become harder or gentler in their approach, more or less specialised, more or less open to the public? Have there been changes in the legislation relating to crowd control?

The police tend to say they have become gentler and lower-profile: Superintendent John Robinson, in charge of Public Order training for London's Metropolitan Police Force said in an interview that public order policing had got "softer" over the last few years. He felt the policing of football violence had got too "soft" and believed that there was less trouble at football matches on the continent because continental police were harsher.

Demonstration organisers tend to say the opposite, that the police have in recent years become more brutal, sinister and powerful.

On the BBC programme "Brass Tacks", broadcast on 31 October 1985, John Alderson, former Chief Constable of Devon and Cornwall, compared the methods used at Orgreave, Great Britain, during the miners' strike of 1984, with the methods which would have been available ten years earlier. At Orgreave, said Alderson, the Chief Constable directing operations had available to him foot police, mounted police and short shield men. Ten years earlier, he said, only foot police would have been available plus one or two long shields to protect police from stone-throwing demonstrators. "The offensive capacity of the police was virtually nil", said Alderson. Winding up the "Brass Tacks" programme, Alderson commented, "We have, in the last few years, seen our police service change from its traditional way of handling public order into what is bordering now on a paramilitary style of policing".

An unnamed Chief Constable on the same programme said public order had superceded crime prevention as a top priority for the British Police.

On 3 July 1986, London's Metropolitan Police took a step towards more forceful crowd control methods when Police Commissioner Sir Kenneth Newman called for new equipment to deal with rioting. A few hours later the purchase of 24 bullet-proof vehicles, 80 personnel carriers, 700 additional radios and 1,500 long truncheons had been authorised by Home Secretary, Douglas Hurd.

In the Netherlands also, methods of public order policing have changed over the last ten years, but perhaps in a more positive direction than in Britain. Willem Van der Ven, staff member of the largest peace organisation in the Netherlands, the Interkerkelijk Vredesberaad, and organiser of massive demonstrations against the deployment of cruise missiles, explained his views in an interview in October 1985. He believed the Dutch riot police (known as the Mobiele Eenhed), had changed its policy over the last ten years, from a large-scale, high-profile policy, to a low-key "flexible response" approach, with officers often not equipped with either helmets or shields. But behind the scenes, said Van der Ven, the equipment was always on hand to deal with trouble, should it occur.

In the Federal Republic of Germany, according to the police of Nord-Rhein Westfalen, public order policing methods have become less hard over the last ten years. This view was supported by Police Director Seifert, the Deputy Chief of Uniformed Police, Bonn, who said that the last truly violent demonstration had been way back in 1975, on the occasion of celebrations held to mark the 20th anniversary of the armed forces of the Federal Republic.

Udo Hanselmann of the Dusseldorf-based Bundesvorstand des DGB (the Union of Trade Unions in the Federal Republic of Germany) said that, in his view, the police had tried over recent years to present a more human image. At one demonstration in the early 1980s, he said, they had carried carnations instead of sticks, as a sign of peace.

Demonstration organisers tend to have a less favourable image of the police. Jutta Ditfurth, a founder of the Green Party in the Federal Republic, focussed, in an interview, on the fact that, in October 1985, Frankfurt demonstrator Gunther Sare was run over and killed by a police water cannon. The police in that city were often brutal, she said. In November 1985, said Ditfurth, the trial process began against a Frankfurt police commander for the way he had handled a demonstration against the building of a new runway at Frankfurt airport in the early 1980s.

Openness of Police Forces

Police forces, especially in the Federal Republic of Germany, the Netherlands and the United Kingdom, appear to have become more outward-looking and open to comment in recent years. Superintendent John Robinson of London's Metropolitan Police admitted that public order training used to be something to be kept secret and said, "Ten years ago we would never have allowed outsiders to look at our public order training".

The Dutch police seem to be the most open in Europe to public scrutiny. They have been very aware of their public image over the last ten years and have made efforts to become more open and responsive to society. They have, for example, invited representatives from peace and ecology groups to talk with police trainees on a regular basis; held open days at training colleges (the most recent of which at the Roermond-based Mobiele Eenhed training college attracted some 20,000 visitors); and invited members of other professions to take part in training courses (the author of this study, for example, was invited to take part in a five-week training course with the Mobiele Eenhed).

Police in several Länder (districts) of the Federal Republic of Germany say they have made efforts in recent years to step up contact with the public. The nation-wide tour which the largest Police Trade Union, the Gewerkschaft der Polizei, say they organised in 1983, to meet with peace and ecology groups throughout the country, is an example of this. However, some peace and ecology activists question whether this tour was a meaningful exercise, and say that it was just "police propaganda".

Legislation

In Spring 1986, the British Government passed a new Public Order Bill which replaced and extended the Public Order Act of 1936.

The Bill increases police powers. For example it enables them to ban a demonstration, or recommend the banning of it, if they have reason to believe there will be any disturbance of public order.

Organisers now have to give the police a minimum of seven days notice of any planned demonstration. The new legislation gets rid of the old offence of "affray" and creates a new offence of "disorderly conduct", which gives the police more opportunity to make arrests.

The Bill has been welcomed by the Police Federation and the Football Association, but it has been widely criticised from other quarters. The Shadow Home Secretary, Labour MP Gerard Kaufman, said that the new legislation would not stop rioting - it would only make arrest easier for the police. It would, he argued, take police away from the beat and set up new strains between them and the community. For the National Council of Civil Liberties, Peter Thornton said the Bill was "disappointing and dangerous". It was a recipe for more, not less, disorder, he said, diminishing the right of peaceful assembly and moving away from policing by consent.

Even the police themselves question whether the 7-day notification of demonstrations rule will help them. Most organisers of demonstrations give much more notice in practice, said police at Scotland Yard. If organisers chose to go by the letter of the law, said the police, they would have much less time to plan their policing strategy.

In the Federal Republic of Germany, in response to pressure from various Lander whose laws forbade demonstrators to be disguised, there has been a recent change in Federal law. Every demonstrator must now, at all times, have his or her face visible, for purposes of identification. Certain Lander have also attempted to make demonstrators pay for the cost of policing a demonstration, and for any damage caused as a result of it. So a demonstrator arrested while causing an obstruction would be required to pay for the police time involved in the arrest, subsequent questioning, etc. An attempt to put this into practice in Baden-Wurtemburg failed, however, because the authorities had to charge so many people that the administration of the penalties became impossible. There are moves to change Federal as well as regional laws to make demonstrators pay, but so far these have been resisted in the Bundestag.

According to training instructors at the police school in Selm, Nord-Rhein Westfalen, the Federal Republic places great emphasis on the right to demonstrate (it is written into the Constitution) - whatever the financial cost. It is the task of the police to ensure that citizens can exercise this right. The police may only intervene if criminal acts are committed, or the right to demonstrate is infringed, through illegal behaviour by one or more demonstrators.

Technology

Ministries of the Interior and demonstration organisers throughout Europe were asked, "Has the use of technical aids increased over the last ten years?" Most of those who answered said the use of such aids had not increased since 1975. Only the Republic of Ireland, Luxembourg, the Netherlands and Switzerland said it had increased. These four countries all thought the increase corresponded to an increase in the number of demonstrations. Only the Ministry of Justice in Norway said they thought the use of technical aids had decreased since 1975.

Police and demonstrators see recent developments from very divergent points of view, the police highlighting the low-profile and softer approach to ensuring public order, demonstration organisers and others stressing their criticism of what they see as harsh and violent practice.

RADIO

Police radio is commonly used in all 21 Member States of the Council of Europe for co-ordinating police actions. Is Police radio a provocative piece of technology? It might not immediately seem to be so, but a youth worker interviewed in Brixton following riots there in 1981, felt that police use of radio could indeed be provocative. Instead of police officers using imaginative dialogue with youths, he said, they tended to resort immediately to the impersonal technology of radio, and as often as not to call up more police, whose arrival on the scene often sparked further confrontation.

WATER CANNON

Water cannon powerful enough to knock someone over at a distance of 100 metres are generally used to disperse large numbers of people. They have been used by the police within the last ten years in Belgium, Cyprus, the Federal Republic of Germany, the Netherlands and Switzerland, according to peace organisations or Ministries of the Interior in those countries.

Peace and ecology organisations in the Federal Republic of Germany deplore the use of water cannon as a method of crowd control. They point to the death, in Frankfurt in September 1984, of 36 year-old Gunther Sare, who was run over and killed by a water cannon during a demonstration. His death triggered further violence between demonstrators and the police.

Many police and demonstrators agree that another disadvantage of water cannon is that it is provocative, and may cause more violence than it prevents. This view was confirmed by the police responsible for planning crowd control at Belgium's Heysel Football stadium before the disaster on 29 May 1985. During planning meetings, the police decided not even to deploy water cannon because they felt the sight of them could have provoked the football supporters into violence.

CHEMICAL GAS

Chemical gas is available, and has been used over the last ten years, according to peace organisations or public authorities, in Cyprus, Denmark, the Netherlands, Switzerland, the United Kingdom and the Federal Republic of Germany. It is available, but has not been used during the last ten years, in Austria, Belgium, Iceland, Italy, Luxembourg, Norway, Portugal, Scotland and Spain.

As to the situation in the United Kingdom, chemical gas has been used in Northern Ireland since 1970. In 1981, after three days of rioting in Liverpool, it was fired at demonstrators on the British mainland for the first time, and so far the last. Some people were seriously injured by the cartridges containing the gas, which were fired from 12-bore shotguns. The public outcry which followed led the then Home Secretary William Whitelaw to tell the British public that this tactic would never be used again. In spite of this statement, at the outset of riots in Brixton and Tottenham, London, which occurred from 6-8 October 1985, Sir Kenneth Newman, the Metropolitan Police Commissioner, said that the use of tear gas in such circumstances might be judged "reasonable or necessary". In the event, however, it was not used.

PLASTIC AND RUBBER BULLETS

Plastic bullets are about 11 cm long and about 4 cm in diameter. The Assistant Chief Constable of the West Midlands Police Force, the latest local force in Great Britain to acquire plastic bullets, speaking on 20 June 1986, described being hit by a plastic bullet as being "like being hit by a cricket ball hit hard by a good player". He said that the bullets would be fired at a range of between 20 and 45 metres and commented, "This particular weapon is lethal under 20 metres". (*The Guardian*, 21 June 1986). Rubber bullets are considerably larger, being only slightly smaller than police truncheons. Because of their size, they are less accurate than plastic bullets. They are generally thought to be less dangerous although they have caused deaths in Northern Ireland. Plastic and rubber bullets are also known as "baton rounds".

According to various sources, plastic or rubber bullets are available to the police and have been used at some stage since 1975 in Belgium, Switzerland, Northern Ireland and Spain. In Spain they were used on 15 December 1985 during a demonstration held in protest at the disappearance, while in police custody, of a Spanish Trade Union leader.

The use of rubber and plastic bullets in Northern Ireland is a matter of great controversy, both in the United Kingdom and throughout Europe. By late 1984, the number of people who had been killed by rubber and plastic bullets in Northern Ireland amounted to 15. Seven of these were children. When asked whether the Dutch police would consider using plastic bullets, the Director of the riot police training school at Roermond pointed to what had happened in Northern Ireland and said they were much too dangerous.

Since the Autumn of 1985, the use of plastic bullets on mainland Great Britain has become much more likely, with the following three developments: - in early October 1985 during riots in Tottenham, London's Metropolitan Police Commissioner, Sir Kenneth Newman, announced that he "would not shrink" from the use of plastic bullets if he considered this necessary. In the event, they were not used during those particular riots; - on 19 May 1986, the British Home Secretary, Douglas Hurd, stated that any Chief Constable, who believed the use of plastic bullets would save more lives than it would endanger, could call on centrally-held stocks, thus by-passing local police authorities, who up till that date had had the power to decide whether or not plastic bullets should be stocked locally; - on 18 June 1986, the Chief Inspector of Constabulary, Sir Lawrence Byford, said in his Annual Report that plastic bullets and CS gas should be available for use by the police in situations of major public disorder.

By mid-June 1986, the following 14 police forces (out of a total of 44 forces in Britain) held stocks of plastic bullets: Metropolitan, Avon and Somerset, Essex, Greater Manchester, Kent, Humberside, Lancashire, Leicestershire, Merseyside, North Wales, North Yorkshire, Sussex, Warwickshire and West Midlands.

FIREARMS - THE LAST RESORT

Firearms are carried as part of regular police equipment in Belgium, France, the Federal Republic of Germany and in several other European countries. In these countries, the police may, as a last resort, use firearms if faced with a violent crowd.

In Great Britain firearms are not carried by the police on regular street duty. But increasing numbers of police are being trained in the use of firearms. Today, one in ten of Britain's 120,000 police officers is authorised to bear arms.

OTHER TECHNICAL AIDS

The police forces of Western Europe have many other technical aids available to them, including the following:

- CROWD CONTROL BARRIERS
- WARNING BANNERS as with the slogan "DISPERSE OR WE FIRE"(Cyprus) or "DISPERSE OR SPECIAL WEAPONS WILL BE USED" (UK)
- GAS MASKS

COMMUNITY DISORDERS AND POLICING

- RIOT SHIELDS. These are an important part of the riot equipment of all European police forces. They may be body-length transparent plastic shields, or small round black plastic shields for use in arrest squads. In Great Britain all 44 local forces have riot shields available to them. London's Metropolitan Police has 5,000 shield-trained officers out of a total force of 27,000. 1,000 shield-trained officers must be available for duty at any time
- REINFORCED HELMETS with visors.
- TRUNCHEONS. In Great Britain, a new long wooden baton is being tested. In the Federal Republic of Germany police have rubber batons, both long and short
- DOGS for deterrence or pursuit
- HELICOPTERS for observation
- IRRITANT added to water in water cannon.
- ARMOURED CARS. In Great Britain a company has offered for sale to the police an armoured car with the following features: small water cannon with dye to mark demonstrators, electric shock waves emanating from the body to ward off attack, gas canister dispensers and rubber bullet dispensers
- ELECTRIC SHOCK BATONS (available in Cyprus)
- HORSES. In Great Britain during the miners' strike of 1984, horses were used in conjunction with arrest squads. A Superintendent at Hendon Police Training College judged the use of horses to be, in certain circumstances, almost as severe as the use of plastic bullets.

Other new devices are reported and are usually said to originate in the United States of America. They include the "photo-driver" (a high frequency flashing light which can have a high-pitched sound-wave attachment); "stench weapons"; "banana-skin liquid"; and the "squark-box". This last item emits inaudible high-pitched sound-waves which make the crowd nauseous, and has reportedly been used by the police at the womens' peace camp at Greenham Common, UK.

Specialists or Generalists?

Who uses the technology described in the previous section? Are the police concerned specialists, whose sole job is the control of crowds and the maintenance of public order, or are they members of the regular police force who also undertake regular street duties? What are the arguments for and against a specialist force whose main task is riot control?

In most European countries, according to answers to questionnaires, public order is the concern of ordinary police officers who also undertake regular street patrol duties.

Crowd Control: Are There Alternatives to Violence?

Only in Austria, Spain and France is it dealt with by police officers belonging to a separate group within the main body of the police.

In the Federal Republic of Germany, Portugal and Sweden, it is dealt with by a combination of the two types of police officer mentioned above.

A police officer from Hendon Police Training College in the UK gave the following arguments for and against the specialist force:

> **on the one hand** a specialist force would be most cost-effective, avoiding the need to train all police officers, as London's Metropolitan Police Authority does at present. In addition a specialist force could undergo more detailed training, including in-depth instruction in subjects such as crowd psychology;
>
> **on the other hand**, officers in a specialist force would have a tendency to over-react when sent out, as maintaining public order would be the only task they would be trained for. Since they would only infrequently be called on, they would often be idle, and this would be a waste of time and of public money. In addition, specialist public order groups are politically highly sensitive.

A new type of unit, the District Support Unit (DSU), was introduced in London following the 1981 Brixton riots, in an attempt to achieve some of the advantages of specialisation without the disadvantages. A DSU consists of one sergeant and ten police constables, transported in a mini-van and equipped with long shields, round shields, helmets, flame-retardant overalls, radios and truncheons. DSUs operate in each of the 24 districts in the Metropolitan Police Authority.

They are on duty from 8.00am to 2.00am seven days per week, 365 days per year. The officers carry out regular foot patrol duties, but can be drawn into any emergency policing activity, for instance a terrorist attack, train crash or riot. DSUs can be called on to help in districts other than their own, but the use of more than one unit requires central permission from the Chief Inspector. The senior officer giving this information thought DSUs had been effective, since their implementation, in controlling local trouble which, he felt, might otherwise have erupted into wider riots.

Another senior officer at Hendon, however, was strongly against DSUs. He saw them as the thin end of the wedge of a much more forceful method of policing in Britain, and referred to them as "a cancer". In the Netherlands, police officers in The Hague said they would not welcome specialist riot control forces because of the risk of violent over-reaction by bored police, eager for action.

Training and Organisation

In Great Britain, police training is organised on a regional basis, each of the 44 local police forces being responsible for its own training programme, and making use of regional facilities. The training programme for the London Metropolitan Police may serve as an example of the sort of training many British police officers now receive.

At Hendon Police Training College, the college for London's Metropolitan police authority, trainee constables undergo a basic 20 week training course. Public order is dealt with during weeks 15 and 16, in a three-day "package". Two out of the three days are devoted to practical training, including the use of shields. The remaining day deals with theory.

In the Netherlands, crowd control training is dealt with by a branch of the police force known as the Mobiele Eenhed (ME). All police are liable to be called upon to do crowd control training with the ME for a period which lasts four weeks for the City Police and five weeks for the National Police. Crowd control is not part of a Dutch police man or woman's basic, 19-month-long training. Ten per cent of the police in any district served by the National Police undergo crowd control training.

The police in the Federal Republic of Germany are organised on the basis of the 11 Lander, and are responsible to the government of their Land. Each Land has its own training school. Police training in the Federal Republic is the longest in Europe, with initial training courses lasting 2 years. Within this period, crowd control training is not a special course, but is incorporated into general training.

Towards Peaceful Crowd Control?

Understanding Crowd Conflict
CAUSES OF CONFLICT

Police authorities and demonstration organisers were asked in our questionnaire to name the chief causes of conflict in crowd situations.

According to the POLICE AUTHORITIES, conflict occurs:

- When police try to prevent demonstrators from behaving unlawfully
- When demonstrators insist on marching to a prohibited place
- When demonstrators damage property or become unruly
- When police or demonstrators use violence .... the police have to try to prevent violence
- When demonstrators don't keep their word, or provoke the

police into violence
- When there is infiltration of uncontrollable elements or agitators into the crowd
- When police show a lack of 'sang-froid' and experience
- When a crowd is aggressive and hostile from the outset
- When there is a cycle of provocation, repression and rebellion
- When there is misunderstanding of one another
- When decisions, taken too quickly, later prove fatal
- When demonstrators and police have fragile nerves
- When demonstrators show disrespect for the law
- When police react to a situation too quickly and forcefully
- When the media, who often portray us unfavourably, only dwell on the arrests, and do not make clear our policy of protecting genuine demonstrators, while arresting criminals
- When police officers have the idea that the tougher and more 'macho' you are, the higher status you will achieve.

According to various DEMONSTRATION ORGANISERS, conflict is caused by:

- Provocation on both sides
- Police provocation
- Disquiet and insecurity
- Anger and hate plus polarization caused in part by the inhuman nature of uniformed police
- Stereotyping by each side of the adversary, calling the other 'sub-human', 'beast', 'brute'
- Mutual lack of information
- The police being unsure of how a crowd will act, and being unsure of how to contain situations which look like getting out of hand
- Sometimes trouble-making demonstrators, sometimes police provocation.

It is well known that the appearance of police technical aids for crowd control can provoke a volatile crowd into violence. Water cannon, for instance, with its obviously unfriendly military appearance, tends to provoke a crowd. For this reason, the authorities before and during the Heysel football stadium disaster in Belgium decided not to deploy water cannon. Police officers from London's Metropolitan police commented that the provocative appearance of this equipment was an argument against introducing it in Britain.

But most of the answers to this question from both police and organisers of demonstrations were brief and without elaboration, which may suggest that neither police nor demonstrators are prepared to look very carefully at the underlying causes of conflict in crowd situations. Only the Norwegian Government gave a fuller answer to this question, listing seven publications about public disorder and its causes, and clearly reflecting a concern with underlying causes at least as much as with tactical control of conflict situations.

What Causes the Police to Behave Aggressively?

The Frankfurt-based Hessische Stiftung Friedens- und Konflikt Forschung (Foundation for Peace and Conflict Research of Hessen) has been trying to find out some of the answers to the question of what causes aggressive behaviour among the police.

In September 1984 two staff members of the HSFK researched causes of aggression during a three-day session with 12 members of the Nord-Rhein Westfalen Police, all aged between 18 and 21. Using role-play, painting and discussion, the session uncovered vivid representations of the way stress can lead to aggression. Members of the group were asked to draw pictures of a very stressful situation they had experienced when dealing with a crowd. One policeman drew a line of policemen with shields, at whom stones were being thrown by demonstrators, and who had been told by their superior officer not to react, but to remain passive. The young officer found this very frustrating, and drew a ball and chain round the feet of all the police, symbolising this frustration. Another drew a punk festival which he had to police. He felt humiliated and angry at having to police what he saw as a frivolous street party, rather than a proper demonstration.

Another had found himself in the front line of police at a demonstration opposite Joseph Leinen, ecology activist and subsequently Minister of the Environment for Saarland. He had started to talk to Mr Leinen, was told not to by his superior, and put right at the back of the police lines, on the other side of the road. He found it intensely frustrating that he was stopped from communicating with the demonstrators. It was often hard, he felt, to know what the superiors wanted. For example, sometimes they would allow the police to fraternise with demonstrators, sometimes not, so creating uncertainty among the police about what sort of attitude they were supposed to take towards the demonstrators.

As a result of this and other exercises, the HSFK found that the police would behave aggressively if they were uncertain of what was wanted of them by their superiors. They were afraid of rebuke from their superiors if they were soft, while if they were hard, they were usually safe, and more likely to get praise and promotion.

Stress

Police in the Netherlands and the Federal Republic of Germany recognise that stress is a factor which causes aggressive behaviour on the part of the police, and, increasingly, they attempt to understand the situation and prevent stress arising. The Dutch police, for instance, have found that if a policeman or woman is away from home and family for more than two days to police an event, this has negative psychological effects. They are liable to use aggressive methods, perhaps in order to try and hasten the end of the event and get home.

It is well-known that people will behave in crowds in ways in which they would never consider behaving as individuals. This phenomenon, called "disinhibition", is a potent factor in triggering violence in mass demonstrations. London's Metropolitan Police are taught that they too are part of a crowd, but during training they are taught to retain their individual decision-making ability, and not to become irrational. Wolfgang Dicke, Executive Secretary of the Gewerkschaft der Polizei, the largest police trade union in the Federal Republic of Germany, argued that the police as a crowd differed from the demonstrators as a crowd, because it is their job to know how being in a crowd will affect their behaviour.

Perhaps demonstrators also have the responsibility to try and understand how their behaviour may be affected by being part of a crowd and some elementary training could help to foster this awareness and self-control.

Training the Police

Raising Thresholds of Tolerance

The course "Verhaltenstraining Zur Konflict-Bewältigung" (behaviour training with a view to overcoming conflict) is run by the police in Nord-Rhein Westfalen, in the Federal Republic of Germany and lasts three weeks. It is taught to those who have already completed their two-and-a-half years initial training at police school and was developed over a period of four years by the Max-Planck Institute in Munich.

This training is intended to help the police control stress in their personal, as well as their professional, roles, since problems in personal life can often affect professional behaviour. In the course of public order work, the police are often provoked and insulted, and those who have gone through this course find such work easier. If the police find themselves able to control stress, their threshold of tolerance is raised and they are less likely to become aggressive. Their behaviour becomes more professional, and their chances of psychosomatic illness are reduced.

The Max-Planck Institute initially taught eight trainers who in turn taught more, so that there are now some 50 qualified trainers. In October 1984, the regular training of police officers started - in small groups of eight - and now approximately 4,000 out of a total of 40,000 officers in the Nord-Rhein Westfalen police have passed through the course at six centres in that Land.

Teaching methods include brain-storming and role-playing, which is filmed and played back, followed by discussion. There is individual work and work in pairs. The trainer is not there to teach, only to lead and guide. Discussion groups are usually carried out sitting in a circle, with the two trainers joining in the circle to generate a feeling of equality. Trainees are encouraged to provide feedback at every stage of the course.

During the first week participants are exposed to stressful situations and do exercises aimed at both recognising, and doing something about, stress within themselves and others. Trainees are encouraged to think how they react to stress - some smoke, some eat, others shout or get aggressive or panic, some remain passive. These are all defined as negative reactions. Others listen to music, speak to others, some pray or even cry - these are defined as positive reactions.

During the second week, trainees learn to develop both short- and long-term methods of coping with stress. Short-term methods include sitting quietly, thinking of something pleasant, doing sport and avoiding stress-inducing situations (avoiding painful reminders, such as a street where the trainee saw a child killed, for instance).

Long-term methods include learning to persuade and instruct oneself to see things in a clearer light, systematic problem-solving, speaking with others, and appreciating that the other party must also be disturbed to cause them to behave as they do. The aim is to learn to raise tolerance levels by enlarging understanding, and to reduce unreasonable reaction wherever this may be possible.

The techniques of speaking with others are particularly relevant to crowd situations. The aim is that police officers should learn to control their verbal reactions, ie to try not to insult demonstrators, even if being insulted or provoked themselves, and also that they learn to listen actively to what other people say, to try to understand them and, if possible, to praise them. Learning these techniques is a long process, helped by some encouraging "rules of conversation":

1. Choose the right time and place to speak. If possible, exercise patience and wait until the other party has cooled down.
2. Listen actively, looking for the real message behind the words.
3. Make sure that verbal and body language are one. For instance, avoid threatening gestures which contradict what you are saying.

During the third week, when trainees know and trust each other, they analyse ways of solving long-term personal problems they may have, such as family problems, or problems with a boss or colleague. The rules of the course are that the five-step action plan described below must achieve results, or the trainee must start all over again.

STEP 1

Recognise the problem, and work out objectively who caused it, even if it was the trainee him/herself.

STEP 2

Write the problem down on paper, eg "Nobody likes me", and list arguments for and against the existence of this problem.

STEP 3

Work out those elements of the problem that something can be done about.

STEP 4

Write down the goal or solution sought, along with a list of ways of reaching the goal.

STEP 5

Carry out the recommended changes in practice and get a family or work partner to monitor progress. On being asked six months later, many trainees said this section of the programme helped them a lot. All confirmed that the reduction in stress which this programme brought about meant they were less likely to be aggressive in crowd situations.

Wolfgang Dicke, Executive Secretary of the Gewerkschaft der Polizei, said he hoped that in future this training would be an integral part of the basic police training course, rather than a supplement, as it is at present. Other Länder are interested in this course, which is very cheap to run.

Non-aggressive Crowd Control

Police authorities were asked the question, "What techniques for crowd control are taught to police which do not involve the use of technical aids?" Their answers were seldom full, but indicated a very uneven picture across the countries surveyed. For the Federal Republic of Germany, for instance, "Oral orders are given to the crowd first, and if these are not obeyed, manual force may be used (such as pushing or carrying). If this fails, technical aids such as water cannon may be used".

In Iceland "the police are taught how to respond to provocative and/or threatening crowd behaviour (both verbal and physical behaviour)". But the essence of the Icelandic response appeared to be training in forming a "human barrier".

In the Netherlands, police training appeared to concentrate on physical means of control: "Unarmed physical constraint and other physical training".

Similarly, in Portugal, where police are trained in "Public order control devices".

In Spain, the response was more ambiguous, the authorities claiming that police were trained in "dialogue and dissuasive techniques".

Only in Norway was the response unambiguous, claiming that "training in mass-psychology is part of the basic educational programme for the Norwegian police, and this promotes reliance on non-aggressive techniques".

In the Netherlands, police have attended week-long training courses in non-violence run by the Volkshogschool in Overcinge, near Havelte.

In the United Kingdom, according to an article in *The Friend* of 23 January 1986, two large police forces requested their local Quaker Meetings to offer them training in non-violence. Regrettably the local Quakers felt unable to answer this need, and this led to a wider debate, still continuing within the Society of Friends, as to whether Quakers should equip themselves to be able to offer non-violent training, should the police request this.

Improving Communication

Before a Demonstration

In many European countries, such as the Netherlands, the United Kingdom and the Federal Republic of Germany, notification by the demonstration organisers to the authorities of their plans is compulsory. It is not compulsory, but usually takes place in practice, in Cyprus, the Republic of Ireland and Luxembourg.

In most countries the level of contact is generally high. In a few countries, however, the level is intentionally kept as low as possible: for instance, in Denmark organisers meet with an "ordinary policeman". This is possibly to give the authorities a free hand subsequently in case of difficulties, as senior officers would not have been involved and implicated in arrangements made at a lower level.

Consultation before demonstrations, between police and demonstration organisers, is a vital way of ensuring that in practice the demonstration takes place peacefully. In addition, it can lead from a psychological point of view to police and demonstrators having a better understanding of each other, thus breaking down the stereotyping that can so easily lead to future conflict.

Most demonstration organisers said they met the police at least once before any demonstration. Some met twice. The content of the meetings included technical and organisational matters such as discussion of the route, traffic security, policing, parking for buses, and, in Denmark, the content of slogans on banners and posters. Both demonstration organisers and police usually agreed that these consultations were valuable.

As to the purpose of the meetings, the Icelandic police commented that they met the organisers "in order to be able to offer sufficient security and assistance".

The Cyprus police commented "Prior consultation gives the police time to get organised and arrange the keeping of the peace. Police cars lead and follow demonstrations and keep any trouble-makers away."

Only two organisers of demonstrations felt there were negative aspects to consultation. A Belgian peace organisation said the police might attempt to impose a different route, which, avoiding key buildings, would reduce the impact of the demonstration. A Swiss peace organisation objected to having to consult, because this seemed to be an infringement of the right to demonstrate. But these objections seem minor when weighed in the balance against the advantages both sides appear to gain from prior consultation in terms of mutual practical assistance and greater mutual comprehension.

In the Federal Republic of Germany, there were 400 demonstrations in 1984, with participation figures ranging from 10 to 100,000. Since the early 1980s there has been a huge demonstration in Bonn each year, in 1983 specifically against the installation of cruise missiles in the Federal Republic. Herr Seifert, deputy chief of the Bonn police, said they always try to have intensive consultation before a demonstration. Before the large demonstrations of 1980 and 1982 they had some ten meetings with demonstration organisers. The police always try to find out the aims of a demonstration and to assess its peaceful intent, but they stress that the responsibility for making sure demonstrations remain peaceful lies with the organisers. In 1981 and 1982 there was one person, representing 100 organisations, who liaised with the police.

It was agreed that it would be the responsibility of the organisers to control blockades and any other actions by potential trouble-makers. Only if they failed would the police go in. Since plans were discussed fully, the police felt able to have a lower presence than in 1983, when there was no clearly identifiable spokesperson for the organisers. That year the police feared disorder and consequently deployed a larger force.

Police Trade Unions can act as intermediaries between demonstrators and the police, where direct communication between these two groups could be difficult or impossible. Mr Kruizinga, Secretary General of the Christian Police Trade Union in the Netherlands, described how, four weeks before one demonstration which was to be a week-long blockade at the site of a proposed nuclear installation, peace group representatives came to the Union and asked them to explain to the police the purpose of the action, in the belief that this would reduce the potential for violence at the blockade.

Together with the other largest Police Trade Union, the Amsterdam-based Nederlandse Politiebond, Kruizinga's union decided to send to all the police who were to be on duty at the blockade a letter which set out the views of the protestors, but did not comment on them. The Unions have acted as intermediaries several times, and although this has been delicate and sometimes controversial work, Secretary-General Kruizinga said the Unions felt they had a duty to try and prevent or reduce violence wherever possible.

Relations over the Longer Term

Building relations over the longer term is as important, if not more so, than consultation before a particular event. This section looks briefly at the way three long-term communication initiatives have developed in the Netherlands, the Federal Republic of Germany and the United Kingdom and asks whether they could usefully be more widely applied.

In the Netherlands, new recruits at the Mobiele Eenhed (the Dutch riot squad) talk with members of many of the groups whose events and demonstrations they will have to police. Four members of the Interkerkelijk Vredesberaad (Interchurch Peace Council) have made about 15 visits, each of about three hours to the Mobiele Eenhed Training Centre at Roermond, Limburg. Willem Van der Ven of the IKV described what usually happens: "They ask us how we see them. We see them as a block. They see us as a block. Each is a threat to the other. By talking we begin to break down our stereotyped images of each other. These meetings have been a good experience for me". Representatives from gay, gipsy, anarchist and other groups also make similar visits to police training colleges. The police regret, however, that some groups never take up the invitation to meet them.

In the Federal Republic of Germany there have been a number of contacts over recent years between the police and ecology organisations. In 1979-1980 there were contacts between the main ecology organisation, the Bundesverband Burgerinitiativen Umweltschutz (BBU), and the largest police trade union, the Gewerkschaft der Polizei. According to the Trade Union, these meetings were set up on their initiative, to improve relations between the police and ecology groups, which had deteriorated badly towards the end of the seventies. BBU representatives, however, said that these meetings had little effect.

In February 1981 there were contacts between the BBU, Churches, the nuclear industry and the administration of the Ministry of the Interior in Bonn, which aimed to work out how to prevent the outbreak of violence in mass demonstrations. These meetings continued on a regional level in 1982 and resulted in a joint statement: "Das Umweltgesprach". This reaffirmed the need for continued dialogue between all sectors of the community concerned with public order. In the summer of 1983, during a tense period while the discussions on Pershing II and Intercontinental Ballistic Missiles were in full swing, the consultations between the police and the BBU were reported in the Federal Republic's press as being a conspiracy, and members of the BBU denounced as "traitors" by many members of anti-nuclear movements. In 1983 the Federal Republic Supreme Court pronounced a judgement on demonstrations which emphasised that authorities should contact organisers of demonstrations beforehand to try to prevent violence. Even if there is some danger of violent conflict, the authorities are obliged to guarantee the right to assemble and speak freely. Meetings continue between the police and various groups: in November 1983 judges, police officers and ecology group representatives met in Hessen to talk about civil disobedience.

But police in the Federal Republic were not enthusiastic in their response to the author's suggestion that they might open up more generally to demonstrating groups in the way the Mobiele Eenhed had done in the Netherlands. The Deputy Chief of police in Bonn, Herr Seifert, said he thought such meetings "would not be very useful".

In the United Kingdom, following riots in Brixton in 1981, "Consultative Committees" were set up to provide a forum for communication between the police and the local community, with the aim of building better relations between the two. Four years later those in favour of these committees argue that they can be a useful safety valve, where causes of conflict can be identified before pressures erupt into the streets. But renewed rioting in autumn 1985 has led to criticism that the Consultative Committees have been ineffective, largely a police "cover", and unrepresentative of the real interests of the local community.

Police in the Netherlands, when asked why riots similar to those in the UK had not occurred there, said social deprivation did not exist to the same extent as it did in the UK. They said also that the degree of involvement between the police and the community is higher in the Netherlands. For example, police in local stations on occasion advise citizens about community matters such as enquiries about social security. Many policemen are also members of community councils which bring together representatives from many sections of society, and watch over social developments in local areas.

Self-Policing of Demonstrations

Effective stewards can play a very important role in keeping demonstrations peaceful. In response to the questionnaire, demonstration organisers said that stewards can have the following functions: - to keep demonstrations on the route agreed with the police; - to diffuse trouble spots by isolating trouble-makers or agitators and dealing with them non-violently; - to act as a 'go-between' or communication link between police and demonstrators.

The London Metropolitan Police remarked, for instance, that sometimes even messages regarding an arrest that was to be made came better initially from stewards than from the police themselves. Police and stewards occasionally cooperated so that arrests could be effected. The police were not always entirely happy with this state of affairs, however, as it sometimes made them feel the stewards were in control of the demonstration, whereas the police felt they should be in control, and be seen to be in control of it.

The London-based Public Order Research Group encourages demonstrations to "police themselves". PORG does this by distributing information about effective methods of stewarding and "self-control" of demonstrations. PORG argues that organisations on the continent are in general better than those in Britain at stewarding, and cites many examples of disastrously inadequate stewarding arrangements in recent years in the UK. For example, during the miners' strike of 1984 there was a demonstration on 24 February 1984, the stewarding of which PORG described as "awful : there were only 40 stewards for some 30,000 demonstrators". Another example was the National Union of Students' rally on 28 November 1984 in London, where there were only 20 stewards for some 50,000 demonstrators.

In Belgium, the Trade Unions and well-established organisations such as Amnesty International and the political parties generally have experienced stewards. The large peace organisations also have stewards who receive briefings in non- violent methods of crowd control as well as legal rights of demonstrators, along with their instructions for a particular demonstration.

In the Federal Republic of Germany it is normal practice for organisers of peace demonstrations to train the stewards. The head stewards are taught to cooperate with each other and with the police in directing the organisation, and assistant stewards are usually given written and oral instructions at the site the evening before the demonstration takes place. The Bonn police said there is always a spokesperson appointed by the police, who communicates through the stewards to the demonstrators.

Outside Europe, the Buffalo project in the United States has taken the idea of stewards acting as peacemakers a step further. In 1972, in the United States, a potentially dangerous situation, arising from the organisation of a rock concert to be held in Harlem, led the Buffalo state police to ask Friends' help in controlling the large crowd expected to attend.

Fifty Friends and 200 others went along to the site of the concert some time before it was due to start and began talking to those around them, creating "pockets of goodwill" which gradually got larger, preventing some of the feeling of isolation and alienation which can result from loneliness in a crowd and which can be a cause of tension and thus violence. The concert passed off without serious incident, and the technique has been used many times since.

The picture which emerges from this brief survey is of very varied experience around Europe, but with a general awareness that improved self-policing by trained stewards could make a major contribution to reducing violence at mass demonstrations. No generally accepted figure emerges, however, for the optimal ratio of stewards to demonstrators; nor does an accepted view on the utility of briefing all demonstrators.

For short-duration events such as mass demonstrations, it is hardly practical to train all participants beforehand. However, for longer-term events, it may be possible. In June 1983, there was in Brussels a week-long protest running concurrently with an electronics and armaments exhibition and trade fair. In this case a peace camp was set up a few days before the fair, and demonstrators spent the time planning their protest actions and learning how to behave non-violently.

In Austria, participants in the 1982 Berlin-to-Vienna peace march were well prepared by a day-long workshop in which they role-played police, military personnel and spectators. This was in order to understand the different behaviour of these groups. Participants were also given legal information about rights and procedures to do with non-violent protest.

It is clear that practice regarding pre-demonstration training is very uneven from country to country and from organisation to organisation, but it may well be that those demonstrations which involve the largest proportion of participants who have had some form of training in advance are carried through with the least risk of violence. Early and prolonged involvement can also reflect a greater degree of responsibility on the part of the organisers, and offers greater chances for cooperation between the police and demonstration organisers.

Conclusions.

Western societies appear to be growing accustomed to a higher level of violence, and this shows also in the behaviour of demonstrators and police where large public demonstrations have been organised in recent years. The trend towards more violent behaviour has been bucked, however, by numerous examples of better understanding, mutual tolerance and sheer good humour in cases of crowd control. There is a fund of useful experience on which to draw to improve the chances of peaceful crowd control in future demonstrations, and it is the responsibility of all parties concerned to build on the best experience of the past to avoid a more violent future.

1. Individuals and groups organising demonstrations should: - learn techniques of non-violent behaviour and train as many demonstrators as possible in these techniques; - take steps to ensure that demonstrations they organise are peaceful by seeing they are adequately stewarded; - create positive centres for expression along the route of demonstrations at key points such as Embassies or government buildings by means of street theatre, music or speakers' platforms, rather than leaving such points unorganised and a target for spontaneous or stimulated aggression; - discuss in detail with the police authorities all aspects of a planned demonstration, as far in advance as feasible; - request permission to visit police training schools to explain the aims and methods of their own organisation and to attempt to understand the police point of view; - learn how to give training in non-violence, and offer such training to the police.
2. The police and in particular police training schools should: - invite representatives of groups whose events they are likely to have to police, to have discussions with trainees on a regular basis, as a part of the training, as is practised already in the Netherlands; - integrate into their training, or at least offer as an optional extra, courses on understanding stress and aggression, such as that run by the Nord-Rhein Westfalen police in the Federal Republic of Germany; - use defensive methods rather than offensive tactics, however much this may go against the grain of traditional thinking in many European police forces; - avoid deploying provocative technology such as water cannons and helicopters.
3. Police Trade Unions should: - undertake visits to groups (peace movements, other unions, football supporters) with which they may find themselves in conflict during a public event; - act as mediators between the police and different groups in cases where it would be difficult for the group to talk directly to the police authorities, as the Dutch Christian Police Trade Union has done; - press for introduction into standard police training of courses such as that run by the Nord-Rhein Westfalia police in the Federal Republic of Germany; - work for their members to have the right to object to, and not be compelled to take part in, the policing of events with whose aims they are in sympathy.

This paper is an abridged version of a report with the same title published by the Quaker Council for European Affairs (50 Square Ambiorix, B 1040, Brussels, Belgium). We are grateful for their permission to use this report.

Chapter Ten

Conflict Management in the Police: A Policing Strategy for Public Order

CHIEF SUPT IAN BECKETT

IN BRITAIN, police officers or 'peace' officers, are recognised as 'keepers of the peace', and 'peacekeeping' has always been a major objective of the professional police service since its introduction in 1839.

However, unlike Crime Prevention, Conflict Prevention has been almost totally ignored as a practical strategy or theoretical concept. Usually police react to existing conflict by trying to reduce it and if this fails then by managing the ensuing disorder to minimise injury and damage.

Unfortunately, the theory of Conflict Management as developed in the field of International Relations is almost unknown in police planning and strategies. In the past police have managed to cope by relying on simple, high profile uniform policing as a method of peacekeeping.

When it comes to major public disorders, however, this is neither appropriate nor effective. On the other hand, it is very difficult to apply theories and concepts, despite their appeal, to actual fast moving street environments as an effective police strategy.

The concept involved is that tension and conflict are not inevitable and therefore can be reduced and even avoided. Each police station can make a realistic assessment of their present environment and own operational practices. Once this has been decided then decisions can be made about the effectiveness of existing strategies and whether or not to move into a preferred category, through police-supported initiatives.

CONFLICT PREVENTION

This is considered the 'ideal' category, where the majority of potential conflict is detected and prevented at an early stage. Such prevention is achieved by normal everyday policing activities involving professional police officers, local community, volunteers and public agencies.

For example, it should be normal practice for domestic and

neighbourhood disputes to be referred to effective Conflict Mediation Services, staffed and supported by volunteers and public agencies.

However, if these types of processes fail to work, or do not exist, then tension and conflict may rise leading to the next category.

CONFLICT REDUCTION

In this type of environment the majority of scarce police resources tend to be directed at reactive attempts to reduce and control the existing high levels of tension and conflict.

Unless police strategies and resource deployment, including the resources of volunteers and agencies, are carefully planned, with a significant investment made in long term prevention measures, then the slide into the next category is almost inevitable.

DISORDER MANAGEMENT

Where there are existing high levels of violence and public disorder, police may be reduced to managing this disorder. This means containing it within defined areas, preventing escalation and generally 'keeping the lid on'.

This type of policing strategy, however effective and well supported by equipment and technology it may appear, will not by itself reverse the upward trend of rising disorder.

It is essential that joint police and public Conflict Reduction strategies are implemented, with the eventual aim of Conflict Prevention processes being effectively introduced and maintained.

The framework described allows events in the environment to be graded by police to decide which of the three categories they are actually in, decide in which direction they appear to be moving and where they would actually like to be.

Due to the fact that Conflict Management covers all policing situations from normality to riot, strategies, tactics and even styles of policing which are appropriate to the actual situation and assist in moving towards a preferred end state can be planned and developed.

Normal Policing

The policing strategies and tactics that are used in riots or serious public disorder have their origins in the every day NORMAL policing provided by a police station.

The LEVEL of policing in operation day to day to a large extent determines the type of police strategy that can be utilised to deal with public disorder.

Levels of policing are dependent on two main factors:

1. Police resources available. Generally, the higher the level the more resources required.

2. The type of geographical area being policed.

Level 1 - Reactive policing

Although this type of policing often receives bad publicity, it is still a basic and essential part of modern policing. Police must provide this basic service and emergency aid to the public in the expected and traditional manner.

First level policing requires the lowest amount of police resources as it restricts its activities to deal with events as they happen. Therefore, this type of policing is most effective when a majority of officers are in motor vehicles for fast response.

Unfortunately, due to the low level of police resources available, there is little or no potential for any preventive strategies including riot prevention. Once a riot has begun officers have to be brought in from a number of police stations and attempt to deal with disorder as it occurs.

This type of riot policing can only be reasonably effective for isolated incidents of disorder, which are not supported by the community and confined to small geographical areas.

Level 2 - Squad policing

This level of policing requires a foundation of effective first level REACTIVE policing supplemented by a number of specialist squads. Usually those squads concentrate on a single objective or problem (eg robbery, burglary, rape etc).

Once again this type of policing can be very effective in the short term, but in the long term has a limited preventive capability, restricted in the main to the arrest of offenders.

With this level of policing, it is possible that the police would have anticipated a tendency for riots by forming riot squads. There is a limited preventive capacity in this strategy introduced by the threat of using these squads and their known effectiveness in dealing with violent riots.

Despite their effectiveness in dealing with riots as they occur, the danger in this type of strategy is its limited riot prevention ability and the danger of escalation. Experience in other countries has shown that rioters may become better organised and equipped until rioting becomes institutionalised (eg Ulster). However, if rioting becomes prevalent and police resources are limited, then this type of riot strategy becomes almost inevitable.

Level 3 - Contract policing (partnership policing)

Third level policing once again requires a foundation of first level REACTIVE policing, supplemented by a small number of level 2 specialist squads. These squads are targeted at the crimes which are causing the most public fear and/or show some evidence of being committed by groups rather than individuals.

The resources committed to first and second level policing are reduced to their absolute minimum, enabling a major investment of resources into preventive policing. This strategy is organised around teams of officers, given multiple objectives in defined geographical areas (sectors).

There are a number of ways of implementing and maintaining this level of policing and a number of names given to these systems; Community Policing, Team Policing, Neighbourhood Policing, Zonal Policing, etc. All of the models have similar structures, methods and objectives and, for the purposes of public order, strategies and tactics are almost identical.

The main advantages of this level of policing with regard to riot strategies are its capacity for introducing effective riot prevention tactics and its flexibility to deal firmly with public disorder should it occur.

Once this type of policing has been established a major benefit is the involvement of the local community in various policing strategies, including riot prevention. The police do not accept that they alone are responsible for dealing with riots or their prevention. The general public and professional bodies must recognise their obligations to work with the police in these matters.

If this type of partnership has been successfully developed then alienation between the police and the public should have been significantly reduced, together with the potential for serious public disorder.

Public Order Strategies

However, a single unfortunate incident or a sequence of events may cause tension to rise. Alternatively, there may have been an outbreak of spontaneous public disorder, which has been dealt with, but tension still remains high. In these circumstances public order strategies must now be implemented.

Before examining these strategies in detail it may be helpful to examine the basic theories on which the eventual strategies are based.

Although there are always a number of common elements in all riots, there are in fact four types of riots, each of which has important implications for the police. (1) Riots with active community disapproval, where local residents actually assist the police, in numerous ways, to prevent and put down a riot. (2) Riots with passive community disapproval, where local residents disapprove, but are too apathetic to assist the police. (3) Riots with passive community approval, where local residents identify with rioters' grievances, but are too apathetic to assist them. (4) Riots with active community approval, where local residents form a significant proportion of the rioters.

The type of riot experienced is directly linked to the level of alienation from the police which existed before the riot. This is why the Normal Policing strategy must include alienation reduction as a major objective. In riots of types two to four, the police alone will be attempting to deal with the riot and any police failure or perceived weakness will encourage more rioting. Active community disapproval has been found to be a major influence on riots or potential riots in a number of 'riot-prone' areas.

Having described the types of riot we should now examine the types of people involved in riots, because this has major implications for public strategies.

Even the most casual analysis of the people involved in riots will indicate that riots are always started by similar groups of people, juveniles in the majority, mixed with older groups of malcontents, criminals and activists. All of these groups can again be split into two types, Locals and Visitors.

Visitors are always influenced in the early stages by the attitude and behaviour of locals who provide them with essential local knowledge of roads, escape routes and the most profitable targets for damage and looting. Visitors need locals to assist them.

Locals are inhibited from becoming too aggressive by local police officers who know them personally and who can deal with them immediately or later. A reduction in anonymity and the certainty of arrest are major inhibiting factors in any pre-riot situation.

Although a number of themes have been put forward regarding the objectives of these groups of rioters, experience has shown that once a riot has started, for whatever reason, its participants have two major objectives:- (1) Injury to police officers and damage to police property. (2) Looting. Knowledge of these two objectives must form a major part of any police strategy designed to put down a riot.

Finally it is suggested that it is very unusual for riots to erupt spontaneously. Riots do not suddenly happen. There is usually a definite sequence to the start of a riot.

First there is a 'High Tension' phase when the embryo rioters are consolidating support and courage for the contemplated riot. Then there is a 'Pre-Riot' phase when several determined attempts will be made to initiate serious disorder and, depending on their success, eventually the riots will begin. Depending on the success and effectiveness of the police, the support of local residents, or even the weariness of the rioters, the riot will eventually move into a 'Post-Riot' phase. This is followed by a High Tension phase and eventually by the re-introduction of Normal Policing. PROVIDING THAT A STRATEGY HAS BEEN PLANNED AND EFFECTIVELY IMPLEMENTED, each of these stages offers police an opportunity to prevent a decline into serious disorder.

There is a simple underlying strategy which co-ordinates all the various tactics that can be utilised in these different stages. The strategy is known as the CONTACT STRATEGY.

In its most basic form this strategy lays down the behaviour of all police officers involved in this type of event. It directs that on the initial contact between all police and the public, the police will take the initiative with:

> TACTIC ONE Be helpful and co-operative, treat the public as a customer. If this is successful then conflict and disorder can be avoided, if not then:
> TACTIC TWO Be firm and restrictive/corrective. If necessary, lawful force will be used in this tactic ie summons or arrest in an early resolution tactic.

Once the public/potential rioters wish to co-operate then the police will immediately switch back to TACTIC ONE whilst retaining the option to revert to TACTIC TWO should the individuals become uncooperative. The police tactic will be determined by public attitudes.

A description will now be given of the specific police strategies and tactics which can be used in each stage of the previously described RIOT SEQUENCE.

High Tension Stage

This usually occurs after an initial TRIGGER INCIDENT or after a number of minor events combining to create a similar incident. Disorder may have already taken place, but usually there will be a lull which enables both the police and COMMUNITY INTERVENERS to work as a team to make a determined effort to prevent serious disorder.

It is important that a deliberate policy decision is made to implement policing appropriate to this level before the situation has degenerated to the stage where disorder is inevitable.

Police strategy in this phase of the riot sequence is very dependent on the 'geographical basis' of the Normal Policing strategy, be it Unit or Sector based. It is essential that wherever possible only local officers are used who are known in the area they patrol.

Local members of the community must now identify themselves to these officers and work jointly with them as a police/public team.

Ideally, by this time, Units will have been established in all potential flash-point areas. There should also be a reserve of Sector officers on normal relief duties who are also well-known by local residents in the Unit areas.

It is most important for police to 'occupy' the geographical areas which have riot potential before the riot begins. The officers involved in this strategy must have a clear understanding of their role at this stage. Both the police officers and the public will be carefully monitoring various TENSION INDICATORS in order to make decisions about the most appropriate police response to the various incidents taking place.

In essence, the Normal Policing strategy quickly evolves into that required for 'High Tension' Policing. A decision is taken as to exactly how many officers can be deployed in the areas without being too provocative and then this number of patrolling officers, usually on foot, will be maintained as required.

The local officers on patrol in the riot-prone areas should be clearly briefed and directed as to their objectives which are PEACEKEEPING and INTELLIGENCE GATHERING. Riots need people; groups have to gather; locals and visitors have to meet and give each other confidence and the impetus for the disorder they contemplate. The officers, being local, can respond appropriately to all incidents in the area.

When the uniformed patrol officers are not dealing with incidents they should be instructed to talk to local residents, reassuring them, conciliating and giving correct information about incidents and rumours. It should be noted that this intensive type of policing is very stressful for all the officers involved and requires careful monitoring from senior supervising officers. The officers should be aware of the existence of readily available back-up.

Where groups of youths and others begin to congregate their size, disposition, and composition should be noted, and, if appropriate, they may have to be dispersed. This can often be achieved by simply standing with the groups and talking to them in a non-aggressive way. The last thing these groups want is to be seen talking to, or in the presence of, non-aggressive uniformed officers.

There is often a temptation to reduce police presence in an area during 'High Tension' periods in an effort to reduce the opportunity for claims of 'provocation' etc. However, it has been found through experience that this strategy is almost always counter-productive. In fact, this is often exactly what the criminals in a riot-prone area want the police to do. It allows them to consolidate their illegal activities in an area, with their blatant criminal activities leading to further alienation of law-abiding local residents against the police.

As well as the important objective of Peacekeeping, there is also a need for careful and structured information and intelligence gathering on a daily basis. Street officers must be carefully instructed what information to gather in these areas and how to do so. The information network should be linked into the police management and planning structure for maximum efficiency.

At this stage of the riot sequence it is almost a 'phoney war' with little obvious indication of the potential for serious disorder. Members of the public will now begin to hear and pass on various rumours which are circulating locally.

These rumours are also an important part of 'High Tension' Policing. If they are allowed to circulate unchecked they will increase the possibility of disorder. Often rumours are deliberately exploited by activists in the area to increase hostility and fear towards the police.

If local residents and their community leaders are committed to reducing conflict they can be of great assistance at this stage - particularly by releasing the facts to the street network. This can contribute significantly to minimising the risk of disorder and has been found to increase police morale.

Whilst this type of policing is being employed, Senior Managers have to be aware of the potential for serious and rapid escalation if this type of strategy is clearly insufficient to return the area to Normal Policing. The basic elements for the next policing strategy in the sequence have already been implemented and should be capable of rapid enhancement once the need arises.

Pre-Riot Stage

Eventually it may become apparent that disorder is inevitable and that attempts to prevent a riot have failed. The public must now be encouraged either to leave the area or remain inside. The police are now responsible for dealing with this situation. Once it is clear that disorder is inevitable, police tactics must change.

Pre-Riot policing has two objectives. First it is a final attempt to prevent escalation into serious disorder and riot. Secondly, the police are 'playing for time'. Experience has shown that even when a riot is expected, there is often considerable delay before sufficient external police resources can be equipped and mobilised. Therefore local police officers have to delay the onset of serious disorder for as long as possible.

On the streets, if Sector Control has not already been implemented, this must be done immediately. This means that each Sector Inspector is now individually responsible for the policing of his Sector. He will already have formulated a contingency plan for this type of event.

Basically, local police officers are all allocated to their own Sector with two objectives: Defence and Enforcement. Remembering the two objectives of all riots, looting and damage to police, all officers on the street must now have access to personal protection equipment in situ. Meanwhile, the Sector Inspector will be defending the vulnerable premises which are possible looting targets and carefully monitoring areas such as housing estates where attempts may be made to attack the police in force. It has been found that it is vital for the police to occupy in a positive manner all known flashpoint areas before the trouble begins. All of these areas should be identified in the prepared Contingency Plan.

At this point, the Sector Inspector will classify his officers into two categories, Defenders and Enforcers:Defenders will be static but have immediate access to full riot protection equipment. Their objective will be to occupy and defend vulnerable areas such as groups of shops or blocks of flats. They will remain within a specific allocated area and will not be re-deployed elsewhere. Their duty is to protect the area to which they are allocated. Once an area has been lost to rioters it is much more difficult to repossess, particularly if barricades etc., have been built.

Enforcers must be mobile with protective equipment in protected vehicles. These Units are to be deployed against roving groups of youths or other disorderly elements, to ensure they are aware of the police presence, and to arrest them where necessary.

The introduction of Sector Control in this strategy, co-ordinated by an Area Control, has been found to be very effective as it introduces a high degree of flexibility and local initiative. This means that many minor incidents are quickly and effectively dealt with before they can escalate into serious disorder. It also reduces the volume of decision making in Area Control, leaving more time for overall strategy co-ordination and control of major incidents.

The Riot Stage

The important point to make about a riot is that it is exclusively a battle between police and law breakers. The law abiding local community, including the COMMUNITY INTERVENERS, should understand there are no such things as spectators at riots. Once they see officers in riot gear and/or hear police warnings to leave the area they must immediately leave the area or go home for their own safety.

Inevitably, the decision to move into RIOT POLICING will be made for the police by the first major violent attempt by the rioters to achieve one of their objectives of looting or attacking the police. However, this does not mean that the initiative has been lost by the police. It only indicates that the rioters are prepared to challenge police effectiveness.

It is at this point that additional, external police assistance will be most urgently required, but it will be almost useless if it is not assembled, equipped and briefed in the most effective manner. Experience has taught that the simplest and most effective system of deploying outside aid is to retain the existing categories of DEFENDERS and enforcers, with all aid being allocated to one of these functions.

Even in the full riot situation, it has been found that retaining Sector Control has many advantages, leaving an Area Control to concentrate on major events. The overall strategy co-ordination and command decisions must be taken by the operational commander, who will be located in the Area Control, close to the scene of the riot.

Should extra Defenders be required by the Sector Inspector, they would be sent directly to the Inspector for briefing and deployment on scene. Superintendents may be required to be in charge of Sectors when large numbers of officers are deployed, but would still utilise the knowledge of local Sector Inspectors in their deployment tactics. Defenders will always remain in static locations to protect vulnerable areas.

If this system is employed at an early stage in the riot it should be successful in preventing extensive looting and, if the patrol officers are properly trained and equipped, they should escape major injury and damage. However, whilst large groups of rioters remain to roam around the area the incident is still not under control. Therefore, it is essential that the majority of the active rioters are detained and removed from the area as soon as possible or persuaded to leave by the presence of police.

Once rioters have found that they are unable to loot or successfully attack police officers or premises, they may well try to stage a violent confrontation with the police in order to injure as many as possible. This type of tactic was tried a number of times at Brixton (1985), particularly in the Moorlands and Stockwell Park Estates. These types of estates with their elevated walk-ways, numerous attack positions and escape routes are ideal for this type of offensive against the police.

However, it was found that if Enforcer Units were employed under the direction of the local Unit or Sector Officer who knew the estates very well, it was possible to regain control of these estates. This was despite the fact that a considerable number of missiles and petrol bombs were directed at the police.

It should be noted at this stage that, should the rioters become extremely violent, then the level of police response will, of necessity, become more violent.

Post-Riot and the Return to Normality

The amount of responsibility accepted by police for a riot starting in the first place is debatable. It is more certain that the putting down of a riot and the return to stability in an area, are valid and reliable performance measures for police.

It is suggested that once a riot has been subdued, however temporarily, the next major task of the police is a planned return to normality. Unless a strategy to achieve this objective is implemented after police success against a riot, it may well flare again into various levels of public disorder.

In this Post-Riot stage, the objective is to maintain a level of stability with the least possible number of police officers. Aid from outside the police station should be returned to 'Reserve' status as soon as possible, leaving local officers to control the streets in normal uniform.

Post-Riot policing is very similar to Pre-Riot policing, with a few important differences:- (1) If the riot strategy was successful, police manpower should be more experienced and confident, but could well be very tired. (2) However, if the strategy is perceived as unsuccessful, Senior Officers and street officers will all be suffering from post-event trauma to some extent. This type of situation requires intervention from outside the police station, introduced into the command structure at various levels. (3) Having once caused major public disorder the participants will be more willing to become involved in spontaneous public disorder at every opportunity. (4) Copy-cat rioting could well erupt or be planned for other areas and therefore intelligence gathering in all riot-prone areas is essential.

Eventually, the immediate danger of rioting is reduced and a policy decision to move back into High Tension policing can be made. The period of time involved in this total sequence and the stress placed on the officers involved make it essential that close attention be paid to the morale and physical health of the police officers involved. It is probably best that this particular monitoring task should be the responsibility of officers from outside the police station involved.

Once an area has returned to 'normal', it is important to remember that the area is still riot-prone and, despite the most enlightened and sympathetic policing, could still erupt into rioting at some time in the future. Until more is known about the causes of riot and some success has been achieved in removing these causes, then police must plan and be prepared for riots in inner city areas. Just because an area has not experienced major disorder for some time, it does not necessarily mean that disorder is now less probable.

If police develop a very effective local policing system which intervenes in conflict situations at an early stage and this is not matched by developments and successes by other agencies, then all policing becomes is a more effective lid on the pressure cooker. Eventually, the social pressure inside the environment will defeat any policing system which is not actively supported by other agencies and the community itself.

SECTION IV:

THE MEDIATORS—
UNITED STATES

The practical application of conflict resolution gained earlier acceptance in the United States than in Europe, so that the construction of training, consultation and conciliation services there is rather more advanced. One suspects that this occurred because of the pluralistic nature of American society, where group conflict is both more evident and more accepted, and where a dominant central decision-making authority is lacking because of the federal structure. This no doubt led American groups naturally to look for other ways of resolving disputes than appeal to authority, which has traditionally been the main response in European countries for several centuries now. This has had the effect of making American society both more violent—when groups looked to adversarial methods of dispute settlement (including precipitate recourse to the more "civilised" but often equally vicious measure of litigation), and more conciliatory - when groups looked to negotiation. Thus Americans tend both to fight and to talk more than Europeans! The centralised authorities in Europe (still enshrined, if only now symbolically, in the monarchies of a few countries) had the advantage of protecting society against internal social violence, which has erupted into large-scale disruption comparatively rarely, but had the disadvantage that communities became over-reliant on "the authorities" to sort out their troubles and seldom developed familiarity with negotiation on their own behalf.

In this section we look at four types of development in the United States that are based on the principles of conflict resolution. The first, in chapter 11, is the local community mediation scheme, primarily orientated to the provision of a facility for resolving interpersonal disputes between neighbours and other acquaintances. These schemes have taken a variety of forms, ranging from the more formal "neighbourhood justice centre", taking most of its referrals on diversion from the legal process, to the more grass-roots community-orientated service, of which the San Francisco Community Board Program is the most well-known. It is this project which is referred to in Chapter 11, written by its founder and former director Raymond Shonholtz. Elsewhere he has been critical of developments which in some cases have become more like a second-class assembly-line form of justice on which overloaded courts can offload what they term their "rubbish cases" (ie the ones from which the lawyers do not stand to make much money). Such mediation can degenerate into a superficial process orientated primarily towards reaching a quick settlement, rather than one which attends to the parties' needs (cf. Harrington, 1985, but also see the criticisms of Harrington in, eg, Marshall 1988).

Shonholtz sees the mediation programme as being for the community, not for the courts. He sees it as a means of empowering local communities to resolve their own internal differences, thereby learning tolerance and a sense of citizenship, and developing a stronger sense of unity through collaboration. In his paper he argues that we all lose out if recourse is had too precipitately to the police or the law: a problem resolved is better than one adjudicated (which may settle blame but offers no forward-looking solution), and a process that involves both the parties and their neighbours is more educative than one which leaves it all to others (lawyers and police officers). The outcome of such mediation (which is carried out by ordinary local residents acting, after training, as volunteers) is more concerned with mending relationships than with sweeping disputes under the carpet, and more concerned with learning to behave with consideration and respect towards others (positive achievement) than with fire-fighting crime or misbehaviour (rearguard reaction). He therefore sees a community-based mediation service as part of the process of establishing democracy and citizenship in society - as much as taking part in elections, and indeed even more so, because the former is more participative. A further advantage is that through training, and involvement from time to time in the resolution of one's own or fellow residents' disputes, members of the community are learning the principles and skills of negotiation that may prove to be an invaluable aid at times of incipient social unrest or major social conflicts. The police, Shonholtz argues, are limited to crisis intervention, in troubles which have already escalated beyond reasoned negotiation, and they are therefore always going to be limited in their impact to the equivalent of first-aid. More substantial control, prevention and resolution can only occur within the democratic community itself, although police forces can encourage and facilitate local neighbourhoods to take responsiblity for localised trouble, to train and organise themselves, and to integrate cooperatively with police activity.

The second type of development is the establishment of a body of skilled mediators and negotiators on a regional or national basis, able to intervene, as consultants, trainers, facilitators or mediators, in conflicts of social importance where relationships have broken down so that conciliation cannot occur naturally. Such a body is the federal Community Relations Service (administratively located in the

Introduction to Section IV

Department of Justice). As Tim Newburn describes in Chapter 12, the CRS was established because of experience of the success of such an approach in labour relations disputes (replicated in Britain by the well-established and highly successful ACAS). Such a body has many advantages. Over time it can acquire experience and hone skills (exemplified in a number of major policy shifts within CRS over the years). It can build credibility as a fair-minded and impartial body which has the best interests of all parties at heart. It can carry out non-crisis relationship-building work in areas where disorder or breakdown are future possibilities, either preventing trouble before it erupts by helping to tackle underlying grievances, or setting up a structure of communication that has a chance to survive localised outbreaks of trouble, or at least providing itself with ready-made contacts and a bank of knowledge for each such area which will facilitate crisis intervention if it comes to such a pass.

In Chapter 13, a former Acting Director of CRS, Wallace Warfield, describes a particular example of CRS intervention. He describes how disorders (riots) arise from social inequality and lack of confidence in authority, but only occur when an additional "trigger" is provided by some particular incident which may bear little obvious relationship to the underlying causes of disquiet - often a shooting incident between police and a resident over what may be some ordinary minor crime or just suspicion. He also sees the degree of tension in a community varying along a scale from co-operation, through a state of peaceful competition, through gradually increasing tension, to overt conflict, and, in the event of some trigger incident, a full-blown crisis. The process of settlement is therefore a long-term one of gradually reducing tension by moving down one step at a time. Resolving a crisis does not remove the conflict, but one cannot start to resolve the latter until the crisis situation is settled. Crisis-settlement is a quick, short-term process, but it is important not to rest on one's laurels at this stage, and to move energetically into the longer-term process of dealing with real grievances and re-establishing relationships. Many of the problems occurring in the policing of the riots he describes - inadequate contingency planning, lack of community mechanisms for social control, insensitive containment policing, failure to use black police officers, rumours getting out of hand - have already been noted in Sections II and III in relation to the Brixton riots in London.

Chapter 14 is a further, and vivid, account of mediation in practice. In this case the intervention occurred at the request, originally, of the police, although it was only able to go ahead, of course, with the full agreement of all the parties involved. The author, Ron Claassen, was the principal mediator in this case, which involved a serious breakdown in trust between the police force and Hispanic communities in Fresno, consequent on a series of incidents including several shootings by members of the police. Claassen was experienced in mediation as

Director of the local programme for mediating between victims and offenders, and he was well known in the locality through the success of this programme. The kind of multi-group high-tension confrontation he found himself in the centre of in this case, however, was very different from the general run of one-to-one victim and offender meetings. Nevertheless, the same general principles run through all kinds of mediation, and, with care, Claassen was able to apply his thorough grasp of these to this special kind of situation.

Claassen is honest and modest about his achievements in this paper, but the success of his intervention is testified to by Wiest (1990), who claims that "Nobody got what they thought they wanted, but everyone got what they really wanted..." as a result of the mediation. She quotes Fresno Human Relations Commission member, Jim Patterson, as saying that "We have today less violence by police than in 1985-86 and no Hispanic people have been shot since that time. ... The concept of mediation does work." By means of a search for common ground (neither the police nor the Hispanic community wanted to see the shootings continue) rather than a focus on blaming, creative solutions emerged that made a concrete difference.

In the remaining chapter, Maria Volpe and Robert Louden describe the problems of mediating under stress, which is typical of policing tasks. Both are experienced in conflict resolution and they are involved in the training of New York police. Robert was himself at one time Chief Hostage Negotiator for the New York Police Department, and this essay draws very much on his experience. Hostage situations put pressure on police forces to negotiate rather than use force, because of the the danger to the hostages, and training for such negotiations is prevalent across police forces of many countries. Any deaths will be seen to be, at least partially, the responsibility of the police, so that every care will be taken to avoid such an outcome. It is interesting how this compares with the typical riot situation, where police use of force can equally easily result in injury and death, often to innocent parties, but where the same constraint on such action does not seem to be felt, perhaps because of the diffuse responsibility that occurs in more inchoate circumstances. It is important that police forces do recognise that their responsiblity is the same in all situations where their action may endanger lives, and that the same care and deliberation are taken with incipient riots as with hostage scenarios. The techniques and strategies are very similar, and the team structures and individual training needed to cope with the stressful aspects of employing conciliation in such conditions are also identical.

References

HARRINGTON, CB (1985) *Shadow Justice*. Greenwood Press.

MARSHALL, TF (1988) Out of court: more or less justice?, in Matthews, R (Ed) *Informal Justice?* . Sage.

WEIST, KH (1990) Another viewpoint. *MCS Conciliation Quarterly*, Summer, 2(4)

Chapter Eleven

The Citizen's Role in Justice: Building a Primary Justice and Prevention System at the Neighbourhood Level

RAYMOND SHONHOLTZ

HOMICIDE AND events resulting in substantial personal injury are commonplace in American life. Contrary to popular belief, the vast majority of these deaths and injuries are caused not by strangers but rather by ex-lovers, former roommates, and business partners. Millions, if not billions, of law enforcement dollars are spent each year to investigate, arrest, prosecute, and try persons charged with causing either death or personal injury to others. These substantial amounts are expended after the fact, that is, after the crime has been committed and the death or injury sustained. Few, if any, dollars are spent to prevent, or foster nonpolice intervention prior to, the eventual homicide or casualty. This absence would of itself not be too surprising if it were not for the fact that the vast majority of potential homicides are known to the police, family members, neighbours, friends, and often fellow members of religious organisations well before the incident causing death or serious injury actually occurs.

Limits of Criminal Justice

In contrast to crimes or transactions between strangers that result in a killing or bodily injury, the significant percentage of homicides and violence in America represent ongoing transactions between the victim and offender. The common situation is an escalating series of interpersonal aggravations between individuals who have an ongoing or prior business or domestic relationship. Generally, these aggravations become known in the general community. Typical is the neighbour who calls the police complaining about the warring family next door. While the neighbour's peace is being disturbed, the real purpose for seeking police intervention is to prevent a further escalation of hostilities within the next-door family. Nearly every police department has a list of families and individuals that are known in the community for their violent dispositions. Certainly, friends and relatives are often quite aware of the conditions in a friend's or family member's home. Yet out of fear, ignorance, sense of privacy, or sheer inability to provide any meaningful assistance, they limit their prevention or intervention role before the predictable and pending violence.

Each of these situations, and the great variations in between, restates the basic theme of the American criminal justice system: if the offence, hostility, or violent behaviour is insufficient to fall within a justice agency's responsibility, then no services are provided. The criminal justice system becomes most operative when hostilities have generated violence, injury, or death to someone. Nearly all agency interventions occur after the fact and are based on legal standards.

The legal basis of agency intervention sets up the great irony and reality in the American interplay between prevention and violence interdiction. In American democratic society, all forms of behaviour are lawful and acceptable except those that violate the criminal law. The criminal law articulates the lowest standard of social behaviour that our society allows. All other forms of behaviour are free from the formal control maintained by law enforcement. The critical point lies in the fact that the state, through its law enforcement system, can only intervene if there is a violation of the criminal law. All other forms of social behaviour, however noxious, are constitutionally immune from the coercive and penal sanction of the criminal justice system. Thus a police officer may be well aware that a house member is at risk, yet be completely unable to do anything about it until the person has been subjected to violence, injury, or death.

Social Disorder:
A Crime Factor Beyond the Criminal Justice System

People's major impressions about neighbourhood or community crime are derived from "highly visible signs of what they regard as disorderly and disreputable behaviour in their community." (Biderman et al, 1967) Many studies have been conducted on the impact of social disorder on the quality of neighbourhood life. "Research indicates [that disorder] sparks concern and fear of crime among neighbourhood residents, and may actually increase the level of serious crime." (Skogan, 1986a)

Disorder has been defined as conditions and events widely interpreted as signalling a breakdown in the realisation of community norms about public behaviour. Their presence appears to provide observable evidence of neighbourhood decline... Disorder is apparent in the widespread appearance of junk and trash in vacant lots, poorly maintained homes, boarded-up buildings, vandalism of public and private property, graffiti, and stripped and abandoned cars in the streets and alleys. (Skogan, 1986b)

This form of disorder and a companion social set that includes public drinking, loitering, and drug use "appear to erode the mechanisms by which neighbourhood residents exercise control over local events and conditions." (Skogan, 1986b) While some sets of problems fall within the scope of law enforcement, others are not so clearly determined; both sorts often present intractable law enforcement problems. Disorder, whether physical or social, has a decidedly negative impact on community life, informal social control, and a community's capacity to prevent more serious crime conditions from emerging.

An important set of responses emerges from communities suffering high levels of disorder. First, the level of cooperation between neighbours often declines. Mistrust and suspicion are high, which serves to undermine cooperative social relationships and common mutual assistance. Second, the crime prevention efforts that do take place relate to self-serving individualised actions such as marking one's property with an identification number.

Wilson and Kelling (1982) argue that communities suffering from social and physical disorder also suffer more serious crime. Many studies support the conclusion that there is a strong relationship between crime and perceptions of disorder. There seem to be very few highly disordered neighbourhoods that are also low-crime communities. Wilson and Kelling make the link between disorder and crime by arguing that disorder promotes domestic crime and encourages the importation of criminal activity from other places. By undermining a community's ability to sustain and maintain standards of social control, social and physical disorder can foster an ever-increasing form of criminality within the community. (Skogan, 1986a)

Moreover, there is a direct relationship between disorder and fear of crime. "We have found that attitudes of citizens regarding crime are less affected by their past victimisation experiences than by their ideas about what is going on in their community - fears about a weakening of social controls on which they feel their safety and the broader fabric of social life is ultimately dependent." (Biderman, 1967) "If 'social control' is the development and enforcement of norms about public conduct, then visible evidence of anti-social behaviour, that local owners and landlords are not maintaining their property, and that the area is becoming a dumping ground, should seem sure signs that the area is out of control." (Skogan, 1986a) Even victimisation studies seem to conclude that disorder generates a heightened sense among the local citizenry of being a victim of crime that is disproportionate to the actual rate of victimisation. Thus the fear of crime and disorder are highly related. "Important neighbourhood factors such as fear of crime or solidarity among neighbours seemed to rise or fall steadily with levels of disorder." (Skogan, 1986a)

Thus, as with homicide and personal injury, research and study reasonably conclude that the ingredients of crime, fear of crime, and victimisation can be found in activities that are either pre-criminal in nature or problematic for law enforcement's control and suppression of crime. Accordingly, a reliance on law enforcement either to break the cycle of hostile interpersonal interaction prior to the occurrence of the violence or homicide or to reduce the factors of disorder is highly questionable. A reliance on formal law enforcement to have an impact in the area of either homicide or social disorder would most likely prove futile, frustrating, and ineffective in reducing the number of people who die at the hands of people who know them or in reducing the disorder factors that lead eventually to greater forms of antisocial conduct or criminality.

The Citizen Intervenor: Building a New Public Policy

Our singular reliance on a formal criminal justice system, ironically, places prevention outside the legal system; formal justice can only intervene after an incident has violated a criminal statute. Accordingly, prevention and early intervention efforts are legally, if not constitutionally, circumscribed. This barrier, which limits governmental agencies from interacting with citizens in the course of their daily activities, is one of the great principles of democratic society and one of America's contributions to democratic thought and practice. It is not the intent of this article to encourage a lowering or changing of this standard, but rather to encourage a recognition that its existence results in a serious social anomaly in a society that increasingly seeks dependency on formal justice for its safety and protection.

If prevention and early intervention are not responsibilities of government and formal justice agencies, then whose responsibilities are they? Prior to a violation of law, all disputes are private and without a formal entry into the legal system. There is only one group in democratic society that can intervene in such conflicts: citizens. Citizens acting and serving in their civic capacity can affect social and private situations provided their intervention is voluntary and without coercion. Citizens working through the informal norms of social control are the only persons who can conduct and sustain an ongoing prevention and early intervention policy. They are the only ones with the proper status to engage their fellow citizens in the informal discussion and settlement of differences.

This approach to prevention has deep roots in American history. While modern thinking views justice as a primary function of agencies, historically Americans turned to community and religious institutions for the early settlement of conflict and the promotion of community social values. In fact, suing or swearing a police oath was considered in many communities to be a violation of individual moral responsibility and a sign that the community was lax in enforcing social norms. The Judeo-Christian base of American democratic thought stressed the responsibilities of individuals and the obligation of society in maintaining cooperative associations and support systems. (Auerbach, 1983)

Historically, primary or civic justice has been understood to be a community undertaking, outside and separate from the more narrow and formal responsibilities of the state's exercise of formal control. To the degree that our Constitution and early American political thinking reflect the then-prevailing religious mores, it is understandable that the early Americans limited the scope of justice to those acts that violated a statute or code, because the larger arena of everyday activity was within the social structure of individuals and voluntary associations to control and maintain informally.

The past few decades have seen a dramatic erosion of these concepts and values and, concomitantly, a significant growth in the adversarial system. The expectations and social norms that had motivated citizens to undertake civic responsibilities began to atrophy in the wake of continued professionalisation of nearly all social services. The result of this transition has been to take - or perhaps, in the concepts of Nils Christie (1977), to steal - from citizens a broad range of social responsibilities and initiatives, leaving many communities, citizens' groups, and individuals feeling more alienated, isolated, and dependent. Moreover, the professionalisation of police work left officers isolated from the communities they were sworn to protect and saddled them with an array of conflicts and conditions of disorder more appropriate for an active, vibrant, civic oriented community to confront and manage.

Communities that fostered a sense of civic norms and common values are no longer cohesive and stable. Though they still need citizen initiative, what is now called for is a modern analogue to the historical experience. The cultural analogue is to develop and implement public policies that will actively encourage citizens to take responsibility for early intervention in conflict and to manage the social and physical conditions of disorder.

Fortunately, the cultural analogue for the concept and practice of the citizen as intervenor in conflict has been the subject of an ongoing and successful social experiment begun in San Francisco in 1976. Recognising that only citizens could intervene in conflicts early and knowing that the vast majority of conflicts were between people who knew one another, the Community Board Programme began to develop an early-intervention, conflict-prevention programme in the neighbourhoods of the city. The themes were the citizens' engagement in the reduction of tension and conflict in their community and empowerment through training to assist neighbours in disputes.

Consistent with the development of the cultural analogue is the articulation of a public policy that formally promotes citizens in their civic role as early intervenors and conciliators of conflicts between people with prior or ongoing relationships. With such a public policy, it is possible to place citizens in a preventive role and to develop a community system for early intervention in conflict. The new community justice system recruits from the neighbourhoods the natural dispute resolvers, provides them with the same training, and advertises widely about when and how to use the new justice system effectively. The community justice model actively engages hostile disputants early in the historical development of their conflict. Using a simple, though highly effective, disputant-empowerment approach, the community conciliators, as modelled and developed by community boards, would apply conflict management methods to de-escalate the dispute and reduce the opportunity for violence and police intervention.

Community as Social Control

While citizens can be trained and organised to facilitate conflict resolution between people who know one another, it is imperative that such facilitation be developed as a community institution. If the civic work stands out as a project of a separate group of people, it will lack the cohesive and impactive relevancy to effect a new dimension in the justice policies of a city. Civic participation is critical for several reasons.

First, as more extensively developed in the final section of this article, community problems and conflicts present an opportunity to engage in civic work. Civic work is the means through which citizens come to know and understand one another and develop social networks. A public policy that promotes civic work elevates its relevancy and makes a policy statement to all citizens within the municipality.

Second, where community institutions are strong and cross-cutting, gossip, social exclusion, negotiation, and even mediation or arbitration by trusted figures can resolve disputes or contain their consequences. However, where community solidarity is so low that there are no viable mechanisms for resolving disputes informally, or where they do not embrace all major local groups, long-standing conflicts may undercut the social and economic forces underlying the neighbourhood stability.... Problem-solving mechanisms which rely upon self-initiated citizen action require community institutions which foster interaction and cooperation. (Skogan, 1986a; cf also Merry, 1981)

This is one of the strengths of community-based, conflict-resolution mechanisms. In order to function, they must build a community support base and develop into a community institution.

Third, it is critical that the community institutions, especially those engaged in justice, have an active and ongoing dialogue with law enforcement. This is the only way for those who advocate a stronger presence for police in acting against and addressing disorder ever to learn what "the neighbourhood [has] decided [is] the appropriate level of public order." (Wilson & Kelling, 1982)

With the development of a community system for the management of a broad range of social disorders, an opportunity opens for both the neighbourhoods and the police. Because many of these disorders fall outside the traditional police mandate, it is essential that a citizen-based institution be available to respond to the local conditions. To achieve a significant impact on social and physical disorder, there must be a three-stage development.

1. The municipality must establish a public policy that views community conflict management as the primary step in the justice system. From this perspective, the municipality would be supporting the community approach as the means of first resort for the resolution of individual conflicts and community disorder concerns.
2. As a complete expression of this justice policy, the community would need organising, training, and service resources to design, implement, and maintain the community justice system effectively.
3. To sustain a working relationship, the police department would be advantaged by developing complementary programmes that positively interact with the community justice process. These might include foot patrols; storefront offices, such as the ones that the Japanese police use; and team policing methods.

Social control by the community requires from the municipality: - a commitment to develop the public policy and resources; - a commitment by the police to be trained in the new model, to support it in appropriate ways, and to refer cases to it; and - an integration of social and police programming that enhances cooperation and communication between the police, the community, and the new justice system in the neighbourhoods.

There are many who argue that the community is too fractured to develop a cultural analogue comparable to the informal mechanisms of social control once prevalent in the World War II community. Experience in community-based conflict-resolution work teaches that this argument is incorrect. Moreover, this form of thinking leaves communities dependent on legally constrained law enforcement providers, who cannot manage either disorder or prelaw violation conflicts. Only individuals operating through community institutions can engage in these activities. If disorder is the basis or a major factor for the expansion of crime in a community and if prior and ongoing relationships serve as the largest statistical pool for homicides and felonious assaults, then it is a social imperative to begin to restore citizens' rights and responsibilities in order to perform their historic civic functions in addressing social disorder and persons in conflict.

A Public Policy for Citizen-Based Community Justice

There really is no choice. It is essential for policymakers and urban mayors to see that they need to support the development of community justice systems. It is the only way we presently know to - reduce the level of violence between people who know one another; - reduce the opportunity for disorder to promote crime and the fear of crime in a community; - restore to citizens a range of civic work that only they can perform anyway; - promote intra- and inter-community cooperation; and - build community institutions that directly respond to the issues of disorder, crime, and violence.

If we are serious about reducing the incidence of violence in our urban communities, it is essential that we address those situations that, statistically, will generate homicide and felonious assaults. These are the cases that on the surface may appear minor or insignificant yet contain the explosive power of homicide. Nearly all violence and death inflicted by people on others with whom they have prior or ongoing relationships have at their point of origin what appear to be minor or petty concerns. In many respects this states the whole point. By viewing the obvious as inconsequential, law enforcement cannot address those very underlying concerns that jettison the situation from an apparent minor matter into greater criminality or homicide cases several months or years later. Communities have the power and the responsibility to address these conditions of disorder and potentially violent situations early, before they escalate further into criminal violence.

How do communities go about this prevention work and reduce the potential for disorder, violence, and criminality in their environment? What is the role of government in this process and how can it serve to enhance and promote the civic work of citizens? And what are the social and communitarian values that encourage citizens to undertake this civic work and complete the cultural analogue modeled so long ago?

A Working Primary Justice System

After ten years of experimentation and practice, community conciliation models and programmes abound in the United States. Many, patterned after the pioneering Community Boards of San

Francisco, the nation's oldest and largest community-based conflict resolution service, have attracted a wide diversity of civic participation by offering to community residents free training in conflict resolution skills; holding community educational meetings; training community residents in how to build a church-community support base; and working closely with local police, school, church, and business associations in support of the community justice system and encouraging referral of cases to it.

The new justice systems receive cases from almost every likely source, though most identify word-of-mouth and school, church, and community organisations as primary sources of referral. It is striking that the types of problems identified in the literature on community disorder are common in community conflict-resolution hearings. These may include the presence of junk and trash in vacant lots, poorly maintained homes, vandalism, graffiti, vacated vehicles, dog litter, gang activity, noisy neighbours, litter, poor garbage handling, neighbours' quarrels, business disputes, conflicts within church or community organisations, and use of mini-parks and social clubs. Moreover, these primary justice systems are being actively used for the peaceful expression and resolution of large group conflicts that include problems between police and youth; problems between gays and Hispanics; and disputes over park turfs, and so forth.

From several different studies (see DuBow and Emmons, 1981), it is now clear that a significant percentage of police cases are precisely the type of dispute or conflict between people with prior or ongoing relationships that is uniquely suited for community justice programmes. From a study of the San Francisco Police Department, conservative estimates are that 12-15 percent of the department's cases are very similar to the disputes going to Community Board hearings. It is important to note that this category, for which the police often neither make arrests nor write reports, absorbs a disproportionate amount of police time compared to cases in which reports or arrests are made. In short, the percentage belies the substantial amount of time these community disorder and nonarrest problems require of responding police officers.

The Municipality's Educational and Support Functions

While the capacity to plan, develop, and execute community dispute programmes lies within almost any urban community, the ability to make case referrals lies most appropriately within a municipality's educational functions. Only the city, through its many and diverse educational units, has the sustainability and ongoing capacity to educate citizens, organisations, and disputants about when and how to access local dispute-settlement services in their urban neighbourhoods. Cities need to appreciate the interrelationship and mutual partnership that exists between the work of volunteer dispute resolvers in encouraging disputants to address conflicts early and the role of the city in promoting early intervention and resolution of disputes. Without the city as a viable promoter of the community justice system, the educational function for conflict prevention and de-escalation becomes de facto the work obligation of the service-providing entity. This is too time consuming and expensive to be borne solely by the dispute-settlement programme. The city's failure to work in tandem with the civic endeavour of the community justice system translates concretely to a limited case load and work opportunity for the locally trained and available neighbourhood conflict managers.

If a city truly desires to put into place a programme that over time will address the underlying causes of disorder in the neighbourhood and reduce the presence of violence in the family, neighbourhood, and school, it becomes critical that it implement and support a process that reaches disputes before they explode and become intractable. Early intervention is the key to thwarting the potential for violence inherent in conflicts between persons who know one another. Communication and education through city instruments are critical to success. Ideally, citizens should be as familiar with the name and function of the primary justice system in the neighbourhoods as they are with the telephone number 911 [999 in British terms - Ed.]. This form of visibility can only be achieved with strong support from the municipality.

Finally, the city must provide some resources for the new justice system. A fully operational community conflict-management system that could effectively manage many of the disorder issues and ongoing relational conflicts that escalate into violence could be fully administered in most urban areas on less than 1 percent of the city's total justice budget. Municipal savings should be most dramatic in how police use their freed-up time, once the police begin to refer the most time-consuming problems to the neighbourhood justice system.

There is little that remains theoretical about the development of a community or primary justice system. The Community Board Centre for Policy and Training has for nearly six years been training volunteers throughout the United States, Canada, and Europe - Ireland, England, and France - in how to plan, develop, implement, and organise for a new community justice system that trains local residents to conciliate conflicts peacefully within the community.

Violence in American cities can be dramatically decreased if municipalities incorporate primary, community-based justice systems as a part of their justice policies and provide disputants with a prevention and early-resolution system for their conflict.

The Foundations of Primary Justice: Citizen and Community

Ownership of civic justice work lies with citizens in the community. While a municipality must provide the general educational, legitimation, and funding support, only the direct involvement of citizens, serving as trained volunteers or as disputants voluntarily using the conflict-resolution process, will achieve the requisite level of support necessary for a noncoercive, voluntary process of conflict resolution. Ownership and participation must cross ethnic, racial, gender, and age lines for the primary justice process to be a comprehensive system relating to all communities within an urban environment.

Community conflict resolution provides people a unique opportunity to perform civic work, reduce community and individual alienation, and prevent violent and potentially violent situations from escalating into the instances of homicide and injury associated with conflicts between persons who know one another. It is this very work that serves to build new alliances and relationships at the community level. By reintroducing civic functions and responsibility into the equation of violence prevention in urban America, a new dimension is added that immediately and effectively relates to a specific group of conflicted persons known statistically to be in a high-risk injury category. By developing a volunteer group of trained residents to assist other residents in the resolution of immediate conflicts, this identifiable, at-risk group can be reached and their tensions and hostilities individually addressed. The placement of public policy emphasis on this identifiable group and the implementation of policies that encourage the development of citizen-managed dispute-settlement processes will in time affect the level and type of violence within the identifiable, at-risk group of known disputants. To achieve this result, the public policy commitment must begin with a new concept of prevention and a clear understanding of the indispensable role of citizens as the primary prevention workers.

Conceptually, prevention is the work territory of the community. It is an area that is not full of regulations and certification requirements. It is not a terrain of professionals or professionalisation. The more citizens actively exercise their civic functions within the realm of prevention, the greater is the social cohesion within their community. In disorder and community-decline studies, the issue of civic participation and bonding is identified as an important factor in what determines whether a community can maintain forms of informal social control or not.

Civic work and commonality of work interests serve as social bonds that cross ethnic and racial boundaries. In many respects, where community ends, law and regulatory schemes begin. The more the community can of itself exercise its civic functions, the more the need for formal law is lessened. In a democratic society, greater social cohesion and community harmony are manifest when actions that qualitatively improve the community are voluntarily undertaken by citizens. Thus conflict prevention and de-escalation are excellent work areas for civic initiative and preventive measures undertaken by groups of trained volunteers. Inextricably entwined with the performance of the civic preventive work is the direct enhancement of the role, function, and skills of citizens. By expanding the boundaries of civic work and by concretely identifying dispute settlement as an important citizen function, the area of prevention is extended and thereby the scope of community is extended as well. Formal law is pushed further away as citizens begin to perform their unique dispute-settlement role, and in the performance of this work the authority and responsibility associated with these civic functions become readily visible and valued. Building a primary justice system at the community level affects not only the conflicts that people have, but the community life of the neighbourhood and the capacity of citizens to work together in common purpose.

It is not unreasonable to argue within the context of the social analogue presented here that all prevention work is within the ambit of civic rights associated with citizenship within a democratic society. Moreover, this is precisely what is constitutionally afforded citizens by the reservation clause of the Ninth Amendment to the U.S. Constitution. The framers saw all around them initiatives and actions undertaken by citizens in their civic capacity. Tocqueville comments extensively on this phenomenon of the new American democracy and expresses the vitality and essentiality of this civic exercise as a keystone to the success of the democratic experience. From this perspective, one can readily appreciate that all opportunities that afford citizens an ability to exercise their civic roles serve to enhance the foundations of the democratic system. Ironically, the performance of these roles is inextricably linked to violence and disorder prevention. Citizens have the unique capacity to intervene in conflicts before the state is constitutionally allowed to do so. Thus the establishment now of community primary justice systems serves as a bridge and social analogue to an earlier time when civic involvement and conflict intervention were connected.

Community prevention systems are the primary, or initial, justice system. Community prevention systems seek to interact with problems as they emerge and to resolve them quickly, before they enter the formal justice system. From this view, the formal, adversarial system is the alternative. Any other policy approach leaves conflicts and disorder to escalate into the after-the-fact justice system and leaves the injured or killed victims as testimonials to the nonexistence of prevention and community justice systems.

This article first appeared in The Annals of the American Academy of Political and Social Science, p.42, November 1987, and is re-published here with permission.

References

AUERBACH, J (1983) *Justice without Law? Resolving Disputes without Lawyers*. New York: Oxford University Press.

BIDERMAN, AD et al. (1967) *Report on a Pilot Study in the District of Columbia on Victimisation and Attitudes toward Law Enforcement*. Washington, DC: Government Printing Office.

CHRISTIE, N (1977) Conflicts as property. *British Journal of Criminology*, 17, 1-15.

DUBOW, F and EMMONS, D (1981) The community hypothesis, in Lewis, DA (Ed) *Reactions to Crime*. Newbury Park, CA: Sage.

MERRY, SE (1981) *Urban Danger: Life in a Neighbourhood of Strangers*. Philadelphia: Temple University Press.

SKOGAN, WG (1986a) Disorder, Crime and Community Decline. Paper presented at the Home Office Conference on Crime and Communities, Cambridge University, Cambridge, England.

(1986b) Executive Summary: Disorder and Community Decline. Paper, National Institute of Justice.

WILSON, JQ and KELLING, G (1982) Broken Windows. *Atlantic Monthly*, March, 29-38.

Chapter Twelve

Police-Community Mediation in the United States: The Department of Justice Community Relations Service

TIM NEWBURN

Background

THE COMMUNITY Relations Service (CRS) was established by the Civil Rights Act 1964, and was originally part of the Department of Commerce (it was transferred to the Department of Justice in 1965). Although it might appear from this date that the CRS was set up in response to the civil disturbances experienced in many major American cities during the 1960s, the establishment of such an agency had been mooted in Congress as early as 1959. The Federal Mediation and Conciliation Service had had a successful history in using mediation and conciliation techniques in the resolution of management-labour disputes, and it was felt by some that such innovations should be extended to the Civil Rights area.

Introducing proposed Civil Rights legislation in 1959, which included the putative CRS, Lyndon Johnson argued that mediation and conciliation were particularly pertinent in this area:

As I understand the concept of civil rights, they cannot undoubtedly be enforced by law. They involve the idea of human acceptance, of human understanding, and of human dignity. The outward manifestations of tolerance can be enforced by guns, clubs and bayonets. But understanding does not exist until the people themselves will it to exist...Controversies involving civil rights have reached a point where they can be paralyzing to whole communities...But somehow life must go on...And a just settlement can be found - if only people will talk to each other. At this point, a conciliator would be worth his weight in gold. (Calhoun, undated)

This bill introduced by Johnson would have established a CRS for four years, but due to pressure of time this part of the Bill was never passed. Early in 1961 Representative Halpern introduced a Bill that would have set up a more narrowly focused agency concentrating solely on problems arising from anti-segregation court decisions. This again fell.

During 1963 an attempt was made to establish a Community Relations and Conciliation Service which would act as 'an independent agency to provide conciliation assistance in communities where peaceful relations among citizens are disrupted and to provide technical assistance in seeking voluntary means to insure all persons equal protection of the laws.' Senator Williams, one of those who introduced the bill, illustrated the necessity for such an agency by arguing that around that time a number of particularly volatile situations in Birmingham, Alabama had been defused by the use of mediation by the Department of Justice's Civil Rights Division. There were a further two attempts to establish a similar agency during this 88th Congress; once again by Representative Halpern like his attempt in 1961, and by Representative Barrett who wished to set up something that would have been called the Federal Human Relations Commission.

Early in the hearings on Civil Rights legislation in 1963 Robert Kennedy, the Attorney General, spoke in favour of the establishment of a Community Relations Service, and strong support was gained when the idea was backed by the President in his message of June 19 1963, in which he spoke of the need for a Service which would 'work quietly to improve relations in any community threatened or torn with strife'. The Bill, with amendments, was eventually passed on the 2 July 1964, and former Governor LeRoy Collins was nominated by President Johnson, and accepted by the Senate Commerce Committee as the Director of the new Service. Title X of the 1964 Civil Rights Act stated that it was the function of the new Service to 'provide assistance to communities and persons therein in resolving disputes, disagreements, or difficulties relating to discriminatory practices based on race, color, or national origin which impair the rights of persons in such communities under the Constitution or laws of the United States or which affect or may affect interstate commerce'.

The CRS Approach

The CRS may offer its assistance when it judges peaceful relations to be threatened, or its assistance can be requested by State or local officials or interested individuals. Central to the CRS procedure is the requirement for confidentiality. The Civil Rights Act states that 'The Service shall hold confidential any information acquired in the regular performance of its duties upon the understanding that it would be so held' (City of Port Arthur v. US., Civil Action No. 80-0648, D.C. Dist Ct., quoted in Chace, undated). The statute also requires that the work of the CRS be conducted without publicity, which explains why

US textbooks on police-community relations rarely mention the work of the agency. No violations of this provision by CRS staff have been recorded, and in the single court case that challenged this position, the court reaffirmed the CRS's need for confidential relationships with its clients.

The Community Relations Service divides its work into three major types; conciliation, mediation and technical assistance. Conciliation it views as a process of communication between two or more opposing factions facilitated by an objective intervenor. It is less formal than mediation which tends to involve face-to-face meetings, and which is attempted only if 'both sides elect to pursue it and if they are dedicated to reaching a clear and durable settlement of critical differences' (US Department of Justice, 1978). The conciliator's role is much more facilitator than mediator. This facilitation may involve arranging meetings between parties, working with parties and law enforcement agencies, helping to establish and carry out self-policing policies for large groups involved in marches or demonstrations etc. The mediator's work, on the other hand, revolves much more around the arrangement of meetings where negotiation over specific issues takes place. Here the CRS representative acts as a formal mediator, establishing groundrules for negotiation, helping to make clear to participants what the major issues are, arranging resource assistance for the parties, helping the parties to observe the procedural rules, and helping to establish the procedure for following-up on any agreement reached. CRS also offers technical assistance to both state and local government. This has involved advice on improving communication with minority communities, training for local human relations commissions, police departments and school officials, and advice on school security.

A Brief History of the CRS

Initially the CRS operated mainly in the South-eastern United States. Early work mainly concentrated on integration of public facilities and institutions eg schools and other educational institutions, hotels, beaches etc. Before the agency was more than a couple of years old major civil disorders broke out in a number of the larger American cities. Even though at this time most of CRS's staff were white, they were nevertheless able to offer assistance in some capacity during the disturbances in Watts, Detroit, Newark, Cleveland and others (see Pompa, 1987). The agency's work in its early years has been characterised as a 'fire-fighting' approach (Pompa, 1987); responding where possible to calls for help.

During the late 1960s this approach was largely replaced by a new system that emphasised the underlying causes of conflict. The greatest sources of frustration for minorities in the US at this time were identified by the CRS as being the administration of justice, education, housing opportunity, economic development and communications/media. Consequently the CRS began to concentrate its resources in providing help in these areas, and this continued until 1972, at which point the Federal Government decided that such support would be better provided by other agencies, and that the CRS should maintain its crisis response approach.

It was at this time that the CRS became involved in conflict resolution, having its staff retrained by organisations like the American Arbitration Association and the Institute for Mediation and Conflict Resolution. Until the mid-1980s the CRS emphasised its crisis response capability, and only in recent years has it begun to emphasise preventive and pro-active work. There is little documentation of CRS's work, and no doubt therefore many of the more noteworthy cases that the agency's staff have been and are involved in will remain unrecorded.

The agency works in a number of areas other than police-community relations. Over the past twenty years it has dealt with disputes within educational institutions, over school desegregation, in industry and in correctional institutions. It has been involved in negotiations over American Indian treaty rights, including the now famous case at Wounded Knee. The CRS has been involved in numerous cases arising from the huge influx of immigrants, particularly Hispanics, into the United States, and was given responsibility for the operation of the 'Cuban/Haitian Entrant Program' (the resettlement programme for the thousands of Cubans and Haitians who came to the United States in the 1980 'boatlifts' and afterwards). The agency also uses its negotiation skills and technical resources in community development, frequently in cases where minority communities feel that city officials are insensitive to their rights and needs. Despite all these other responsibilities and concerns, the CRS remains the only large organisation that uses conciliation techniques in dealing with police-community disputes.

CRS and Police-Community Relations

What types of police-community disputes does the CRS become involved in? The answer is almost any type of dispute as long as it is related to 'discriminatory practices based on race, color or national origin..' Thus the CRS has been involved in conflicts ranging from the most serious urban disorders to more minor allegations of harassment or abuse. The following examples will give some flavour of the work of the agency, as well as illustrating the potential for mediation and conciliation in police-community relations and public order.

As has already been suggested not all of the agency's work in the area of police-community relations is related to major incidents or crisis situations. Nevertheless as histories of disturbances and riots show, it is frequently seemingly small incidents that 'trigger off' major problems, and consequently almost all of the work done by CRS in this area can be seen as crisis-prevention. There have been a number of occasions, for example, where relations between Hispanic communities and their local Police Department have reportedly become particularly tense, and conflict has seemed inevitable unless communication could be established. In one case in Plainview, Texas, the Hispanic community accused the police department of harassment, abuse and excessive use of force. In another case in West Liberty, Iowa, Hispanic leaders argued that police officers were unlawfully dispersing groups of Hispanic citizens. In both cases meetings were arranged between Hispanic community spokespeople, city and police officials. Agreements were reached, which included the establishment of new lines of communication, civil liability as well as civil rights training programmes for police officers and provision by the community for translation services and Spanish lessons for the Police Department (Annual Reports of the CRS, 1982 & 1985).

Lack of communication between the police and minority communities, particularly in the form of language problems, is frequently an area in which the CRS works. Communication difficulties may be both the surface manifestations of more deeply-seated police-community conflicts, or may be the underlying cause of other tensions and complaints.

In one case in Providence, Rhode Island, a request for help from the Hispanic community with communications problems actually hid a series of other concerns: alleged police brutality, cutbacks in federal funding and a poor bilingual education programme. This was set against a background of poor communication both within the Hispanic community and between them, the police and the city. As frequently happens in multi-party work the CRS mediator had to begin by organising the Hispanic community leaders, so that they could effectively present their concerns to the other parties. The newly organised Hispanic community coalition gained support from the National Urban League and the Providence Human Relations Commission before presenting its case. A meeting was arranged with the Mayor, one of the results of which was that the Mayor committed half of the police academy training program - designed to increase minority enrolment - to Hispanic-Americans. A programme in English as a second language was also initiated, and the Police Department's hiring policy was reviewed by the city's equal opportunities officer. Although the CRS were involved in the arrangement of meetings with city officials in this case, their primary role was not as a mediator. This case illustrates the problems that many communities face in communicating their grievances or concerns to the appropriate authorities. The CRS mediator had to work with upwards of thirty Hispanic community leaders in order to facilitate a broad and representative approach by the community. Working as a quasi-community organiser the CRS mediator was able to help the community to articulate its concerns and thereby improve local police-community communication (Annual Report of the CRS, 1982).

Work with communities and police departments need not always be concerned with conflict or potential conflict. In some cases it may simply be that the community or neighbourhood in question does not feel that the service being provided by the Police Department is adequate. The CRS consequently is involved in much work with Police Departments, conducting assessments of recruitment and promotion programmes, identifying models for effective citizen participation and helping to design and/or improve police community relations units. After the MOVE conflict in Philadelphia (see Assefa and Wahrhaftig, 1988) a new Commissioner of Police was appointed and one of his initiatives was to set up a new approach to police-community relations in the City. The local CRS office was important in arranging for representatives from the Philadelphia police department to visit other forward-looking community relations divisions in Boston and New York. In this way the CRS were directly involved in the setting-up of a new community relations agency, called the Conflict Prevention and Resolution Team within the local Police Department.

Other disputes may involve conflict over the way in which particular laws are enforced. Through an agency like CRS, grievances over particular policing styles or methods can be communicated to the Police Department concerned. In Alamosa, Colorado, complaints were made during a council meeting over the way the police were implementing the state 'drink-driving' laws. Also causing concern was the perceived readiness of police officers to display their weapons when investigating minor traffic offences. CRS help was requested by the city manager, and the CRS mediator who became involved in the case met with the mayor and the chief of police as well as the city manager. As a result of CRS advice an assessment team comprising a Police Chief from another part of the state, a Police Captain from California, and the CRS police specialist was set up. After a five day review, forty three recommendations were made, most of which, it is reported, were implemented by the police (Annual Report of the CRS, 1984).

The most serious breakdowns in police-minority community relations in the United States tend to result from the use of deadly force by police officers. On occasion, fatalities resulting from the police use of firearms have been the spark that has set off widespread disorder (cf. the shooting of Cherry Groce, leading to the 1985 Brixton riots in London, as described in Chapter 4). At these times the CRS's crisis response approach to disputes is put to the test. CRS responds in a number of ways to such problems, and the following examples give some idea of the approaches taken.

In 1976, in Springfield, Massachusetts, a Puerto Rican man was fatally shot by a white police officer whilst he was allegedly running away from the scene of a burglary. The following night 400 police officers in riot equipment were stationed in the area and a number of arrests were made. The charges brought included possession of a 'Molotov cocktail' and inciting a riot. The community wanted the suspension of the officer involved in the shooting and the investigation of the incident forthwith, as well as making a number of other demands. Having been called in, CRS suggested negotiations between city officials and a coalition of minority community organisations. Initially, face-to-face meetings could not be arranged so the CRS mediator used 'shuttle diplomacy' to convey respective ideas, demands and proposals for action. Eventually it was agreed that an advisory committee consisting of representatives from minority groups, the Bar Association, labour organisations and the clergy be set up, and that this group would monitor the work of the local Police Department. A further committee was established to investigate the effectiveness of the Police Department's internal investigations unit. Although face-to-face mediation had not taken place, what appeared to be an effective agreement had still been negotiated by the CRS mediator (Annual Report of the CRS, 1976).

The approach that the CRS takes is most graphically illustrated on those occasions when widespread disorder does eventually break out. In August 1984, Lawrence, Massachusetts, was the site of two nights of rioting. Although the 'triggering incident' did not involve the police, it appeared that many of the underlying grievances that fuelled the consequent rioting did relate to poor police-community relations (Walsh, 1986). CRS learnt of the rioting from the media and immediately sent one of their conciliators to the scene. The town of Lawrence had experienced considerable racial tension in the years leading up the riots, and CRS had already been involved in work in the community over a number of issues. Consequently they had experience with the environment and familiarity with many of the influential figures on both sides and, in particular, the agency already had some credibility with some of the major players in the dispute. With rioting still occuring when the fieldworker first arrived, the first task, the CRS argued, was to attempt to contain or reduce the violence and to get people to the negotiating table.

The CRS conciliator began by walking the streets, and meeting with community leaders, as well as police, civic, religious, minority and municipal representatives. The conciliator argued that the first priority should be to establish a perimeter around the riot area, and then allow the community to organise a 'community public safety patrol', essentially a self-policing initiative. This involved internal community leaders taking responsibility for talking with residents, and attempting to calm the situation. In this case the CRS advice was rejected, and a 'show of police force' strategy was adopted. According to the CRS report of the incident, this led to a second night of rioting, this time mainly directed at the police and city officials. The following day the CRS conciliator again recommended the setting up of a community safety patrol, as well the establishment of a rumour control centre (which would provide accurate and up-to-date information about the crisis). This was undertaken, together with meetings between leaders from the Hispanic community and city officials. There was also a curfew instituted, and enforced by the Community Public Safety Patrol. The result was a successful de-escalation of the tension and no further violence.

Having been through periods in which either the 'fire-fighting' approach or the more pro-actively oriented planning approach were given priority, the CRS now attempts to combine the most positive elements of both. It attempts to work pro-actively largely by assessing the potential for conflict in particular communities. The way in which the CRS as an organisation conceives of the etiology of conflict is central to the way in which it 'measures' such potential, and therefore also to the likelihood of the agency becoming involved in particular disputes. As Warfield explains in the following chapter, the CRS employs a theory called the 'two tap roots and a triggering incident' with which to understand those factors that contribute to racial tension and conflict. The two tap roots provide the general conditions which may, if existing with sufficient intensity, and sparked by a 'triggering incident' result in (racial) conflict. In the conceptualisation used by CRS 'tap root one' is a general perception of inequality (it need not be real) by a segment of a community. 'Tap root two' is where the same section of the community lacks confidence in the will of the government, or other such institutions, to redress their grievances. Triggering incidents vary, but are often related to the administration of justice, and on many occasions have centred around the police use of deadly force. The use of such a theory, has enabled CRS to build up profiles of the levels of tension within communities, and successfully to predict the outbreak of disorder.

The cases such as the few that have been described in this paper (and Warfield's in the following chapter) point to the ways in which an agency like the CRS can successfully intervene in major public order crises. A combination of systematic pro-active fieldwork and then, when necessary, mediation, conciliation, shuttle diplomacy and so on may facilitate better police-community relations. This tends to be a long-term process, however, and rests on the ability of the staff of the agency to establish good working relationships with all the organisations and communities they come into contact with. As Gil Pompa has argued: "Our people have to be sensitive...and to deal with...groups and organisations in such a way that they do not ruin their credibility and perhaps, get themselves 'blown out of the water'. Credibility is our most effective weapon in negotiating".(emphasis added) (Pompa, 1987).

References
ASSEFA, H and WAHRHAFTIG, P (1988) *Extremist Groups and Conflict Resolution.* Praeger.
CALHOUN, FL (undated) *Legislative History of the Community Relations Service.* The Library of Congress.
CHACE, J (undated) *Groundrules and Procedures Governing Mediation of Court-Referred Disputes by the Community Relations Service.* U.S.Department of Justice. (unpublished).
POMPA, G (1987) The community relations service, in Sandole, DJD and Sandole-Staroste,I (Eds) *Conflict Management and Problem-Solving.* Frances Pinter: London
US DEPARTMENT OF JUSTICE (1976-85) *Annual Reports of the Community Relations Service.*
US DEPARTMENT OF JUSTICE (1978) *CRS: A National Review.* US Govt. Printing Office.
WALSH, M (1986) The 1984 Riots in Lawrence, Masachusetts, in *Bringing the Dispute Resolution Community Together.* Proceedings of the 13th Annual Conference of SPIDR.

Chapter Thirteen

Triggering Incidents for Racial Conflict : Miami, Florida Riots of 1980 and 1982

WALLACE WARFIELD

A SIMPLE theory has emerged that has aided in guiding those of us in the Community Relations Service in our understanding of factors that lend themselves to racial tension and conflict. By and large we conclude that the origin of most racial conflict stems from what we describe as Two Tap Roots and a triggering incident. Tap Root One is a general perception of inequality by a particular segment of the community. It is not necessary that the perception be real. If it is perceived enough to be institutionalised in the psyche of a class of individuals, it is just as deadly.

Tap Root Two is the lack of confidence by those same racial and ethnic minorities in the interest and capabilities of government and other institutions to provide redress for their grievances. Interaction of the Two Tap Roots, perception of inequality coupled with lack of confidence in redress, creates a chemistry that produces a potentially volatile condition.

The most frequent triggering event that sets off this condition is often an incident that relates to the administration of justice system. These factors were certainly involved in the Miami riot of 1980 and its sequel in 1982.

The comfortable view of community dispute resolution is one where parties to a dispute (usually a segment of the community without much power vs. an established entity) attempt to negotiate their differences in an atmosphere of tension but within boundaries of behaviour accepted by both sides. In Miami, events leading up to the May 1980 riot and even afterward suggest that boundaries of acceptable behaviour surrounding issues in dispute were abrogated.

In examining the events in Miami, it might be well to keep in mind the Laue-Cormick model of an interactive society which I have modified to be more descriptive of the range of community conflict.

THE LAUE-CORMICK MODEL
Cooperation<—>Competition<—>Conflict<—>Crisis

Cooperation is as reflected above.

Competition exists when the legitimacy of power is questioned, or the allocation of resources is in question.

Conflict arises when the existing power arrangements are seen as nonlegitimate and resource allocation is inadequate. No quid pro quo exists. The status quo is challenged through a series of actions, eg, strike, sit-in or work stoppage.

Crisis occurs when conflicting groups undertake unusual action to make their desires or fears known. This is often violent action, or some method of inaction carried to the extreme that traumatizes the system. (The Boston school crisis would be an example.)

Most communities exist somewhere along this continuum and indeed this is not a static situation. The opposing arrows are meant to suggest that communities frequently move back and forth along the continuum as they react to various internal and external events. It should be noted that it is the rare community that remains stabilised in an existence of cooperation. Given today's economy and scarcity of resources, a status of competition is the norm.

THE MODIFIED CONTINUUM
Cooperation<—>Competition<—>Heightened Tension<—>Conflict Crisis

The modified continuum adds heightened tension as an interim stage between competition and crisis because it more accurately reflects the deterioration of dialogue between parties in a community dispute.

Heightened tension is distinctive because parties at this stage are in a posture of noncommunication or abortive communication. Incidents have occurred and parties or adversaries are levelling charges and countercharges through the media.

Background

There were a number of destabilising events leading up to the May 1980 riot that have their origins in the Tap Roots as well as building the pressure on the trigger that by 1982 had become crystallised.

1980 saw the beginning of the Cuban Haitian refugee migration which caught the city-country infrastructure unprepared to deal with the sudden influx. Dade is a county with over 2 million residents to which 110,000 refugees have been added. At one point, thousands of Cuban refugees were erecting tent cities under highway overpasses and in some cases sleeping in the streets.

From the early 1960s to 1980 there existed what many observers

Triggering Incidents for Racial Conflict: Miami 1980 and 1982

describe as a kind of uneasy coexistence between blacks and Cubans. Evidence indicates that blacks were originally supportive of the Cuban plight. They were seen as fellow third-world people fleeing a political philosophy that conservative, southern blacks were ambivalent towards at best. Blacks supported Cuban candidates for local office and refused to support a local referendum that passed in the fall of 1980 to prohibit the expenditure of county money for the "purpose of utilising any language other than English or promoting any culture other than that of the United States." Many blacks felt this had racial overtones.

But when the second wave of refugees - the "Marielistas" - came in ever-increasing numbers, there were expressions of resentment that social services, generated by both public and private agencies directed to meet the need, were never mounted with such enthusiasm for blacks. Leadership in the black community, however, was reluctant to aim anger and criticism towards Cubans.

Reflecting back to the continuum, the equilibrium that hovered around the competition point was shattered and Miami entered a state of heightened tensions.

Another factor in black fragmentation is that the civil rights movement that swept the country in the 1960s never really touched Southern Florida. As a consequence, unlike Atlanta and some other cities, blacks had made only limited inroads into the political power structures of the city and country.

Underscoring the fragility of blacks in visible positions of power, a high- ranking school official and a black judge were indicted on separate charges.

In addition to this, there was the traditional high level of black unemployment coupled with the absence of a large employer or group of employers on the order of G.M. or Kodak that could draw a large, diversified workforce together. Rather, Miami is a Balkanized city with blacks living in one area, Cubans in another and whites in a third. There is little social interaction between them. All of these circumstances came together to create a kind of siege mentality for blacks, reinforcing the perception of Tap Root Two - that government was not interested or capable in providing redress.

While these occurrences were building the sense of Tap Root injustice, there were a number of alleged police use-of-excessive-force incidents heightening tensions and putting pressure on the trigger. These incidents culminated in the beating death of Arthur MacDuffie and the riot in May 1980 pursuant to acquittal of the police officers involved.

The Role of the Community Relations Service

CRS, operating from the regional office in Atlanta, had been in and out of Miami for a number of years on short-term conciliation efforts. Regional staff saw the pressure on the trigger building, warned local officials, but unfortunately could not sustain these efforts until the May 1980 Riots. It was at that point, CRS was able to open an office and hire additional staff.

Some dispute resolution theorists suggest that it is borderline unethical for interventionists to "cool a situation out" and not deal with the underlying issues as though to do so would be to lend oneself to cooption. As an ultimate progression of dispute resolution, I agree. However, you will never get to those underlying issues unless you deal with the crisis at hand. In fact, your actions at this level are being mentally recorded by the actors in the dispute and how you handle the situation at this point will determine the level of trust accorded to you later.

Post-Riot Analysis of Contingency Planning

The riot that took place in the Liberty City section of Miami in May 1980, resulted in a number of deaths, scores of arrests and hundreds of millions of dollars in damages. Part of the difficulty in developing an effective contingency plan rested with a cumbersome administrative infrastructure existing between the county, the City of Miami, and Miami Beach. Each have their own police forces and at the time of the riot there was:

1. No contingency plan for mass arrests, interdiction and use of force;
2. Community alleviating mechanisms were ad hoc, "out on their own," or ignored;
3. Police practised containment, resulting in fires burning out of control and trapping noninvolved residents who were often unable to get to essential services;
4. Black police officers were not used effectively.

CRS staff, on the scene shortly after the disturbance began, recommended greater use of "salt and pepper" police patrols and putting black police in more visible command positions, and also helped to set up a rumour-control mechanism.

Post-Disturbance Analysis Contingency Planning

The method of local governmental and police response to the ongoing events created a seemingly no-win situation. A heavy police response often resulted in public criticism of alleged police abusive behaviour while low-profile police response brought charges that police were not interested in protecting individuals' constitutional rights. The two following examples will clearly demonstrate the difficulty of contingency planning prior to the implementation of the Special Events Coordinating Council. In 1981, local community activists announced a protest march commemorating the Liberty City riots. The march commenced in Dade County with a heavy police response for the procession which included traffic control at intersections. However, when the marchers reached the city boundary, the County police discontinued its involvement and no city police officers could be seen anywhere. Traffic control became a problem and civilians began serving in that capacity. Because of all the confusion, the potential for danger to nonparticipating motorists or passers-by was obvious.

The other incident involved a rally at a downtown park followed by a protest march and rally in front of the Immigration and Naturalisation Service. The organisation organising the march had previously obtained a permit from the city and was complying with its provisions. However, a counterprotest group, in favour of current federal immigration policies arrived and physical confrontation between individuals from both groups occurred with no uniformed police in the immediate area. Civilians from the Community Relations Board intervened and averted further conflict. When a uniformed officer finally arrived, he was not aware that one group had a permit to march and threatened police action.

On December 28, 1982 a Cuban police officer shot and killed a black male in the Overtown section of Miami. Although not on the scale of the Liberty City riot, the resultant disturbance left two killed, 26 injured, 38 arrests, and considerable damage.

Recognising that lack of coordination between law enforcement entities and between these entities and civilian peacemaking groups could trigger renewed incidents in a still volatile atmosphere, CRS arranged to bring representatives of county and local police, the county manager's office and the County Community Relations Board to Washington to meet with officials of the D.C. Special Events Planning Task Force. The two-day workshop dealt with multijurisdictional contingency planning and response.

The components of this group returned to Miami and formed the Special Events Coordinating Council (SECC). Now SECC meetings have become institutionalised in Dade County, and local and State officials have come to rely upon SECC in an effort to avoid unnecessary confrontation. Contingency planning meetings are called upon first notice that an event is scheduled and the potential for community relations problems exists. Other SECC meetings have been called to plan for activities or protests involving INS, military recruitment offices, and city and county government. SECC meetings are also scheduled to plan for youth-related problems during major holidays and some extraordinary events, such as parades and rock concerts.

On a long-term basis CRS has met with the Dade County Independent Review Panel to make recommendations on firearms policy; did an analysis of police-community relations for the city of Miami which resulted in change in police command structure, patrolling, and establishing store front policing; and recommended the use of a simulator training device for police to curb excessive-force incidents.

This paper was originally published as part of the Proceedings of the Thirteenth International Conference of the Society of Professionals in Dispute Resolution (SPIDR), October 27-30, 1985. It was written when the author was Associate Director for Field Coordination of the CRS. The article is reprinted here with permission.

Chapter Fourteen

Creating Space for Dialogue

RON CLAASSEN

IN A period of thirteen months, my community of Fresno, California experienced 15 police shootings. Three of these resulted in deaths, all of Hispanic youth. On January 1, 1985, Paul Rangel Jr., a teenager, was carrying a gun and threatening suicide. The family called the police for help. Somehow he was not contained inside the house. When police felt threatened, they shot and killed him. Within twelve minutes after the call to police, Rangel had approximately 35 entry wounds.

On Janurary 24, 1986, Ronnie Lopez, another teenager, was shot and killed by police. Lopez was in his house with a gun. A neighbour called his mother, who was at work, and the police were called. The police arrived first. By the time his mother arrived, approximately 10 minutes later, Lopez was dead on the doorstep of his home, with one bullet through the heart. Lopez was a cousin to Rangel, their mothers are sisters. In between these incidents, another youth, Anthony Garcia, had also been killed by a shot in the back of the head. No other shots were fired.

Each incident generated a great deal of public concern and calls for "justice". Shortly after Lopez's death, the media coverage and citizen demonstrations became intense. It was at this point that I was asked to intervene as a "mediator". This paper will describe and reflect on the processes which evolved.

The first "mediation" involved bringing the Chief of Police and several support officers together with the two sisters, whose sons had been killed, and their support group. These meetings were shortly after the second death. They were very private.

The second "mediation" was about a year later. It involved facilitating a public forum attended by over 300 people, in which members of the Hispanic community addressed the city council on their concerns about "the excessive force of the police against the Chicano community".

I believe I was called on to get involved in these "justice" concerns in the community because of my own involvement in the Victim Offender Reconciliation Program (VORP). In Fresno County, those of us involved in

175

VORP had been working since 1982 at developing the structures, the training, and the credibility to make it possible for volunteers to work at justice and peacemaking concerns primarily with victims and offenders of crime.

The initiative for the first meeting, between the Police Department and the two mothers, came from Chief of Police Max Downs, in a request to Metro Ministry. Walt Parry, director of Metro Ministry and a trusted person in the community, asked me if I would be willing to convene and facilitate such a meeting. After hearing a mixture of support and discouragement from people whose opinions I sought, I agreed. Parry agreed to work with me as a support person. I had never led a meeting like this before and I prayed a great deal during this time.

Since the Chief had initiated the meeting, I wanted to meet first with him and any others he wanted to represent the Department. We met with him and five of his immediate subordinates. I said that if we were to have a meeting, it was important that everyone came voluntarily, that we have a common purpose, and that everyone agree to ground rules. Then I read the ground rules and purpose I had developed:

Purpose

To seek peace and justice for both sides. To give opportunity for family and police to meet face to face, to express and recognise feelings and experiences, to ask questions, and to clarify concerns:

1. The first meeting will be one hour in length and everyone agrees to stay for the duration. (The last 10 minutes will be devoted to deciding when and with whom future meetings might be held.)
2. All agree to allow the facilitator to regulate the conversation. (Fairness is important. The discussion may be interrupted by anyone to discuss fairness of process.)
3. All agree to allow the facilitator to ask for clarification and to work together to make our points as helpful and clear as possible.
4. All agree to summarise or restate the comments of the others at the request of the facilitator.
5. All agree that there will be no name calling and that they will avoid those statements which each of us knows will get the other side immediately angry. We will not avoid the issues, but will try to raise them by describing experiences rather than by judging and condemning the other side. We all know how to push the other side's "buttons" and will try

to avoid this.
6. The facilitator may caucus with either or both parties if it seems helpful.
7. No tape recorders.
8. No press.
9. No attorneys representing someone present. (We recognise that a family friend who is an attorney might be present and might at a later time represent one of the parties.)

After some discussion, I explained I would need to hear from each of them individually that they would support this purpose and abide by these ground rules. Chief Downs immediately assured me that he was in agreement and that this meant they were *all* in agreement. I told him that was probably the case, but that I would need to have approval from each of them individually before I could proceed. He agreed; all of the others individually agreed.

Parry and I then met with the mothers, Mrs.Rangel and Mrs.Hernandez, and about five support persons, including family, a pastor, and a friend who is also a civil rights attorney. Again, I laid out and we discussed the proposed purpose and the ground rules and I asked for approval from each individual. The civil rights attorney immediately slammed his papers on the table. He saw the ground rules as obvious and just another example of racial discrimination. He said that if they were Anglos, there wouldn't be a chance in the world that I would spell out the rules in such detail and then ask each individual for agreement.

I deferred to Parry, who told of our experience at the police department. After hearing this, the attorney said that he agreed with the ground rules and recommended going ahead with the process. All agreed. After discussing some concerns and possibilities for the meeting, we amended the first part of the purpose statement to read "That this meeting lead in a direction of greater understanding so that the shootings of Chicano youth in particular and all youth will not happen in the future. The bigger purpose being that justice will be experienced by all people." I later called the Chief and he agreed to the amended purpose statement.

Our first joint meeting was at a church in the area of the shootings. Mrs.Hernandez, whose son had been shot only about one month before, didn't come to the first meeting. We talked about whether we should go ahead. The Chief said that he wanted to be clear that he was not trying to force anyone to meet. I caucused with the family group, then left them alone to make their decision. They soon decided to go ahead.

We sat around a table and each person wrote on a folded card the name by which they wished to be addressed. After introductions, I again asked each person if they were in agreement with the purpose statement and ground rules. They all agreed. After getting permission to refer generally to the two sides as "police" and "family", I asked someone from the family to share an experience or concern.

Mrs.Rangel explained how she felt when the police had recently surrounded the house of an Anglo who had a gun, waited him out for 8-10 hours, and ended the incident peacefully without even firing a shot. Her son had been threatening to kill *himself* and she had called the police for help. Within twelve minutes, he was dead. I asked the Chief to summarise, and there was some discussion on the idea of containment.

The Chief shared what it feels like to be an officer, called in to help, finding yourself looking down the barrel of a loaded gun. There is no time to wait. This was summarised by someone from the family, and there was discussion of the concern of guns in the hands of youth and how police respond to perceived threats from someone with a gun.

Towards the end of the meeting, everyone acknowledged the low trust between the Hispanic community and the police and that this was a growing problem that needed to be turned around. Everyone agreed that the discussion had been helpful, that there should be a second meeting, and that Mrs.Hernandez should be invited again.

Before the second meeting, I called Mrs.Hernandez and we talked for nearly an hour. She was particularly distressed at how police and the press had labelled her son as a neighbourhood bully and drug addict.

She came to the next meeting and shared that when her son would drive truck with his uncle, he would call home to let her know if he was going to be late. Just about a week before he was killed, he had been with her and several of his friends in their living room. He had walked over to her and hugged her and told her how much he loved her. She appreciated it when members of the police team summarised this.

We also discussed an incident that had almost escalated into a major problem. Police had driven by the Hernandez home several times and slowed down. The first couple of times, Mrs.Hernandez told another son and his friend, who were painting the house, to turn down their radio. About the third time, out of fear, she brought them into the house, closed the drapes, and watched the police by peering through the curtains. The police had received a call of loud noise at the Hernandez home. The first couple of times they drove by, they had seen the boys painting, thought the noise wasn't that bad, and had gone on. Then they received another call and went by again. This time they noticed the boys had gone into the house, had drawn the curtains, and were peering through. Out of fear, the police interpreted this as being called into an ambush situation. ("Kill a cop" had been threatened at some demonstrations.) They called in reinforcements and met about two blocks away to discuss their strategy. Mrs.Hernandez took the boys with her to Mrs.Rangel's house. She saw the police gathering and tried to talk to them, but they saw her coming and moved to another location. She called Chief Downs' office to talk about what was happening, and the incident stopped. It was a classic case of fear escalating into violence.

Also discussed were the problem of drugs in the community, the general lack of trust between police and youth, and some possible steps toward working on these. The police committed themselves to reviewing policies and procedures in light of these discussions. At the conclusion of the second meeting, all agreed that the problem was larger than this group alone could address.

Soon thereafter, the incidents disappeared from the papers and the demonstrations ceased. Had I helped privatise the incidents and minimise them? Or had this process of "mediation" set in motion new channels of dialogue on how "justice will be experienced by all people"?

During this general time period, the Hispanic (later called "Chicano") Civil Rights Network formed in Fresno. They approached the city council about listening to the concerns of the Hispanic community in a public forum. Also during this time, a local Human Relations Commission was developed. The city council asked the Commission to organise a forum. The purpose of the forum was to give people a chance to address the large issues of excessive force by police in the Hispanic community.

Based on a request from the Hispanic Civil Rights Network, I was asked to mediate. I proposed ground rules that called for citizen statements, limited to seven minutes each. One council member or several woring together would summarise each statement. The Human Relations Commission formed a task force, including police and Hispanic Civil Rights Network members. They approved the ground rules in a slightly modified form and these also received approval from the city council itself.

During the planning stages, the task force discussed the concern of security at the forum. The police, the highway patrol, and the national guard were considered as possible options. We finally decided to emphasise the cooperative focus and the reconciling intention of the meeting by inviting clergy from the community instead. All clergy were invited and were recognised during the opening of the forum.

Members of the Hispanic community had been present at the planning meetings and were supportive of the proposed format. I also requested a meeting with the city council to explain the format and help them understand the intended spirit of the meeting. I was told that they would meet with me one-half hour before the forum.

When time for that meeting came, only one council member showed up. The city attorney informed me that my effort to meet with the council members ahead of time would be in violation of the state "open meetings" law. This was very unfortunate. It meant I had opportunity to work on the process and spirit of the meeting with only one of the members of the city council.

When we went into the forum hall, at the Mosqueda Center, approximately 300 chairs were set up. Most were filled and many people were standing. The city council members were on a slightly raised platform in the front. A speaker's table was in front of them. Seated at that table were the timekeeper and an interpreter. A third chair was provided for the speaker to sit. Also provided was a table podium for those who preferred to stand.

My podium was off to one side. The other side was filled with cameras and television, radio and newspaper reporters. I had already been anxious before the meeting, and now I was feeling high stress.

After some introductions, I had a brief time to explain the ground rules and try to develop the spirit of the meeting. When the community speakers began, the reports were highly charged and difficult for the council to summarise.

One reported observing an incident late one night, in front of his house. Two officers were beating a young person with their sticks and dragging him on the street. "When I asked them to stop, they told me to get away or I'd be next," the speaker said. "Then I went in and got my Fresno City College identification showing I was a professor. The punishment stopped immediately."

Another person, through an interpreter, told of an incident when he called police about a hit and run accident in front of his house. "When the police arrived, they frisked me, took away my pocket knife, and pushed me around. They finally let me go when an English-speaking neighbour explained that I was the one who lived there and had called the police."

Another said, "I was driving home from a barbecue one day, and my clothes were dirty from the day's activity. I was pulled over and told my car was weaving. I was pushed around, frisked, and talked to in a very derogatory way until I produced by California State University/Fresno faculty card."

After each statement, I would turn to the city council members for their summary. The summary was intended to let the community know that they had been heard. It was not intended to say that the council agreed with or had no questions about the details. However, they were instructed not to cross-examine the speakers.

Some city council members accepted the format and worked hard at this difficult assignment. Some others did not participate at all. Less than an hour into the three-hour meeting, the mayor asked me to change the rules to eliminate the summaries. At the same time, I received a note from the audience asking me to have the council summarise the statements more thoroughly. I stuck to the ground rules as we had previously agreed.

The evening went in a very orderly fashion. After about an hour,

Creating Space for Dialogue

the television cameras left. Forty-two community members signed up to speak. Only about 22 were able to talk that first night.

At the end of the evening, several of the city council members were upset about the format, and refused to participate further. For the second meeting, the Human Relations Commission became the listening group, and the ground rules were changed somewhat to adapt. I was again asked to moderate. I was told later this was because of insistence from the Hispanic community. At this second meeting there were fewer people present overall and less media coverage. About 20 speakers presented reports.

After the forums, in November 1987, a subcommittee of the Human Relations Commission presented a report to the Commission with findings and recommendations for improving the relationships between the Hispanic community and the police. This report was later submitted to the city council and raised a lot of controversy.

Shortly after this first report was released by the Human Relations Commission, my wife and I received an invitation to a meeting with the Chicano Civil Rights Network. They said they wanted to honor us. The meeting was held in the home of the civil rights attorney who had been skeptical of the original private mediation sessions, described earlier. To our surprise, the gathering was actually a worship service. Sister Angela Mesa started by talking about "shalom" and how God intends for all people to live together in safety, in love, and in justice. We sang some songs, and the civil rights attorney, who had slammed his papers down in that first meeting months before, read *Matthew* 25:31-46.

Then Mrs.Rangel, the mother of one of the young men who had been shot and killed, stood up and took a plaque off the wall. She explained that his plaque was a favourite of her friend, the attorney, and how it was often referred to in their meetings. She presented it to me. It said:

THE ART OF PEACE

Peace is God on both sides of the table in a conference. It is putting the power of good will to work. It is sanity, maturity and common sense in human relationships. It is open-mindedness and a willingness to listen as well as to speak. It is looking at both sides of a situation objectively. A quality of the heart as well as the head, it is a mighty faith in the goodness of God and the potential greatness of man.

To Ron Claassen muchas gracias 11-30-87 C.C.R.N.

It had seemed to me that I had not done very much. Some of the process which had happened could have certainly been improved. The group, however, affirmed the process, commenting on how good it felt for the power to be balanced for at least a short time.

Some time after the forums and the report were completed, the Human Relations Commission was again asked to move the process forward. After much debate, certain recommendations for change were agreed to by all parties. One was to have an ombudsman review complaints of excessive force by the police. Previously there had been no outside person or group reviewing citizen complaints against the police. Despite some delay by the city after making this agreement, an ombudsman has now been hired to handle police complaints from community members. In this way, what began as a private mediation did evolve into a process which encouraged a broader, systemic response to charges of racism - and some long-term institutional change.

This paper previously appeared in the Mennonite Conciliation Service Conciliation Quarterly *Spring-Summer 1990, and we are grateful for permission to reproduce it here.*

Chapter Fifteen

Negotiating and Mediating in Stressful Situations

MARIA R VOLPE AND ROBERT J LOUDEN

Introduction

INDIVIDUALS INVOLVED in the handling of conflicts are confronted with some stress in virtually every situation they experience. The stress, however, does vary from situation to situation. Some situations are much more stressful than others. Furthermore, the amount and nature of the stress may not be steady throughout the entire conflict situation.

Since we believe that various skills and strategies are transferable from stressful setting to stressful setting, the field of dispute resolution has much to learn from interveners working in diverse settings. Overall, if one were to examine stressful situations along a continuum, conflict situations encountered by criminal justice professionals, particularly police, certainly fall at the upper end. While police agencies have a long way to go before the average officer is amply trained in negotiation and mediation skills, much can be gained from examining the skills and procedures used by selected police components, notably those specialised in the handling of hostage negotiations and domestic disputes. Officers handling such matters often experience conflict situations when stress levels are highest due to the context within which the conflict occurs. This paper is an effort to draw from the work of those officers who engage in hostage negotiations.

Police Hostage Situations

For hostage negotiators employed by police departments, conflict dramas usually begin before they are called to the scene. Typically, one or more individuals are being held captive by a captor or captors who more often than not have some agenda they are attempting to advance. The calling of attention to themselves by holding others against their will sets the stage for uncertainty, high emotions, as well as potential danger to many, including the captives, the interveners, and others on the scene as well as the captors.

Stressful hostage situations may vary. It could be a husband holding his 3 year old daughter captive in an effort to gain his estranged wife's attention. Or, it could involve a trio of political activists who seek to dramatise their views to the public by holding an office full of employees captive until the media arrive to hear and report on what they have to say.

An initial response to any of these situations would be for the police department to be alerted. Upon investigation that a hostage situation is in progress, a designated officer or officers are then summoned to the scene to take charge of the negotiations. It is these individuals who are usually referred to as hostage negotiatiors.

By the time the hostage negotiators arrive, however, even if within several minutes, some actions may already have been taken by the police personnal who responded or by the many others who may be on the scene merely by accident, such as neighbours, friends or curiosity seekers, or in an official capacity, such as emergency medical personnel. Furthermore, things may have been said or promised that need to be addressed. For example, a neighbour who was called by the captor may have been asked to get a carton of cigarettes and personally bring it to the door as soon as possible. Since the neighbour promised to do so, s/he may be insistent on following through.

Upon further assessment, decisions have to be made regarding what else or who else is needed. For example, some background information on the hostage takers is essential, such as police records, psychological information, etc. In addition, details about the building's layout, a specific political group the captor is affiliated with, etc may be essential for planning an intervention approach. During the course of the assessment, it may be determined that there is a need to alert selected others to come to the scene, such as religious personnel, a news reporter, building superintendent or political official.

Besides those who are more directly involved in the hostage situation, it is not uncommon for such incidents to attract the media's attention. Hence, the unfolding of the conflict drama often occurs in settings where the actions of interveners can be carefully scrutinised by others, step by step as they are taken. When local and possibly national radio and television crews respond, it is not unheard of for the captors to have a radio or television set at their disposal, where they too can assess what is being said about them or done to them.

Due to the complexity, urgency and potential danger of many hostage situations, it is common for police to work in teams. Exchanges about information collected and strategies to be used are shuttled back and forth between the primary negotiator and backup units. Moreover, depending on department procedures, the decisions about any concession may have to be cleared with supervisory personnel who may or may not be on the scene.

The vast majority of hostage situations involve a confrontation at a location where the police attempt physically to secure the scene before, or simultaneously with, the start of the negotiations. The ensuing negotiations may take place face to face, by telephone, or through some barrier or barricade with or without voice amplification.

Despite all of the activity depicted here, uppermost for the police negotiators is the need to settle the conflict safely. The loss of any life would be seen as a failure.

Sources of Stress

As was mentioned in the above depiction of hostage situations, many foreseen and unforeseen circumstances contribute to the stress. While the vast majority of negotiators and mediators will not experience such scenes, many of the same sources of stress are shared, including the following:

Uncertainty

Since the handling of conflict situations is not rehearsed, no one is quite sure who will say or do what. Dispute resolvers are often confronted with the unexpected, which generates considerable anxiety.

Emotional state of disputants

Disputants are likely to experience high emotions and lowered reasoning abilities as they relive their experiences and attempt to deal with them. Such conditions may be manifested through many forms of resistance, including irritability, intolerance, restlessness, and vociferous interactions, to name a few.

Reputation

It is not unusual for dispute resolvers to be concerned about their reputation. An unsuccessful outcome may well damage their reputation. For example, they may feel failure in the eyes of significant others, particularly colleagues, or interested parties such as the press.

Lack of information or expertise

Dispute resolvers may not have all the necessary information nor the requisite expertise to proceed in an informed manner. For example, they may lack the skills necessary for a particular process to work with a new issue s/he is tackling. Similarly, s/he may lack substantive knowledge about an issue that has come up at the table. Such situations can create considerable uneasiness. In some circumstances, the situations may raise concerns about liability.

FEAR OF VIOLENCE

The potential that violence will occur is a reality in many conflict situations. If dispute resolvers are aware of a past history of violence by disputants, the anticipation of potential harm to themselves and other parties may be uppermost in their minds.

PREVIOUS EXPERIENCES WITH DISPUTANTS

Having had some experience with disputants may colour the way in which one anticipates the current session. A negative experience will most definitely be seen as more stressful than if one has had a positive experience. That is not to say that the latter cannot also be stressful, particularly if one is concerned about recreating the same successful outcome.

USE OF TIME

How time is perceived in any given situation may be very stressful. For example, if deadlines are imposed, the need to meet them can generate considerable stress. Disputants can also use time in such a way that increases the pressure experienced by the dispute resolvers. For example, if a mediator feels that in order to proceed properly in a session, a particular format ought to be followed and one of the disputants insists on finishing up within the hour, the mediator may experience substantial stress.

ROLE OF WITNESSES, LAWYERS, OTHERS IN ANY SESSION.

Depending on the role that others play before or during a session, they may increase the tension in the room. An attorney who insists on using legalese or a witness who coaches his/her friend to withhold or embellish information may make the session much more stressful.

DISPUTANTS' EXPERIENCE WITH DISPUTE RESOLUTION PROCESSES

The previous experiences of disputants with any negotiation or mediation process may influence their interactions. Those disputants who have had negative experiences may not trust the process and manifest more resistance than those who have had positive experiences.

PHYSICAL SETTING

Not having control over the physical setting, including size of room, shape of table, air quality and so on, can be very discomforting for those managing the intervention process.

DISPUTANTS' COMPLIANCE WITH AGREEMENTS REACHED

Mediators routinely report feelings of uneasiness in those situations where they feel that disputants may be reaching an agreement that they may well not be able or willing to comply with in the future. In such situations, mediators are often concerned that non-compliance may well reflect on their work and credibility, hence adding to their stress during the process.

OBSTACLES PRESENTED BY DISPUTANTS

During the course of an intervention process, any number of challenging barriers may surface. Some of them may be anticipated by the dispute resolver. Others may spring up without any forewarning. Depending on what arrangements have been made to handle them, the intervention process may be quite stressful. For instance, when language difficulties surface, if one was able to provide for interpreters, the situation may be stressful in worrying about the literal translation of messages, but at least one feels covered. If one does not have translators, and the parties speak very little of the official language, the stress level increases markedly.

For hostage negotiators, the context within which the negotiations must be conducted is very stressful. In addition to the aforementioned concerns, for hostage negotiators, the hostage taker has the power of life and death over the victims. For any number of reasons, the police are unable or reluctant to intervene immediately using physical tactics.

The stress comes from a variety of sources. The most obvious probably involves thinking about a degree of responsibility for the life of the captive. The next comes from an informed awareness about the physical danger which may be present for the negotiator and/or for other police personnel present. A lack of familiarity with the disputants as well as with the physical surroundings adds more pressure. The fact that the event is being conducted in a public setting, witnessed at a minimum by supervisors and peers, and perhaps by relatives and/or acquaintances of the captive and/or captor, and conceivably in the eye of the local, if not national, media, adds to the more mundane stress that we all experience when we want to perform well and accomplish our goals.

Learning from Hostage Negotiators

Third party interveners, particularly mediators, may find that some of the skills and strategies used in hostage negotiations may be of great value. In high stress situations, it is extremely important for dispute resolvers to remain calm, be flexible and very resourceful.

Mediators already have a large toolbox of skills from which to draw when confronted with high stress situations (eg see Moore, 1986). In the following section, we will elaborate on several skills and strategies common to hostage negotiators that might be of use to mediators.

ANTICIPATION, RECOGNITION AND TOLERANCE IN DEALING WITH STRESS ITSELF

The stressors noted above are present in all police hostage situations. For the most part, absent the immediate threat to life, similar stressors are present in the more common-place conflict which most interveners become involved in. Among the ways the police negotiator is able to persevere and succeed are a good sense of self (warts and all); a reminder from Hippocrates that although we may not be able to solve all problems, "make a habit of two things - to help or, at least, to do no harm"; a recognition that calm is usually contagious; and, that help is available in the form of our own personal support system or from professional sources.

CONTROL OF THE ENVIRONMENT BEFORE AND DURING THE SESSIONS

Hostage negotiators are extremely sensitive to their surroundings. For the most part, such negotiations occur on unfamilar turf with little advance notice. Before negotiations begin and with the assistance of many others, the negotiators secure the area to maximise survival of all, including hostages, police, bystanders, as well as the hostage takers. This may mean barriers, barricades, or the use of a myriad of other tactical strategies. As the negotiations progress, these strategies can change.

During the negotiations, it is often necessary to control the environment. Some have referred to such actions as manipulation. In hostage negotiation work, this is absolutely vital. Such actions may include, for example, depriving someone of cigarettes, turning down the air conditioner on warm days, delaying the arrival of a much sought after beverage and so on. For the third party intervener, many manipulations are simply too draconian and even inappropriate or unethical. Nonetheless, there are imaginative steps which may be taken by third party interveners that are not so extreme. Though difficult to achieve, a few suggestions may include, for example, holding sessions in highly air conditioned rooms to make sure that parties will stay alert, particularly if one fears that some may be inattentive or doze off during potentially long sessions, or minimising the availability of food or beverage in order to keep the parties from enjoying the process too much and perhaps unintentionally delaying settlement due to comfortable accommodations.

USE OF TEAM APPROACH

Although at times cumbersome and a source of stress, the use of others in working through diverse, multi-faceted problem situations could be a valuable resource. Hostage negotiators may use experts, superiors, significant others and whatever talents are needed in order to bring negotiations to a successful closure, that is, the saving of lives. Much of the interaction around such concerns is accomplished by using non-verbal communication, such as previously agreed signals or codes, or through the use of written notes. Third party interveners can consider pairing up with appropriate talent, calling for recesses to confer with others on a regular basis, or have the equivalent of a coach, runners or relay team, who will be able to access or gather information in a fairly systematic and timely way. This team effort needs to be carefully orchestrated before the session begins so as not to be overly disruptive.

TUNING OUT DISTRACTORS

Hostage negotiators are frequently confronted with bystanders, hecklers, acquaintances, family members and others who may intentionally or inadvertently become a distraction. It is a necessary yet delicate task to exclude such persons. This must be accomplished without creating a void and/or without reinforcing the distractor, in part because the excluded person may be useful later in the process. Interveners may experience a similar situation when witnesses, friends, family members or significant others show up and want to become involved in their sessions. Not knowing if they will become potential distractors or assets, it could be extremely advantageous for interveners to spend some time with them at the outset of the sessions and be very clear about the process and each participant's role. This permits interveners better control of the setting while leaving open the possibility that they may be called back to contribute.

Conclusion

There are no easy formulae for handling high stress situations. Dispute resolvers need to keep themselves and their surroundings in mind when contemplating the next critical move. While no one skill or strategy works all of the time, it is nonetheless crucial to be extremely resourceful about alternatives that may be used by those practising in other specific areas. The aforementioned thoughts were presented in an effort to begin the cross-fertilisation of ideas between police hostage negotiations work and that of third party dispute resolvers.

This article is an expanded version of a presentation made at the SPIDR International Conference in Washington, DC, October 1989, and of the written text prepared for the SPIDR Conference Proceedings .

Reference

MOORE, CW (1986) *The Mediation Process: practical strategies for resolving conflict.* San Francisco: Jossey-Bass.

SECTION V:

THE MEDIATORS— GREAT BRITAIN

In this section we take a look at seminal developments in mediator- (or third party-) led initiatives in this country. In Chapter 16, Dave Ward, a social worker and lecturer, describes a unique style of intervention in youth/community and youth/police conflict. By helping the youngsters implement the basic principles of constructive conflict resolution, Dave and his associates were able both to defuse a growing "crime" problem and enable the community as a whole to resolve the underlying grievances that created the problem. The story exemplifies the need for cooperation between the police and the community, the involvement of all concerned parties, taking reconciliation as one's ultimate aim, not just trouble-shooting, and problem-solving rather than confrontation as the basis for the process. It is also noteworthy that eventual success was achieved by intervention on one side only. By empowering the youth group to analyse its own problems, devise a strategy of involving the rest of the community in resolving them, and to use the communication skills that would encourage cooperation, the workers were able to withdraw and allow the youths to take responsibility for their own problems. The workers remained in the background, able to assist when major obstacles sapped optimism, or when differences of interest among factions of the youth group itself threatened to undo all that had been achieved (cf. remarks on the Notting Hill carnival in the Introduction to Section III). The workers' care not to direct proceedings or take responsibility enabled all involved - youth, adult residents and police - to develop basic civic skills of democratic (participative) collaboration, just as Ray Shonholtz advocated in Chapter 11. The writers point out, too, another crucial lesson: the danger of "pathological" explanations of crime and disorder. By leading one to dismiss a particular individual or group as having an immanent defect inevitably leading to deviance and antisocial behaviour, such an explanation rules out any attempt to negotiate the problem in favour of the superficially easier process of trying to "stamp it out" by force or punishment. As the writers remark, people have an inherent capacity to create social improvement, if only they can be helped to realise this (mentally and practically) in themselves and in others.

The experience of the longest established of Britain's own community mediation schemes in working with the police is described by Pauline Obee (Newham Conflict and Change Project) in Chapter 17. The project is a grass-roots initiative in a borough of London with a vast mix of recently settled ethnic groups along with long-standing residents. With all the usual inner city problems of social disadvantage, unemployment, community disruption and crime, Newham has not been the scene of any major social disorder, although it has had a serious problem of racial harassment. The project was started because a group of residents wanted to find a way of developing relationships between all the different groups and building a sense of community. That they sought this way out from their problems may be part of the reason why there has been no major public disorder, for the group soon picked up the ideas on conciliation and reconciliation that were being developed in America, especially by San Francisco Commmunity Boards. Concerned to keep a truly local flavour and to develop a programme that would genuinely serve residents' needs, the group did not slavishly copy any of the American schemes, but took training in conflict resolution and adapted these principles to their own needs in fashioning a unique project which is owned and managed by the volunteers who work for it.

The Newham Conflict and Change Project provides a number of conciliatory services, all aimed at building up a positive community. One is a mediation service for individuals or organisations in dispute, as in San Francisco, although in the case of Newham the mediation is much more loosely structured and informal. Another service involves training in the principles of conflict resolution in schools, an activity which San Francisco also pioneered. If one sees oneself as establishing a basis of skills for democratic citizenship, where better to start than in the educational system? Such intervention can begin as early as primary school, from the age of eight upwards at least, using class discussion, "cooperative games", drama and role-play which children find enjoyable. Youngsters readily pick up the idea that there is an alternative to either running away or standing up fighting. (See Marshall, 1987; FIRM, 1989.)

Newham also provides a training service for other organisations that may need to handle conflict internally (eg a club) or externally (eg social workers, housing officers). As part of this activity, Newham have been commissioned to provide training for local police forces, and it is this service upon which Pauline Obee concentrates here. She shows how it has led to a two-way learning process for both police officers and community members, with many surprises to the preconceptions of both. The collaborative training continues to mutual

Introduction to Section V

advantage and is helping to reduce the barriers between residents and the agencies that exist to serve them.

Chapter 18 describes a further scheme for police training in community relations. Although not formally based on conflict resolution principles, it is quite compatible with these, and also uses some experience from America. The scheme is described by its author, Robin Oakley, who has been involved with race relations training for many years. It takes a more formal shape than the previous example and is integrated into standard police training and sector organisation (see Chapters 7 and 10) in the London Borough of Haringey, where Yvonne Craig (Chapter 6) is also resident. The training component described here takes the form of facilitated workshops (for more examples of which see Chapter 22), with equal representation from local community members and police officers. The workshops are separately organised for officers of different rank - Inspectors, Sergeants and Constables - thus ensuring that the experience is shared at all levels of management. The programme was started at the request of the police, seeking to gear themselves to the new "service" orientation described in Section III. The workshops focus on the first of the conflict resolution skills outlined in Chapter 1, that of active listening, and of discovering common ground, although the workshops are not geared to resolution of conflict so much as building relationships and hence preventing conflict. The importance of having a "neutral" third party facilitator is stressed by Robin Oakley. It enabled the groups to deal with feelings that would otherwise be destructive, and also led to the adoption of a concrete problem-solving task which gave the workshops meaning and relevance, which may have helped towards the surprising degree of commitment and support which was evidenced by individual participants. Robin stresses two important factors in his conclusion: that to be effective any interchange between the police and the public must take the form of a genuine partnership - learning from the community, not just about it; and such interchange must also be underpinned by empowerment of the local community, via social policies quite aside from policing, if the consultation is ever to be really free, equal and responsible. Like many of the other contributors to this collection, he emphasises the fact that the police alone cannot be given the responsibility for reforming society.

The final chapter of this section concerns training usually provided for social workers, although available and relevant to any other group of people liable to have to deal with inter-personal violence in the course of their work, which would *a fortiori* include police officers. How an aggressive person behaves is affected by how one reacts to the signs of impending violence, a point made in Chapter 1. The training course that Pat Sawyer provides combines consciousness-raising (awareness of the nature of conflict and of one's instinctive reactions to it) with skills training (how to control one's own behaviour to optimise the outcome). Like Wallace Warfield, she divides crisis intervention from the more analytical phase which may follow, and emphasises the need for contingency planning.

When crises occur, there is no time for reflection, so one needs to have thought in advance how one would ideally act, to have sorted out the problems and dangers in one's mind beforehand, not wait until it is too late to do anything but react by instinct. The principles behind the training in handling individual aggressors are identical to those of conflict resolution generally as outlined in Chapter 1.

There are several courses of this kind available across the country, especially for social workers. Others provide what is essentially the same training for those who may initiate violence themselves. Jim Murtagh and others (including many Quaker groups) provide non-violence workshops, especially for men guilty of domestic violence, and the American Alternatives to Violence Project (AVP) enters prisons to provide the same kind of participative training for violent offenders.

References

FIRM (1989) *Conflict in Schools*. Bristol: FIRM.

MARSHALL, TF (1987) Mediation: a new mode of establishing order in schools. *Howard Journal*, 26(1).

Chapter Sixteen

Letting Young People Have Their Say

DAVID WARD

IN ITS response to the recent Green Paper 'Punishment, Custody and the Community' (Home Office 1988), FIRM (The Forum for Initiatives in Reparation and Mediation) proposed that:

> certain principles of practice need to be adopted by all those working with offenders. These are: (a) Breaking down barriers: the process should not be artificially separate from society. Decisions should not be based on 'legal' criteria alone but take into account personal, social and economic implications. (b) Involvement: of all relevant parties. Certainly opportunities should exist for both victim and offender. Preferably, their families as well, and possibly other significant community members. (c) Reconciliation: despite the need to identify and denounce an offender, and impose certain restrictions, the ultimate aim should be to plan actively for a return to acceptance in society. (d) Problem-Solving: the apportionment of blame and penalties is not the resolution of crime: crime is a problem shared between the parties involved (including the state) and needs to be addressed by a process that is essentially problem-solving. (FIRM 1989)

These are worthy statements, ideals from which few would demur. However, if they are to be more than high sounding but empty words, if they are to convince an ever sceptical public, assailed by a tabloid press baying for harsher sentences, and a governing party whose instincts and preferences are to tune to what it interprets as a punitive popular mood, such principles need to be backed up with demonstrably effective practice. The purpose of this paper is to outline an approach to working with young people that meets these standards.

I shall begin by describing in some detail one project that has taken place in Nottingham, but which is representative of an approach that has been developing steadily for the past decade (Ward 1979, 1982; Burley 1982; Connelly & Woolman 1982; Fleming et al 1983; Badham et al 1984, 1988; Mullender & Ward 1985, 1989; Keenan & Pinkerton

1988; Badham 1989; Ward and Harrison 1989). Then I shall draw out the essential features that make the method both distinctive and effective.

The Ainsley Teenage Action Groups

This started life in the autumn of 1979. A group of teenage lads had offended together on the council estate where they lived. One or two had served sentences of custody while others were under supervision, had been fined, or simply had not been caught. Their offences had been mostly related to break-ins at local factories and the disposal of goods stolen. Their probation officer along with two other workers decided to help the young people to work together as a group to improve leisure facilities on the estate, the lack of which had been, in the teenagers' view, an important factor behind the offences. Rather than taking the young people out of their community and treating them on the basis of an outside professional assessment of their needs, the aim was to help the young people to understand and to deal with their own problems on their own home ground. In the event, the work touched upon many issues way beyond the rather predictable starting point of "we've nothing to do, and nowhere to go".

To remain consistent with this approach, much of the story that follows will be in the words of the young people themselves.

> The club started when several Ainsley teenagers got in trouble with the police and had to appear in court. There we met Colin Butcher who is a probation officer. We told him about our boredom and the idea of setting up a youth club. From the word go he took an interest in the group.
>
> A few weeks later the group began to meet weekly with Colin, Dave Ward [a volunteer] and Mark Harrison [a youth worker]. We decided we would have a go at getting youth facilities for the teenagers of the estate. As one of the first things, the group agreed to get a petition to see if the majority of the estate agreed with us that there are not enough play facilities. We collected over 400 signatures from residents on the estate.

The petition was preceded by a distribution of leaflets around the estate, announcing the existence of the group and its intentions. Both the leaflets and the petition forms were drawn up by members. A mother typed the stencil skins which were run off at the local university.

> Councillor Stone and Councillor Marshall are local councillors for the Ainsley estate. They visited us because we sent them a

letter inviting them to come down to Robert Shaw primary school. We wanted them to come to look at our petition and give us help. When they came we told them about the estate and about the good points, but especially that there is nothing to do for young people. We said that we had been in trouble and are not angels. They agreed with us and made plans for us to meet the Sheriff to present our petition.

One Saturday we made our way to the Council House where we met the Deputy Sheriff and his Lady, along with the councillors. We talked about our project and aims and brought forward our petition. Then we had coffee and biscuits. As we were drinking the Sheriff said he would take the petition to a higher authority or someone who can deal with our problems. The Sheriff and his Lady signed the petition. Then we had our photo taken with the Sheriff and his wife.

The press were told about our petition and came to one of our meetings to find out what we were meeting for. We talked about how we first formed the club and what made us form the club. He wanted to know what we did in our spare time and hear about the facilities we have. He said he would write an article in the *Evening Post* and send a photographer round to take pictures of us.

We talked to the pressman about the club's problems and having no place where we can meet. The two councillors were also present and they told him that they support us. They also said we had a good chance of getting the wasteland down by the bridge for a youth hut, which is what we would like to start with. The following week the press camera-man came and took some pictures of us.

The newspaper article and the attendant picture, presenting the group in a very positive light, made quite an impact locally, and members quickly saw the value not simply of publicity, but of representing their cause and themselves.

They immediately produced a news sheet, the *Ainsley Youth Express* (AYE!) examining themselves and detailing their activities in a series of short articles. To our astonishment, some of these articles (in part reproduced above) were by members who had been written off by teachers as illiterate. On completion of the draft, and after discussing the general layout and subtitles, four members went to a local community printer. While he typed the text, they laid out titles and subtitles with letraset and pasted up and printed off the news sheet on the printer's offset litho machine.

Their next step had the same 'outreaching' purpose:

> We organised a jumble sale to gain our respect back; because people on the estate did not like us, we did not seem to have any. First of all we collected jumble from people of the estate. We kept the jumble in Darren Smith's shed and moved it to the school the night the jumble sale was held. We also held a raffle of goods given to us by firms we had written to. This and the jumble sale raised £55, and we had some jumble left over. We sold that to a junk man for £10.
>
> We gave a display of our work on a model and a map with photographs of the estate. We took round leaflets asking for any jumble. There were two types of leaflets: one to tell people what we were collecting for, the other when the sale was on. We drew posters, put them in the shop windows on the estate and got the jumble sale mentioned on the local radio.

The jumble sale required quite an effort both in terms of production and coordination. More unusual aspects of work surrounding the jumble sale were the photographic display and the model of the estate. For the display a small group toured the estate taking black and white photos of features they regarded as significant with regard to their aim of getting a youth hut, eg graffiti, 'keep off' notices, areas of unused land. Then they developed and printed the photos at an arts and crafts centre, mounting them on display boards back at the group meeting.

The model was suggested by a worker from the Education for Neighbourhood Change Unit (Gibson 1979), based at Nottingham University, who came to visit the members. They quickly took up the idea. Using materials from the unit's resource kits and with the support of the worker, they quickly built up a scale model of the estate, which in a different way reinforced their arguments as to what was lacking and what could be achieved.

This was a period of total involvement and high excitement for members. Among the various tasks there was something for each member to get her/his teeth into (a number of girls had joined the group); something which offered the satisfaction of a worthwhile job well done and a chance for all members to demonstrate publicly their positive sides. The tasks were firmly attached to an issue which they saw as relevant and important to their daily lives. Then,

> Councillor Marshall said that if we wanted a club we would have to have parents and teenagers on a committee. We sent out a leaflet asking residents of the estate to come to a meeting. This was a bit of a failure; only a few residents came and some officials gatecrashed.

Letting Young People Have Their Say

>After this we went round the estate and asked personally people who we thought would be likely to support us to come to another meeting. At this second there were just residents and teenagers. The adults said they would support us either by being on a committee or by helping with the running of a club. Soon after we had another meeting with officials, which the same residents came to. People were very angry that there were no facilities on the estate - a committee was formed. The committee consisted of six parents, four teenagers, one councillor and the secretary of the local Association of Boy's Clubs as secretary."

However,

>Not a lot was achieved. The officials and councillors made promises on several occasions, such as providing disused prefabs for the club, but we got nothing. What was achieved from the committee was a letter from the council saying that there was the possibility of using the school field for a portable building.

>We got nowt to do and all the work towards the club was taken over by the councillors and adults. They said we couldn't do anything because we are not old enough, so we have to put ideas up to the committee and they will follow them up. We were not happy about this. They said we were ungrateful if we complained about being left out.

The adult chairman of the original committee resigned, after which an atmosphere of genuine co-operation reemerged, and the committee's applications for local authority funds and other forms of support looked more convincing. In a matter of weeks commitments for some £4000 in cash and material aid flowed in leaving the committee to raise another £1000 itself so that a portable building could be erected. A good start to this was made by a second jumble sale, styled as a mini-market, which was organised and run by teenage members and adults together.

For a long time the committee was held back by leasing details, having successfully applied for planning permission for a site at the heart of the estate. However as a temporary measure the young people arranged twice weekly youth club sessions at the primary school, using an equipment grant they had obtained. They used this interim club to develop membership and make plans for future activities in their own premises.

With this underway and the committee operating successfully, it was decided with the young people that two of the original workers, Dave and Mark, should withdraw. The young people were proving they could help themselves and work with adults on the estate. The worker team had been involved for over two years. Development work of this kind is inevitably a lengthy and painstaking process, with many peaks and troughs. As the local probation officer with a range of contacts on the estate, Colin continued to be available to provide support and consultation to the young people involved.

However, the success of the school-based club lessened the incentive to pursue vigorously the work for the independent club building, and the committee became all but defunct. The commitments for funding lapsed. It took teenage action to get momentum back.

In the autumn of 1982, two teenagers and two adults put together an Inner Area Programme application for funding a club house to begin in the 1983/84 financial year. The councillors reaffirmed their support, and with their backing the application was successful. £21,000 capital now became available, with £3000 p.a. running costs for four years. The youth service were to provide 25% of the funding and to administer the money. A new committee had to be formed but because some of the original, but still active, members had now passed the age of eighteen, and could be considered as 'adults', it was overwhelmingly made up of group members. In consultation with the youth service the committee worked out rules and running procedures. The building was opened in October 1984. Purpose built, it was a simple but sound shell with water, heating etc. - but no frills - which the members equipped themselves.

For about a year the club was opened 4 nights a week, with hirings for weddings etc. bringing in additional income. Attendance regularly reached 100. The older members saw to the day to day running, supported by regular discussions with Colin who also showed his face at the club from time to time.

By mid-1985 a change could be discerned. Commitment was again waning and the club opening less frequently. There was some vandalism to the building and trouble at discos. A number of the older committee members were moving away from the estate. Responsibility had fallen on the shoulders of two girls who had been original members and were now nineteen years old. They were not prepared to do everything - but none of the younger people attending the club seemed prepared to help out.

However history repeats itself. Over the winter of 1986 a group of about a dozen of these younger members began to get together and expressed dissatisfaction that they were being 'shut out'. The club was not opening as they wanted and they could not get on to the committee. They blamed the two girls for 'controlling' the club. This group was showing similar characteristics to the original group, getting into trouble and appearing in court. Meetings were held. It was agreed that the girls hand over responsibility to this younger new group, and that support would be provided by a detached youth worker.

Thus the process continues. Through 1987 and 1988 the club opened regularly and remained very popular. Young people continued to carry responsibility for it themselves. At the time of my last contact in 1988, they were negotiating with the county council for mainstream funding, as the Inner Area running costs were shortly to expire.

Young People and the Police: From Conflict to Involvement

One particular episode in the life of the group highlights more than any other what is at stake both in working with young people in this way, and in the management of 'disorder and conflict'.

In the group's first year the number of police arrests, prosecutions, and court appearances for Ainsley young people reduced dramatically. During this period there were no official reports of group offences of burglary, theft, or taking and driving away vehicles. However by mid-1980, the teenagers were giving vague, frustrated accounts of conflict with the local police, about being harassed and arrested on the estate for no apparent reason. Police arrest referrals were beginning to increase and the nature of the offences were violations of public order eg threatening behaviour, breach of the peace and abusive language. It was noticeable that police arrest action was confined to two or three constables, one of whom was designated community constable for the estate.

The young people (and in due course the police inspector concerned) will now take up the story (BBC 1982).

> About 5 or 6 months ago the police activity on the estate was large. I think the reason for this was when we was together on the estate we always used to keep together, perhaps about ten of us. We used to actually split into two, the younger ones and the older ones, and we used to hang about on the estate and people used to get annoyed by the presence or the noise, and the police used to come down more or less every night - clearing us off. But instead of just coming and asking us to move, we got a lot of lip, and we got pushed around a lot and, well, we resented this.

As workers we attempted to encourage the group to take constructive action rather than remain frustrated and angry. However, feelings on the estate were running high and a group of four teenagers stoned an unoccupied police car in July 1980.

This incident became the main focus of the next group meeting and the members decided to make representations to the sub-divisional police headquarters, to invite the police inspector responsible for police operations in the area to meet them. On their own initiative they visited the police station, only to find no chief inspector available; returning to the estate they prepared a letter describing the conflict with the local police, and invited the chief inspector to a meeting.

> Well, what we decided to do was we contacted the local police station, the Canning Circus police station, because the main source of trouble was one officer. While we was running this group, about 5 of us went up, but when we got up there they was not showing much willingness to help us, so we actually had to write a letter. We invited the chief inspector down and told him the problem.

They circulated interested adults asking them to give support at the meeting. The chief inspector met the teenagers who were supported in their demands by a number of adults.

> Well, when Chief Inspector Coote came down we had a meeting together. He did a lot of talking about the olden days, but we did manage to get our point over, and we emphasised that this one officer was mainly to blame for the trouble, and he said he would see what he could do about it. Subsequently this police officer was moved off the estate which is really a great thing for the estate because since then the trouble has gone down, and there hasn't been so much police activity on the estate.

The chief inspector moved the beat constable from the estate and introduced a community liaison constable to work with the group and to help with the youth club campaign. He made a bargain with the teenagers to make policing changes and to adopt a lower police profile in the area, but in return expected the group to take their part of the bargain seriously and reduce the number of incidents and neighbourhood complaints. There was clearly a good deal of mutual respect between the teenagers and the chief inspector.

Chief Inspector:

> Well, they complained about the police patrolling and they felt they were getting unjust attention. It was obviously generally thought that they'd got a complaint and because of this I decided to alter the patrol requirements for the area.

> After that and after we'd altered the patrolling requirements our community constables visited together with myself, and I think after that visit when I'd spoken to the children and asked them to cool the tempo, to try to assist us to assist themselves, they felt there was a genuine effort on our part, and I feel to some extent we're more acceptable to them, and since then we've visited fairly regularly and in fact the children have asked me to attend at the adults' meeting which follows the meeting they have at the school.

Crime has gone down in the past 12 months, certainly. And in the past 4 months nuisance and vandalism has gone down tremendously. We don't get the calls from the people in the community complaining about them.

The chief inspector attended the monthly committee meetings, actively putting forward points raised by the teenagers and was at times their advocate. Two community liaison constables became fully involved in the group, working with the interim youth club at the primary school. Further conflict with the operational police was minimal.

It is significant that the police's involvement came as a result of the young people taking an initiative, and not as part of police strategy. The workers regarded responding to the reports of harassment as a priority, as it was what the members saw as important. This issue developed as an integral part of their campaign to help themselves.

COMMENT

The Ainsley case study provides an example of what has become known as 'social action' or 'self-directed groupwork' (Ward 1982, Mullender & Ward 1985). Clearly there are many issues and questions one could take up from the case study. However its purpose in this paper is first and foremost to provide a 'live' example of this method, which I will now go on to explain and outline in a more systematic form, and to show that such work can be effective. The Ainsley project was successful not only in the terms of the four principles proposed by FIRM mentioned at the beginning of this paper: breaking down barriers; involvement; reconciliation; and problem-solving; but also, in meeting the more clear-cut expectations of public, media, and government to 'do something about crime'.

The Social Action Groupwork Approach: Resetting the Agenda

Basically Social Action groupwork is an approach which aims at empowering people to define and meet their own needs. It is located in theory, in values, and in practice experience gained in working with groups like that at Ainsley. The approach provides an alternative to other methods which are seen as clinging to pathological explanations of behaviour, in which the entire burden of change is placed on the client (Thorpe et al 1980, McGuire & Priestley 1985). It is accepted that individuals do sometimes need to change, but this change must not be wrapped up in pathology. Instead practice should be based on an understanding that social structures and the way particular societies are organised, their norms and their institutions, are the source of a good deal of human suffering.

The starting point is that groups have an inherent capacity for bringing about social change and together with this, personal betterment. However to work in this way means making an attempt in practice to bridge the gap between individuals and social institutions, that is between private troubles and public issues (Wright Mills 1970). It involves simultaneous concern for both but affords primary attention to the way in which public issues penetrate private troubles (Longres & McLeod 1980:271-272). Only when these connections have been made explicit can people begin to break out of the disablement and frustration brought about by carrying responsibility for problems which are not at root of their own making. They can then begin to experience their own potential and utilise their energies to bring about change in the outside world and in themselves.

From Theory to Values to Practice

Grounded in this theoretical position, the social action approach is founded upon a set of values from which flow the goals and activities of the work. Fundamentally it is the explicit nature of these values - and the practice principles which emerge from them - that gives the approach its distinctive flavour.

At the core of this value position lie the following assumptions:

- Young people are not in themselves THE problem. They are caught in a wider web of problems including lack of opportunity, resources, facilities, and adverse attitudes and prejudice against them.
- They are not 'inadequate'; they have skills, knowledge and experience which can be drawn on to help address the problems they face. They have much to teach us if we are prepared to engage with them in dialogue. They can be partners with workers and other members of the community in finding solutions to problems located in the wider social world. They have rights, including a right to more control over their lives.
- Our role as professional workers is to facilitate the process through which learning, development and change can take place. We do this by starting from the issues, ideas and understanding of the young people with whom we work, rather than our professional definition of 'their' problems.
- This involves a working relationship in which there is a commitment to equality and non-elitist forms of leadership in which special skills and knowledge may be employed but do not accord privilege. As a group worker, one assumes responsibility for oneself and responsibility to others.
- As workers we need to take into account and address ourselves to the endemic racism and sexism that exists in our institutions and practices.

These assumptions lead to a number of principles for practice in working with groups of young people:

- Group members have the freedom to set their own agendas: to identify and work on issues which are relevant to themselves.
- Workers relate to group members as equals; they are given responsibility rather than being remoulded, contained, treated or overprotected.
- Group members set their own timetable and work at their own pace.
- Group members locate resources and negotiate for these and policy changes for themselves; they develop negotiating skills, and learn to find their way around and deal with complex organisations.
- Group members make their own decisions and take responsibility for carrying them out and facing the consequences.
- Group members control their own resources. They are responsible to their colleagues for handling group resources including money and hardware.

The Social Action Groupwork Model

These principles provide the underpinning for social action groupwork. Workers usually come to this approach having tried and rejected other methods of work which they have found ineffective, as well as in conflict with the values they hold. They discover in social action a real and viable alternative.

In drawing out the distinctive and specific social action methodology of practice, it is possible to identify a process through which social action groups pass (Mullender & Ward 1985). It falls into three stages, each with a number of steps.

The steps of the basic three stage model are as follows:

STAGE 1. TAKING STOCK

The potential workers begin by spending time reaching an agreement about the values which motivate their practice - values akin to those which have been outlined above. This is the point at which they choose to work along social action lines, opt for an alternative approach, or decide they do not constitute a compatible worker team.

Once the workers have reached an agreement on these matters, they can begin to engage with young people with a view to inviting them to develop a group. The young people become partners with the worker team in seeking solutions to the problems they will go on to define.

STAGE 2. TAKING ACTION

The Three Key Questions Moving from recognition to action: exploring

'WHAT', 'WHY', and 'HOW'. The workers facilitate the group setting its own agenda of issues:

> ASKING THE QUESTION - 'WHAT' are the issues/problems to be tackled? The workers help the group to analyse why the problems on its agenda exist.
> ASKING THE QUESTION - 'WHY' do the issues/problems exist? The workers enable members to decide what actions to take. (Workers do not impose their own ideas for action, except to say they will not do certain things like working towards racist goals.) The group members share out the tasks.
> ASKING THE QUESTION - 'HOW' can we bring about change? The members take those actions for themselves. These stages may recur several times during the 'Taking Action' stage.

Asking the question 'WHY?' is the keystone in the process. Without it, there can be no awareness of wider scale oppression, no moving beyond blaming oneself for one's problems, into raised consciousness and the pursuit of rights. To jump straight from identifying WHAT is wrong, into the practicalities of the HOW of achieving change, is to collude with a process in which explanations and responsibility for problems are usually sought in the private world around the individual and family.

Asking the question WHY gives group members the opportunity to widen their vision and to bring social and public matters on to their agenda. These, in turn, can point to new and unanticipated options for action. A spin-off of turning the spotlight outwards in this way, and thus taking the pressure off members as individuals, is often a marked improvement in personal morale and self-confidence. This is also very much assisted by the successful completion of tasks on behalf of the group, and becomes a self-reinforcing process.

STAGE 3: TAKING OVER

Perceiving the connections between WHAT? WHY? and HOW? The group reviews and reflects on what it has achieved, identifying new issues to be tackled: REFORMULATING 'WHAT?'; perceiving the links between the different issues tackled: REFORMULATING 'WHY?'; and deciding what actions to take next: REFORMULATING 'HOW?'

These steps become a recurring process for as long as the group continues. The group members gradually gain some control over their own lives and realise that they have a right to more. They are now active in tackling the roots of their own problems. In Stage Three, the workers can be seen to have moved into the background.

Conclusion

Experience shows that the process methods and techniques of social action groupwork are tremendously effective and powerful in encouraging young people to participate. However, one concern is that this methodology should not be misused, and converted into an instrument of control. For this reason practice must be firmly embedded within the overall values and purposes of social action. It is in the explicit value base of the approach, providing a springboard into practice, and fixing its parameters, that this insurance lies.

I am not suggesting that the social groupwork approach can provide a panacea. Indeed the values are open to challenge from those who will approach their work from different, but equally genuine starting points. The methodology as stated here is inevitably only a sketch, and experienced, practice-hardened workers will point to how employing organisations can put up obstacles to new ways of working. It can be argued that the openness and equality, stressed so strongly, is inevitably to some degree illusory if professional, state funded, workers are involved. In this paper I can do no more than flag these issues - although some have been addressed elsewhere (Burley 1982, Keenan & Pinkerton 1988, Mullender & Ward 1985, 1989a, 1989b) - and sincerely invite a continuing process of reflection and debate, and further work in the field. These are all necessary if this, or any approach to practice, is to move forward.

However I would assert that the respect for young people's own opinions and acknowledgement of their real abilities, often gained through hard experience, which are embedded in the social action approach, can point us in directions towards genuinely meeting their legitimate aspirations. In so doing we can stem the processes of alienation that contribute to offending. In this way social action provides us with an opportunity of working towards real change, as opposed to allaying what are only surface symptoms. The social action approach provides an effective and accessible methodology - and a way forward.

References

BBC (1981) Grapevine (transcript of interviews used in television programme).

BADHAM, B (Ed.) (1989) Doing something with our lives when we're inside: self-directed groupwork in a youth custody centre. *Groupwork*, 2(1), 27-35.

BADHAM, B, FLEMING, J, PERRY, A and WARD, D (1984) Chronicles of confusion. *Community Care*, 29 Nov, 18-21.

BADHAM, B, BENTE, M and HALL, P (1988) Nowt to do and always getting into trouble. The Bulwell Neighbourhood Project: a social action response. *Groupwork*, 1(3), 239-251.

BURLEY, D (1982) *Starting Blocks: Aspects of Social Education Groupwork with Young People*. Leicester, National Youth Bureau.

CONNOLLY, P, and WOOLMAN, T (1982) The confidence trick. *Youth in*

Society, 73, 16-18.
FIRM (1989) *Punishment, Custody and the Community: A Response to the Home Office Green Paper*. Beaconsfield, Forum for Initiatives in Reparation and Mediation.
FLEMING, J, HARRISON, M, PERRY, A, PURDY, D and WARD, D (1983) Action speaks louder than words. *Youth and Policy*, 10(3), 16-19.
Home Office (1988) *Punishment, Custody and the Community*. Cmnd.424, London, H.M.S.O.
GIBSON, T (1979) *People Power*. Harmondsworth, Penguin.
KEENAN,E and PINKERTON, J (1988) Social action groupwork and negotiation: contradictions in the process of empowerment. *Groupwork*, 1(3), 229-238.
LONGRES, J and MCLEOD, E (1980) Consciousness raising and social work practice. *Social Casework*, May, 267-276.
MCGUIRE, J and PRIESTLEY, P (1985) *Offending Behaviour: Skills and Strategems for Going Straight*. London, Batsford.
MULLENDER, A and WARD, D (1985) Towards an alternative model of social groupwork. *British Journal of Social Work*, 15, 155-172.
MULLENDER, A and WARD, D (1989a) Challenging familiar assumptions: preparing for and initiating a self-directed group. *Groupwork*, 2(1), 5-26.
MULLENDER, A and WARD, D (1989b) Gaining strength together. *Social Work Today*, 20(50), 14-15.
THORPE, D, SMITH, D, GREEN, C and PALEY, J (1980) *Out of Care: The Community Support of Juvenile Offenders*. London, Allen & Unwin.
WARD, D (1979) Working with young people: the way forward. *Probation Journal*, 26(1), 2-8.
WARD, D (Ed)(1982) *Give 'em a Break: Social Action by Young People at Risk and in Trouble*. Leicester, National Youth Bureau.
WARD, D and HARRISON, M (1989) Self-Organised Employment Initiatives and Young People: A Social Action Approach. Paper presented at an International Workshop, May, University of Bielefeld, West Germany.
WRIGHT MILLS, C (1970) *The Sociological Imagination*. Harmondsworth, Penguin.

Chapter Seventeen

Conflict, Change and the Police: Shared Experiences in the Borough of Newham

PAULINE OBEE

Introduction

THE NEWHAM Conflict and Change Project was set up in the London Borough of Newham in 1984, after a year of widespread exploration of conflict situations in the area. Behind it lies the belief that our society is in a state of transition, in which differences between people can become the focus for stresses and uncertainties created by change. It exists to help people learn about conflicts and changes in Newham: these might be conflicts in which they are themselves involved, in which case our role is usually that of an impartial third party; or they may be conflicts in general, in which case we design appropriate events and courses.

Membership of the project is open to anyone living in Newham, and is as mixed in terms of race, age, class and gender as the population as a whole. All members are volunteers, who go through an induction and training programme and then commit themselves to an average of 2 hours a week for the project. They act as "conciliators", form the management committee, provide supervision, support colleagues, design and run training and other events, and employ staff. They are also all directors of Conflict and Change Ltd, our legal entity, which is a company limited by guarantee and a registered charity.

Newham

The London Borough of Newham was founded in 1965 by amalgamating the old boroughs of West Ham and East Ham. It covers about 10 square miles, between the Thames, the Lee Valley and the River Roding. The population of approximately 213,000 is one of the most racially mixed in the United Kingdom. There are seven different Indian language groups, people from most Caribbean islands, from Africa, Eastern Europe and China, and there are six major religions. Because the more socially mobile people move out of Newham, the elderly and low income groups make up a large proportion of the population.

Housing is very high density, ranging from terraces and detached houses to flats and tower blocks. The southern part of the Borough is on docklands, where there is much redevelopment. The area comes within the Metropolitan Police "K" District, one of the most hard-pressed districts in the city.

Life is changing all the time in Newham - the people change, as do the work situation and the buildings. The necessary work skills have changed and the possibility of long-term unemployment makes it difficult to find a place in society. This kind of uncertainty affects lives and makes it easy to distrust anyone who is different to oneself and to see difference as a form of opposition. Often minor differences seem to burst with the built-up anger of other frustrations, and problems presented in conflicts are not always the major issues - but rather a response to uncertainty and insecurity within the community.

The Conflict & Change Project

The main areas of work within the Conflict and Change Project are:

> Reconciliation Service: the provision of impartial volunteer mediators in disputes between people in Newham
> Education Programme: events and courses for schools and other groups to examine conflicts and to provide training in conflict management skills
> Consultancy: to assist members of organisations to manage both change and conflict in their work and within their organisations.

The Reconciliation Service

The Reconciliation Service is offered free and on a confidential basis to all residents of Newham, and deals with conflict between: neighbours, friends, landlords/tenants, community groups, agencies/clients, employer/employee, co-habitants and so forth. We also come across cases between husband and wife, parents and children, but this kind of work is very delicate and needs mediators skilled in these specific areas of conflict. If we know of appropriate agencies we try to refer such cases on. Third party referrals are not accepted and agencies are asked to send the parties to us directly.

After the first interview some decide not to proceed further for various reasons such as:

1. Having told their story to someone in the office they feel there is, after all, nothing to worry about. They are satisfied that someone had the time and patience to listen to them, and feel that the problem is no longer overwhelming.
2. To some people the fact that conciliators are volunteers raises doubts about the quality of their work.
3. A small percentage are disappointed at the fact that the Project is

not a law enforcement agency and cannot put pressure on the second party. Some are annoyed that an instant solution is quite impossible. NCCP will only agree to proceed with a case on the understanding that it is up to the parties themselves to take responsibility for any changes that may be needed for a proper resolution.
4. First parties often express the conflict in quite clear, simple terms. It is easy to fall into the trap of accepting a one-sided view until a visit to the second party produces quite a different story. The discussion with the second party helps to put things in perspective. This can be difficult for the first party to accept, and they may then be unwilling to proceed.

Those who decide to continue, also do so for various reasons:

1. Some need assistance with language and ask the Project to intervene and help them talk to their neighbour. The NCCP have a good mixture of conciliators speaking almost all the main languages used in the Borough.
2. Having acquired help from other establishments such as solicitors, police, or community centres, they may resort to NCCP because of the time and money that would otherwise be involved.
3. The fact that NCCP have an informal, innovative approach to conflict management attracts quite a number of people.
4. In a substantial proportion of cases the Project works only with one party, because the second party does not agree there is a problem or refuses to work with NCCP. However, the fact that they know of the Project's involvement often influences their relationship with the first party.

If it is agreed that NCCP may be able to help in a dispute two conciliators are assigned to the case. Some cases go on for months, while others are closed immediately after the first visits to one or both parties. This variation occurs in all kinds of case regardless of the initial presented issues. The duration of involvement in a case depends more on the attitudes of the parties eg whether they agree on what the problem is, or whether they see the possibility of a solution.

Following the initial interviews and visits some cases eventually come to a formal mediation session. This is a process to bring all parties involved to a neutral place and help create communication in a way that clears the emotions and misunderstandings. Enough time is given to all parties involved to say whatever they wish, and help is given to continue the discussion in a constructive manner, ensuring that it does not develop into an argument.

Taken in the context of people's lives, the process of resolving a conflict is itself a major task, often requiring changes of attitude as well as behaviour. This is especially true in a conflict that has gone on for a long time, involving a lot of different people and leading to abuse, violence and bad feeling. Often all that can be hoped for is to help turn the tide so that the parties themselves can begin to approach each other and the situation differently. This might not appear very dramatic at the time, but it is nevertheless a vital role in any community.

Another use of mediation sessions is to establish normal verbal communication between people of different cultures and ethnic origins. Racism, misunderstanding and prejudice often make it difficult to form a relationship where the differences between people appear so marked. A fairly formal meeting with mediators can help clarify what these differences really are, and to establish a basis of trust and respect.

The Education Programme

The main aim of the Education Programme is to help individuals develop their natural ability to manage conflicts. Conflict management is carried out in many different ways in different societies. Our aim is to develop these methods in order to work with the variety of people who need the service. Under the Education Programme the project undertakes the following activities:

1. Work in schools
2. Training courses
3. Public workshops
4. Police induction workshops
5. Women's groups
6. Newsletter and information
7. Lectures and talks.

Training Courses

These courses are for anyone interested in gaining conflict management skills. Each course lasts 18 hours and three courses are provided during the year to cater for all needs by having one evening course, one daily course, and one weekend course, each divided into six sessions. These sessions comprise:

1. Conflicts in the community, and case studies. A variety of conflicts are examined, the presenting and underlying issues discussed, and role plays developed on the basis of real situations.
2. Differences. This session examines the differences that exist among us. It is a space for people to find out about other cultures, religions, traditions, etc.
3. Prejudices. This is a continuation of the second session. Prejudices are mainly based on our previous knowledge or experience. Existing prejudices are used as a tool to build or acquire

knowledge about conflict and cooperation.
4. Communication skills. Mediators need specific communication skills. Listening and understanding the differences between facts and feelings are the main features of this session.
5. The last two sessions are designed to practice formal and informal mediation.

Working With the Police

When the Newham Conflict and Change Project was just a sapling, the local Police Liaison Officer became interested and our first link with the police was formed.

Many of the disputes to which the police are called are recognised as being unsuitable for police intervention. The NCCP emphasis on the importance of the parties concerned examining the root of the problem and coming to a mutual understanding was quickly recognised by the police as having great value, and within a short time referrals were being made.

As a "holding institute" for conflicts (see following section), Conflict and Change felt they could also offer an opportunity to the police to share in a process of reflection whilst themselves learning more about the police framework, powers and training.

An exchange programme began with four senior officers participating in a four hour Community Workshop with six Conflict and Change workers and six members of the public who had expressed an interest in becoming volunteers with the Project. The success of the event prompted the police to invite eight NCCP volunteers to attend a video training session on counter procedures.

The role play following the video was designed to show both the attitude of the person who enters the police station and reports a problem and the police response to that report. The latter is found to be very responsive to the attitude assumed by the person reporting. Different attitudes were acted out in role-play.

This session was followed by an introduction to legislation and police powers which helped dispel some misunderstandings and assumptions. Riding in a police van at a time when the pubs were turning out proved to be a harrowing experience, with black volunteers within the van experiencing the same verbal abuse as the police officers. A substantial number of calls revealed the police response often to be a temporary holding of a conflict, while little could be done to address the emotional content of the conflict or its underlying causes. Conflict and Change was able to demonstrate within the training session the possibility of a deeper, more active type of intervention.

This initial work was established with senior members of the force, but a meeting with the Street Duties Officer prompted a change of direction, and in 1986 the Project became one of the community-based organisations that work with police probationers during their second year street duties course. In the resulting workshops, each police officer was encouraged to approach the exercises from an individual stance, rather than attempting to think as a group or "force": how does the area in which you live change when you become a police officer? Where do we "fit" as individuals into the Newham "community"? Exercises included:

- Listening for feelings as well as for facts
- Need to be open about prejudice.
- The Newham map and how we fit.
- Working together.
- Combination of roles.

The nature and pattern of calls for police assistance vary tremendously and the police response obviously varies according to other obligations, time of day, and so on. From observation and discussion it seems clear that the police give low priority to domestic disputes and tend to regard them as inherently frustrating. Intervention is primarily designed to abate the immediate conflict and rarely attempts to address the underlying issues due to pressures, time and assessment of possible outcome.

Without some form of intervention the incidents are likely to recur, often escalating in violence. Arrest by itself could act as a deterrent, but only if an opportunity is given to examine the source of the conflict, which is often deeply embedded. If, on a formal basis, access were given to a conciliation agency such as Conflict and Change, it would provide an alternative for effective intervention, complementing and extending the actions of the police.

Approximately 40 officers attend the workshops each year for a session of three hours, in which mutual trust is built between the police and the community, and issues of difference among cultures, stereotyping and prejudice can be examined. Informal lunchtime meetings have also enabled an exchange of ideas when the local police station have invited members to introduce themselves and the work of the Project.

Conflict and Change and the police have much in common. We both work in the community and are usually called to situations in times of trouble, although once there the similarity ends, as the police exercise legal and state authority, whilst Conflict and Change take a consultative role. Mutual respect has grown from the above exercises in cooperative learning and there has been a steady increase in the number of cases of dispute introduced to the service by the local police.

It has become very apparent that there is a need within the police structure for a confidential territory like that provided by the Conflict and Change office, without fear of ridicule from senior colleagues or other repercussions, an issue which is developed below in the final section of this paper.

The Importance of Neutrality

(Extracted from a discussion paper written by Project founder-member Paul Regan.)

Newham Conflict and Change was set up to offer a service to those who find themselves caught in a conflict which they find destructive or unacceptable. In order to be able to do this Conflict and Change cannot allow itself to be a party to conflict. As we say in our publicity, "We are not here to take sides". This is not to say that we do not have conflicts within our own membership and organisation, which we try to recognise, confront and work at as they arise. But if we allow ourselves to become part of someone else's conflict we cease to be able to operate effectively in the role of conciliator.

One of the essential parts of the service is to create a "space" in which people can look at their conflicts from another perspective. This space could be physical - a piece of neutral territory, a safe room at our centre at Christopher House, for instance. But it is more than that. It is also a psychological and emotional space in which individuals can "stand back" from the issues that are winding them up. Having stood back you can sometimes see things more clearly.

As an example, we sometimes speak of "ground rules" which help to define the way in which communication can happen: "You will each be given an equal amount of time in which to express your point of view. In response we ask that while the other person is speaking, you do not interrupt....". These ground rules are particularly apparent when we have a formal mediation panel before which disputants appear. But even in informal conciliation similar conditions prevail.

An important part of the organisation of the service we provide therefore is knowing how to define the ground - how to set the rules - so that people are protected from attack and from the danger of their own feelings getting out of control. In this way people can hear and be heard.

Our authority and responsibility is to manage and control the environment within which conflict can be safely expressed, analysed and managed. It is not our responsibility to express or manage it. The authority and responsibility for that lies only with the parties to the disputes. We cannot solve other people's conflicts. We can, however, provide the conditions within which it may be easier for them to do so.

An example of this occurred recently when we were invited by the police to attend a meeting at which a number of representatives were being asked to examine incidents of racial harassment in the community. This is a very serious issue covering a wide and deep-seated level of conflict which makes life intolerable for many black residents in Newham. However, we recognised that such a meeting would not find it easy to agree on the nature or extent of the problem, nor on the best method of dealing with the issue. To attend such a meeting would mean participating in the ongoing debate about how much racial incidents should be dealt with by the police. But it is not our role to take part in such a debate. If we have any distinctive contribution to make it is not in debating the problem with the police or the community. Our role would be to offer a controlled space in which the police and the community could negotiate possible approaches. In order to remain free to play this role we decided we could not accept the police invitation to be their guest at the meeting they had proposed. Instead we decided that it may be appropriate for us to invite the police and/or the community into "our" space to look at the issue to see whether it could be managed in a different way.

It is such reasoning which has impelled us not to join other associations in Newham which it would otherwise have been natural for us to join. (From time to time we have attended meetings as individuals, since it is important that we know what is going on in our community. However, this is for our benefit rather than any benefit for the meeting concerned.)

Another example of creating "space" is where we undertake a consultancy to an organisation which is experiencing internal conflict which it finds difficult to manage. Here we would normally define a clear task for the consultancy and agree this with the organisation concerned before accepting the contract. The task provides a focus for the work to which the organisation may need to give attention if it is to find a method of managing the conflict better.

In this sense it becomes clear that Newham Conflict and Change is a very "controlling" organisation, as someone put it at a recent residential event we ran. But we do not control the people. Nor do we control the decisions. What we control are the conditions within which they can think clearly about their problem and make decisions which are appropriate for them.

Chapter Eighteen

Learning from the Community: Facilitated Police-Community Workshops at the Local Level

ROBIN OAKLEY

Introduction

POLICE FORCES in Britain increasingly aspire to present themselves as a public service. At least until recently, most police officers have tended to see their 'service role' as something separate from the proper business of policing - that of law enforcement. Service meant 'being kind to old ladies or people who had lost their way', an unwelcome distraction forced on police by a misguided public or by government. The loss of consent, which Lord Scarman felt lay at the root of the disturbances of 1981, was in police eyes a problem of public relations: if only the public understood better what police were trying to do, the problem of consent would be resolved. Police knew best, and the problems of policing were primarily technical and financial ones which inhibited police effectiveness in catching criminals.

The last few years have seen a definite shift away from this position (particularly at senior management level) towards an ideology of policing as a 'service' to the public generally - an approach more characteristic of some continental European police forces (eg Oakley, 1990). Perhaps the most striking indication of this has been the introduction by the Metropolitan Police of their 'Plus Programme'. A further indication has been the acknowledgement by police generally, and by police associations in particular, of the findings of the recent Operational Policing Review, which documents the major gap between police and public perceptions of policing priorities and preferred styles (Joint Consultative Committee, 1990; cf. Levi & Jones, 1985). If the emphasis on 'public service' is to become not just an ideal but a reality, then police organisations will have to develop their institutional capacity to listen more effectively to what the public feel they need, and be able to respond in a manner which is more accountable to the public while safeguarding professionalism and the requirements of the law.

Although it has taken until the 1990s for them to become clear at the national level, the key issues here originate with the disturbances of 1981, even though more specific preoccupations (eg. with public order and with 'race relations') have to some extent clouded them. Indeed, it has been the black community (with its unique experience of racism and predominantly inner-city residence) that has played a major part in bringing the issue of police-community relations to national attention. It is for this reason that it is still appropriate to speak of 'community and race relations' in this context, ie. to emphasise both the specific and the general aspects, as well as the relationship between them. Coming to terms with the multi-racial and multi-cultural aspect of society is not just a key but also a trigger component of the challenge for police (and all other public service agencies) to come to terms with changing communities generally.

From the Scarman Report onwards, a variety of measures have been advocated for the improvement of police-community relations, covering areas such as recruitment, training, complaints procedures, discipline, lay visitor schemes, and community consultation. Despite the many initiatives and achievements, relationships between police and communities in many of Britain's multi-racial cities remain cool at best, with conflict persisting or erupting in numerous locations. The challenge to police forces to become more sensitive and responsive organisations may (in the light of the Operational Review) be substantial enough anywhere, but in the inner cities where trust and community solidarity are lowest it is at its most acute. Good classroom training may be undermined by cynicism and harsh experience on the job; management-led policies are dismissed as unrealistic or 'soft'; use of disciplinary procedures against racism is resented and avoided; formal consultative groups are felt to be 'talking-shops' and too remote.

If in these circumstances police forces aspire to advance the 'service' aspect of their role, what further can be done? The answer to this question must lie in working from and with the experience of the officer delivering the service 'on the front line' - whether this be on the street, in the police station, or visiting people's homes. The focus must be on operational police constables, and on the immediate supervisors and managers of their work. The answer must also lie in recognising that a 'public service' is provided to all members of the public equally and fairly, and with sensitivity to their diverse needs. This will involve not just fairness and understanding towards those who are suspected, or victims, of crime, but also (especially the more that preventive work is to be emphasised), relating confidently to, and with the respect of, all sections of the community. Where normal contacts are restricted to a limited cross-section of the community with whom an officer comes into contact through work, and where (as is often the case) officers do not live in or are not familiar with the kinds of areas they may police, the need to foster sensitivity, understanding and confidence in relating to the local community as a whole is a need which it is essential for senior police managers to address. It is a need, moreover, which cannot be satisfied simply through isolated classroom training nor through the formal procedures of a community consultative group, but calls instead for a design which cuts across some of the conventional categories of institutional provision and response.

Background

It was with such considerations in mind that the author was pleased to be invited in 1987 to develop a programme of work along these lines in a division of the Metropolitan Police serving a multi-racial population in an inner-city area of north London. The division was that of Tottenham, in the London Borough of Haringey, and it included (as one small part of its area) the Broadwater Farm Estate, the scene of a major disturbance in 1985.

At the time, the author was on the staff of the Centre for the Study of Community and Race Relations at Brunel University, an independent specialist support unit set up by the Home Office in the wake of the Scarman Report to assist police forces nationally in the development of the community and race relations aspect of training (Oakley, 1989, 69-72). Moreover, the approach was made through the Metropolitan Police Training School at Hendon, and for these reasons the author conceived of the programme of work as a 'training initiative'.

The divisional commander's view of what was required was more specific than, and slightly different from, this. Keen to improve police-community relations on the division, he was concerned for local police managers to meet with members of the local community in order to 'learn what police officers were doing wrong'. More than this, however, he was seeking what he called a 'double exposure': for the public to learn more about the police, as well as the other way around. Among his own officers, a particular concern was to give those from outside London (a majority in the Metropolitan force as a whole) an opportunity to get to know Londoners better, especially those from ethnic groups with which they might not have been previously familiar.

He had also just introduced a scheme for 'sector policing' on the division, whereby each of the four 'relief' teams (among which rotate the three daily shifts) would take 'geographic responsibility' for one of the four 'sectors' of the division, and he wished to bring the officers of each relief into closer relationship with members of the community on their own 'patch'. All these objectives might seem closer to the idea of 'consultation' than to the idea of 'training'. However, the training concept was also present if only due to pressures from outside. In the first place, the Metropolitan Police had recently decentralised its training strategy, allocating greater responsibility and resources for training provision to divisional level. Secondly, the Report of the Broadwater Farm Enquiry had advocated improved training for local police officers (Gifford, 1986; see also Gifford, 1989, p26). The challenge therefore was to meet training objectives within a format appropriate to divisional circumstances and needs.

The role of the author was agreed from the start to be that of consultant on the design of the programme and of facilitator of the meetings or events to be held. The police view was that, given the history of police-community relations in the locality, strong feelings could be aroused and expressed at such meetings, and if learning by police participants was to be achieved, independent facilitation of the group process in the meetings was essential. Although not professionally trained as a facilitator, the author had considerable experience of running such events in police and other professional contexts, and through experience of working with police officers and in community organisations (outside the local area) felt capable of empathising sufficiently with participants from both of the intended groups.

General Strategy

The strategy eventually adopted for meeting requirements at the local level involved a three-stage programme of meetings between police and invited members of the local community, involving Inspectors, Sergeants and Constables in succession. The general aim of these meetings was defined as: "To promote awareness and understanding of each others' perceptions of problem areas in police-community relations, with a view to enhancing police service to the public within the local area".

All Inspectors on the division, whether managers of sector policing teams or in other posts, were involved first, in a set of two workshops organised on a divisional rather than sector basis. Subsidiary aims here were to establish commitment to the principles of the programme, familiarity with the approach and confidence in its utility.

Sergeants were involved next, not simply as rank-holders, but together with their own 'relief' Inspector as members of the sector management team. Four such meetings were organised on a sector basis, with community members and locations drawn from within the team's own area. Subsidiary aims were to promote knowledge and awareness specific to the sector, and to enhance the commitment of the management team as a group to a service- and community-oriented approach.

While the first two stages have already been carried out, the third stage, involving police constables from each relief, is currently in process of implementation. Apart from being restricted to constables, the design is flexible, with Inspectors as sector managers undertaking primary responsibility for identifying the most appropriate means to advance the broad goal.

Format of Meetings

The initial format, employed in the two Inspectors' meetings, was that of a one-day workshop, led by the independent facilitator. Although training aims were implicit, the day was not designed according to a conventional training format, and the facilitator gave no direct instruction nor offered substantive expertise. The facilitator's role was simply to assist communication and mutual learning between police and community participants, and manage the group process. However, since one of the aims of the divisional commander in setting up the programme was to enhance the awareness by local officers of the concerns of the community, a consultative aspect was clearly present. In these circumstances, the author advised that the involvement and commitment of community members would be enhanced if a role could be offered that went beyond simply 'expressing concerns' in one-way communication, and allowed police officers and community members to work jointly to suggest practical ways of enhancing police-community relations that could be implemented directly and locally. The workshops were accordingly designed in such a way as to include achieving a set of such suggestions as an explicit objective. Training and local consultative functions were therefore integrated within a single design.

Each Inspectors' workshop thus brought together half of the divisional Inspectors (5 in each case) and invited members of the local community. The intention was to keep numbers sufficiently small for participants to interact on a personal rather than a collective basis, and to maximise the opportunity for interpersonal interaction by having police and community members work together in pairs. The aim therefore was to obtain an equivalent number of participants from the local community. In practice, circumstances ensured that numbers proved difficult to balance, and in most cases slightly more community participants than police were present at the meetings, requiring a corresponding flexibility in workshop design.

The workshop programme was therefore planned to meet these various requirements, and involved the following sequence. After personal introductions (with police introducing community members and vice versa), the divisional commander made a brief presentation to explain why he wished to hold the workshop, and what he hoped to achieve, after which he withdrew from the workshop proceedings. Police and community participants were then given a brief opportunity to work separately in order to share and then formally list their respective concerns. The intention here was to achieve awareness and ownership of the general differences (as well as similarities) in police and public perceptions of policing issues, and also to allow the community participants (who, unlike the police officers, had usually not previously met) to get to know one another a little and gain in confidence as a group.

The middle stage of the proceedings then involved police and community participants working together in twos (or threes) discussing issues of mutual concern, with the aim of identifying both the reasons for any differences in points of view, and the potential for common ground on which a way forward could be based. Where time allowed, participants would change partners in order to extend personal contacts and to discuss other issues of concern.

Finally, participants reconvened as a group, to report back on their deliberations, and to discuss, and where possible agree, on practical suggestions for improving police service to the public and police-community relations. The intention was for participants by this stage to be able to understand better and respect both differences and similarities in police and community viewpoints, and to be able to explore the merits of different practical suggestions as individual members of the group as a whole rather than as members of separate categories in conflict with one another. Shortly before concluding, the divisional commander then rejoined the workshop in order to hear the practical suggestions and give initial comment, to be followed by more detailed consideration subsequently. Participants were later informed by letter what action had been taken on the suggestions made.

The format for subsequent stages has followed similar lines but has been deployed more flexibly, and adapted to the need to hold evening meetings to draw in an adequate cross-section of members of the local community.

The format for the second stage, of meetings primarily for Sergeants, was planned to follow the same workshop design, but with the relief Inspector responsible for the geographical sector taking charge of organising the meeting and acting as its sponsor (in place of the divisional commander) during the proceedings. These second stage meetings fulfilled the divisional commander's original concept precisely, in that community participants were always drawn from those residing or working in that particular geographical sector. These meetings therefore brought together the local police management team (of Inspector plus Sergeants) with representatives of the public they directly serve. However, although two of the four such meetings successfully deployed the full one-day workshop programme, it soon became clear that day-time events were not succeeding in drawing the representative cross-section of the public that was desired.

The fourth meeting of this stage was therefore re-scheduled as a three-hour evening workshop (running from 6 pm to 9 pm), which proved far more successful from the point of view of local community participation. Despite its shorter duration, the workshop still retained its essential structure: viz. identification of issues (though in the group as a whole), followed by pair discussions, and concluding in plenary with a report back and identification of practical ways forward.

This evening format now constitutes the basic model for third stage meetings involving officers of constable rank. Flexibility, however, is likely to be needed, as for example in the planned scheduling of a day-time meeting with students at a local further education establishment.

Location and Selection of Participants

From the start it was accepted by all parties that the location for the workshops should be away from and independent of police premises. Locations used have consisted mainly of church halls and community centres. Finding appropriate locations has not proved difficult, despite the requirement of kitchen facilities and of seating sufficiently comfortable to be conducive to an informal and relaxed atmosphere. From the second stage onwards, locations have always been within the sector area.

The selection of participants has at all stages been undertaken by police, though with the advice on criteria for selection from the facilitator. Three such criteria have guided the selection of participants for invitation. The first is that participants should attend as individuals, and not as official representatives of organisations or groups. This is in accordance with the emphasis placed on personal interaction within the workshop design, as described above. The second is that participants as a set should be representative of the various groups present in the local population as a whole. Obviously with such small numbers this is only feasible to a modest degree, but the criterion requires participation by those of different age-group and sex, as well as of the main ethnic groups present in the locality. The third criterion is that the individuals should be willing to be both critical and constructive in their approach: critical in that informed judgements on current policing practice are required, and constructive in that the workshop aims are to promote learning and identify practical ways forward.

No great difficulty appears to have been found in identifying appropriate members of the local community to meet these requirements. Some nervousness was apparent initially at senior management level about the risk involved in inviting those who have expressed negative criticisms, but due to the support of successive Community Liaison Officers and the positive experience of the first workshop, such concerns appeared soon to have evaporated. Indeed, the concern of many police participants (as is noted below) has been that the selection of community participants has not been sufficiently adventurous to make the most of the opportunity provided. This was perhaps less justified in the case of the Inspectors' workshops, where the community participants were drawn from a wide range of groups and organisations active across the division as a whole. Where the workshops have been sector-based, the pool has been smaller, and greater emphasis has been placed in bringing in residents known to Home Beat Officers as opposed to those working in the borough in a professional or voluntary capacity. It is here that the restrictions imposed by day-time meetings proved most disadvantageous, since so many residents were excluded from potential participation by their domestic responsibilities or by employment elsewhere. The use of evening sessions is intended to overcome this limitation on adequate community participation.

Briefing by the facilitator on the aims and style of the workshop was planned for both police and community participants prior to the event taking place. While this appeared to be found useful by the community participants (who were usually strangers to one another), it proved difficult to arrange for this group and was not continued subsequent to the initial stage of Inspectors' workshops. Responsibility for briefing of community members thus passed to the divisional Inspectors. Prior contact with and briefing for police participants by the facilitator was continued (so far as police duties permitted) in advance of all of the meetings.

Participants' Evaluation

The workshops were subject to a formal evaluation which was conducted by means of a short questionnaire sent to participants shortly after the workshop had been held. Given the differences between the workshops it would not be valid to aggregate the statistical results as a whole, and indeed in some respects the judgements differed substantially from case to case.

In all workshops, however, the tendency was for the workshop to be judged 'fairly successful' in achieving its overall aim, though on the police side there were some who judged negatively in this respect. Views were more positive so far as the specific aim of increasing mutual awareness and understanding was concerned, but sometimes less so (particularly among police participants) as regards the aim of producing practical suggestions. Although most police officers found the production of suggestions constructive (and some have indeed been acted upon), there was a tendency to express cynicism that such suggestions were uninformed and had been heard many times already.

Comments from community participants tended to welcome the holding of such dialogue at all, even though there was some scepticism (or at best suspended faith) as to whether the suggestions would be taken seriously. Community participants also expressed satisfaction with the opportunity to learn more about policing, and to discover that police officers beneath the uniform were also fellow human beings.

The format of the workshop generally met with firm approval, chiefly for the opportunity it provided for personal contact. There was some negative criticism from both police and community members, however, of the practice of having each group work separately at an early point, this being felt to be divisive in its effect. Where whole-day workshops were run, this session was retained for reasons already given, but where a shorter period was used, this session has been dropped.

The representativeness of participants was judged differently from workshop to workshop, though (as noted above) a general feeling was that the selection of participants could benefit from being more adventurous. The absence of young people from the local area was the main concern of both police and community participants, an issue that is currently being addressed at the third stage. Women participants from the community also expressed concern on occasions when no woman officer was present on the police side.

The style of facilitation of the workshop was generally seen as appropriate and successful, especially among community participants who had experience of similar events. Some police officers expressed disappointment that there had not been any 'expert' input, but younger officers familiar with facilitative and student-centred learning styles appeared happy and at ease with the approach adopted.

Finally, all participants (with very rare exceptions, solely among police officers) expressed firm support for the continuation and extension of the initiative, and expressed willingness to participate further in it. There was a widespread view (especially among community participants) that the programme should draw in other police officers on the division, and especially those new to the area and all those working directly on the street.

Concluding Observations

Similar initiatives to this programme of police-community workshops may have taken place elsewhere, though none to the author's knowledge with the particular aims, level and format described above. Within the Metropolitan Police District and elsewhere, formal consultative groups are of course well established, but quite apart from their different geographical level, they are different in aim and format as well. On the training side, a recent Metropolitan Police initiative at the Peel Centre bears some comparison, whereby under the 'Reciprocal Training Scheme' members of different social groups and associations participate jointly in role-plays and discussions with new recruits as part of their initial training (Community Involvement Unit, 1989). While this scheme is close in spirit to that described above, and complements it, it is very different again in its format and context.

Focussing instead on the local level and on operational policing, the holding of 'surgeries' by Home Beat Officers in certain areas of London has similarity to some degree with the consultative aspect of the initiative just described. Where some form of neighbourhood or sector policing is in operation, a 'sector forum' or equivalent meeting may be regularly held by the sector Inspector (eg Safe Neighbourhood Unit, 1987). Although such meetings may successfully bring the communication process down to local or neighbourhood level, they still retain a strictly consultative format, with police likely to be in total control. The training aspect and some degree of independence are both absent.

It is the combination of training and consultative functions, operating at the local level, and with a degree of independence from full organisational control, that jointly make the initiative described above distinctive in character. The initiative seeks to move forward into an area where structured learning is not just about the community, nor simply with the community, but from the community and on a community base. From this perspective, training and consultation merge and become indistinguishable, both being seen as an active learning process essential for any profession (or agency) that aspires to serve the public's needs. 'Learning from the community' therefore needs to be adopted as a basic principle for any public-service organisation, and structured in appropriate ways that can best turn into practice this ideal.

The extent to which the present initiative implements such a principle is limited to say the least, and for a number of reasons. In the first place, whatever the kind of service involved, a balance must always be found between the requirements of professionalism and professional responsibility, and the needs and demands of the client group. Professional responsibility includes the responsibility to ensure and manage learning, and in this sense it is perfectly appropriate that 'learning from the community' should be to some degree professionally or organisationally controlled. The fact that the initiative described above is police-initiated and -managed, therefore, is not necessarily an obstacle, but may be seen as a virtue instead.

The key issue is how far the organisation is in control of the process, and how far power is shared by the professionals with the public they serve. From this perspective, 'learning from the community' needs to take the form of a partnership between the two groups - two groups in a relationship which has always a potential for conflict as well as for common interest.

The need for some kind of facilitation or mediation of this learning process is therefore inherent whatever the agency or professional group. Partnership, however, is a relationship between equals, and police-community relations are relations of a different order. 'Learning from the community' in the policing context is therefore bedevilled not just by the history of police and community experience, but by the constitutional inequality between the two sides. Much as police seek to pursue a service ethos, their duty to the Crown is to enforce the law, and to this degree their role is neither as partner nor 'servant' of the local community. The inequality experienced and perceived in this relationship by the population of multi-racial inner-city areas such as Tottenham only highlights the significance of the dimension of power.

Key issues around the accountability of the police arise at this point, and cannot be elaborated here. For present purposes it must suffice to say that initiatives such as that described above may be limited in their capacity to realise the principle of 'learning from the community' when as yet so little influence over the learning process, and the uses to which such learning is put, lies in community hands. If 'learning from the community' is to become effective, then community involvement in the design, management and subsequent use of such learning needs to be increased up to at least 'partnership' level in appropriately institutionalised ways. This was in large part the message of the Police Training Council Working Party Report on Community and Race Relations Training for the Police (P.T.C., 1983), a view endorsed strongly by community participants in the workshops in their response to the evaluation questionnaire. The present type of initiative is undoubtedly a positive step forward in this direction, even though it is still in a developmental stage. To maximise its potential will require time, and progress also on other fronts. If the workshop format and an idea such as 'learning from the community' are truly to reflect an ethos of partnership and public service within the police organisation, then they will need to be supported by power-sharing initiatives in other appropriate spheres and levels as well. Both facilitation and mediation will be needed to play a key role in any such developmental process.

Acknowledgements

The author would like to thank Ch.Supt.Graham Mathias and Ch.Insp.Roger Outing for their assistance in setting up the initiative in Tottenham, and Ch.Supt. Dick Stacey for providing the opportunity to carry out the programme and for continued support. Views and judgements expressed in the article are the author's own.

References

COMMUNITY INVOLVEMENT UNIT (1989) *The Metropolitan Police Reciprocal Training Scheme*. Hendon: Metropolitan Police Training School.

GIFFORD, LORD (chair) (1986) *The Broadwater Farm Enquiry: Report of the Independent Enquiry into the Disturbances of October 1985 at the Broadwater Farm Estate, Tottenham*. London: Karia Press.

(1989) *Broadwater Farm Revisited: Second Report of the Independent Enquiry into the Disturbances of October 1985 at the Broadwater Farm Estate, Tottenham*. London: Karia Press.

JOINT CONSULTATIVE COMMITTEE (1990) *Operational Policing Review*. London: Police Federation.

LEVI, M AND JONES, S (1985) Public and police perceptions of crime seriousness in England and Wales. *British Journal of Criminology*, 25, 234-250.

OAKLEY, R (1989) Community and race relations training for the police: a review of developments. *New Community*, 16(1), 61-79.

(1990) *Policing and Race Equality in the Netherlands*. London: Police Foundation.

POLICE TRAINING COUNCIl (1983) *Community and Race Relations Training for the Police*. London: Home Office.

SAFE NEIGHBOURHOOD UNIT (1987) *Landsdowne Green Report*. London: Safe Neighbourhood Unit.

Chapter Nineteen

Managing Aggressive Behaviour: A Workshop

PAT SAWYER

TRAINING INITIATIVES is one of a number of programmes providing workshops in Britain for developing conflict resolution skills in the context of managing aggression, coping with stress, and so on. The workshops are designed for people who work in an environment where there is the possibility or probability that they will be under some physical and/or emotional attack.

The actual content of each workshop is dependent on the specific profession of individual participants and the needs of the group.

Between 15 and 20 is an optimum number. Go down as far as 12 and some participants might lose the option of selective anonymity from the rest of the group. Over 20 and it becomes more difficult to cater for individual needs that might emerge.

For many people, the subject of aggression and violence is an emotive and challenging area to explore. And the workshops are very much about exploration. Exploration of our pre-conceptions about ourselves, about other people and about how we all affect each other.

The participants with whom I work are professional carers, social workers, residential and day care personnel. Some are highly trained people, some trained many years ago when the 'aggressive scene' had a much lower profile. Yet others are totally untrained. They came into the work because they care about people who are dependent on others for help.

These might be the people who manage aggression and violence on a daily basis or they may have never had to confront a situation. The common denominator is their concern about their ability and/or confidence to manage an incident competently in a positive and safe manner for all concerned. And that's the basis of the work that I do with groups. I believe that, by gaining some understanding about the subject area and by exploring our own reactions to situations as well as looking at the behaviour of others, we become more equipped to manage the incident that we all hope will never happen.

The main underlying aim of any workshop is to develop the climate for open and free discussion. People are meant to feel safe to talk.

Theories

So where does the workshop start? Theories and definitions are always a good starting line. Pre-course handouts ask participants to think about, and relate to their own experiences, the major theories that abound. The main aim is to stimulate thinking and questioning. One lady I remember well said no, she had never been involved in an aggressive incident in her life. About half way through this session, she suddenly 'remembered' that her ex-husband had beaten her so badly that she had ended up in hospital twice. It was something that her mind had conveniently stored away. There have been many similar - if not so dramatic - occurrences.

The theories covered include:

1. Freud believed that aggression is INSTINCTIVE in all of us. It is a drive in the same way as sexuality is a drive. Freud went even further in his thinking to make distinct links between sexuality and aggression.
2. Albert Bandura led the theoretical following of those who believed that aggression is created out of SOCIAL LEARNING. We learn as small children to use aggressive responses to manipulate the environment around us. That learning process can then continue through childhood into adulthood.
3. FRUSTRATION is seen by some as being the major contributor to aggressive behaviour. While all frustration does not result in aggression, the theory suggests that all outbursts are preceded by frustration.
4. Avoidance of an unpleasant situation can lead to an aggressive incident. This can be seen as fitting into the AVERSION theory camp.

This session within the workshop is not designed to be informative about any particular theory and in no way attempts to look in any detail at any of them. It is meant to provide an overview.

Other aspects that can beneficially be linked into the theories are those such as the way in which personality and environmental factors can affect an individual situation. Expressive and Instrumental aggression is of interest to some groups of people and may provide another hook on which to hang an idea.

Given the fact that the workshops are anything from one to five days, it's necessary to provide some information and lots of pointers for future investigation.

Definitions

In some manner, an agreement on definitions needs to be reached at an early stage. What do we mean when we use terms like aggression, violence, conflict, abuse? We all hold pre-conceived ideas and concepts. Time needs to be spent on airing these notions and agreeing the use of terminology.

As citizens, it probably matters little that we talk glibly about the 'manager having an AGGRESSIVE approach' or about 'needing to be more AGGRESSIVE if they want to win the league'. As professionals who have the care of others firmly held in our hands, it matters very much how we use and misuse such terminology. This session develops a heightened awareness of the use of definitions within our thinking and within our subsequent responses and action.

The Model for Analysis

Having agreed that we are all talking the same language (if not the same dialect), the next stage of the workshop is to provide a framework on which to work and develop. The 'incident' is presented as going through a period of growth and decline.

Trigger and Build Up

The growth aspect looks at the period before the crisis where a trigger sets off the whole process of feeling at odds with the world, feeling wronged, aggrieved, angry. We all have such days but for those who, for whatever reason, have a predisposition towards aggression and/or violence to solve their problems, this trigger point might be the start of an irreversible road to a crisis. If allowed and encouraged to fester, the trigger point can grow out of all proportion and even get lost as the natural chemical reactions within our bodies begin to take over and we become more and more agitated.

During the workshop, I use video clips to encourage exploration of those aspects of our environment and our reactions to people that might inadvertently accelerate the build up to a crisis. One of the video clips allows us an insight into the thought patterns of a young lady who lives 'in care' before following her through a series of encounters with peer and staff members. The culmination is an 'unexpected' attack on one of the staff members. A different video shows the problems of a woman with two children and a pram in getting to a probation office that is situated on the first floor with no lift.

Such video clips are intended to stimulate thinking and discussion about that aspect of others' lives that we are not a party to. As professional carers, we may not be a party to it but we are often the recipient of the sudden, out of the blue, response to frustrations and/ or learnt behaviour that says "I will feel better if I expel my built up feelings on YOU". As previously suggested, there is a normal chemical reaction happening inside the person who is getting frustrated, angry, upset. It's the same reaction that happens when people get stressed. The result is that breathing becomes more shallow, the heart rate increases, tension builds up, in short, we are preparing for either running away from the situation or fighting it. In understanding that we will also have a similar response to the aggressor, we can begin to see ways of affecting the behaviour of others. (See section on stress management.)

Role play is used to demonstrate practically the different ways in which people who are highly agitated or angry can be defused, deferred, calmed. Participants are encouraged to explore different ways of approaching and talking to people. Given that the responses are genuine (or as near as possible during role play), this type of session can be an invaluable way for people to discover how their behaviour affects other people. An essential factor to note within these exercises, however, is the vulnerability of participants. They may be learning things about themselves that they did not previously know. And they may not necessarily be positive things. It is interesting that there is always a percentage of participants on every course who are very angry, uptight or aggressive in their general manner. Sometimes these people have been sent rather than having volunteered, which understandably adds to their potential anger and aggression.

The Crisis

If we have been unable to divert/defuse the build up, the crisis will occur. The analogy that I use within workshops is that of the pan of water on an electric cooker. The bubbling is gentle at first, getting more and more agitated until, finally, the lid is thrown off.

During this period, whether it is a physical or an emotional crisis, the role of the professional worker is to protect: protect the aggressor, anyone else in the vicinity and themselves. We don't sit and analyse where we've gone wrong while the water continues to boil over the top of the pan, we act in a way that will solve the immediate problem; we turn the heat off or remove the pan. We analyse what went wrong later. This is the approach that I advocate in the workshops. Manage the situation that you are confronted with in as safe and as controlled a manner as possible. You'll make mistakes; by removing the offending pan from the heat, you may spill the contents over you. Likewise, you may appear to aggravate rather than calm a situation that you are attempting to manage. The main pointers to follow relate to control. Maintain control over yourself, stay calm, don't act like a bull in a china shop. Take a split second to think of your alternatives for action. Even with the ill-fated pan of water, you've got two choices.

During this session within the workshop, we look at issues like personal space, methods of approach, the importance of relaxation (not tension). Where appropriate to the group, I also work through a practical workshop that demonstrates methods of restraining people that maximises the dignity and minimises the physical hurt that is given to the aggressor.

Recovery and Post-Crisis Periods

For working out a long term programme for the reduction of recurring incidents, this is probably the most relevant area.

To describe the recovery period and its effect, I'd like to go back to the pan of boiling water. Having reached the crisis, our way of management is to turn off the electricity. The contents don't suddenly stop moving. The heat is retained for quite a long time. Turn the electricity back on again and the contents will very soon be boiling again.

The same principles apply to the person who has been through a crisis. The feelings that led to the crisis don't just go away. They bubble and seethe near the surface for quite a long time. The timing will vary with the person and type of incident, but 45 minutes is average. During this period, people need to calm down, need space to allow their feelings and reactions to settle. Interject too soon and you're likely to set the bubbling off all over again.

Another vital point that we explore within the workshops is the fact that such reactions will be felt by everyone who is involved with the incident; other staff members, clients, the aggressor as well as the recipient of aggression.

Using video clips, discussion and role play, participants are asked to determine the type of support that is required for all involved both at this point and at the stage where everything has settled and people are beginning to feel a little foolish, upset, confused, hurt.

In the vast majority of cases, aggressors will have some reaction to their outburst. The time to support, counsel, question is during this post-crisis depression. This is the time for analysis and plans.

The importance of adequate support for staff cannot be stressed enough. The alternative could result in the loss of staff to sickness, burn-out or resignation.

Self Control

In looking at improving the management of aggression, we are probably looking at three distinct areas for change: the environment, other people and ourselves.

The environment in some cases could be relatively easy to change (the average social services or DHSS waiting room would benefit from some simple yet effective alterations). In other ways, the environment poses a major stumbling block.

A lot of time and resources are spent in changing the behaviour of others. Probably the easiest and most accessible change to make is within our own behaviour.

During the workshops, time is spent to some degree or another on issues like:

POWER AND CONTROL

How do we exert this over other people and how do they then react to you? Exercises are used to encourage participants to question this issue of power and control especially over those people who are less independent and/or able than ourselves.

STRESS MANAGEMENT

in ourselves is of vital importance. Long term strategies for the control of stress make us more relaxed and able to meet the difficult situation. 'First aid' strategies help us to remain calm and controlled during the crisis. Such techniques include breathing exercises, positive thinking, body checks.

ASSERTIVENESS

Assertiveness is a skill that is of great benefit in the management of aggression. Being assertive is having the ability to respect your own rights while acknowledging the rights of others. Other people have the right to be angry; they don't have the right to abuse the rights of others and neither do you.

ANGER MANAGEMENT

Anger management is about recognising the anger inside yourself and having the ability to retain control over that anger. As with a lot of instinctive reactions, the most important thing is to acknowledge its existence and recognise the onset.

ASSESSING THE RISK

Risk assessment is essential for those people in a caring and/or controlling situation. An immediate response to a crisis is commendable if it is the most beneficial action to take and if the resources match the demand. A large percentage of incidents, however, need an urgent but not necessarily immediate response. Minutes spent on assessing the risk and in thinking about and planning for it might make all the difference. The more we think about possible situations and of how we would theoretically manage those incidents, the better we are prepared for the real thing.

CREATIVE THINKING AND PROBLEM SOLVING TECHNIQUES

These are very important areas to explore for most groups of staff. Our thinking and therefore our ability to solve problems in a creative way, can be greatly inhibited by preconceptions, inaccurate interpretation of stimuli that we receive through our senses. This is a session to heighten awareness to the things that are misread or just missed on an everyday basis. We also look at practical implications of a range of problem-solving techniques that utilise creative thinking.

Summary

The main aims of the workshop are to develop a level of understanding and interest that will result in participants taking a new sense of awareness back to their work base: awareness of themselves, their reactions and their feelings; awareness about the environment in which they work and how that might affect behaviour. They should also develop some insight into the possible reasons for aggression and violence in others.

Awareness is an essential component but, on its own, has very little practical use for the professional who has to return to a work base and manage an aggressive incident. The workshops are also designed to provide a toolbox of skills that can be stored away until the appropriate time of use. It's not a complete toolbox. If a new job crops up, you might have to go out and acquire something totally new. But at least you have the basics. You probably have something in the box that will allow you to 'make do' until the more appropriate tool is acquired. You have contacts who might be able to assist with practical help or a confidence-boosting comment.

For those who are faced in their professional life with aggression and violence, there are a number of responses that they can develop over a long term period. They can become hard and present the 'macho image' of not really caring about being abused (it's all in the job!). They can develop a skill in avoiding any situation of conflict (someone else is more able to cope). They can leave the work all together and go and work in a less demanding job (it wasn't for me after all). Or they can develop skills to be competent and confident professionals who are well able to support and manage those people who, for whatever reason, use aggression and violence as part of the normal, regular repertoire of behaviour. The workshops aim at encouraging participants to develop those skills and the confidence to use the skills to their maximum benefit.

Recommended Reading

BANDURA, A (1973) *Aggression : A Social Learning Analysis*. Englewood Cliffs, N J: Prentice Hall.

BREAKWELL, GM (1989) *Facing Physical Violence*. BPS Books.

DOLLARD, J et al (1939) *Frustration and Aggression*. New Haven, Conn: Yale University Press.

KAPLAN, SG and WHEELER, E G (1983) *Survival Skills for Working with Potentially Violent Clients*. Social Casework.

STORR, A (1968) *Human Aggression*. Penguin Books.

SECTION VI:

OPENING THE DOOR

TONY MARSHALL

Chapter Twenty

The Analysis of Social Conflict

CONFLICT CAN be seen as just another way of saying "I cannot get along without you". If we can get what we want without someone else's help, then there is no conflict.

This is the most important fact about conflict, and when people get caught up in it, this is the first thing they tend to forget. As Kreisberg (1982) says, "...social conflicts are social relationships. This means that at every stage of conflict the parties interact socially; each party affects the way the others act, not only as each responds to the others but also as each may anticipate the responses of the others. Even the ends each party seeks are constructed in interaction with adversaries."

It is a universal feature of social relationships that no-one can exercise complete control. However complete physical dominance may be, there is always some option remaining to the other party that may frustrate the first's intentions - if only something as extreme as suicide. In German-occupied Norway during World War II, the degree of defiance embodied in nonviolent resistance was quite remarkable and completely undermined the authority of the Quisling government. To continue with Kreisberg's (1982) remarks: "...no one party determines the outcome of any conflict. As any group pursues its aims, they are modified in interaction....The outcome embodies new elements unanticipated by any side....Many other social forces and processes help shape [outcomes], including nonconflicting aspects of the relations."

The fact that lack of control is especially obvious in conflict situations is one of the most frightening aspects for those involved or merely observing. Emotion runs high and reduces control even more in a vicious spiral of confrontation. However,

> If you can keep your head when all about you
> Are losing theirs and blaming it on you,
> If you can trust yourself when all men doubt you,
> But make allowance for their doubting too;

> If you can wait and not be tired by waiting,
> Or being lied about, don't deal in lies,
> Or being hated, don't give way to hating,
> And yet don't look too good, nor talk too wise:"
>
> (Rudyard Kipling "In the Neolithic Age")

then each party is far from being completely powerless and at the mercy of every wind of change. Because conflict is a relationship, "...every conflict unit can influence what its adversary seeks and how the adversary goes about getting it. Hence we can shape our own enemies." (Kreisberg, 1982).

Complexity may daunt, old memories haunt, and present fears taunt, but the motility of conflicts allows each party considerable scope for intervening unilaterally to divert the process, whether to escalate or placate. As Fisher and Brown (1989) have recently argued, one can pursue a relationship from one side. One cannot, of course, guarantee that the other side will respond, but one can ensure whether or not the conditions are favourable for such a response if it will come. The door to negotiations can always be left open. Rapprochement can always be on offer. It would be unusual if such conditions did not affect decision-making by the other side, and thus the first step has been taken towards regaining order and control - control not by any particular party but mutually agreed structure, which is the only form of control in a relationship. Not only is such action always a possibility, it is also a responsibility. Order (on the right terms) is the ultimate goal of all groups, and none can attain even their immediate aims without the eventual cooperation of those with whom they share their conflicts. Simply for the sake of their own interests, therefore, they have a responsibility to seek a collaborative, negotiated solution, as long as conditions make more or less equal participation feasible.

This book is about the opening of doors to such solutions. The results cannot be predicted - nothing can in social action - but the previous chapters have given instances of the success of many well-considered and well-intentioned attempts at opening doors. One thing can be guaranteed: if the door is not open, no-one will have access. As Waddington et al (1989) observe: "Our evidence and other studies provide examples of moments when leaders of police or protestors seek to make contact with the other side to defuse the situation. For example, concessionary gestures by the police, such as the release of an arrested person, can de-escalate conflict. But if either or each side issues ultimata, then one side has to choose to resist or back down. This is rarely achieved without the occurrence of disorder".

Conflict Analysis

The open door is one aspect of the first and most basic principle of conflict resolution: OPENNESS. Openness implies being ready to receive new information, a "willing suspension of disbelief", dispassionate evaluation of one's own and others' positions and interests, taking time to analyse rather than surrendering to instinctive gut-reaction, acting without moral judgement of others, being flexible in one's stance, and attentive to innovative ideas for settlement. Such an attitude not only allows one to make conscious rational decisions on the basis of one's own real interests, but also encourages others to do the same. Few people can kill or injure in cold blood. Violence is a product of the unthinking moment, of strong emotions, pent-up frustrations, the exultation of the crowd's surge, or fear. Let them pause, give them hope, give them trust, and few will not be grateful for the chance to reconsider. Only do so insincerely, cynically, and for short-term advantage only, and one just as assuredly increases the violence of the next episode. "By and large," Nieburg (1968) says "all violence has a rational aspect ... The 'rational' goal of the threat of violence is an accommodation of interests, not the provocation of actual violence. Similarly, the 'rational' goal of actual violence is demonstration of the will and capability for action, establishing a measure of the credibility of future threats, not the exhaustion of that capability in unlimited conflict."

Openness means being honest and committed to the search for a pragmatic solution. Most basically of all, openness means facing up to the fact that there is conflict and that one is involved: "It seems to me that people should not deny the existence of conflicts or seek to end all of them, since such efforts are often refusals to recognise the interests of other groups." (Kriesberg, 1982.)

Analysing a conflict is not an easy or straightforward task. If one is a party, or has some social connection with the parties, it may seem that one's interests are clear. But this is rarely so - aims tend to be confused with "positions" (ie the state one wants to attain is identified with one of many possible means of reaching it); one's conscious aims tend to be complex blends of unconsidered prejudices, subconscious desires, mistaken assumptions, and suggestions by others, as well as real interests. It takes an effort of both will and imagination to disentangle all these and to see clearly where one's interests really lie. In the heat of conflict one may easily assume that one's over-riding aim is winning the present battle, when it is in fact finding a satisfactory ending of the war. Or the need to "save face", to give vent to emotions, may be temporarily dominant, when this has nothing to do with one's practical intentions and may well hinder or destroy them. In previous chapters we have seen how "trigger" incidents (or "precipitating factors" if we use the term of Smelser, 1963) may give rise to overt conflict which really relates to quite separate long-standing grievances. The tendency is to see the conflict in limited terms, as being about the trigger incident only, so that efforts at resolution are confined to these narrow issues - usually, in the context of public disorders, ones of police policy, methods and training. But the real conflict is still there, unaddressed because it passes beyond anything the police or any other of the parties involved can resolve alone (general racial discrimination, unemployment rates in particular areas, etc). However superhuman the efforts of police at being controlled, understanding and "professional", mistakes will happen and will trigger public unrest again. Indeed, the more reliance placed on policing as a solution, the more oppressive the social circumstances of the aggrieved become, and the greater the scale of disorder when it does erupt.

It is not sufficient, moreover, to be able to know what one's real interests are, and to be able to keep hold of these throughout the series of decisions one has to make about handling the conflict. One must also obtain some idea of the real interests and intentions of other parties. In a conflict situation this is not easy because each party tends to erect a "smokescreen", or even to resort to deliberate disinformation, in order to obtain some imagined "advantage" in the struggle. I say "imagined" because lack of trustworthy information is a decided disadvantage to any party that wants to achieve a satisfactory resolution. One of one's own aims is easily forgotten in conflict - the need to be able to live in peace with the other party after the dispute. If one can keep hold of the fact that the relationship - in some form (it may simply be the terms for communicating or sharing family responsibilities after a divorce) - is necessary and is part of the conflict, one can more easily divine both one's own real interests and those of other parties. By putting oneself in the role of the other party, one can get a clearer picture of what they want - often better than the one they have themselves. But just as one has to abstract one's instinctive emotions to see one's own aims clearly, so one must be able to abstract one's prejudices and preconceptions of "the others" in understanding them. Prejudices are not simply bad in themselves - they are also not in one's own interest in comprehending the reality of others. Without this understanding one cannot predict their reactions and therefore cannot devise sensible strategies of one's own.

In social conflicts (ie conflicts that involve more than two individuals) the analysis of interests can be extremely complex. Even identification of all the relevant parties can be difficult. Groups exhibiting a united front may in fact be divided into any number of different interest groups. Sometimes these divisions are wider than those between the opposing factions and it is the rivalry within the groups which keeps the factions from discovering their common interests. Failure to identify all the parties, or the conflict within groups, can leave the process of rational conflict resolution open to sabotage - for instance, if in creating consultative mechanisms between the police and a local community one only involves those members of either group who are willing to volunteer to participate. Such consultation will only involve a part of the totality of interests, issues and positions and any agreements can easily be sabotaged by those who feel unrepresented. Lack of participation - even by choice - may leave such parties feeling that sabotage is, indeed, the only weapon left to make their voices known.

One needs to know, also, the type of issue that is predominant. Aubert (1963) distinguishes between consensual and dissensual issues. Consensual ones involve disagreement on objective matters of "distribution" - who has more or less of a proper share of goods equally valued by all. Dissensual issues involve fundamental differences in norms, values and beliefs between the parties. The distinction is important because consensual issues can be resolved, potentially, by compromise or appeals to commonly held values of justice or fairness. Dissensual issues are usually not at all responsive to such approaches. Resolution of these is a matter of increasing understanding and tolerance, building lines of communication and agreement on forms of relationship. Consensual issues can be resolved relatively quickly and the conflict dissolved in a short time - eg a contractual dispute between two commercial companies, a boundary dispute between neighbours, a dispute over rights to the use of water from a river that passes through a number of independent states. Some consensual issues, however, occur in the context of deep-seated conflict involving dissensual issues as well. The latter may interfere with what on the surface appears to be a straightforward resolution process, although success in solving the more limited dispute can contribute to the building of relationships of respect, trust and understanding needed to resolve the more dissensual issues. In the context of "race riots", the trigger incident is usually a factual, consensual dispute with a limited number of parties; the typical dissatisfaction with social conditions is in part a further consensual issue, but one that involves social policy generally and therefore an indefinite array of potential parties; but the feelings of injustice or of discrimination, and clashes of life-style, relate to dissensual issues that pertain to relations between major social groups. Each of these issues requires a different strategy for resolution, but each strategy needs to interrelate with the others if lack of progress on one problem is not to spoil success in other aspects.

Phases of Conflict Resolution

The achievement of openness depends on confidence. It is difficult to maintain such an attitude to conflict if one is unsure of one's own position, if there are major divergences of opinion within one party, or if one does not trust the other party. In this the parties can assist one another by being clear and assertive, but not aggressive, in stating their case, and attentive and affirming in receiving that of others. From a rational standpoint there would seem to be little to be lost in doing so. In practice, it is unlikely that one or the other side will initiate such an exchange, and it is often up to third parties to facilitate more effective communication - by playing the part of an intermediary, or by training one or several parties in the techniques of controlling violence and setting the conditions for constructive resolution. When the conflict is complex, as most social conflict is, an intermediary may also be needed to identify and contact all relevant parties and to begin constructing the process of consultation.

The role of mediator at this stage, can be particularly helpful in working through the emotions and tensions, which will initially be intense and obstructive. Rational discussions cannot proceed until the level of feeling has been reduced to manageable levels by the provision of means of expression and of communicating emotions between the parties without at the same time increasing their sense of threat or confrontation. What has to be conveyed is the existence of such emotions and their relevance to solving the problem, giving them legitimacy while separating them from "blame" or "accusation" which involve judgements. The parties must be able to differentiate upset, which is legitimate, from hatred, which is unhelpful, because the first is capable of being received, understood and respected by other parties, while the second of course is not. Attention needs always to be paid to the emotional level of a conflict, which may rise and fall several times over the course of consultation, and deliberate efforts must be made to release tension periodically. There is a natural tendency towards escalation in inner feelings that is never easy to stem. Once a party has resorted to a particular technology - eg the use of firearms - for the first time, it is always easier to employ them again a second time. Thus we find a gradual building up of an arsenal of technical aids by the police (see Sally Sadler's chapter), first used in desperation but subsequently becoming more and more conventional unless deliberate policies of restriction are adopted. The same process occurs among oppositional community groups, with even fewer possibilities for exerting control.

Once the emotional temper of the debate has subsided, it is unusual for consultation not to lead to the discovery of some common ground. Such shared interests are virtually synonymous with the existence of a relationship which, as we have seen, conflict implies. Continuing violence and disorder is one thing virtually all parties will share an interest in avoiding (this was the basis for mediating in the Fresno example described in Chapter 14). Platt (1987) quotes Dolly Kiffin, one of the local leaders in the Broadwater Farm estate, London, where a serious riot occurred in October 1985, as saying "We didn't want a riot then, and we don't want one now. We just want to get on with building up our community and creating jobs." And, of course, every other party - the police, other groups of residents - could equally well have expressed such sentiments. What was lacking was any realisation that such feelings were shared, that major disruptions could occur without any of the major groups involved wanting them to. Platt also quotes another lady who addressed the platform at a Broadwater Farm Defence Campaign press conference: "The police want a riot. You people want a riot. We don't - we live here." Such perceptions - that one's own side only has just and peaceful intentions, and that the others do not share them - are typical, but often completely erroneous. They reflect the realisation that, in attempting to further their own interests, some groups may take actions that make violent confrontation more likely, but fail to recognise that such confrontation is not necessarily what they want.

When one has moved a dispute through the stages of consultation, ventilation of feelings, exchange of information and discovery of common ground, the process of collaboration on resolving the real issues can begin, in conjunction with the process of increasing respect and understanding. This is the problem-solving stage which will largely be carried forward by the parties themselves, and will need to be if it is to be successful. Neutral intermediaries may still, however, be of assistance in helping remove "mental blocks" by brainstorming alternative solutions, facilitating round-the-table conferences when a substantial number of different parties are involved, assisting groups that are having difficulty resolving internal differences, finding acceptable representatives to speak on behalf of unorganised parties, and attending to hiccups in the process when emotions threaten again to get the upper hand.

Such is the theory! If only we were all saints.... But we are not, and not everyone is going to be well-intentioned. A realistic policy has to confront the possible failures and the very probable obstacles. The rest of this chapter will be devoted to the problems encountered in applying the above principles, as manifested in real situations such as those described by several of the writers represented in this book. We shall do so in relation to three stages of conflict, in much the same way as Ian Beckett does in Chapter 10.

Stages of Conflict

Rubenstein (1988) distinguishes crisis resolution from longer-term processes. In the event of a crisis, a breakdown in public order, the immediate need is for a quick temporary settlement that will save lives and property. The above principles of conflict resolution apply only in a limited way, although intervention should be carried out in such a fashion as to minimise obstacles to later more systematic attempts to resolve the underlying problems. Action at this stage will be rapid, relatively coercive, with limited objectives and options. It takes the form of what may be termed "conflict management". It does not attempt to resolve the issues behind the confrontation (although it should be knowledgeable of, and sympathetic to, these), but will seek the achievement of sufficient practical order, the extinction of immediate threats of violence, and the calming of anger. It seeks, in other words, to establish a situation where consultation can take place. This phase is characterised by a primary police role, although in situations where the police themselves tend to be identified as one of the parties themselves (as in many of the inner city disorders discussed in this book) their natural role as order-restorers may be compromised by lack of community confidence. In such cases a mediating agency may have a crucial role to play, even at the crisis stage, as we have seen from descriptions of intervention by the American CRS. An agency such as this may be able to facilitate the restoration of order through the leadership resources of the community itself, with the police taking a less interventionist, containing role, while sufficient legitimacy is re-established for introduction of a uniformed presence (perhaps under agreed conditions mediated by the third parties). The early establishment of some form of communication and involvement is crucial for the second-stage process. Assefa and Wahrhaftig (1988) have documented the result of the total breakdown of police-community communications in one area of Philadelphia, when the authorities felt that their only way out was to bomb the residential neighbourhood occupied by a radical group (MOVE) practising an extreme "alternative" lifestyle. This was a truly lose/lose "solution" demonstrating that both sides always have a shared interest in maintaining communication and an open door to negotiation, however desperate the conflict (as Nelson Mandela's role in trying to resolve the conflict over South African apartheid has made abundantly clear).

When the crisis has been defused, one moves to a much longer stage of the process, attempting to analyse and reduce the issues in dispute (problem-solving proper). Some of the actions necessitated in the first "law and order" phase may make this process more difficult. Even if the police had not previously been a party to the conflict, they probably will be now. The requirement of quick, effective action may well have led to complaints of unnecessary police violence or action against "innocent" bystanders (which, from the police perspective, as Beckett notes, do not exist), such complaints as we see in Chapter 4, for instance. Two elements are crucial at this stage:

1. that the conflict should be squarely faced for what it is, and not swept under the carpet just because the critical threat has passed (ie openness). As Warfield remarks in Chapter 13, it is vital to move on from crisis-intervention to long-term resolution, a role which the CRS has espoused, although it has at times been restricted to a "fire-fighting" role alone. It is, however, pointless setting up countless firefighting organisations without providing resources for follow-up. The problem has not ended - it has

merely moved to a state where it can be tackled constructively.
2. that there should be an effective neutral intermediary presence to help resolve the tangled complex of parties and issues that will inevitably be involved in any major social upheaval, with particular attention to the need to re-establish feelings of trust and confidence that the parties unaided will find difficult to attain. It is especially important that the police are not seen to bear the primary responsibility for this phase, which involves skills and methods for which they neither have the training nor the resources, and which sits uneasily with their crime-prevention and crisis-intervention roles.

A third stage also needs to be differentiated. This is one of conflict prevention. Logically it should precede the other stages. Moreover, it is not a response to conflict at all. Nevertheless, even when there is no manifest conflict, it makes sense to be sensitive to the need to maintain good relationships among community groups and between them and statutory agencies, of which the police force is an important member. The measures that might be taken are generally similar to those that will be discussed under the second stage processes, but it is necessary to be aware of the need to proceed with such measures as a normal part of social life. All organisations and communities should have the capacity and the mechanisms for coping with conflict when it occurs. It is too easy to assume that, because one knows one is well-intentioned, that one will never come into conflict with other persons or groups. It is necessary to demonstrate those good intentions by paying attention to the needs and anxieties of others before they exhibit themselves in conflict. Conflict prevention is the most important stage of conflict resolution, but the one most often forgotten.

Chapter Twentyone

Crisis Intervention

IT IS not easy to draw up a precise definition of "disorder" or "crisis". One can, however, say that community disorder is likely to be characterised by:

1. Imminent threat (or actual occurrence) of bodily harm or damage to property;
2. Involvement of a "large" number of people (crowd);
3. A sense that emotions (anger, excitement, enthusiasm, desperation, aggression, fear) predominate over rationally planned activity;
4. A sense that events have moved beyond normal measures of control;
5. A recent occurrence that has stimulated widespread sense of grievance;
6. Unpredictability.

These features are largely subjective, so that in cases where a full-scale riot is not already in progress there is considerable scope for differences of opinion as to whether a situation is one of disorder or not. This is especially so in the run-up to a riot. When does an angry crowd milling around in a public space become a disorder? The Lambeth Consultative Group (Chapter 4) was critical of what they saw as a police failure to identify a nascent riot, but in other situations the police have been accused of over-precipitate reaction which was self-justifying by inflaming tempers and increasing participants' sense of threat or injustice, and thus causing events to get further out of hand. This has particularly happened on the occasion of mass picketing by strikers or of mass demonstrations, when some of the above features will generally be present (especially 2, 3, 5 and 6), and when it may seem to uninformed observers that events are beyond control when they are not (item 4) and a sense of threat may easily be imagined (item 1). One may think, for instance, of the militaristic police response in some years to the midsummer hippy convoys converging on Stonehenge. In Chapter 10, Ian Beckett adopts a technical definition of riot in essentially criminal terms, but other parties may well operate with other definitions.

There is no answer to the question of when disorder has actually begun, or when it is imminent. Therefore it is necessary to think in terms of continua rather than either/or situations. A possibility of disorder is always present, but usually to a trivial degree only. Normal police patrolling, relatively unobtrusive, hopefully unthreatening, is a sufficient response to the normal level of threat, especially if carried out with sensitivity to the need for maintaining positive community relations. As such a threat becomes more probable, so policing policy will also need to move up the scale of intensity and awareness (cf. Chapter 10). The crucial feature is not the increasingly active response, but the nature of that response. Normal community policing, as Ian Beckett argues in Chapter 10, should already have set up "antennae" among local residents that could relay information about critical events and give police, in conjunction with community leaders, a chance to take measures to calm emotions and prevent any actual breakdown. This sort of information exchange and consultative decision-making seemed to be lacking in the run-up to the 1985 Brixton riot, which might have been preventable by a few simple conciliatory responses. Understanding of the gravity of the situation, however, seemed to be lacking among local police during the few critical hours when preventive action might have been taken - or else the signs were ignored in the dangerous hope that the problem would just "go away" of its own accord. This was despite the positive moves that local police and community groups had made since the earlier riots in the area to normalise relationships and prevent just such a re-occurrence. What improvements there were in day-to-day police/community relations were not sufficient to bear up under more stressful conditions such as, in this case, a police shooting of a resident.

As Pat Sawyer says in Chapter 19, in a crisis there is no time for analysis or elaborate decision-making: there has to have been contingency planning for such events, so that the structure for action is already there and the major decisions already made about the type of policy to be adopted in various circumstances. The 1981 riots in London had led the MPD to carry out just such contingency planning, but in Brixton in 1985 it was learnt that even these plans were not foolproof - largely, I would suggest, because there was inadequate provision for community consultation under crisis conditions and no plans for the use of the community's own resources for control and pacification. In such an eventuality as this, where the police were implicated in the trigger event itself, it was crucial that they should be able to act through pre-established links and not offer themselves as direct targets. As Chapters 7, 8 and 10 show, the MPD has continued to refine its contingency planning in the light of experience, but the number of contingencies is so large that this is inevitably a gradual process.

In the case of Brixton, as in so many other cases here and in America, the police had in the end to respond to a situation already out of hand by means of the use of force and try to limit the spread of the conflagration. Once forced into such a policy, the police are essentially in a no-win position. The Lambeth Group in Chapter 4, for instance, claim that a cordon should have been established to prevent others (whether innocent bystanders or agitators wanting to augment the disorder) from swelling the numbers in the affected area, but Wallace Warfield's experience (Chapter 13) leads him to point out the danger that uninvolved residents of the riot area will thereby be trapped. In the Handsworth riots of 1985, police avoidance of the use of weaponry led "to complaints that they failed to protect the public", while "withdrawal...in an attempt to avoid provocation" was blamed for riots getting out of hand both there and in Tottenham in the same year (Waddington, 1987, p.43).

Constructive Policing During Crises

One may legitimately speculate whether any riot need occur if the right action is taken in the pre-riot phase, but even when order has finally broken down there are still options for the use of constructive techniques. As has already been stated, the right decisions are dependent on having adequate information and promoting the flow of this by making sure it is two-way. The police certainly seemed to have been cut off from adequate inside information in the 1985 Brixton case, but they could also have given out information (concerning the trigger event) which might have stemmed some rumours. Both Beckett and Warfield stress the role of rumour control in crisis situations.

Police confidence in their role and their capacities is typically low in crisis situations - leading many officers to be over-reactive and indiscriminate in the use of force. Advances have been made in training recently, as evidenced by several writers in this book, especially Chapter 18, but it is still nowhere near widespread or substantial enough to bolster the necessary action during episodes of disorder. Attempts to remove themselves from apparent blame, too, may result in denigration of some of the groups the police are facing - only adding fuel to the fire. Traditional resort (documented, eg, in Skolnick, 1969, and Platt, 1971) to the mythology of "agitators" (who are powerless without a situation already ripe for their demagogism) and pathological explanations (see Dave Ward, Chapter 16) is not helpful, and government pronouncements should also avoid the same trap. As the former Chief Constable, John Alderson (1984) states, "If we are to seek the cause of most disorder and violence in Britain over the last 15 years,...we must not look for a 'criminal fraternity'", and certainly the President's Commission (1967) seeking causes of the American race riots of the sixties were led to observe that "The studies show that the rioters were not preponderantly wild adolescents, hoodlums, racial extremists and radical agitators, as is sometimes asserted, although such people undoubtedly did take part." Public statements from agents of authority should avoid blaming and scapegoating, which merely serve to close the door to a negotiated settlement. Respect for the grievances of the rioting groups is essential if they are to be persuaded to use the negotiating table rather than the brick and bottle. Discrediting such highly-charged emotions can only heighten the sense of grievance and the perception that things can only be changed by force - because violence appears to be the only thing that the authorities will take seriously. It is not easy, however, in the front-line of riot control, to keep in mind these realities behind the situation, faced as the police often are by the most violent and extreme elements who are seeking confrontation, as one can see from reading Ian Beckett's account.

We have already discussed the need for collaboration with the community. Even at the height of a riot, only a minority of citizens will be actively involved in disorderly behaviour. There is always the possibility, therefore, of working through established community channels. Both Sadler (Chapter 9) and Warfield (Chapter 13) write about the use of stewards, the first in the context of demonstrations, to avoid having to use too close a uniformed presence that might provoke violence, the second in the context of rioting no-go areas from which the police may more appropriately withdraw as long as some means of re-asserting control can be established through accepted community members. Long-standing protest organisations like CND (Campaign for Nuclear Disarmament) in the United Kingdom have developed sophisticated stewardship policies and are able to prevent trouble by fringe groups (personal communication from Fran De'Ath). Key points on a march where trouble is likely should be actively targeted by stewards, who can be more effective than the police in diverting the excesses of breakaway groups because they can more readily be identified as being "on the same side" and are less likely to be themselves a target of violence. Such lessons had not, unfortunately, been learnt by the organisers of the poll tax protest march in central London on 31 March 1990, which passed by the obvious flashpoint of Downing Street (the Prime Minister's official residence), barriers across which were manned solely by police with no stewards present to help prevent groups actively seeking violent confrontation from trying to break through. The fighting and arson to which this eventually led could almost certainly have been contained by better planning and control by the march organisers in consultation with police.

In less desperate situations, as Ian Beckett stresses, it is important for local police to stay in place as long as possible, in a defensive/protective role. Especially where the police themselves are not a primary target - in clashes, say, between different ethnic groups or political factions - a police presence may be quite able to establish order as long as it can contrive to be non-threatening by the avoidance of weaponry and the use of officers known to the community in question. Platt (1987) notes that in Broadwater Farm, where the local police had made considerable efforts to fraternise with residents and work with them, familiar officers were quite acceptable to help quell disorder when there was, on the other hand, great resentment of "police specials" and "CID" drafted in from outside. The policing of the recent Miners' Strike also provided examples of the increasing militancy that results from the use of "stranger" forces from other parts of the country that have no natural ties with the communities being policed. Officers who know they are going to have to deal with the same persons later on, in normal everyday situations, are less likely to be tempted to the use of undue force, as well as having the confidence when dealing with familiar faces that they can cope by persuasion rather than coercion. One of the problems with using defensive armour (helmets, shields), even though they may be less provocative than weapons of attack (such as batons), is, Sadler points out in Chapter 9, that they can disguise even those officers who might be known and depersonalise the police force in such a way as to make an aggressive response easier. Waddington (1987, p.41) argues that such defensive technology may reduce fear on the part of police officers and hence give them confidence to reduce their use of force, but it may be that the measures above provide a better, and more realistic, means of raising confidence. Similarly, where part of the problem is racial, the use of black police in predominantly black areas may be less inflammatory, Warfield suggests in Chapter 13, although this is not currently a realistic option in Britain, where black recruitment to the police has been so limited. There is also a tendency, given that there are so few black police officers, for them to be rejected even by their own communities as "Uncle Toms" who have sold out to the "other side", a situation which will only change through the recruitment of much higher numbers.

At the crisis stage in any conflict the main aim must be to cool the emotional temperature, which takes the situation beyond the application of rational problem-solving appeals. The experience of policing demonstrations in West Germany has led Ruckriegel (1986) to conclude that "...there is a considerable connection between police intervention and use of violence....If police, the judicial administration, and politicians show a problem-conscious attitude, this nearly always has a violence-reducing effect, whereas undifferentiated harsh actions on the part of executive organs and judicial administration regularly lead to solidarization and increase the preparedness to use violence." Thompson (1979) describes a case where a jury in 1833 was even led to return a verdict of "justifiable homicide" in the case of a police constable killed in a riot on the grounds that the situation had been improperly managed, explaining their decision in these words: "We find a verdict of justifiable homicide on these grounds - that no Riot Act was read, nor any proclamation advising the people to disperse; that the government did not take the proper precautions to prevent the meeting from assembling; and that the conduct of the police was ferocious, brutal and unprovoked by the people...".

A primary aim for police forces, even when having to intervene to protect people and property, must therefore be to respond to the demonstration of hurt that motivates the disorder. We have already referred to the avoidance of denigration in order to show respect for such grievances. The minimisation of the use of force and coercion will also help to defuse the crisis (cf. Marx, 1970; Boskin, 1976) - to the point of temporarily suspending some kinds of intervention that would otherwise be normal practice: eg action against trade in drugs or against noisy parties. Effective control over behaviour which is formally illegal but widespread in the community can only be carried out through well-established community relations in any case (see Yvonne Craig on war-time Bermondsey, Chapter 6). In the case of Brixton 1985 a public police apology - even if combined with an explanation of the exonerating features of the situation - would probably have been sufficient on its own to have saved all the injury, damage, and harm to police-community relations (only tenuously re-established since 1981).

If police forces are to incorporate such lessons into practical policy, there will have to be a substantial supportive training effort, as many of the writers here have argued. Training generally will be considered in the next section. Here we are concerned with training for crisis situations alone. Pat Sawyer (Chapter 19) gives an example of the type of course that might be appropriate, combining workshops to heighten awareness of the nature of conflict (and to reduce fear of conflict) with training in the skills of managing one's own reactions and controlling those of others - stress management, assertiveness without aggression, control of anger, risk assessment, accurate perception, creative problem-solving. Other such courses (largely provided at present for social workers in this country) have been described by Pugh (1988), Foster (1989) and Phillips and Leadbetter (1990). Training in the handling of hostage negotiations (see Maria Volpe & Robert Louden in Chapter 15) also incorporates many of the same elements as are needed in crisis situations more generally. In some American police forces officers are trained in crisis-management of domestic (interpersonal) disputes, which form a high proportion of call-outs and can be extremely volatile, if not, indeed, dangerous (see Bell et al., 1969). Such facility would no doubt be useful in other sorts of crisis too, such as public disorder.

Police action, effectively, as mediators in domestic disputes raises the issue as to how far their role should be extended in that direction. Volpe (1989) points out that the police are called to domestic crises because they have access to the use of force, plus a measure of authority, which itself helps to calm emotions, redress power disparities, and incline individuals to reflect on their behaviour. (Note how one's speed decreases on the motorway when a police car hoves into view!) It may be difficult to combine such features with the approach of the mediator (acceptance of whose services should be entirely voluntary). A temporary arrest, rather than trying to resolve the problem when emotions are still extremely roused, may be the most effective strategy (see Sherman and Berk, 1984), with referral to an independent mediation centre for further action, post-crisis. Nevertheless, as Volpe says, police can use the skills of mediation in any personal encounters. Even if the police do not have the time or resources, and do not operate in the appropriate conditions, actually to help resolve conflicts, they can at least lay the groundwork by a calming, diffusing approach that orientates parties to problem-solving rather than confrontation. Even if police officers should not be viewed as mediators, their work nevertheless involves them continually in situations where conflict resolution skills would be invaluable. Evidence from interviews with police leads Lawson (1981) to observe that "...many officers felt a vast majority of their policing activities centred on solving somebody else's troubles....They are acting as social brokerage agents involved in cooling out participants in public disputes...[and] much of police work is a direct reaction to, or strategy for adapting to, the ongoing hostility and antagonism that officers experience as they attempt to be public mediators."

With regard to the police role in larger social disorders, one senior MPD officer has argued that "The first option to be considered by any police commander is one of mediation. By far the most successful way of dealing with the threat of disorder, and the least damaging in all respects, is to bring events under control peacefully rather than by using force." (Moore, 1986). Waddington (1987) considers that the force's role as a mediator depends on the establishment of credibility and legitimacy, which, he argues, stem from being able to demonstrate their impartiality and from the restrained use of force. In many of the major disorders considered here, police impartiality could not have been claimed, given that they were actual or imagined parties in the conflict to begin with. However, even were they not, Jefferson (1987), in his reply to Waddington's paper, points out that another element in their legitimacy as intermediaries is the perceived legitimacy of the society which the police are seen as representing and protecting. In many cases nowadays (as Craig shows in Chapter 6) the rioters' grievances are against that social order with which the police must side, and this discredits their impartiality in the eyes of rebel groups. Any mediating institution must, therefore, be able to demonstrate its independence from the state and any particular political allegiance, a task which is more within the power of a body such as the U.S. CRS, although it has had to work hard to earn such credibility, operating as it does from within the government Department of Justice.

Third Party Crisis Intervention

A body like the CRS (see Chapters 12 and 13) is capable of being much more than just a crisis intervention resource. By specialising in public conflict it can build up experience invaluable for future intervention, consultancy and training for agents of other organisations. The CRS, for instance, according to Salem (1982), has all these objectives:-

1. To end or prevent violence.
2. To ease tension and establish an effective basis for negotiations by improving communications between the disputants.
3. To resolve differences over the incident which precipitated the dispute.
4. To bring the parties to an agreement on a plan of action.
5. To develop conflict resolution mechanisms.
6. To bring about the development of improved plans, policies, procedures, standards or personal practices to deal with inequities.
7. To develop or conduct training (eg of school or police personnel).
8. To provide technical information.

The CRS has regional offices covering the whole of the United States. Although its brief is strictly limited to ethnic conflicts (as ACAS is to industrial relations only), other bodies in America provide mediation services for different arenas of public conflict, while neighbourhood justice centres for interpersonal disputes are also widely distributed and highly successful for removing from prosecution what are essentially civil squabbles (although no less serious for being so), moving from a punitive to a remedial solution (see FIRM, 1990).

It is particularly useful if an established body with advanced conciliation skills is available, but other agencies or persons may be able to act successfully as mediators on an ad hoc basis, as Sally Sadler indicated in Chapter 9. The only such intervention which I have been able to discover in the literature on the British riots was by the probation service in Toxteth (Liverpool) in 1985 (Bowe et al.1987). The service had been trying to build up good relationships between the local community and criminal justice agencies since earlier riots in 1981, and were aware of rising tension in the summer of 1985. A number of incidents involving the police and black residents led to particularly serious disturbances in October and intervention by non-local special police which resulted in many allegations of violence and racism by officers. The probation service management had a policy of working with all other statutory agencies, including the police, in an attempt to prevent civil disturbances, but the experience of community-based field staff was that "the level of suspicion of the Police by local people" was so high "that to consider forming organisational links with the Police pragmatically made work tangibly more difficult, quite apart from the fact that, in such a setting, it was often impossible to justify or condone activities of the Police force....Clearly, a considerable gap in perception exists between field and management on these issues. Firstly, Management's easy acceptance that the Service had a role to play in preventing disturbances was not universally shared and understood. Secondly, knowledge of the area led the field to be sceptical about forums in which management invested great importance; for example, the majority of black-community groups in Liverpool 8 boycott Police community forums due to their irrelevance. Thirdly, Management's preparedness to adopt a preventative mantle entailed that, in October 1985, a mixture of permanent and MSC [Manpower Services Commission] staff were requested to be physically deployed at the point of the disturbances, in a soft-policing role." (Bowe et al.1987.)

This example illustrates the problems that can exist for non-independent agencies trying to act as intermediaries. Natural statutory ties with the police made it difficult for the probation service to establish credibility with the local community. Moreover, while we have already seen how divisions of opinion within parties to a dispute can hinder attempts at negotiated settlement, this is an unusual example of conflict within the intermediary body itself, with management having to be clearly seen to be cooperating with the police while their own field staff were more closely relating to local residents in the proper fulfilment of their liaison role. If this rift could have been identified and resolved, the contradictory pressures from statutory and community sources might have made the probation service a natural mediation resource, having strong links with major parties, but they were unable to establish such a role.

The Community Role at the Crisis Stage

Although, in the event of a disorder crisis, the police force will inevitably have to play a primary role, the preparedness of the community and its own inherent social control mechanisms is also crucial. Although crowd violence is usually imagined with much trepidation, as a phenomenon beyond control - a belief responsible for many of the rash responses that have frequently been witnessed the world over when agents of authority have faced a threatening crowd - empirical studies have shown that crowd behaviour has its own order, less recognisable as such than that of ordinary social life, but far from being "out of control" (cf.Marsh, 1978). The actions of a crowd are highly volatile and responsive to minor stimuli - a fact which makes them both unpredictable and potentially manipulable by small numbers of "leaders" or even single individuals. The description of his own experiences by Jim Murtagh in Chapter 3 gives a good impression of this volatility and uncertainty of aims in a crowd situation and the way individual acts can inflame or cool out the crowd's behaviour. A few individuals out to cause trouble can easily exploit this aspect of the crowd - as happens in football hooliganism; at the same time Murtagh shows that individuals with the opposite motivation - seeking to avoid violence - can be equally successful. Individuals generally have a horror of violence and, even if that horror is somewhat suppressed in the excitement of mass phenomena, they will respond surprisingly well to the offer of reasonable alternatives, as long as respect seems to be shown to their grievances.

Policies and techniques of non-violence were particularly developed by Gandhi in India and by the civil rights movement in the United States, where people like Martin Luther King saw that the violence and militarism of some black groups, despite their justifiable sense of outrage, was only leading to their further rejection and marginalisation, and was thus ultimately failing to achieve their own desired goals. The mediator Adam Curle (1971) has asserted that an initial phase of attempting to get grievances resolved, especially where disadvantaged groups are concerned, is to seek majority acceptance that they have a case at all, to gain credibility in other words, and that phase may well be marked by confrontation, publicity-seeking and dramatisation, even the threat of violence if the majority resort to mere suppression of the problem. But having gained public recognition that a problem does indeed exist, the stage is set for negotiation and problem-solving, when confrontation, a high public profile, and dramatic action may be more obstructive than helpful. While we tend to think in terms of a natural escalation in violence, once one has set down the path of confrontation, this is in fact far from inevitable and social groups are usually quite capable of recognising when a change of tactics is called for (as Meer, 1990, documents in the case of the African National Congress recently in South Africa). Widespread violence only tends to occur when recognition is refused by continuous suppression or a series of superficial responses that merely serve to demonstrate a basic unwillingness to treat the matter seriously.

Bickmore et al. (1984) contrast violence and non-violence in the following way:

Crisis Intervention

	Violence	**Nonviolence**
Goals:	To defeat opponent ....Must humiliate, injure, corner, &/or destroy opponent.	To solve the problem. To work with the opponent or change her/his understanding to achieve a mutually satisfactory settlement.
Attitudes:	Requires a strong hatred & fear of opponent....	Requires courage to think and act clearly with self-control
Techniques:	Attack so strongly that opponent has no alternatives or choice....	Offer many options for both sides to save face & yet reach a solution.
	Avoid one's own suffering at all costs & inflict suffering on other.	Completely reject the use of violence. Be willing to suffer but not to cause anyone else to suffer.
	Use all resources to get victory as soon as possible.	Use persistence & patience...
	Use public relations to distort truth where it serves own purposes....	Keep conduct & public relations as exemplary and truthful as possible to create sympathy & understanding by the public & opponent.
	Act arrogantly to instil hatred and fear.	Act with integrity & humility to instil respect & sympathy.
	Be harmful.	Be helpful.
	Relies on...physical resources.	Relies on...mental, creative & moral resources.
	Ignore or suppress a problem.	Positive action for change...

Gregg (1959) compares nonviolence to "moral jiu-jitsu" which throws an attacker off balance. Violence only achieves its aim when the object of the violence assumes the role of victim. The nonviolence practitioner refuses to assume such a role, refuses to accept the simplified "black and white" picture of the problem that is being forced upon her/him, and refuses even to define the other as an "opponent". Such an approach, Gregg argues, forces the attackers to confront their own assumptions and motives, and to face up to the complexity both of the problem and of its possible resolution. The uncertainty created makes the original aggressor more amenable to change. A violent response to violence, on the other hand, only serves to reinforce preconceptions and to polarise attitudes.

Dorothy Cotton and Captain Alphin took part in the US Civil Rights campaign alongside Martin Luther King. According to Gosling and Mahendran (1984), their strategy of conflict resolution through non-violence consists of six steps which overlap considerably with the general principles outlined in Chapter 1 and the beginning of the present chapter:

INFORMATION GATHERING

> The ability to find and communicate the truth about a problem is the most important skill of the non-violent practitioner.... The idea was to learn techniques for achieving self-control, for releasing tensions and for anticipating responses prior to meeting opponents....

The main elements of this stage are:

1. Formulate a clear statement of the problem.
2. Test the validity of the problem statement.
3. Collect and disseminate information about the problem.
4. Understand how the opposing parties view the problem.
5. Determine the level of conflict between the opponents.
6. Study the history of the problem and attempts at resolution.
7. Examine the resources available to each opponent."

EDUCATION

Conveying one's views of the problem to the public generally.

PERSONAL COMMITMENT

> viewing oneself as a social healer, having a vision of what one wants to accomplish ("I Have a Dream..."), being open to the truth, and being teachable.

NEGOTIATION

1. Parties seek a win-win solution.
2. Means exemplifying ends. (In other words, the end does not justify the means).
3. Parties affirm each others' humanity.
4. The truth may be held by either side [or, more likely, partially by both].

5. Parties are flexible but firm on principles.

DIRECT ACTION

Tactics include "boycotts, marches, rallies, rent-strikes, work slowdowns, and various acts of civil disobedience. They are successful to the extent that they permit the opponents to save face and evoke their good will".

RECONCILIATION

Although past wrongs are not forgotten, they should not be allowed to "serve as a barrier to a relationship".

The practice of non-violence in situations where feelings run strong is no easy option. It requires considerable education and practical training comparable to that described in Chapter 19. Bickmore et al. (1984) is an example of the kind of training manual available, widely used in America. More widespread knowledge of the alternatives to violence and the principles of conflict resolution would not only complement attempts by the authorities to encourage de-escalatory techniques and reduce resort to violence, but would empower local groups and communities to act in a way that is more effective in achieving their own goals. The Lambeth Consultative Group (Chapter 4) recognised the value of having such resources within the community, and especially the value of "openness" in providing information to the police about potential trouble that would allow time for rational planning and help avoid the knee-jerk response of those who are surprised into rapid action. Warfield makes the same appeal for the use of community mechanisms for stemming disorder, as less provocative than intervention by an "external force", especially one regarded with huge suspicion as the police tend to be in riot-prone areas. In Chapter 11, Shonholtz outlined a whole strategy for returning social control generally to the community as far as is possible, employing the police as a last rather than a first resort. More recently, at a Conference organised by the Forum for Initiatives in Reparation and Mediation in June 1990, Jim Murtagh himself has argued for the creation of local neighbourhood groups of people willing to be trained in the techniques of non-violent intervention, who would be prepared to try to prevent violence happening in their own community by interceding in personal quarrels that have deteriorated to violence or in group conflicts that seem to be getting out of hand (see Marshall, 1990).

Chapter Twentytwo

Post-Crisis Intervention and Prevention

REGARDING CRISIS intervention, it was inevitable that the police role should have been centre-stage, for the application of controlled force may be necessary once violence has got out of hand, and the saving of lives and destruction are the main aims in the short-term. Even in that context, however, it was emphasised that the role of the community and of independent third parties was not inconsiderable.

This point applies even more strongly to the post-crisis resolution phase, and to preventative action. Several chapters (eg 2, 6, and 13) referred to the typical combination of deprivation and injustice that provide the underlying fuel of major social confrontations, as distinct from the immediate causes. (In Benyon and Solomon, 1987, five features were found to be common to the British riot situations: racial disadvantage and discrimination; unemployment; environmental and household deprivation; political exclusion and powerlessness; mistrust of and hostility to the police.) The resolution of these issues inevitably passes beyond the capacities or the remit of the police, and even beyond the capacities of the local area altogether. As Alderson (1984) remarks, concerning the 1981 riots, "...the idea that problems of social disorder could be cured by the police was a gross error." "Difficult though the task may be,...we should avoid the trap of regarding a strong repressive police arm as a substitute for greater social justice and the amelioration of conditions..." "The police system should be seen in its rightful place as operating on the margins." In chapter 10 of this volume, too, Ian Beckett supports the fact that the police alone cannot be responsible for dealing with public disorder. As another former police officer, Holdaway (1984), observes, "We have virtually asked for the eradication of crime from our society: for an orderly society devoid of any visible conflict. The police cannot deliver such goods; the degree to which they can co-operate with other people and organisations, working towards the reduction of crime and creation of public tranquillity depends upon government policy and, importantly, upon a public realism about what our police can and cannot accomplish."

Chris Leeds (Chapter 2) particularly featured the role of

government policies, and the Lambeth Consultative Group (Chapter 4) complained about economic and social policies that gave over-encouragement to selfish attitudes in the general population, reducing the strength of the community as a medium of control and the potential for constructive conflict resolution, which depends on attitudes of respect, tolerance, patience and trust. It is factors such as these, Kim (1987) argues, that account for the strong police-community links in Japan, rather than any particular techniques used by the police force (which is, in any case, organised along lines developed by American advisers of the occupying forces after the Second World War). With increasing Western cultural influence, the author sees these strong and effective ties breaking down.

Ray Shonholtz (Chapter 11) sees the police as a negative force per se - representative of the breakdown of community mechanisms for self-help and social control and hence the necessity to resort to institutionalised violence. Although this power would seem inevitable, in the background, for maintaining the modern state, its representatives should not be called in to resolve issues that do not absolutely require the application of force. There has been a tendency to restrict the response to the major riots of 1981 and 1985 to reforms of policing methods and police/community consultative arrangements. Necessary as these might be, they are essentially side-issues in the major resolution scenario that has never really begun. Keith (1988) argues that by delegating responsibility for consultation to the police, the government was able to distance itself from the problem and avoid taking direct action itself. The police are thereby left, quite unfairly, to "carry the can" for failure to alleviate the root grievances of certain social groups like the ethnic minorities or detached youth (cf.Chapter 15). In the words of Greta Brooks (Chapter 5), the major conflagrations of the early eighties provided an "opportunity" for demythologisation and reconstructing social relationships that has hardly been grasped at all, except in isolated initiatives by small community groups and by certain police divisions. The section on major government initiatives that might have complemented the other sections of this book - the police, the community and independent parties - does not appear simply because there is nothing to include within it. The government has assumed a low profile in relation to these problems, as Leeds points out in Chapter 2, thus emasculating the process of resolution as a whole. There are many promising initiatives around, but they need to be encouraged more widely, to be resourced and integrated into a concerted effort, and to be underpinned by social policies congenial to the establishment of a peaceful, just and humane society.

Police Initiatives

Out of considerable experience of resolving public disputes and consultation with both police forces and disadvantaged communities, the CRS in the United States has formulated a useful document on the "Principles of Good Policing: avoiding violence between police and citizens" (CRS 1987). Recognising that initiatives at one level may well not percolate through to another (either up or down the hierarchy) and may even meet concerted resistance (cf. Rose, 1990), the document places a primary emphasis on the creation of a pervasive departmental culture favourable to enhancing community relations and democratic accountability, including a fundamental orientation to negotiation rather than confrontation. Such a culture would consist of a set of clearly articulated values and a system for ensuring that they were operationalised in practical terms within the organisation, by formal training, informal socialisation, regulations, appropriate rewards and reinforcements, and public statements. The seven prime values of good policing identified by CRS are:

Democracy (protection of rights)
Preservation of human life
Crime-prevention
Involvement of the community in service delivery
Accountability to the community
Professionalism in operations
Integrity.

The CRS recognises that the dangers and social isolation (eg because of shift-work) endemic to the police job lead to a sense of togetherness, which can provide a valuable commitment to the organisation and to colleagues, but which tends also to lead to defensiveness and closure of ranks in the face of external threat or criticism. Holdaway (1984) also mentions the isolation which results from the public having too high expectations of what the police can deliver and the tendency to abnegate responsibility totally in favour of the police, which further heightens the stress of policing and the defensiveness of the force. Such a set of values as that above, which imply an openness to external influence and accountability that violate the defensive tendency to organisational closure, requires both a concerted effort, promoted powerfully from the top, and active public support and cooperation.

In the short term, the introduction of a new and distinct police culture is likely to cause unsettlement and insecurity, but such are the problems that must be faced and resolved if policing is to move back into mainstream social acceptance, regain credibility and gain the attributes of professionalism (effective self-regulation, accountability, clear objectives and priority-led operations) demanded of any social agency in the late twentieth century. Hunt (1987) has demonstrated how the best of efforts to tackle police institutional racism, for instance, have often failed because they have not gone beyond the analysis of the problem and the formulation of remedies to make "provision as well for anticipating impediments to the application of these remedies and the formulation of remedies for these impediments." In particular, he points out, a purely "rationalist" approach is unlikely to work. As the principles of conflict resolution would predict, and as he discovered, one must deal openly with the conflicts that change brings and the emotions that form an important part of the original problem and the reactions to change. As they are part of the problem, so feelings must also be accommodated in the solution.

Such a major management re-orientation has begun within the Metropolitan Police. Some of the strands have been portrayed in the third section of this book. These initiatives have recently begun to cohere in a consistent plan to try to counter the so-called "canteen culture" that at times supported extra-legal corner cutting, anti-community attitudes, and corruption of overall goals. The attitude has been taken - contrasting with the traditional management defeatism in the face of the ingrained canteen culture - that "How officers perceive both themselves and the role they perform...are inexorably linked to the way in which the organisation and its management seem to contribute towards the achievement of corporate goals. How managers provide resources, reward achievement, sanction misdemeanours, and facilitate efficiency are very important variables which affect the performance of the service as a whole." (Street, 1990.) This effort is part of the Plus Programme (mentioned in Chapter 7 by Alec Marnoch, who is in charge of it). According to Street (1990), the programme is "concerned with developing a common service-orientated bond; improving the quality of performance; increasing efficiency; and presenting the end result clearly and honestly to the customers." Giving coherence to the programme is a "statement of common purpose and values" that is not unlike the CRS "prime values" above:

> The purpose of the Metropolitan Police Service is to uphold the law fairly and firmly; to prevent crime, to pursue and bring to justice those who break the law; to keep the Queen's peace; to protect, help and reassure people in London; and to be seen to do all this with integrity, common sense and judgement. We must be compassionate, courteous and patient, acting without fear or favour or prejudice to the rights of others. We need to be professional, calm and restrained in the face of violence and apply only that force which is necessary to accomplish our lawful duty. We must strive to reduce the fears of the public, and so far as we can, to reflect their priorities in the action we take. We must respond

to well-founded criticism with a willingness to change.

A virtually identical statement has since been adopted by the Association of Chief Police Officers for the whole of England and Wales.

Part and parcel of value-reorientation efforts must be practical policies which give them effect. Those mentioned in the CRS document are:

RECRUITMENT AND SELECTION PROCEDURES

A major goal should be to attain representation of all minorities in the police force in proportion to their local populations. There have been a number of drives in Britain to increase minority representation, but without marked success. A recent lowering of height requirements might have a marginal effect for a few groups, but the main influence on recruitment is the image the force has in a particular community. It is likely that programmes such as "Plus" will have to be further down the road - and demonstrably successful - before the suspicions of most minority groups can be overcome. Another consideration in selection should be the psychological suitability of applicants. Modern police work requires flexibility, creativity, confidence, receptivity, tolerance, and even humility (cf. Bickmore et al., 1984, above - techniques of non-violence). More attention to careful selection may lead to problems in the recruitment of sufficient numbers of personnel initially, but the consequent upgrading of the quality of membership would itself increase the attraction of a police job.

HANDLING OF COMPLAINTS FROM CITIZENS

Complaints need to be seen to be handled fairly, respectfully and with due seriousness. The complaints mechanism - and its outcomes - are an important source of credibility and trust for any profession or organisation. The CRS is cautious about recommending an independent complaints system for a variety of reasons, and the issue as to how far complaints should be investigated and judged by the police force alone is still strongly debated. Whatever form such a system takes, however, it will have to be able to obtain the confidence of both police officers and the community, and arrangements for consultation and representation from both sides will be crucial. Openness and honesty will need to be cornerstones of an effective system, and the attainment of this will be a sign that the old defensiveness of the police force is on its way out. In current British procedure there is allowance for "informal settlement" for minor complaints (ones that would not lead to major disciplinary consequences if proven against an officer), and there is room there for more participative modes of resolution. The use of conciliation in such cases was proposed recently by the Lambeth Consultative Group, but the idea has not so far gained general acceptance.

PUBLIC INFORMATION POLICY

The CRS recommend the use of the mass media in a constructive way, in order to affirm community values and relationships, and to underline the democratic and accountable nature of policing philosophy. The media should not be used simply to present a "police view", to be defensive or to attack other groups.

DEVELOP A CONFLICT-MANAGEMENT PLAN FOR THE COMMUNITY

This would include contingency plans for major disorders (so that even urgent action can be taken on the basis of rational planning and minimal escalation - see discussion in Chapters 13 & 21). It could well involve combined training for police and citizens (of all local groups) for the containment of violence, and should certainly encourage the development of community-based mechanisms of control, independent of, but linked to, police operations. The development of such plans would of necessity have to be a freely collaborative exercise between the police and community groups, an exercise in itself of value for all parties as a learning experience.

TRAINING

The CRS document emphasises that training is not an automatic solution to the problems of policing discussed here. Training tends to be the easiest response - it can take up relatively little in the way of time and resources and is not so demanding as measures involving interaction with external groups. Training can also be entirely superficial, a technical requirement that leads to rote-learning of standard phrases the real meaning of which has never been really understood or assimilated in terms of behaviour. Training, if it is to have effect, must be integrated into the departmental culture and operational policies. It cannot, in other words, be itself a force for change, as many have perhaps hoped, but can only be a means of putting into effect changes already agreed upon and incorporated into practical philosophy. Training also should not be confined to classroom lectures, for however much theory one has imbibed it is useless unless one has also learnt how to put it into effect. Training methods should therefore be participative and practical - using role-plays, simulations and other exercises that ensure participants are learning behavioural skills not just rationalisations. The scope for conflict resolution training in police-work is widespread and little exploited so far in this country, despite the examples here in Chapters 10, 16, 18 and 19. Our police officers are given little guidance on how to manage any of the non-crime aspects of their work, even though these comprise up to three quarters (Cumming et al., 1964; Murray, 1988) of all calls on their time. Chapters 9 and 19 give examples of the elements which could usefully be incorporated into such courses, aimed at any number of different problems, such as general community "interfacing" (cf.Chapter 18); the handling of arrests and questioning on suspicion; domestic disputes; persons in custody; use of firearms; hostage confrontations; and so on.

POLICE-COMMUNITY PARTNERSHIP

> One suspects that a principal reason for the widespread international acceptance of the community policing innovation is that the term means whatever police administrators want it to mean. (Munro, 1987)

Or what police constables who have to carry it out make it mean. Like training, police community liaison can be the lynch-pin of a pervasive system of democratic policing, or it can be a superficial effort, unsupported by other actions, that may eventually cause more harm than good. "Token or artificial efforts toward enhancing public image will quickly be recognised as an insincere gesture, which can only invite public ridicule and repudiation....The public must be convinced that the department's concern for community relations is not just a priority for administrators or community relations officers, but a serious concern that enjoys the commitment of each officer" (CRS, 1987). Public liaison is not an adjunct to policing - it must be policing. As Brown (1981) puts it: "...the essential nature of policing is a continual process of interaction and reciprocation, or as some would say, a form of social contract, negotiated, and constantly renegotiated, between two active and ever-changing elements, police and society." If collaboration by the community is sought, it must also be earned by real sharing ("means exemplify ends"). "When we talk of community involvement we mean bringing the public in, not only at the implementation levels but at the decision-making levels....It is no use bemoaning the lack of community support for the implementation of policies which communities do not feel to be their own" (Clifford, 1983). Similarly, "A well-developed community relations effort should be the product of careful construction, designed by the police and the public together, and should not be the result of an emotional reaction to a temporary crisis in the community" (CRS, 1987). Isolated, short-term projects are capable of attaining nothing lasting - just as they are not integrated into overall policing policy, so they will also fail to become integrated into local culture and community action.

The same applies to specialist community relations divisions: "Specialist community relations work often proves of value; but the more it is used to compensate for failures in operational contact between police and public, the less credit it will be to both, serving to expose the gulfs between police words and police deeds" (Brown, 1981). A study by Phillips and Cochrane (1988) of Community Liaison Officers in several non-Metropolitan forces showed many of these problems. There was often a tension between the need to locate such officers at a sufficiently local level for meaningful community contact and the need to create high-level representation in the police force to give solid backing, status and credibility to their work. Training was often inadequate and the work discredited by the "canteen culture" - those officers who saw police work as apprehending criminals rather than "helping old ladies across the road". Other officers saw community liaison as "day-to-day policing" that "in an ideal world everyone in the police force would be doing" (Phillips and Cochrane, 1988, quoting a police officer), but was not done because of lack of time or inclination or encouragement. There is then "a danger that members of a target community may fail to perceive the CLO as a representative of 'The Police'. They may see the officer as, at worst, an individual, and at best, a representative of part of the Force (the 'goodies') whilst retaining a negative image of the rest of the Force (the 'baddies')" (Phillips and Cochrane, 1988). The activities of CLOs, moreover, normally avoided the types of two-way communication or collaborative work which might have had some impact on the community by offering them some initiative or influence. Youth work, crime prevention, school visits, talks, and inter-agency liaison were the most typical activities - concerned rather with "selling" a positive image of the police force than with attending to the concerns of residents. In most areas the researchers found that they fail to make any meaningful "grass roots" contact and still adhere to a crime-orientated confrontational approach. They conclude that "Only a determined and prolonged campaign with support from the highest levels can make it possible for planned, purposeful and defined community liaison initiatives to co-exist with the reactive side of policing.

Examples of this failure are legion. Let us look at two examples here, the first American, the second British Project COPE (Community Oriented Police Education) in Philadelphia was an ongoing 16-week course involving "small groups of police officers and Philadelphia community residents in an intensified classroom experience aimed at improving police and community relations, and community crime prevention efforts" (Greene and Decker, 1989). Topics included institutional racism, communications, values and ethics, team building and community problem-solving, etc. According to Greene and Decker (1989), "Discussions are often heated and focused on police and community tensions. The central aim of these communications and discussions between the police officers and community residents is to show the officers that the community has a legitimate interest in improving police services and that the officer's attitudes and behaviour toward primarily minority residents can be either facilitating or disruptive. For citizens such programming provides them with a glimpse of the police officer's oftentimes frustrating work environment, and an understanding of the community's responsibility for crime and disorder prevention." The programme was started in response to increasing tensions between police and black communities in certain areas through the 1960s and 1970s, although it was later established city-wide.

The authors administered pre- and post-course questionnaires to police and community participants. Over the research period, officers' perceptions of citizen support declined significantly, as did residents' perceptions even more dramatically. Measures of officers' job satisfaction also deteriorated significantly. These results may have reflected serious public disorder and policing problems occurring during the period of research, but they do at least indicate that the experience of the education programme alone was insignificant in its impact relative to these wider influences, and may indeed have reinforced them by forcing officers to face up to residents' criticisms and apparent distrust, inadvertently increasing their "siege mentality" and defensiveness. This example is instructive in reminding one that a lack of confidence in one's own position, or in one's ability to represent that position to community residents in a favourable light, will lead to an inability to absorb criticism in a constructive way, and immunity to educational initiatives. Instead, officers' levels of confidence dropped and the experience was negative.

The Lozells Project was a statutory initiative in the multi-ethnic Handsworth area of Birmingham, which effectively started in 1979, well before the riots of 1981 and 1985. According to Cumberbatch & Tadesse (1987), "The project had three main stated aims:

1. to develop closer links between the police and the community;
2. to encourage people living in the area to participate with local agencies solving problems within the community;
3. to give support to the numerous groups and agencies working within the community who strive to improve the quality of life.

... The focal point for the project and the main source of expenditure was a community centre which opened in September 1980 with a police-run youth club....Over the years...it became a very active resource for the area.... Apart from the community centre, the project financially supported a wide range of groups and agencies in the area, provided intensive police input to the local secondary school, organised regular swimming and football events..., supported an intermediate treatment group for young offenders and later opened a second youth club." The Project "was described as the 'icing on the cake' by one senior police officer who was very committed to community policing. Unfortunately", the authors add, "this is exactly what the project remained rather than being an essential ingredient of police work in the area. Thus one of the original aims included increased foot patrols which were never forthcoming. Doubtlessly lack of manpower was the main reason for this".

The Project itself was only vaguely related to the overall aims. The steering group comprised middle managers from statutory agencies with inadequate knowledge of the local community, which was extremely diverse and complex. Taking a cautious line, "local groups and agencies were kept at arm's length for over a year after the project started. It is true that a number of these were given financial support by the project, but these were almost entirely groups either in or closely allied to the statutory sector." The imbalance was redressed later, but the damage had been done, resulting in a "serious lack of community interest and involvement....The resistance occurred at many levels but principally at the level of public passivity rather than at the level of ideological resistance." Insofar as there was such resistance, this was increased by the lack of involvement of community groups at the earliest stages. Even at the youth club, police contact with youths was very infrequent, and neither that experience nor that in the school initiatives, led to any changes in the attitudes to the police of young people, who were quite able to differentiate between the acceptable officers participating in the community activities and the general run of officers encountered on the street, whose behaviour and attitudes were no different from those they had always encountered.

These examples show that change in a large organisation cannot be produced by innovation in one part, which thereby becomes special and different and hence irrelevant to the mainstream. Partial isolated changes of this sort are easily recognisable as such in the community and, for all their good intentions and welcome ambitions, are easily dismissed as window-dressing. We have the icing, so where is the cake? Even with the backing of the whole system, such projects are greeted with suspicion or exploited as a means of aggressive confrontation. This is only natural in neighbourhoods where relationships have become extremely tenuous for particular local groups, and initial reluctance and tensions can only be dissolved through skilled and sensitive facilitation of the kind a body like CRS is able to supply. The fact that an initiative is instigated by one "side" will be sufficient reason for the others to treat it with caution; the role of the intermediary can be crucial in making the breakthrough at this stage. The other limitation on police policies for enhancing community relations, even in the context of widespread operational change, is that they cannot begin to address the problems of disadvantage and discrimination felt by many inner city communities, even though, as the main representatives of the state with whom residents come into contact they will be the agency that has to bear the brunt of such grievances.

The whole concept of community relations is ambiguous anyway. Potter and Reicher (1987), in a study of accounts of the first of the eighties riots in Britain (St Paul's district of Bristol) showed how the term was used in innumerably different ways to mean very different phenomena. There are those, moreover, like Chatterton (1973), who point to an inherent conflict between the crime and non-crime duties of the police, between the operations of "legitimate force" on behalf of state control and the community helpers at hand to guide people through various crises and calamities. One can observe comments in Chapters 7 and 8 about the complications for building community relations that derive from the need at the same time to detect and prosecute crime - a source of tension that was certainly part of the trigger events in both St Pauls and Lambeth, and probably elsewhere too. Potts (1982) goes so far as to see the conflict deriving from the endemic tension between the governed and the governors in a democratic state, and that it is only in the Anglo-American legal tradition that the police are encumbered with the responsibility for bridging the gap. He argues that "Police-community relations programs often aim directly at overcoming the negative connotations of law enforcement. The programs may seek to replace the negative image of the police with a positive image. Since, however, the negative image is rooted in the nature of the society and the political culture and not in police behavior, transformation of the image cannot be effected solely through police efforts." Even in the Bermondseys of Yvonne Craig (Chapter 6) the consent of the governed was always, as Brogden (1979) puts it, "tentative rather than absolute", and this has always been so (with respect to the nineteenth century see Storch, 1975).

If one takes into account the deeper social tensions, one will approach police-community relations in a more sanguine fashion. The archetypal photograph of the "local bobby" dancing arm-in-arm with the black women at the Notting Hill carnival represents a dream of relations that is at best a temporary highpoint and highly conditional. It represents a state of relations that could never be a feasible goal of everyday policing. Any such conception of what police-community relations is about is doomed to manufacture frustration and despair. Community relations is a much more mundane affair: it is an occupational requirement which derives from the fact that policing is about interaction with the citizenry, an interaction, however, that is always restricted to particular operational aims. It is a partial relationship between people in roles - police officer and victim/ criminal/suspect/help-seeker/informant etc. No-one imagines an idyll where doctors dance with patients - why should one expect it of police officers? A good relationship with one's doctor implies a lack of friction in relation to health-related consultations, not that one enjoys his/her company as a compatible personality. So also good relations between police officers and residents refer only to the quality of interaction in connection with policing jobs. The implication of this is that what we are seeking in good police/community relations is a means of carrying out the functions of policing in liaison with lay citizens without friction and without obstruction, and, more positively, that active collaboration should occur in support of those functions. In building community relations, one is not trying to increase the liking of individuals for one another, but constructing lines of communication, encouraging mutual respect and understanding, creating structures for active consultation. Restricting oneself to such aims would help avoid the vagueness of a Lozells Project (and a multitude of others) that had, in practice, the aim of somehow demonstrating police "cordiality" and "friendliness", and lacked any direct connection to the policing job itself. Enjoyable as youth clubs and sports activities may be to some officers and some youths, they have nothing to do with policing and it is hardly any surprise that they have no impact on the relations surrounding that job.

The promising approaches to police/community relations directly arise from operational requirements - developing community conflict-management plans (see above), action to eliminate police racism, etc. Two developments deserve specific mention. Chapter 7 describes the development of one of the more successful "consultative groups" recommended by Lord Scarman in his report on the Brixton riots of 1981. These can serve a number of the principles of collaborative problem-solving discussed in this book, always assuming that they are used for a genuine sharing of views, ie with the active intention of putting the ideas that arise into practical effect, and that there is a wider culture amenable to collaboration to which they can relate. To work well, however, members of the group - police or citizens - require training in the effective use of such opportunities, to build their confidence and skills in the face of a task that at times can be frustrating and threatening. (Note Alec Marnoch's observations on the "obstructionism" of the early ventilation phase, which could have been anticipated as a normal and even valuable part of the exercise, instead of tending to lead members back to defensive positions.) Another requirement of such groups is continual work on the "representation" problem (see Keith, 1988; Stratta, 1990). Not all elements of the community will be equally prepared to participate, and development work in the area (not a police job) is needed to improve the representativeness of the consultative committee and to create channels of communication between such representatives and their rather inchoate constituencies - a means, in other words, for the mass of people to ensure their views are transmitted via those who actually attend the meetings. Stratta (1990) also makes several other important points, based on a study of the actual working of such committees, including the necessity for adequate resourcing and a commitment to a proper power balance, for he found that the police side tended to control the agenda, so that consultation became "a reinforcement, rather than an exploration and a questioning, of the police point of view."

The other development worthy of note is that of "contract, partnership or neighbourhood policing", introduced, in the Metropolitan Police, at Brixton by Ian Beckett. Whatever the term used to describe the activity, the intention is to maximise officer availability within the community and familiarity of one with the other. Murray (1988) describes a development of this ("contact policing") which attempts to structure patrolling so as to achieve more meaningful public contact and use patrolling time more constructively, instead of being an aimless meandering "waiting for something to happen". In Chapter 10, Beckett himself touches on this briefly, emphasising the fact that such policing is a style of normal policing, not a supplement. He argues that this style of police work alone is capable of being preventative, flexible and receptive to community involvement. As he infers, however, such a style has its costs, in that greater resources are needed to operate in this way than in a purely reactive fashion or through specialist squads. We can only get the policing for which we pay. Research in America (Pate et al, 1986) has shown that contact policing can have measurable effects, and replication of this in Britain (in Birmingham and London) by Bennett (1990) also showed that it was feasible, effective in increasing police-public interaction and in improving public confidence, and acceptable to the police officers involved.

These developments are hopeful because they arise from practice and directly relate to requirements of the policing job. It is crucial that police community relations is not imagined to be some additional type of work for which special arrangements need to be made. It must evolve together with day-to-day practice.

Third Party Initiatives

We have already made the point that post-crisis conflict resolution is not just a matter for, or even a primary task of, the police. Insofar as policing policy can assist, as discussed above, there are various ways in which third party assistance is really required to make the police initiatives more effective.

The mediator is particularly useful in relation to he emotional and psychological aspects of conflict, for these are difficult for those involved to handle themselves. Adam Curle, an international Quaker mediator of very wide experience, has this to say of what he terms the "ideology of suspicion" typical of serious conflicts:

> When quarrels rise to a certain pitch of violence the difficulty of reaching a peaceful settlement seems to increase sharply. This

applies, in my experience, both in war and in family or marital feuds. Certainly the shedding of blood in the former marks a steep escalation of anger, resentment and blind chauvinism that inhibit any moves towards peace. This is particularly tragic in those cases where both sides really want a negotiated settlement.

These violence-induced and -inducing attitudes tend rapidly to harden. Fantasies, originally based on reality but rapidly soaring far beyond it, develop concerning the barbarous wickedness of the enemy, making it increasingly hard to end the conflict other than militarily. More and more, as a result, does the task of peace making become a psychological one of changing these distorted perceptions, and less one of dealing directly with the territorial or other issue that precipitated the strife. This, of course, remains an issue, probably very serious, but one that is certainly exacerbated and mythologised beyond all reason. However, whereas there can obviously be no single resolution to the innumerable possible substantive occasions of war, and therefore few generalisations to be made, the psychological forces they generate follow a more regular pattern." (Curle, 1986.)

The ideology of suspicion is reinforced by a number of factors Curle encountered at the national level which would apply equally well to disputes between groups within nations. Psychological blocks to pacific conflict-resolution that, from a dispassionate point of view, would be in the party's own interests include:

Perceived threats to one's ego, through identification with a community, culture, etc which is under attack.
Sense of guilt because of past acts of violence or rash behaviour.
Reinforcement by mass media presentations that insist on over-simplification of issues, portrayed in black/white oppositional ways and represented by extreme views.
Political considerations for leaders (who may benefit from dramatisation and media coverage).
Fear of showing weakness; wishing to "preserve face"; desiring to "negotiate from strength" - all of which lead to an endless competition for advantage.
Lack of information about the "other side", leading to exaggerated notions and illusions about their behaviour, intentions and motivation.

Mediators can help break down these emotional blockages (which, from the point of view of negotiating in one's own best interests, are in fact weaknesses, because they prevent rational decision-making) by working to improve communications, providing independent information, bolstering the parties' confidence by personal support and "talking through the issues", and helping the parties through negotiations.

We have already made a case for an independent body skilled in conflict resolution to act as intermediary in crisis situations. Such a body would also be available to facilitate longer-term negotiations in public conflicts that have passed the crisis stage or have not so far reached it, as Newburn indicates in Chapter 12, or in helping to build up positive relationships and credibility. Rubenstein (1988) differentiates two modes of facilitation of direct negotiations: a public formal mediation approach and problem-solving workshops. In addition, a mediatory body might work separately with both sides in order to enhance understanding, often in preparation for one of the direct mediation modes. The CRS might employ any of these methods at different times.

Indirect mediation, often called "conciliation", as used by CRS, is described by Salem (1982) as "a process in which an outside party uses skills of persuasion, a knowledge of the dynamics of conflict and human behavior and technical information to ease tensions between disputants and move them toward voluntary resolution of their differences." He notes that "The arrival on the scene of the outside intervenor often alters the behavior of the parties and at times just the presence of the conciliator helps to lower rhetoric levels....While working to reduce tensions, the conciliator begins to address the substance of the conflict - both the precipitating incident and the underlying issues - recognising that it is often more difficult and less important to resolve differences over the precipitating incident...than the underlying issues....In meeting separately with the parties, the conciliator is aware that their perceptions of the problems are as important as the facts, and that intensive discussion of the issues can help close the gap between conditions as they exist and as they are perceived by the parties." Interestingly, Salem observes that protest leaders have, in America, become increasingly sophisticated over time in their approaches, controlling demonstrations and clearly articulating demands, while the authorities have tended to show more conciliatory responses and be better prepared to meet with protesters and enter into negotiation. This may have been the effect of bodies like CRS - including mediation projects and nonviolence practitioners - that have been familiarising American organisations with constructive conflict resolution over the last decade and a half, although it may also have been simply a matter of accumulated experience, or "learning by mistakes" to avoid over-reaction and leave doors open. For whatever reason, Salem believes that, as a result, CRS intervention has tended to be more concentrated in the formal modes as time has gone by.

Formal mediation is described as "a structured process in which the mediator helps the disputants negotiate their differences and reach agreement" (Salem, 1982). It "usually entails face-to-face negotiations over a written agenda addressing the precise issues which divide the parties. The agreement defines future behavior by the parties, is signed and usually publicised." Salem lists particular advantages to formal mediation of this kind:

1. a "signed, publicised agreement is likely to be more binding than one reached during informal conciliation";
2. "the formal process legitimises the protest group, making it easier to open negotiations if there are future disputes";
3. "the structured mediation process helps sensitise the parties to each other's positions and tends to increase understanding between divergent groups".

He admits, however, that certain conditions need to be fulfilled if such a process is to be successful. The issues have to be specific, the emotional temper sufficiently lowered, the political climate favourable, the parties ready and able to commit themselves, and all the major or more powerful parties involved. (See also Chalmers, 1974.) If these conditions are not satisfied, public mediation can do as much harm as good. Rubenstein (1988) points out the dangers of public forums:

> It is difficult, to begin with, to induce the participants in a multiparty forum to participate in a no-holds-barred analysis of the problems generating conflict. But even where this is possible, the problem-solving options generated in such a context may be explicitly or implicitly limited by the forum's terms of reference or by the intervenor's desire to obtain a settlement. Thus, intervenors are often asked to help resolve housing or school disputes without any commitment of significant new public resources for housing or schools, or to help resolve police-community disputes without any possibility that public authorities will agree to restructure the relationship between law enforcers and disadvantaged communities.
>
> Worse yet, mediators may be employed by government agencies as a substitute for making such commitments - a method, as it were, to 'manage' conflict without confronting its basic sources. These implicit limitations on the options available to the parties can feed back into the dispute-resolving forum, with the result that third-party intervenors in public policy disputes focus more on improving communications and decision-making procedures than on discovering or dealing with the root causes of group conflict. They are often tempted to select both the dispute to be mediated and the representative

parties with an eye out for the achievement of a 'practicable' settlement, and to assist in the discovery of options that appeal to the moderates on both sides, while isolating the extremists."

Rubenstein fears that the process could be more a matter of "short-term peacemaking" than "long-term problem solving". These problems are well known to mediators and techniques for circumventing some of them continuously being developed, while others can be over-stressed. Sometimes a partial resolution is better than none at all, and an interim settlement may assist the longer term process of resolving underlying issues (some of which cannot be resolved, anyway, except through political action). Just as we have counselled against over-reliance on policing initiatives to solve all ills, so we should not rest unrealistic hopes on the mediator. Social problems severe enough to cause threats to social order are not going to be solved overnight.

The option preferred by Rubenstein - the problem-solving workshop - occurs out of the public eye, is small-scale, is sequential (involves a long series of meetings that approach the problems incrementally) and focuses on the expansion of options through interaction, rather than on a settlement per se. This process is most applicable to those conflicts that are intermediate between the conditions appropriate to conciliation and those appropriate to public mediation. Antagonisms are not so serious that the parties cannot meet for discussions, but considerable relationship-building and problem-analysis remains to be accomplished.

The technique has been most fully developed in the context of international mediation and is described in Mitchell (1981) under the rubric "third party consultation". The most distinctive feature of consultative workshops is "externalisation" of the conflict, in that the participants are "not the actual parties to an ongoing dispute but merely some segment of a party, representing, in some unspecified degree, typical attitudes and beliefs of the entire party" (Mitchell, 1981). This feature enables the group to be more relaxed and open in its exchanges, because the outcome will not commit in any way the parties to the actual conflict. The options generated - perhaps evaluated and weighted on a number of criteria - can, however, be submitted to a wider forum, such as a formal mediation. The consultations are distinct from the police-community consultative groups described above in not being public (and thus avoiding the posturing and rhetoric to which such groups are prone), by having a more clearly defined problem-solving aim, and by the presence of a the third party facilitator. Apart from the externalisation of the actual conflict, Mitchell also describes such workshops as sharing the following characteristics:

A workshop setting involving a high level of informality and non-committing, analytical discussions that provide maximum opportunities for problem solving.
A third party acting in a consultative role and relying upon formally recognised expertise for any recognised authority within the workshop.
Non-directedness throughout the whole exercise, the parties participating under no form of duress and able to withdraw at will.
Tactical objectives of removing some of the atmosphere of fear, mistrust and hostility that customarily surrounds the relationship between parties in conflict.

The problem-solving workshop blends into a number of other techniques such as T-groups, encounter groups and sensitivity training, which however tend to focus more on Mitchell's last feature above - relationship building - than on problem-solving as such. These other forms also tend to be used for therapeutic purposes - to change the behaviour or attitudes of the participants - which is not a goal of the consultation workshop.

The use of such techniques in the police/community context has been concentrated on attitude-change, awareness of others, self-awareness and so on. One of the earliest experiments (Bell et al., 1969) followed episodes of violence and hostility between the black community and police in Houston, Texas. Several series of workshops, each involving between ten and fifteen police officers and the same number of lay citizens, meeting for one three-hour session each week for six weeks, were organised at community centres and at the Police Academy. Attendance by the officers was required, but that by citizens was of course voluntary, while attempts were made to recruit a representative cross-section of the whole community. The groups were led by psychologists experienced in group therapy. "The major goals of the program are to promote a cooperative relationship between the community and police and to effect greater mutual respect and harmony. In order to achieve these ends the group sessions are structured so as to have the police and community first examine the damaging stereotypes they have of each other; second, to consider the extent to which these stereotypes affect their attitudes, perceptions and behaviours toward each other; third, to look at the ways in which each group reinforces these stereotypes in the eyes of the other; and fourth, to develop a cooperative, problem-solving attitude directed towards resolving differences and reducing conflict to a level where both groups can work together constructively" (Bell at al., 1969). Questionnaires completed by participants after the course indicated "enthusiastic acceptance by the participating community and grudging to moderately good acceptance by the police." Most community "representatives" reported a positive change in feelings towards the police, but only just over a third of officers indicated more positive attitudes to the community. The community members felt they had a better appreciation of the police as individuals instead of members of an undifferentiated group, and the police members were gratified by the fact that their role and capacities were now better appreciated.

The programme suffered from problems of inconsistent participation by citizen members. After attending the first session to let off steam and express their grievances they often failed to return. The police, for their part, were reluctant but coerced attenders who often sought to sabotage sessions by, for instance, refusing to join in discussions or by deliberate belligerence. There was even a problem of turnover among group leaders, some of whom found the sessions stressful or took hostilities personally. Given these problems, it is hardly surprising that there seemed to be no appreciable behavioural change in the longer term. Several of the problems could have been resolved, however, by, for instance, having leaders experienced in mediating group conflicts (rather than in directing therapy groups of psychiatric patients), better definition of aims and a clearer problem-solving orientation, participant-control rather than leader-control of the agenda, and voluntary attendance on both sides. Even so, the function of such workshops could hardly be to alter behaviour in the community, as too few would experience them, and the more combative would have exercised the option of non-participation. Such an aim was unrealistic, and the goal of option-expansion associated with problem-solving workshops or consultations proper would have been more fruitful. Klein et al. (1971) had a similar experience and commented particularly on the "boundary maintenance" problem - the fact that the group could not be insulated from the "socially explosive local situation", which thus sabotaged its aims. It is inevitable that people who feel strongly about a problem will impose their own agenda on the situation, or leave if they cannot, and it is the duty of the group facilitator to incorporate such agendas in preference to his or her own.

A later attempt followed riots at Stanford University in 1970, when students and local police officers were brought together in a variety of contexts to promote better understanding and reduce campus tensions (Diamond and Lobitz, 1973). The project sought to achieve this by arranging for "nonviolent, communicative interactions" between the two groups. Three contexts were provided: riding together in squad cars on a regular beat (one officer and two students together for 4-8 hours); informal dinners and discussion sessions in students' homes and dormitories (typically one or two officers and 3-4 students for 2 hours); encounter sessions, or small group discussions, at a local high school, views being shared in threes, sixes and then in the entire group (each session lasting 3 hours).

According to the researchers "The results indicate, in general, the project achieved its hypothesized objectives of increasing understanding...between police and students, depolarizing police and student attitudes towards each other..., and changing students' intended behavior [as indicated in questionnaire responses] towards police in a positive direction." Of the three modes of contact, the encounter sessions seemed the most efficient and were associated with "liberalization of police attitudes" (Diamond and Lobitz, 1973).

The use of volunteers only in this project undoubtedly contributed to its greater success. The authors admit: "It is doubtful that such changes would have occurred among non-volunteer police and student subjects." How far such workshops could change behaviour "on the outside" is still dubious, because of the limited numbers who can feasibly take part and because the more extremist elements would not be included. This sort of experiment, focused on improving relationships, is thus of limited use. Of more benefit would have been to have passed beyond the sharing of experiences and views to the collaborative construction of possible solutions to the community and inter-group relationship problems identified by the participants as underlying the continual outbreaks of disorder. This would at least have provided a concrete outcome to share with non-participants and become the basis for further resolution exercises of more practical import. Turner and Brown (1981) have, moreover, adduced evidence for the idea that, when major negative prejudice exists between groups, greater familiarity without some kind of cooperative task is ineffective in reducing the stereotypes they have of one another, and can make them worse.

Chapters 17 and 18 demonstrate how the idea of consultative workshops, facilitated by skilled independent third parties, can be more successfully applied in the context of police community relations in the British context. Based on different models, these two schemes show how there is a wide range of options for using this basic principle of facilitated consultation, adapted to local exigencies and needs.

The account by David Ward (Chapter 16) provides another approach open to the intermediary. The work in this case was almost entirely with one "side" in the conflict, and took the form of advice, exploration of issues, and suggestions, often akin to "training" in conflict resolution skills, but in an informal way and focused on a particular existing dispute. The approach was therefore far more practically-orientated than the encounter sessions just described. The third party role was one of empowerment by expanding the options of the group and by providing information and skills. The intervenors were very careful to stand back and retire once the touchpaper had been lit, to ensure that the group learnt to rely on its own resources and honed its skills through experience, to prevent any tendency to become dependent on their leadership. In the course of the project, the group imbibed such principles of conflict resolution (although not in any didactic way) as openness (exploration of the causes of their problem instead of blaming others, admitting their own past offending), assertion (especially the use of publicity, increasing confidence in their own capacity becoming self-reinforcing), affirmation (admission of the good things about the estate, thereby not alienating other groups), participation in resolving their own dispute, and taking responsibility for this. The intervenors had to return from time to time when internal conflicts threatened the survival of the group and its achievements. It is very important that any facilitative resource is not offered on a temporary basis only: there will be times when reinforcement is needed. Even when the third parties have retired from direct involvement, they should remain available as a resource to help through future crises. In this case, the reception of the youths' overtures by the authorities and the community was favourable and responsive; in other cases, where attitudes were more entrenched, a mediatory effort by the third parties might have been necessary to break down barriers on the other side as well.

Other work of great value is being pioneered in Northern Ireland, where the centuries-old antagonism between Protestant and Roman Catholic communities, with colonialist and militarist overtones, presents a particularly entrenched conflict, engrained deeply in the group-consciousness of every citizen of that warm but tragically torn country. While political conditions may facilitate or hinder rapprochement, ultimately resolution will depend on reconciliation between the two communities, both practically and mentally. The separation in this case is so severe, that very little accurate information passes across the divide to challenge partisan prejudices and preconceptions. Schools, for instance, are largely segregated - "oases of calm" as Tyrrell (1989) has described them, "cushioned...against the reality outside, daily happenings are not discussed." At the expense, of course, of understanding.

Mediation work in the province concentrates particularly on fostering discourse across the sectarian divide in safe conditions. The Community Conflict Skills Project uses workshops for "experiential learning", where groups are enabled to discuss their feelings, encounters and ideas about the "troubles", increasing positive attitudes of toleration and respect, communication and understanding between communities. Fitzduff (1988), whose handbook gives many examples of exercises for focusing such group work, argues that "It can often prove more productive to promote intra-community discussion...than to attempt inter-community dialogue in the first instance. Indeed it should be noted that there is evidence to show that groups are likely to increase their hostile attitudes towards each other if thrown straight into political dialogue unless adequate work is first done on both developing their confidence to speak as a group, and on providing an unthreatening atmosphere within which dialogue can take place." Such workshops, she believes, "may be an essential first step in tackling sectarianism and can increase the possibility of communities eventually developing agreed frameworks of justice, cultural plurality and political responsiveness."

Many other groups pursue the same objectives in the schools. "Education for Mutual Understanding (EMU)" is a guide for teachers developed from individual school initiatives and aims to enable young people to "learn the importance of resolving differences and conflict by peaceful and creative means" (Tyrrell, 1989). Workshops are carried out within schools as a preparation for work between schools. The Quaker Peace Education Project, based at the University of Ulster in the town which aptly symbolises the sectarian divide by being known as Londonderry by one side and Derry by the other, provides conflict resolution training in the schools, and carries out "prejudice reduction" workshops, based on the work of the American Cherie Brown. These workshops start by building pride in one's own background, and recognition of the mistreatment and stereotyping one suffers because of the divide, to give groups the confidence to accept the pride of others and to see their suffering because of one's own prejudices.

Others, like the Nonviolent Action Training Project and the Northwest Youth and Community Project, are employing similar techniques, but more direct contact between the communities is encouraged in an increasing number of non-segregated schools and holiday associations. The Corrymeela Community has brought representatives of the two sides together for weekends in a rural area remote from the city to encounter one another's views and discover common ground in shared suffering and hopes.

Such techniques are equally applicable to basic conflicts in any society. The Corrymeela Community is based, indeed, on an Israeli reconciliation project (Neve Sharon) for Jews and Arabs. Similar school-based projects are being pursued in England for tackling problems like bullying and racial discrimination.

In general, one can conclude that there is a variety of options for intervention open to the mediator or facilitator, and these should be used according to the situation - eg. according to the emotional climate, the degree of entrenchment of opinion (racist or sexist attitudes being particularly impervious to change), cultural factors, political sensitivities, parties' sophistication and accustomedness to nonviolent action, etc. Their approach will change over time - more or less interventionist, or from one mode of intervention to another. Rather than prescribe a particular approach, one should encourage flexibility and creativity in line with the general principles of conflict resolution. However, the experience so far inclines one to a few tentative conclusions:

1. Intervention which is problem-focused is likely to be more effective than that which is purely relationship-focused (while admitting that situations exist where the latter is the only feasible step open initially, to prepare the ground for subsequent problem-solving).
2. Intervention should not be in the form of short-term "projects". Conflict-resolution is long-term: as each specific dispute is settled, wider issues come to light. Conflict is not a "sudden" occurrence, but a process over time, continually changing shape and oscillating between periods of calm and crisis (cf. Marshall, 1988). Third party assistance may be needed at a number of stages and should endure as a potential resource, to be accepted as parties feel they need it.
3. Conflict is a normal feature of any society, and institutions for assisting in its constructive handling themselves also need to be planned on a permanent basis. Mediation as crisis-intervention only is prone to the accusations of superficiality and "keeping the lid on" conflict. Mediation bodies also acquire more sensitive skills and credibility through experience accrued over time and this advance needs to be consolidated by ensuring continuity.
4. Conflict-resolution is assisted by familiarity of its principles among parties to disputes. While skilled third party intervenors are needed to guide protagonists through emotional complexes, there is no need why citizens and professionals of all persuasions should not receive education in the appropriate principles and practice in the skills, whether as part of occupational training, voluntary community-based workshops or, even better, as part of basic schooling.

There are a number of potential sources of intermediaries. They can be ad hoc and particular to specific situations (as in Sadler's example in Chapter 9), or individuals and groups who have specialised in "neutral third party" intervention. The latter include national organisations like CRS and local mediation projects, like Newham Conflict and Change Project (Chapter 17). The latter may take referrals of interpersonal disputes (police "domestics") or inter-group disputes for mediation, or provide training in conflict resolution skills for any who request it. Some local projects specialise in training and "conflict-awareness" workshops. There are also local mediation projects that arrange meetings between victims and offenders ("reparation schemes" - Marshall and Merry, 1990), which may be of service in disputes involving crime. (See FIRM, 1989, for lists of such facilities in Britain by region.)

Several of these latter schemes in America have been involved in helping to resolve situations where public disorder was breaking out; for instance, the case described by Claassen in Chapter 14 and a sniper shooting case in New York state described by Umbreit (1986). In this case, a depressed young man, high on drink and drugs, had been firing a rifle across the main street of a rural town. After his arrest, a meeting was first arranged between the man and two victims who had been shot and nearly killed. This was followed, after lunch, by a meeting of these three "plus seven community representatives consisting of a minister from a church near where the shooting occurred, a former judge, a housewife involved in promoting drug abuse programs, the investigating police officer at the time of the shooting, a realtor, and a local attorney. Particularly since this very violent offense, which had received banner headlines in all of the local newspapers, had frightened the entire community, it was believed that the direct involvement of a number of community representatives was important in terms of working toward some level of reconciliation between the community at large and the offender" (Umbreit, 1986). Such local mediation projects can play an important part in public order problems because they are at hand, have developed credibility with local groups and agencies as independent parties, and have the requisite skills (which are essentially the same across all contexts of conciliation).

The Contribution of the Local Community.

During outbreaks of public violence and disorder the local community is the major victim. It is in their interests, therefore, for neighbourhood groups to seek a degree of self-imposed control and to develop mechanisms for pursuing grievances both forcefully and peacefully, as Ward's teenagers did with great success (Chapter 16). Ray Shonholtz, in Chapter 11, was especially concerned to argue for local communities taking responsibility for control and breaking their reliance on external authorities, through training, organisation and cooperation with the police and other agencies (whose responsiveness to community initiatives is an essential source of encouragement).

Such ideas form the basis of "neighbourhood (or community) justice", a concept explored in a particularly illuminating way not only by Shonholtz, but also by Scheingold (1984). The latter justifies this kind of community development by appeal to Berger and Neuhaus's (1977) idea of "mediating structures" (employed also, in relation to crime, by Woodson, 1981). As Scheingold explains, "The theory of mediating structures focuses on the alienating quality of modern life in which individuals, particularly the poor, tend to to be caught between the oppressive certainty of large-scale bureaucracies...and the contingent existence of private life....Mediating structures, it is argued, can reduce 'both the anomic precariousness of individual existence in isolation from society and the threat of alienation to the public order'." (Scheingold, 1984, quoting Berger and Neuhaus, 1977.) The neighbourhood, family, church, voluntary associations, ethnic groupings are examples of such mediating structures that provide meaning (values), structure and effective participation for the individual. Such structures must be autonomous and culturally diverse, but, "as the essential, noncoercive integrative mechanism of modern society", they create a "unity growing out of diversity" (Scheingold, 1984). Mediating structures like neighbourhood justice, therefore, are the source of order between the disorderly poles of "everyone for oneself" and totalitarianism. Such structures appear to be what former Chief Constable John Alderson (1984) is seeking when he refers to "more democratic participation...at small community level, more confidence engendered in 'local' government'" and "an adequate political forum at community level in which to discuss local issues", without which "people are often brought into conflict with the law and the police"; "Some people suffer prosecution, humiliation and social ostracism as they feel obliged to protest" and "a nation will become more reliant on police power and the criminal sanction....".

We have already noted the grassroots growth of community groups in Northern Ireland working through their feelings, conceptions and experiences to a better understanding of their own needs, those of others, the common ground between them and the need to develop better - pacific and respectful - mechanisms for reconciling group differences. Sally Sadler (Chapter 9) also propounds the need for the training of community groups, empowering them to adopt a rational and effective approach to the resolution of their own problems. We have seen, too, the capacity of people to learn and put into practice (even in the fear-provoking context described by Jim Murtagh in Chapter 3) the principles of nonviolent action; and not just the more socially resourceful individuals, for the Alternatives to Violence Project is teaching the same skills to offenders imprisoned for violent behaviour, enabling them too to discover they have unrealised inner resources for self-control and hence greater control over what happens around, and to, themselves - what AVP terms "transforming power". The principles of this power listed by AVP are not distinct from those we have already outlined for constructive conflict resolution:

1. Seek to resolve conflicts by reaching common ground.
2. Reach for that something in others that seeks to do good for self and others.
3. Listen. Everyone has made a journey. Try to understand where the other person is coming from before you make up your mind.
4. Base your position on truth.
5. Be ready to revise your position if you discover it is not fair.

6. When you are clear about your position, expect to experience great inward power to act on it.
7. Do not expect that this response will automatically ward off danger. If you cannot avoid risk, risk being creative rather than violent.
8. Surprise and humor may help transform.
9. Learn to trust your inner sense of when to act and when to withdraw.
10. Work towards new ways of overcoming injustice.
11. Be patient and persistent in the continuing search for justice.
12. Help build a community based on honesty, respect and caring."
(Alternatives to Violence Project handout.)

Apart from learning new skills, communities can actively strive to reduce the rifts and tensions within, work for a greater sense of neighbourliness, and make positive efforts to enhance communication with the police (as the Lambeth Consultative Group propose, Chapter 4, and as other contributors like Jim Murtagh and Yvonne Craig also support). The community can go even further and provide help with, and participation in, police training in conflict handling skills, as Sadler argues (Chapter 9). Conciliation resources can also be developed locally - as has happened in both Newham and Lambeth for instance, as well as elsewhere in London and the rest of the country - employing ordinary residents as volunteer mediators after appropriate training, utilising the sources of goodwill, social responsibility and local knowledge that are inherent in any microcosm of society. Such developments could be supported and aided by government resources that would reap a profit in public-spiritedness and peace far outweighing the cost (FIRM, 1990).

While striving for mechanisms of natural order, "community self-control", it is crucial, however, not to forget the other needs: to end injustice and exploitation, and to eliminate, as far as possible, suffering and degradation. Inability to resolve our conflicts constructively is one problem; the other is our inability to stem the grievances which cause them and will go on causing them if not addressed. How far can one apply the principles outlined here to the endeavours of grassroots activists seeking social change on behalf of the downtrodden? To a degree, one certainly can, as long as one appeals to the basic principles and not to the superficial forms - such as mediation, problem-solving workshops - they may take. There can be no doubt that a realistic, unblinkered perception of what the problem is, what a group's fundamental interests are, and where the bottom-line of acceptable achievement lies - openness, in other words - are invaluable assets to any proponent of change. Only if one is clear where one is coming from and where one is going can one take rational decisions about appropriate action. In theory, too, many activists would accept that collaboration is preferable to - and even more productive than - confrontation. BUT, they will argue, quite correctly, that collaboration must take place on the basis of equal participation and a balance of power, and this, as far as disadvantaged groups are concerned, is manifestly not so, as Oakley says at the end of Chapter 18. (Yvonne Craig reminds me that "collaboration" became a dirty word during the Second World War for the very reason that it was associated with the lack of such preconditions.) MOREOVER, collaboration cannot occur from one side only (one hand clapping) - one cannot begin such a process unless the other "party" is willing and able to recognise that there is a problem. The work of the organiser of disadvantaged groups is focused around building power and publicising grievance. Even this much can be derived from the principles advocated here. But if power-building and public expressions of discontent involve confrontation, involve criticising the role of dominating groups, involve blame, are we not then deviating from such a "grand design" and does this not indicate a fundamental weakness in it?

In the United States, where mediation and mediators have been more prevalent and more pervasive than in Britain so far, political activists have been imbibing the ideas behind them for a while, to the extent that many are now trained in conflict resolution techniques. Yet there is still a fundamental ambivalence, which gave rise recently (June 1988) to an exploratory conference at Ann Arbor, Michigan, attended by six grass roots organisers and ten members of Conflict Clinic, Inc. and Program for Conflict Management Alternatives, two mediation bodies also concerned with social justice and social change, and many of whom had been themselves at some stage involved in community organisation. The account of their discussions has been published by PCMA and CCI (Cunningham et al., 1990). Although there was no attempt to resolve all their differences, some common ground was found - "All agreed that there is no virtue in false agreement, superficial management of conflict, suppression of conflict, or avoidance of social justice concerns."

One of the concerns voiced, however, was that community organisers tend to be blamed for "creating" conflict. Bringing problems to the surface, focusing attention on them, is not, of course, to create them. It is the essential first step towards solving them. Every group tends to have its reputed "trouble-maker" or "stirrer", who tends to be unpopular, but may, in fact, be playing an important social role as an "early warning signal" of problems which, if left unattended, may sooner or later threaten the survival or the efficiency of the group. One may argue that there are indeed people who do seem to create conflict, who spur people to disputes by picking unnecessary fights. But given that this is so, it will almost certainly be a matter of displacement - the creation of one conflict in order to relieve tensions derived from a real but latent problem which passes unrealised or unadmitted. Even displacement, then, can act as a sign of conflict that needs to be brought into the open and addressed. It is up to the other parties to root out the real causes of the antagonism, and not to take the overt situation as necessarily the only problem. The problem is less with the "troublemaker" than with those who seek to discredit or dismiss him/her.

At the Conference there was a division between those whose primary orientation was towards resolution and those who did not regard this as a necessary goal. One of the arguments of the latter was that one's purpose might be to create open conflict in order to alter power-relations in favour of less powerful groups. At times confrontation can achieve short-term advantage which might be valued above the loss in mutual esteem and trust. This focus of many activists on building power rather than collaborative relationships can lead them to criticise the intervention of mediators who "took away too much of the power that community groups worked so hard to obtain".

These issues may only be resolvable in specific instances. It is apparent that mediators need to be peculiarly sensitive to issues of power imbalance and to allow disadvantaged groups to take responsibility for handling their own conflicts. If the latter is a major issue, the more appropriate role for a third party may be as consultant, trainer or facilitator, rather than the more actively interventionist one of conciliation or mediation. This was the approach described by David Ward in Chapter 16, concerned always to take a sideline position and to leave actual negotiations to the parties alone. It was found to be the only feasible approach in relation to unorganised extremist groups in the MOVE conflict (Assefa & Wahrhaftig, 1988), where a "middleman" position was utterly distrusted and untenable. The last word should perhaps rest with the American Chicano organiser who addressed mediators thus: "The people know what they want and what they need. They have always known. We don't need you to tell us what we need. But you can help us figure out how to get it." (Quoted in Nicolau and Cormick, 1972.)

Chapter twentythree

Conclusions

THIS BOOK is not intended to provide answers so much as possibilities; nor explicit techniques so much as orientating principles. Nevertheless, certain recommendations emerge relatively clearly from among the various contributions, written as they are from a great variety of standpoints:

1. The levels of hostility and violence in any confrontation are the separate responsibility of each of the groups involved. Restraint in response, clarity in intention, and openness to conciliatory opportunities are the principles that should inform the management of public disorder crises.
2. Such responses depend on preparedness and thorough training in both skills and, just as important, attitudes (including attitudes to oneself or self-control). The principles of openness, assertion, affirmation, participation, collaboration, the resolution of emotions and creative problem-solving are common to a wide variety of well-developed and tried approaches to handling conflict, whether as an involved party or a third party "neutral". Understanding of these principles of conflict resolution should be a part of the basic education not only of professionals such as the police and administrators, but also of citizens generally.
3. Appropriate responses also depend on confidence in oneself and one's organisation that comes from having clear goals and high morale. Individual skills can only be exploited fully in the context of good management, attention to which should be a major priority of any establishment.
4. Police forces have a vested interest in maintaining good public relations. Community liaison should not therefore be simply a peripheral function, but one of the main central roles of every police officer. As such it should comprise a major part of the training and job specification of all officers.
5. Good community relations depend on reciprocity, power-sharing and collaboration. In this context, too, the "community" cannot

just be seen as the conforming and the participating, but must be understood to include the activist and the detached members, to reach whom will require a more dedicated effort.
6. Although police forces can, and should, play a role in fostering community peace, they cannot be expected to overcome the effects of widespread discrimination, sense of injustice, social disadvantage and group alienation. Although the police may on occasion make mistakes that can trigger off major incidents (they are human, which is a positive attribute), they cannot be held to blame for the sense of grievance and despair that fan the flames into a full-scale conflagration.
7. Government policies play a crucial role in the causation and prevention of public disorder, by their effects on the socio-economic well-being of different groups, the credibility of authority relations, the overall ethos of trust and responsibility, and the resources available to statutory agencies and local communities for creating a viable, lasting and universally acceptable system of social control. In particular, the government should ensure that police authorities, local communities and minority groups have the confidence in their own powers as agencies or citizens of a democracy, and in the fairness of the political system as a whole, to enable them to take a secure part in the process of peaceful protest and conciliation.
8. In the event of a crisis, governmental bodies tend to respond with a great deal of activity, but most of this tends to consist of "the great and the good" talking with one another in an attempt to resolve a problem which they cannot understand without listening directly to those who are involved in it. It is not sufficient to listen to Chief Constables' interpretations of what is happening in their areas. The voices of representatives from the local communities themselves, including the more rebellious groups, also need a sympathetic hearing and a designated role in the problem-solving process. Policy cannot be effective without a true grasp of the nature of the problem and without the commitment of those who are part of it. The government should give a lead in openness for the police, local authorities and other bodies.
9. Local communities, especially those characterised by a rich mixture of cultures and group-identities, need strong indigenous mechanisms for conflict-resolution and prejudice reduction, including both conciliation services and skills training, the latter preferably incorporated into, but not limited to, basic school education.
10. A national body of experienced and highly trained mediators is required that can intervene in major social conflicts where aggression has got the upper hand. They would be empowered to

Conclusions

institute training in constructive approaches to conflict, to advise parties in dispute, to facilitate direct negotiations or problem-solving workshops, to conciliate among parties to conflict, or to carry out formal mediation, according to their judgement and the views of all the parties.

References to Section Six

ALDERSON, J (1984) *Law and Disorder*. London: Hamish Hamilton.
ASSEFA, H & WAHRHAFTIG, P (1988) *Extremist Groups and Conflict Resolution*. Praeger.
AUBERT, V (1963) Competition and dissensus: two types of conflict and conflict resolution. *Journal of Conflict Resolution*, 7, 26-42.
BELL, RL, CLEVELAND, SE, HANSON, PG & O'CONNELL, WE (1969) Small group dialogue and discussion: an approach to police-community relationships. *Journal of Criminal Law, Criminology & Police Science*, 60:2, 242-246.
BENNETT, T (1990) Getting back in touch. *Policing*, 6:3, 510-522.
BENYON, J & SOLOMOS, J (Eds) (1987) *The Roots of Urban Protest*. Oxford: Pergamon.
BERGER, PL & NEUHAUS, RJ (1977) *To Empower People: the role of mediating structures in public policy*. Washington, DC: American Enterprise Institute for Public Policy Research.
BICKMORE, K, GOLDTHWAITE, P & LOONEY, J (1984) *Alternatives to Violence: a manual for teaching peacemaking to youth & adults*. Akron, OH: Peace Grows Inc.
BOSKIN, J (1976) *Urban Racial Violence*. Beverly Hills: Glencoe.
BOWE, J, CRAWLEY, L & MORRIS, J (1987) Inner city disturbances: lessons from Liverpool 1985. *Probation Journal*, March, 10-12.
BROGDEN, M (1979) 'All police is cunning bastards' - policing & the problem of consent. Paper to the British Sociological Association Conference.
BROWN, J (1981) The functions of communities in police strategy. *Police Studies*, 4:1, 3-8.
CHALMERS, WE (1974) *Racial Negotiations: potentials and limitations*. Institute of Labor and Industrial Relations, University of Michigan - Wayne State University, Ann Arbor.
CHATTERTON, M (1973) Sociology and the police, in Alderson, JC & Stead, PJ (Eds) *The Police We Deserve*. Wolfe.
CLIFFORD, W (1983) Policing a democracy. *Police Studies*, 6:2, 3-21.
COMMUNITY RELATIONS SERVICE (1987) *Principles of Good Policing: avoiding violence between police & citizens*. Washington, DC: US Govt. Printing Office.
CUMBERBATCH, G & TADESSE, M (1987) Community policing in crisis, in Shaw, JW, Nordlie, PG & Shapiro, RM (Eds) *Strategies for Improving Race Relations*. Manchester: University Press.
CUMMING, E, CUMMING, I & EDELL, L (1964) Policeman as philosopher, guide and friend. *Social Problems*, 276-286.
CUNNINGHAM, HV, CHESLER, MA, ISRAEL, B, POTAPCHUK, W & BLECHMAN, F (1990) *Strategies for Social Justice: a retrieval conference*. Fairfax, VA: Conflict Clinic Inc.
CURLE, A (1971) *Making Peace*. London: Tavistock.
——— (1986) *In the Middle: non-official mediation in violent situations*.

Leamington Spa: Berg.
DEWDNEY, M (1988) Police negotiation - 'it stuns us but it works!' *Alternative Dispute Resolution Association of Australia Newsletter*, December.
DIAMOND, MJ & LOBITZ, WC (1973) When familiarity breeds respect: the effects of an experimental depolarization program on police & student attitudes toward each other. *Journal of Social Issues*, 29:4, 95-109.
FISHER, R & BROWN, S (1989) *Getting Together*. Business Books.
FITZDUFF, M (1988) *Community Conflict Skills: a handbook for anti-sectarian work in Northern Ireland*. Cookstown, CoTyrone: Community Conflict Skills Project.
FORUM FOR INITIATIVES IN REPARATION AND MEDIATION (1989) *Directory of Mediation Projects & Conflict Resolution Services*. Bristol: FIRM.
——————— (1990) *The Need for Community Mediation Services*. Bristol: FIRM.
FOSTER, C (1989) Coming to terms with panic & temper tantrums. *Social Work Today*, 2 March, 12-13.
GOSLING, J & MAHENDRAN, J (1984) *Report of Visit to USA, 1984*. London: Newham Conflict & Change Project.
GREENE, JR & DECKER, SH (1989) Police & community perceptions of the community role in policing: the Philadelphia experience. *Howard Journal*, 28:2, 105-123.
GREGG, RB (1959) *The Power of Nonviolence*. New York: Schocken.
HOLDAWAY, S (1984) Policing the city. *Christian Action Journal*, Summer, 11-13.
HUNT, RG (1987) Coping with racism: lessons from institutional change in police departments. In Shaw, JW et al (Ed) *Strategies for Improving Race Relations*. Manchester: University Press.
JEFFERSON, T (1987) Beyond paramilitarism. *British Journal of Criminology*, 27:1, 47-53.
KEITH, M (1988) Squaring circles? Consultation & 'inner city' policing. *New Community*, 15:1, 63-77.
KIM, Y (1987) Work - the key to the success of Japanese law enforcement. *Police Studies*, 10:3, 109-117.
KLEIN, EB, THOMAS, CS & BELLIS, EC (1971) When warring groups meet: the use of a group approach in police-black community relations. *Social Psychiatry*, 6:2, 93-99.
KRIESBERG, L (1982) *Social Conflicts*. Englewood Cliffs, NJ: Prentice-Hall.
LAWSON, PE (1981) Mediation of social order: police use of law, myth & mystifications. *Police Studies*, 4:2, 9-20.
MARSH, P (1978) *Aggro: the illusion of violence*. London: Dent.
MARSHALL, TF (1989) Out of court: more or less justice? in Matthews, R (Ed) *Informal Justice?* London: Sage.
MARSHALL, TF (1990) Conference supplement. *Mediation*, 6:4.
MARSHALL, TF & MERRY, S (1990) *Crime & Accountability*. London: HMSO.
MARX, GT (1970) Civil disorders & agents of social control. *Journal of Social Sciences*, 26:1, 19-57.

References to Section Six

MEER, F (1990) Negotiated settlement: pros and cons. *Race and Class*, 31:4, 27-37.

MITCHELL, CR (1981) *Peacemaking & the Consultant's Role*. Aldershot: Gower.

MOORE, T (1986) Public order; the police commander's role. *Policing*, 2:2, 88-100.

MUNRO, JL (1987) The decision for community policing: the cases of Victoria & South Australia. *Police Studies*, 10:3, 140-153.

MURRAY, JD (1988) 'Contact policing' & the role of the constable. *Police Journal*, January, 76-90.

NICOLAU, G & CORMICK, GW (1972) Community disputes and the resolution of conflict: another view. *Arbitration Journal*, 27:2, 98-112.

NIEBURG, HL (1968) Violence, law, and the social process. In Masotti, LH & Bowen, DR (Ed) *Riot and Rebellion: civil violence in the urban community*. Sage.

PATE, AM, WYCOFF, MA, SKOGAN, WG & SHERMAN, LW (1986) *Reducing Fear of Crime in Houston and Newark*. Washington, DC: Police Foundation.

PHILLIPS, R & LEADBETTER, D (1990) Violent sessions in the classroom. *Social Work Today*, 1 February, 22-23.

PHILLIPS, SV & COCHRANE, R (1988) *The Role & Function of Police Community Liaison Officers*. London: Home Office (Research & Planning Unit Paper 51).

PLATT, AM (1971) *The Politics of Riot Commissions*. New York: Collier.

PLATT, S (1987) Troubled waters. *New Society*, 27 March, 9-10.

POTTER, J & REICHER, S (1987) Discourses of community and conflict: the organisation of social categories in accounts of a 'riot'. *British Journal of Social Psychology*, 26, 25-40.

POTTS, LW (1982) The limits of police-community relations programs: a cross-national perspective. *Police Studies*, 5:2, 10-20.

PRESIDENT'S COMMISSION ON LAW ENFORCEMENT & ADMINISTRATION OF JUSTICE (1967) *The Challenge of Crime in a Free Society*. Washington,DC: US Govt.

PUGH, R (1988) How to build a system for managing violence. *Social Work Today*, 1 September, 14-15.

ROSE, D (1990) Forces of change. *The Guardian*, 21 February, 21.

RUBENSTEIN, RE (1988) *Group Violence in America*. Fairfax,VA: Center for Conflict Analysis & Resolution (Working Paper 2).

RUCKRIEGEL, W (1986) Police operations at demonstrations. *Police Studies*, 9:3, 148-150.

SALEM, RA (1982) *Community Dispute Resolution through Outside Intervention*. Washington,DC: Society of Professionals in Dispute Resolution (Occ.Paper 82-3).

SCHEINGOLD, SA (1984) *The Politics of Law & Order: street crime & public policy*. London: Longman.

SHERMAN, L & BERK, R (1984) The specific deterrent effects of arrest for domestic assault. *American Sociological Review*, 49, 261-272.

SKOLNICK, JH (1969) *The Politics of Protest*. New York: Simon & Schuster.

SMELSER, NJ (1963) *Theory of Collective Behaviour*. New York: Free Press.
STORCH, RD (1975) The plague of police locusts: police reform & popular resistance in Northern England, 1840-1857. *Int.Rev.Social History*, 20, 61-90.
STRATTA, E (1990) A lack of consultation. *Policing*, 6:3, 523-549.
STREET, R (1990) A quiet revolution. *Criminal Justice*, 8:1, 10.
THOMPSON, EP (1979) Law and order and the police. *New Society*, 15 November, 379-340.
TURNER, JC & BROWN, RJ(Eds) (1981) *Intergroup Behaviour*. Oxford: Blackwell.
TYRRELL, J (1989) Developments in conflict resolution in schools in Northern Ireland, in Forum for Initiatives in Reparation & Mediation *Conflict in Schools*. Bristol: FIRM.
UMBREIT, MS (1986) *Victim Offender Mediation with Violent Offenses*. Valparaiso,IN: PACT Institute of Justice.
VOLPE, MR (1989) The police role, in Wright, M & Galaway, B (Eds) *Mediation and Criminal Justice*. London: Sage.
WADDINGTON, D, JONES, K, & CRITCHER, C (1989) *Flashpoints: studies in public disorder*. London: Routledge.
WADDINGTON, PAJ (1987) Towards paramilitarism? Dilemmas in policing civil disorder. *British Journal of Criminology*, 27:1, 37-46.
WOODSON, RL (1981) *A Summons to Life: mediating structures & the prevention of youth crime*. Cambridge,MA: Ballinger.

NOTES ON THE CONTRIBUTORS

Ian Beckett is the Chief Superintendent at Battersea Police Station and was the Chief Inspector (Operations) during the successful introduction of the Neighbourhood Policing Project. He also established and implemented the police tactics first tested in the public disorders of 1985 at Brixton.
Greta Brooks has, since 1965, been Secretary of the Lambeth Churches Coordinating Committee. She is a member of the Brixton Council of Churches. She chaired the sub-committee of the Lambeth Community/Police Consultative Group which negotiated with the Home Office the pilot scheme for Lay Visitors to Lambeth Police Stations. She has chaired the Panel of Lay Visitors and the Consultative Group. She is also an elected member of the Executive Committee of the Forum for Initiatives in Reparation and Mediation, and initiated the Lambeth Mediation Service.
Ron Claassen is the West Coast affiliate of the United States Mennonite Conciliation Service and directs the Fresno County, California, Victim Offender Reconciliation Program (VORP). He also serves as co-director of the new Institute for Peacemaking and Conflict Studies at Fresno Pacific College.
Community/Police Consultative Group for Lambeth is made up of representatives of local voluntary and statutory bodies, police and politicians. It has an open policy both in its representation and in the opportunity given to non-members to take part in discussion during meetings. Useful work is done by small sub-committees, made up of relevant members of the community and police, in preparation for major items on the agenda at Group meetings.
Yvonne Craig has been a community worker and counsellor in Bermondsey and Haringey. She is editor of "Mediation", and on the editorial boards of "Counselling" and "Self and Society". She is also a Justice of the Peace and is currently researching an MA Public Order (Race Relations) at the University of Leicester Centre for the Study of Public Order.
Sir Christopher Leeds is a Senior Lecturer, University of Nancy II, Lorraine, France. He graduated with a BSc in Economics from the London School of Economics, and gained an MA in International Relations at the University of Southern California. He has been a long-term member of the Conflict Research Society and the International Association for Conflict Management. Publications include Understanding Conflict (Teaching Resources Folder) (1975), Peace and War (1987), and English Humour (1989).
Robert J Louden, MA, is Associate Director (Training) at the Criminal Justice Center, John Jay College of Criminal Justice, New York. He was formerly Chief Hostage Negotiator with the New York Police Department.
Alexander Marnoch is a Commander in the Metropolitan Police and was the last District Commander for Lambeth before the reorganisation of the

Metropolitan Police District removed the post. As such he had overall responsibility for the policing of that Borough, which includes Brixton, in the aftermath of the 1981 riots and the re-establishment of police credibility along with reduction of the high levels of local crime.

Tony Marshall was Director of the Forum for Initiatives in Reparation and Mediation at the time of editing this book. Before that he had been a member of the Home Office Research and Planning Unit for 15 years. He is author or co-author of many articles and books, including Alternatives to Courts, Crime and Accountability, Counselling and School Social Work, Bringing People Together, etc. He received his MA in Social Anthropology from Cambridge University.

Jim Murtagh is involved with training in non-violence techniques and produces an "alternative" newssheet, Whose World?, which deals with ecological and non-violence issues, and alternative life-styles generally.

Tim Newburn gained his PhD at Leicester University for his thesis on "Permission and Regulation: sexual morality and the criminal law in post-war Britain". He currently works as Director of the Hillsborough Project at the National Institute for Social Work. He was previously a Senior Research Officer at the Home Office Research & Planning Unit, where his major research interests were in policing and victims of crime.

Dr Robin Oakley is a sociologist who specialises in research and professional training in ethnic relations and equal opportunities. Since 1984, he has been closely involved with the development of police training in community and race relations, both nationally and in particular with the Metropolitan Police Training School at Hendon. He is at present Academic Director of the Centre for Community and Race Relations Training at Turvey, Bedfordshire, and is also a visiting Fellow at the Institute of Criminology, University of Cambridge.

Pauline Obee, JP, BBO, is Administrator of the Newham Conflict and Change Project, Fundraising Chairperson for St.Francis Hospice, and a dance & drama teacher. As the first Administrator at NCCP in 1984, her duties have expanded with the growth of the organisation, which offers Reconciliation, Education and Consultancy services. Her skills in fundraising and teaching are particularly valued as a major contribution to the Project's comprehensive programme.

Lawrence Roach is a Commander in the Metropolitan Police. When in command of the operational element of No.6 Area (West) within London, he was heavily involved with Deputy Assistant Commissioner Paul Condon (now Chief Constable of the Kent Constabulary) in the planning of the policing of the annual Notting Hill Carnival - seeing their efforts rewarded by reductions in both crime and disorder.

Sally Sadler has lived in Brussels for 8 years, working as a freelance radio and print journalist, specialising in social issues, women's concerns and leisure. Before that she worked for the BBC Brussels office and for the Wall Street Journal. Her first job in Brussels was as programme assistant at the Quaker Council for European Affairs, an information and lobby office specialising in peace, human rights and development.

Pat Sawyer was employed for 15 years by Social Services Departments before setting up her own agency, TRAINING INITIATIVES, in 1989. She now designs and implements courses for private, voluntary and statutory agencies around the country on a variety of subjects. Her primary interest is in the understanding, control and management of aggression and violence in self and others. Training Initiatives can be contacted at 28 Beacon Close, Rownhams Park Estate, Rownhams, Southampton SO1 8JR.

Raymond Shonholtz, J.D., is an internationally recognised expert in the field of conflict resolution, having founded one of America's first and most influential community and school conflict resolution systems, Community Board Program, Inc. A former criminal trial attorney, Dr Shonholtz has written and lectured extensively on conflict management, in the United States and abroad. As President of Partners for Democratic Change, Dr Shonholtz is actively involved in developing conflict resolution systems and training programmes in the Soviet Union and Poland. He is an Executive Trustee of the Eisenhower Foundation and a Juvenile Justice Commissioner in San Francisco.

Maria R Volpe, PhD, is Associate Professor and Coordinator of the Dispute Resolution Program at John Jay College of Criminal Justice, New York. She is also a vice-president of the Society of Professionals in Dispute Resolution.

David Ward is a Senior Lecturer in Social Work and Co-director of the Centre for Social Action Groupwork at Nottingham University. Following a degree in Law and VSO in Africa, he trained for social work and worked in the Probation Service. His particular interest is groupwork with young offenders, in which he maintains an active involvement through practice, consultancies, and project management as well as teaching and research.

Wallace Warfield is a Senior Associate of The Conflict Clinic, Inc., and Assistant Professor at George Mason University, Virginia, USA, providing process design, mediation, training and facilitation services with a particular emphasis on complex public policy issues. Prior to this he served as a Distinguished Visiting Fellow at the Administrative Conference of the United States, where he was responsible for helping Federal agencies build alternative dispute resolution processes into their administrative systems. Earlier, Warfield worked for the Community Relations Service as Acting Director, and has worked with community groups and street gangs in New York. He has written several recent articles on conflict resolution.

Index

A

abuse 28, 59, 61, 162
    verbal 213
ACAS 20, 90, 143, 256
accountability 83, 98, 217, 227, 265
active listening 19, 89, 120, 193
activists 17, 83, 92, 136, 288, 289
adversarial methods 19, 141
adversarial system 149, 156
adversaries 239
Advisory, Conciliation and Arbitration Service
    see ACAS
affirmation xiii, 19, 244,283, 291
African National Congress 89, 258
Afro-Caribbeans 25, 26, 28, 77
    relationship with police 79
agenda 203, 206, 278
aggression xii, 1, 2, 5, 7, 8, 10, 12, 13, 16, 17, 18, 21, 31, 33, 56, 67, 82, 84, 89, 118, 128, 229, 254, 292
    environmental factors 230
    philosophy of 6
    ritualised 6
    theories of
        aversion 230
        frustration 230
        instinctive 230
        social learning 230
aggression in crowd situations 121
aggressive behaviour 118
    diverting 96
aggressive tendencies 39
agitators 61, 126, 251
agreement(s) 163, 256, 278
agreements, compliance with by disputants 186
aims 123, 241, 242, 281
Ainsley estate. 196
Ainsley Teenage Action Groups 196
Ainsley Youth Express 197
Alamosa, Colorado 164
alarmism 28
Alderson, John 66, 78, 108, 251, 263, 287, 295
alert 58
alert systems 66
alienation 14, 17, 34, 58, 63, 80, 127, 132, 135, 155
All Saints Road 105
Alphin, Captain 260
alternative dispute resolution 82
alternative lifestyle 246
Alternatives to Violence Project 21, 194, 287, 288
American Arbitration Association 162
American cities 13
Amnesty International 126
amplification 11
analysis 231, 232, 233, 266, 278
anger 7, 36, 54, 62, 83, 210, 246
anger management 234
Ann Arbor, Michigan, conference 289, 290
anomie 13. 15 See also violence: theory of
anonymity 15, 94, 133
antagonism 63, 64, 67
anti-nuclear movements 125
anti-segregation 160
apology 54, 254
Arabs 284
arbitration 150
Archer 15
armed forces 36
arrest(s) 56, 59, 66, 106, 110, 126, 131, 133, 137, 153, 165, 201, 214, 269, 286
arrest rates 81
arrest squads 106, 114
arson 26, 252
arts 67
Asian(s) 25, 26, 35
Asian cultures 42
assault(s) 8, 152
    verbal 57
Assefa, H & Wahrhaftig, P 164, 246, 290
Assefa, H 167
assertion 283, 291
assertion of authority 66
assertiveness 14, 19, 234, 243, 254
assessment(s) 164, 184
assessment team 164
assimilation 27, 79
Atlanta 171, 172
attitude 12, 94, 213, 241, 243, 259, 280, 291
attitude change 84, 280
attorneys 177
Aubert, V 243, 296
Auerbach, J 157
Australia 20
Austria 112, 115, 127
authority 6, 13, 84, 214, 255
authority relations 292
awareness 119, 187, 220, 222, 224, 231, 234, 235, 280

B

Babylon 42, 77, 78, 79, 83
Baden-Würtemburg 110
Badham B. 195, 207

303

Bandura, A 7, 230, 235
Banks 10
Bar Association 165
Barrett, Representative 160
barriers 17, 113, 195, 203
baton rounds 57, 58, 112
Beckett, Ian v, 88, 90, 91, 249, 251, 252, 263, 275
behaviour training 119
behavioural skills 268
Belgium 111, 112, 113, 117, 123, 126
Bell , R L 254
Bell, RL, Cleveland, SE, Hanson, PG & O'Connell, W 295
Bellis, EC 296
Bennett, T 275, 295
Benyon & Solomos 79, 263, 295
Berger, PL & Neuhaus, RJ 286, 295
Berk, R 255, 297
Berkowitz 7, 10
Berlin-to-Vienna peace march 127
Bermondsey 42, 77, 78, 80, 83, 84, 254, 273
Bickmore, K 258, 261, 267
Bickmore, K, Goldthwaite, P & Looney, J 295
Biderman, AD 146, 147, 157
Birmingham, Alabama 160
Birmingham, England 35, 271, 275
black activists 83
black community 32, 96, 218, 257, 280
black community groups 257
black cultures 42
black fragmentation 171
black middle class 37
black MPs 37
black people 29, 30, 32, 34, 35, 63, 82, 171
black police officers 143
black youth(s) 31, 81, 83, 84, 93, 94
blame 39, 54, 142, 144, 195, 251, 289
Blau 15
Bleckman, F 295
Blitz 42
body language 120
Bonn 108, 123, 124
Bonn police 126
Bootham 82
Boskin, J 254, 295
Boston school crisis 170
bottom line 288
Boulding 33
boundary maintenance 281
Bowe, J 256
Bowe, J, Crawley, L & Morris, J 295
boycott 97, 257
brainstorming 120, 245
Brass Tacks 108
Breakwell, G M 235
Bricklayers' Boys 78
bridges 17
Bristol 26, 273

Britain 15, 25, 29, 87, 93
British Association of Sound Systems 105
Brixton 35, 40, 53, 87, 88, 93, 95, 97, 98, 99, 112, 125, 138, 143, 164, 250, 251, 254, 275
 unemployment in 35
Brixton Council of Churches 73
Brixton riots 9, 32, 34, 53, 73, 74, 115, 274.
 See also riots
Broadwater Farm Defence Campaign 245
Broadwater Farm Enquiry 220
Broadwater Farm Estate 42, 82, 219, 244, 253
Broadwater Farm Revisited 81
Brock 27
Brockwell Park 98
Brogden, M 273, 295
Brooks, Greta 41, 264
Brown 5, 80, 269, 282
Brown, Cherie 284
Brown, J 295
Brown, RJ 298
Brown, S 296
Brunel University 219
Brussels tragedy 11
Buffalo 126
bullying 284
Bundestag 110
Bundesverband Burgerinitiativen Umweltschutz 124
Bundesvorstand des DGB 108
Burgess 14
Burley D 195, 207
Butcher, Colin 196
Butler 29
Byford, Sir Lawrence 113

C

Calhoun, F.L 159, 167
calm 59, 188, 266
campaign 203
Campaign for Nuclear Disarmament 252
Campbell 5
Canada 20, 154
Canetti 57
cannabis 31, 94
Canning Circus police station 202
canteen culture 81, 266, 270
capital punishment 3
Caribbeans 79, 101
caring 288
carnival 102, 103, 104, 105, 106
Carnival and Arts Committee 104
Carnival Arts Committee 105
Carnival Support Group 106
catharsis 7
caucus 177
causation 32, 154, 292
CCI 289
census 94

Index

Centre for the Study of Community and Race Relations 219
Chace, J 167
Chalmers, WE 295
change 206, 209, 266
Chatterton, M 273, 295
chemical gas 112
Chesler, MA 295
Chesshyre 27, 84
Chicano Civil Rights Network 179, 181
Chicano community 175
Chicano youth 177
child abuse 8, 14
child-rearing 13
children 20
Children in Conflict 78
chimpanzees 6
Christian Police Trade Union 123, 128
Christie, N 149, 157
CID 253
citizen demonstrations 175
citizen education 291
Citizen Intervenor 148
citizen participation 164
citizens xiii
citizens' responsibilities 152
citizens' rights 82, 152
citizenship 142, 192
city council 179, 180, 181
City University 87, 90
civic work 150, 152, 155, 156
civil disobedience 125
civil disorders 34, 161
civil rights 159, 258
Civil Rights Act 1964 159, 160
Civil Rights campaign 260
civil rights movement 171
civil rights training programmes 163
civilisation xiii, 16
Claassen, Ron 143, 286
Clapham Common 98
class 14
classroom training 219
clergy 165, 179
Cleveland 161
Cleveland, SE 295
Clifford, W 269, 295
Clutterbuck 5
co-operation 82, 84, 94, 199
co-operative 78
co-operative policing 82, 83
co-operativeness 134
Cochrane, R 269, 297
Cockneys 78, 79
code of practice 81
coercion 9, 10, 253, 254
coexistence 171
Cohen 10, 11, 13
collaboration xii, 19, 87, 142, 191, 245, 252, 274, 289, 291

collective behaviour 15
collective violence 25, 33
Collins, LeRoy 160
colonial imperialism 78
Commission for Racial Equality 27
commitment 18, 98, 151, 193, 200, 220, 265, 278, 292
common ground 73, 144, 176, 193, 222, 244, 245, 284, 287, 289
communication 17, 19, 87, 91, 97, 105, 118, 122, 151, 154, 161, 163, 211, 215, 221, 243, 256, 270, 277, 278, 283, 288
communication skills 8, 191
communication, structure of 3 143
community xii, xiv, 6, 9, 14, 30, 53, 93, 94, 102, 104, 106, 125, 132, 134, 141, 142, 143, 145, 149, 150, 152, 153, 155, 160, 164, 165, 166, 170, 179, 180, 191, 192, 194, 196, 210, 212, 214, 216, 244, 250, 252, 256, 263, 264, 269, 270, 283, 286, 287, 288, 291, 292. See also: neighbourhood; public ... ; social ...
community, responsibility of 41
community accountability 265
community activists 82, 173
Community Boards 153, 192
Community Board Centre for Policy and Training 154
Community Board Programme 149
Community Boards of San Francisco 152
community centre 271
community collaboration 269
community complaints 203
community conciliation 152
Community Conflict Skills 283
community conflicts 77, 212
community constable 201
community consultation 218, 250
community consultative group 219
community councils 125
community development 162
community goals 104, 105
community groups 55, 73, 90, 244, 247, 250, 272, 287, 290
community initiatives 286
community interveners 134, 137
community involvement 91, 98, 103, 227, 265, 275
Community Involvement Unit 226, 228
community justice 150-154 *passim*, 157, 286
community leaders 30, 56, 136, 163, 250
community liaison 291
community liaison constable 202, 203
Community Liaison Officers 224, 269
community mediation 16, 20, 84, 96, 192
community mediation scheme 141
community mediation services 83, 91
community members 91, 193
  political and non-political 99
  professional 99

305

community norms 146
community objectives 87
community organisation 289
community organisations 84, 96
community organisers 164, 289
Community Oriented Police Education 270
community participation 95
community peace 292
community policing 29, 56, 57, 61, 65, 66, 78, 82, 84, 91, 201, 250, 271
Community Public Safety Patrol 166
community relations 166, 173, 193, 250, 254, 265, 269, 272, 274, 282, 291
Community Relations Board 173
community relations divisions 269
community relations, police training in 193
Community Relations Service 21, 90, 142, 159, 160, 161, 169, 172, 246, 256, 265, 267, 269, 277, 285, 295
community relations units 164
community representatives 54, 101, 281, 286
community responsibility 271
community safety patrol 166
community solidarity 218
community stewards 89
community support 151, 269
community values 268
Community Workshop 213
community-based policing 99
community-based workshops 285
Community/Police Consultative Group 40, 87. 96
Community/Police Consultative Group for Lambeth 53, 96, 97
competition 170, 276
complaints 20, 105, 163, 164, 246
complaints against the police 58
complaints, neighbourhood 202
complaints procedures 218
complexity 39, 240, 260
compromise 243
concessionary gestures 240
concessions 5
conciliation 16, 37, 88, 135, 141, 144, 161, 162, 166, 192, 277, 286, 288, 290, 292, 293
conciliation agency 214
conciliation, informal 215
conciliation procedure 66
conciliation resources 288
conciliation services 292
conciliation techniques 159
conciliators 150, 159, 165, 209, 210, 211, 215
conciliatory opportunities 291
conciliatory responses 250
Condon, Deputy Assistant CommissionerPaul 102, 103
conferences 245

confidence 65, 84, 143, 219, 220, 222, 229, 235, 243, 246, 247, 253, 277, 284, 291, 292
confidence, lack of 166
confidence-boosting 235
confidentiality 160
conflict xii, 8, 9, 16, 20, 28, 30, 33, 41, 82, 91, 122, 125, 128, 129, 130, 134, 136, 139, 143, 148, 149, 150, 151, 152, 154, 156, 162, 166, 170, 183, 185, 201, 209, 211, 213, 222, 227, 235, 239, 277, 278, 279, 280, 284, 285, 290, 291, 293. See also: social conflict
  stages of 245
Conflict and Change 213, 214, 216
conflict, awareness 193, 285
conflict, causes of 116, 161, 278
Conflict Clinic, Inc. 289
conflict de-escalation 156
conflict, deep-seated 243
conflict, entrenched 283
conflict, externalisation 279
conflict handling skills 288
conflict management 3, 36, 82, 84, 129, 150, 151, 154, 211, 212, 246, 268, 274
  theories of 17
conflict management, skills of 210
conflict managers 154
conflict prevention 106, 129, 149, 154, 156, 193, 247
Conflict Prevention and Resolution Team 164
conflict reduction 91, 130
conflict resolution 1, 19, 36, 39, 91, 141, 144, 150, 151, 155, 162, 192, 194, 241, 242, 243, 245, 247, 256, 264, 266, 275, 276, 277, 284, 285, 291, 292
conflict resolution skills 77, 153, 229, 255, 282
conflict resolution techniques 289
Conflict resolution, theory of xi, 1, 17, 87
conflict resolution training 268
conflict school 33
conflict theories 25
conflict, visible 263
conflict-resolution principles 285
confrontation 19, 26, 37, 59, 111, 185, 191, 244, 245, 246, 252, 255, 258, 265, 272, 289, 290, 291
Connolly P, & Woolman T. 195, 208
consciousness-raising 193
consensus 102, 104
consent 106, 217
Conservative policies 25, 28, 31, 34
conspiracy 125
constables 87, 88, 95, 218. See also: police
constitution 28, 110, 149, 160
constructive conflict resolution xiii, 1, 18, 40, 41, 191, 201, 223, 225, 244, 287
Constructive Policing 251
consultancy 210, 216, 256

Index

consultants 122, 142
consultation 96, 97, 99, 123, 124, 125, 141, 193, 200, 219, 226, 243, 244, 245, 246, 267, 290
  maintaining initiative 98
  objectives 98
  two-way 98
consultation workshop 280
Consultative Committees 125
consultative group v, 65, 88, 274
consultative mechanisms 242
consultative role 214
consultative workshops 279, 282
contact policing 91, 133, 275
contacts, increasing 88
containment 130, 165, 172, 178
contingency planning 55, 105, 106, 136, 143, 172, 193, 250
control xii, 5, 16, 19, 74, 105, 126, 146, 147, 200, 205, 206, 216, 227, 239, 240, 244, 249, 250, 286, 287
control of anger 254
controlled verbalisation 89
controversy 112
cooling out 255
Cooper 9
cooperation 19, 20, 29, 67, 127, 147, 150, 151, 152, 170, 191, 213, 240, 286
cooperation, police/community xiv
cooperative associations 149
cooperative conflict resolution 20
cooperative games 192
cooperative learning 214
cooperative relationship 280
cooperative task 282
coordination 173
Coote, Chief Inspector 202
Cope 270
coping with stress 229
copycat violence 26, 32, 139
cordons 58, 60, 105
Cormick, GW 290, 297
corruption 266
Corrymeela Community 284
Coser 33
cost of policing 110
Cotton, Dorothy 260
councillors 90, 96
counterculture 81
counterprotest group 173
CR, CR principles See: conflict resolution
Craig, Yvonne 6, 42, 193, 254, 255, 273, 288, 289
Crawley, L 295
creative problem-solving 291
Creative thinking 234
creativity xii, 19, 20, 284, 288
credibility 66, 165, 167, 187, 241, 255, 258, 277, 285, 286, 292
Creighton, Sean v

crime 14, 29, 32, 34, 36, 42, 62, 83, 88, 93, 94, 95, 97, 102, 104, 106, 142, 146, 152, 191, 195, 203, 263, 285
crime, minor 143
crime prevention 80, 88, 95, 96, 97, 108, 129, 147, 247, 265
crime prevention officers 105
crime rate 30, 63, 88
crime-fighting 88
criminal behaviour 25
criminal elements 104
criminal fraternity 251
criminal justice 20, 145
criminal justice agencies 256
criminal justice system 146, 148
criminal law 146
criminalisation 82
criminality 33, 152
criminals 92, 105, 135. See also: offenders
crises 251, 283
crisis 143, 166, 170, 172, 231, 232, 233, 234, 245, 269, 292
crisis intervention xii, 142, 246, 247, 249, 263, 285
crisis management 254
crisis prevention 163
crisis resolution 245
crisis response 162, 164
crisis stage 246
Critcher, C 298
criticism 97
  constructive 53
crowd 15, 40, 56, 59, 61, 119, 241, 249
crowd conflict 116
crowd control 89, 107
crowd management 10
crowd psychology 115
crowd violence 257
Crown Prosecution Service 84
CS gas 113
Cuban Haitian refugee 170
Cuban/Haitian Entrant Program 162
Cubans 162, 171
culture 11, 12, 28, 29, 83, 284, 292
culture of poverty 13
Cumberbatch, G & Tadesse, M 271, 295
Cumming, E, Cumming, I & Edell, L 268, 295
Cunningham 289
Cunningham , HV, Chesler, MA, Israel, B, Potapchuk, 295
curfew 166
Curle, A 17, 258. 275, 295
Curtis 8
cynicism 97, 225
Cyprus 111, 112, 122, 123

D

Dade County 170, 173
Dahrendorf 33

307

damage 116, 133, 138
danger 33, 102, 184, 187
dangerous behaviour 16
de Tocqueville, Alexis 156
de Waal 6
de-escalation 1, 6, 150, 154, 166, 240
deadlines 186
deadly force 164, 166
De'Ath, Fran 252
decision-making 240, 250
decision-making authority 141
decision-making procedures 278
Decker, SH 270, 296
Declaration of Independence 33
defence 136
defenders 136,137
defensive armour 253
defensiveness 271
  avoidance of 98
definition 204, 250
democracy 20, 33, 82, 142, 292
democratic accountability 265
democratic society 65, 146, 148, 156
demonstration xii, 83, 108, 109, 110, 111, 122, 124, 127, 128, 161, 178, 249, 252
demonstration organisers 107, 109, 111, 117, 122, 123, 125, 127
demonstrators 56, 90, 108, 110, 111, 112, 114, 116, 117, 118, 119, 123, 126, 127
demythologisation 264
denigration 251, 254
Denmark 112, 122, 123
Department of Justice 143, 159, 256. See also: Community Relations Service
depersonalisation 253
deprivation 13, 26, 34, 36, 84, 93, 263
  relative deprivation 42
Derry 284
despair 25, 32, 292
destabilising events 170
detached youth 264
detached youth worker 201
deterrents 31
Detroit 26, 161
  riots 26
development 200, 286
deviance xii, 10
Dewdney, M 296
dialogue 64, 84, 111, 125, 170, 175, 204, 225, 284
Diamond, MJ & Lobitz, WC 281, 282, 296
Dick, Ch.Supt. Stacey 227
Dicke, Wolfgang 119, 121
differences 209, 214, 222
direct action 261
disadvantage 82, 272
disadvantaged groups 5, 258, 289, 290
discipline 32
discontent 32
discrimination 13, 14, 17, 79, 243, 272, 292

discriminatory practices 160, 162
discussion 120
discussion, non-committing 280
disempowerment 41
disillusionment 41, 94
disinformation 242
disinhibition 119
disorder 62, 93, 95, 98, 99, 101, 102, 104, 105, 106, 110, 123, 134, 136, 137, 139, 149, 152, 154, 155, 156, 164, 166, 201, 244, 249, 251, 254, 257, 282, 286
disorder management 130
disorder, pathological explanations of 191
disorderly conduct 110
disorderly elements 91
dispersal 55, 56
displacement 36, 289
disputants 150, 153, 155, 185, 186
dispute resolution 8, 169, 172, 183
dispute resolution processes 186
dispute resolver 185, 187, 189
dispute settlement 141, 155, 156
dispute-settlement services 153
disputes 9, 37, 142, 160, 162, 164, 165, 169, 210, 211, 213, 214, 255, 276, 278, 289
disrespect 81
District Support Unit 115
distrust 31, 210
Ditfurth, Jutta 109
divorce conciliation 20
Dobash 12
docklands 42
Dollard, J 7, 34, 235
domestic conflict resolution 87
domestic disputes 183, 214, 255, 269, 285
domestic relationships 145
domestic violence 8, 12, 194. See also violence: family
Domestic Violence Unit 85
dominant morality xii
Downing Street 252
Downs, Max 176, 177, 179
drama 192
drug dealing 84, 102, 105
drug traffickers 104
drugs 11, 179
Dublin 34
DuBow and Emmons 153
DuBow, F 157
Dunhill 80
Durkheim 14, 31
Dusseldorf 108
dynamics of conflict 277

E

early intervention 148, 149, 150, 154
early warning signal 289
ecology organisations 124
economic recession 34
Edell, L 295

Index

education 35, 37, 153, 154, 212, 260, 261, 285
Education for Mutual Understanding 284
Education for Neighbourhood Change 198
Education Programme 210
effectiveness 129, 131, 165
efficiency 20
Einstadter 15
Elephant Gang 78
Elias 16
eliciting factors 6
Elliott 56
emergency policing 115
Emmons, D 157
emotion 10, 18, 20, 39, 40, 183, 211, 213, 239, 244, 245, 249, 255, 291
emotional climate 284
emotional level 244
emotional state 185
emotional temper 5
employment 78, 93
empowerment 82, 142, 150, 191, 203, 287
encounter groups 280
encounter sessions 282
enemy 16, 30
entrenchment 283, 284
environment 78, 231, 233, 235
environment, control of 188, 215
equal participation 289
equality 204, 207
escalation 8, 9, 10, 11, 16, 18, 37, 58, 91, 130, 131, 136, 137, 145, 157, 214, 244
estates 94, 138
esteem, mutual 290
ethnic conflicts 256
ethnic minorities 29, 30, 35, 264
ethnic minority groups 93
ethnicity 14
ethnocentricity 28
ethologists 6
Europe 25, 90, 154
evaluation 224, 227
exaggeration 11, 16, 18
excessive force 59, 64, 171, 179
excitement 13, 15, 33, 56, 57, 62, 198
expanding options 282
experience 117, 165, 282, 285
experiential learning 283
experimental approaches xi
exploration 229, 231
externalisation 279
extreme behaviour 15
extremist groups 290
extremists 279
Eysenck 31

F

face saving 241
face-to-face meetings 82, 161, 165
facilitated workshops 193

facilitation 161, 175, 176, 204, 206, 220, 225, 244, 272, 277, 293
facilitator 88, 142, 176, 220, 221, 223, 224, 279, 284, 290
factions 191
Fairbairn 97
fairness 16, 83, 176, 218, 243
"Faith in the City" 65
familiarity 6, 58, 165, 187, 220, 282, 285
families 20
family problems 120
Farley 31, 33
Farrer 82
fatalism 13
Feagin 33
fear xii, 7, 11, 36, 39, 40, 136, 240, 253, 280
fear of crime 146, 147
fear of violence 186
Federal Mediation and Conciliation Service 159
feelings 176, 193, 201, 214, 233, 283, 287. See also: emotions
feelings, destructive 193
Felson 10
Ferguson 7
Ferracuti 13
Field 26, 33
fighting 1, 6, 13, 18, 59, 192
fire-brigade policing 30
fire-fighting 92, 246
firearms 113, 164, 269
firearms policy 173
Fisher, R 17, 296
Fisher, R & Brown, S 240, 296
Fitzduff, M 283, 296
Fleming J 195, 208
flexibility 91, 132, 137, 223, 261, 284
flexible response 108
flight 1, 18
Florida 169, 171
Follett 17
Football Association 110
football hooliganism 6, 10, 11, 13, 258
football supporters 112
football violence 107
force 17, 61, 134, 144, 192, 251, 254, 255
force, excessive 163, 175
Forum for Initiatives in Reparation and Mediation v, xiii, 19, 83, 192, 194, 195, 203, 208, 261, 285, 288, 296
forums 84, 182
Foster, C 296
Foundation for Peace and Conflict Research of Hess 118
Fox 6
France 113, 115, 154
Frank 5
Frankfurt 109, 111, 118
Fraser 78
freedom xii, 32

309

freedoms 16
French 5
Fresno, California 143, 175, 244
Fresno Human Relations Commission 144
Freud 7
Friend, The 122
friction 273
Friends 126
frustration 1, 11, 13, 34, 36, 95, 118, 161, 210, 241, 273
Frustration Hypothesis 7
functionalism 31
funding 163

G

Galtung 30, 33
gangs 6
Garcia, Anthony 175
Gartner 15
Geen 11
George Mason University 87
Germany 108, 109, 110, 111, 112, 113, 114, 115, 116, 119, 121, 122, 123, 124, 126, 253
Gewerkschaft der Polizei 109, 119, 121, 124
Gibson T 198, 208
Gifford, Lord 81, 82, 220, 228
Gluckman 6
goals 104, 121, 259
Goldstein 8
Goldthwaite, P 295
Gosling, J & Mahendran, J 296
Gosling, Jonathan v, 260, 296
government 62, 65, 152, 166, 169, 171, 264, 278
  policies 1, 25
Grant 81
grass-roots initiative 141, 192, 287
grassroots activists 288
Greater London Council 64
Green Party 109
Greene, JR & Decker, SH 270, 296
Greenham Common 114
Gregg, RB 259, 296
grievance 58, 249, 252, 292
grievances 5, 37, 92, 132, 169, 254, 255, 258, 264, 281, 286, 288
Groce, Mrs Cherry 40, 54, 61, 62, 164
ground rules 161, 176, 177, 179, 180, 181, 215
group alienation 292
group behaviour 15
group conflicts 20, 141, 153
group consciousness 283
group disorder 9
group identity 79
group interests 288
group process 220
group review 206
group therapy 280

group work 283
group worker 204
groups 280
groups, disadvantaged 290
groupwork 203
Grunwick dispute 30, 59
guilt 15, 276
Gulliver 6
guns 57, 178
Gurr 5, 15

H

Hague, The 115
Hahn 33
Haitians 162
Hall 11, 79
Halloran 11
Halpern, Representative 159
Hamnett 17
Handsworth, Birmingham 28, 29, 31, 35, 65, 271
  unemployment in 35
Handsworth riots 32, 35, 251
Hanselmann, Udo 108
Hanson, PG 295
harassment 30, 162, 203, 216
Haringey, London Borough of 77, 193, 219
Harlem 126
Harrington, CB 11, 142, 144
Harrison M. 78, 196, 208
Havelte 122
health 29, 139
Heath 28
helicopters 128
helmets 108, 114, 115
Hendon Police Training College 74, 95, 114, 115, 116, 219
Hernandez, Mrs. 177, 178
Hessen 125
Hessische Stiftung Friedens- und Konflict Forschung 118
Heysel football stadium 111, 117
high rise blocks 94
Hillfields 9
Hippocrates 188
hippy convoys 9, 249
Hirschi 14
Hispanic communities 143, 153, 163, 166, 175, 178, 179, 181
Hodges 29
Hodgson 26
Holdaway, S 263, 265, 296
holding institute 213
holiday associations 284
home beat officers 55, 60, 224, 226
Home Office 40, 53, 195, 208, 219
Home Secretary 96
homicide 145, 152, 155
honesty 241, 267, 288
hooliganism 25, 32, 34

310

Index

hostage confrontations 269
hostage negotiations 183
hostage negotiatiors 144, 184, 187
hostility 28, 80, 81, 84, 136, 280
housing 26, 29, 32, 35, 37, 83, 93
   sub-standard 94
Houston 280
Howells 9
Human Relations Commission 144, 163, 179, 181, 182
human relations commissions 161
human rights 28
humour 127, 288
Hunt, RG 265, 296
Hurd, Douglas 32, 108, 113

I

Iceland 112, 121
identity crisis 12
ideology of suspicion 275
Imbert 81, 82, 84
immigrants 29, 34, 78
immigration controls 32
impartiality 255
impediments 266
imprisonment 1, 9
India 27
induction course 95
industrial relations 20
inequality 166
infiltration 117
inflation 29
informal social control 14, 147, 155
information 117, 135, 166, 189, 241, 250, 251, 282, 283
Information gathering 260
information, lack of 185
inhibitions 7, 15
initiation ceremonies 12
initiatives 42, 203
injury 133, 138, 145
injustice 34, 66, 243, 249, 263, 288, 292
inner city xii, xiv, 9, 13, 36, 62, 63, 65, 78, 88, 90, 139, 192, 246, 272, 277
inner city decay 93
inner London 42
insecurity 117, 210, 265
instinct 6, 16, 18, 31, 34
Institute for Mediation and Conflict Resolution 162
institutional ombudsman 20
institutional racism 270
integration 29, 161
intelligence gathering 106, 135, 139
inter-community dialogue 283
inter-group conflicts 89
inter-group disputes 285
interaction 17, 88, 150, 239, 268, 281
Interaction theories 10. *See also* violence: theory of

interest groups 242
interests 242, 245, 288
interests, shared 244
interim settlement 279
Interkerkelijk Vredesberaad 108, 124
intermediaries 90, 244, 245, 247, 255, 272, 277, 282
internal conflicts 283
internalisation 7
International Relations 129
interpersonal disputes 141, 254, 256, 285
interveners 161, 183, 184, 187, 189, 278, 282
intervention 143, 146, 148, 187, 191, 192, 213, 214, 256, 284
interventionists 172
intimidation 64
intolerance 10, 185
intra-community discussion 283
involvement 19, 125, 142, 195, 198, 201, 203, 272
IRA 5
Ireland 20, 27, 78, 79, 111, 122, 154
Irish Post, The 79
isolation 1, 94, 127
Israel, B, 295
Israeli reconciliation project 284
Italy 112

J

Japan 264
Japanese police 151
Jarrett 83
Jefferson, T 33, 82, 255, 296
Jews 284
Johnson 36
Johnson, Lyndon 159
Joint Consultative Committee 217, 228
Jones, K, 298
Jones, S. 228
Joshua 33
judgements 244
judges 32
justice 6, 67, 175, 176, 177, 243, 284, 288
justice, administration of 166
justice, formal 148, 156
justice, social 289
juveniles 92, 133

K

Kaplan, S. G. and Whee 235
Kaufman, Gerald 110
Keenan E & Pinkerton J. 195, 208
Keith, M 264, 274, 296
Kelling, G 157
Kennedy, Robert 160
Kerner Commission 26
Kestner 82
Kettle 29
Kiffin, Dolly 244

311

Killian 15
KIM, Y 264, 296
King, Martin Luther 258, 260
Kinsey 36
Kipling, Rudyard 240
Klein, EB, Thomas, CS & Bellis, EC 296
Kraybill 89
Kriesberg, L 17, 239, 240, 296
Kruizinga 123

L

Labelling 10. *See also* violence: theory of: sociological
Labour government 34
labour organisations 165
Labour Party policy 34, 97
Lambeth 32, 40, 90, 92, 93, 94, 95, 96, 98, 99, 273, 288
Lambeth Borough Council 73, 96, 97
Lambeth Consultative Group 249, 261, 264, 267, 288
landlords/tenants 210
Lane 27
language 35, 211
language difficulties 163, 187
latent conflict 30, 36
latent problems 290
Latin America 13
Laue-Cormick model 169
law 18, 33, 142, 156
law and order 53, 60, 61, 246
law breakers 13, 137
law enforcement 13, 145, 146, 147, 148, 151, 161, 173, 211, 217, 273
Lawrence, Massachusetts 165
Lawson, PE 296
lawyers 142, 186
lay visitor schemes 97, 218
Layton-Henry 84
Le Bon 15
Lea 9
Leadbetter, D 254, 297
Leadership 171
leadership, avoidance of dependence on 283
learning 232
learning experience 268
learning opportunity 225
Leeds 41, 82, 264
Leeds, Chris 263
legal rights 126
legal system 148
legislation 109. 213
legitimacy 4, 12, 84, 246, 255
legitimate force 273
Leinen, Joseph 118
Levi, M. & Jones, S. 228
Lewis 13
liaison 37, 60, 274
liberalism 31, 35

Liberty City 173
life-style 243
Limburg 124
listening 181, 210, 213
listening skills 74
litigation 141
Liverpool 32, 35, 112
Lobitz, WC 281, 282, 296
local authorities 35, 37, 105, 292
local beat officers 105, 273
local government 172, 287
Local Government Act (1966) 34
local initiative 137
local people 41, 88, 93, 95, 133
location 223
Locke 33
Lofland 9
London 26, 27, 28, 32, 34, 37, 40, 42, 53, 87, 91, 115, 126, 192, 250, 275, 288
Londonderry 284
Londoners 102
Longres J & McLeod E. 204, 208
Looney, J 295
looting 26, 55, 61, 62, 91, 133, 138
looting targets 136
Lopez, Ronnie 175
Lorenz 7
Los Angeles 15, 26
lose/lose "solution" 246
Louden, Robert 144, 254
Lozells Project 271, 274
Luxembourg 111, 112, 122

M

MacDuffie, Arthur 171
machismo 13, 60, 117, 235
Mahendran, J 260, 296
male-domination 13
management 291
management defeatism 266
management style 98
Manchester 40
Mandela, Nelson 246
manifest conflict 36
manifest violence 37
manipulation 188
Manpower Services Commission 257
manual force 121
marginalisation 30, 34, 258
marginality 14
Marielistas 171
Marler 6
Marnoch, Commander Alec 40, 88, 266, 274
Marnoch Report 58
Marsh, P 6, 9, 11, 258, 296
Marshall, TF 16, 20, 83, 142,144, 192, 194, 261, 285, 296
Marshall, TF and Merry, S 285, 296
Marshall, Councillor 196, 198
Marx 5, 33, 254

Index

MARX, GT 296
masculinity 12
mass media 11, 32, 54, 67, 81, 99, 104. *See also* violence: theory of
mass picketing 249
mass psychology 122
mass society 16
material aspects 18
materialistic values 11
Mathias, Ch.Supt.Graham 227
Matthews, R 296
maturity 42
Maurer 8
Max-Planck Institute 119
McConahay 15
McGuire J. & Priestley P. 203, 208
McLeod E. 208
McNee 59
media 31, 54, 67, 117, 125, 181, 184, 185, 187, 195, 197, 276
mediating agency 246
mediating structures 286
mediation xiii, 16, 20, 37, 82, 142, 143, 150, 159, 160, 161, 165, 166, 213, 255, 283, 285, 286, 288, 290
mediation centre 255
mediation, formal 215, 278, 279, 293
mediation, international 87, 279
mediation, private 182
mediation projects 90, 285
mediation resource 257
mediation services 130, 256
mediation session 211
mediation skills 42, 87
mediator 77, 84, 90, 128, 142, 161, 164, 186,187, 210, 255, 258, 275, 278, 284, 290, 292. See also: third party conciliator
police as 79, 255
mediator initiatives 191
mediator stress 186
mediators, volunteer 149, 153, 210, 255, 287, 288
Meer, F 258, 297
meetings 97, 175, 177, 178, 181, 198, 200, 215, 220, 286
open 96
Members of Parliament 96
Merry, S 16, 285, 296
Merry, SE 157
Merton 14
Mesa, Sister Angela 181
Metro Ministry 176
Metropolitan Police 87, 90, 95, 102, 103, 107, 109, 112, 114, 115, 116, 119, 126, 217, 219, 226, 266
Metropolitan Police District 40, 88, 103
Miami 173
middleman 290
Miles 36

militancy 253
military policing 9
Miller 13
Mills, Wright 33, 204, 208
miners' strike 9, 108, 114, 126, 253
minority communities 161, 162, 163
minority groups 267, 292
minority representation 267
mistrust 28, 97, 147, 280
misunderstandings 39, 117, 211, 213
Mitchell, CR 78, 87, 90, 279, 280, 297
Mobiele Eenhed 108, 109, 116, 124, 125
moderation 77
Mods and Rockers 10
monitoring 139
Montagu 34
Moore, CW 189, 255
Moore, T 297
moral judgement 241
moral reasoning 8
morale 60, 139, 206, 291
morality, dominant xii
Morris, J 295
mounted police 108
mugging 11, 34, 93, 102
Mullender A. & Ward D. 195, 203, 205, 208
multi-agency action 85, 105
multi-ethnic society 83
multicultural society 29, 77
multiple deprivation 78
Mungham 6
Munich 119
municipal support functions 153
Munro, JL 269, 297
murder 8. *See also* assault
Murdock 11
Murray, JD 10, 268, 275, 297
Murtagh, Jim 39, 91, 194, 258, 261, 287, 288
Muslims 40
mutual assistance 147
mutual esteem 290
mutual understanding 213

N

National Council of Civil Liberties 110
National Front 5, 29
National Union of Students 126
National Urban League 163
Nationalist parties 27
Native Americans 162
Nederlandse Politiebond 124
negative mode 88, 97
negative reactions 120
negotiated settlement 252, 257, 276
negotiation 8, 19, 37, 141, 142, 150, 161, 165, 167, 169, 201, 216, 260, 265, 276
negotiation skills 142, 162, 205
negotiations 89, 144, 165, 240, 256, 278, 293

313

293
negotiators 142
neighbour 141, 145, 147, 148, 210
Neighbour conflicts 20
neighbour disputes 18, 150
neighbourhood 164, 287. See also: community
neighbourhood conflicts 37
neighbourhood crime 146
neighbourhood disputes 130
neighbourhood groups 286
neighbourhood justice 154, 286, 287
neighbourhood justice centres 20, 141, 256
neighbourhood mediation project 41
Neighbourhood Policing Project 99, 103
Neighbourhood Watch 99
neighbourliness 66, 67, 288
Netherlands 108, 109, 111, 112, 115, 116, 118, 121, 122, 123, 125, 128
Neuhaus, RJ 286, 295
neutrality xiii, 90, 193, 215
Neve, Sharon 284
New York 13, 144, 164, 286
New York Police Department 144
Newark 26, 161
  riots 26
Newburn, Tim v, 143, 277
Newham 214, 288
Newham Conflict and Change Project 210, 216, 192, 209, 285, 296
Newham, London Borough of 192, 209
Newman, Sir Kenneth 56, 78, 81, 108, 112, 113
Newson 5
Nicolau, G & Cormick, GW 290, 297
Nieburg, HL 297
no-win situation 172, 251
non-committing discussions 280
noncommunication 170
non-directedness 280
non-provocative communication 89
non-racial society 29
non-verbal communication 189
non-violence 122, 128, 259, 261
non-violence practitioners 277
non-violence training 90
non-violence workshops 194
non-violent action 287
Non-violent Action Training Project 284
non-violent intervention 261
non-violent protest 127
non-violent resistance 239
Nord-Rhein Westfalen 108, 110, 118, 119, 128
Northern Ireland 15, 27, 30, 79, 112, 131, 283, 287
Northwest Youth and Community Project 284
Norway 20, 111, 112, 122, 239
Norway, German-occupied 239

Norwegian Government 118
Notting Hill 28, 88, 89, 101, 102, 104, 105
Notting Hill Carnival 83, 88, 89, 101, 106, 191, 273
Nottingham 28, 195
Nottingham University 198

O

Oakley, Robin 193, 217, 219, 228
Obee, Pauline 192
obscenity 11
obstacles 187, 245
obstruction 110, 274
O'Connell, WE 295
offenders 19, 287. See also: criminals
offenders, violent 194
O'Leary 15
ombudsman 20, 182
openness xii, 18, 20, 39, 207, 214, 241, 243, 246, 261, 267, 283, 288, 291, 292
Operation Kingfisher 83
Operation Trident 105
Operational Policing Review 217
operationalisation of objectives 87
opponent 18, 19, 260
opportunists 92
opportunity 13, 34, 204
opposition 98
oppression 33, 66
option-expansion 281
options 74, 206, 239
organisational management 18
organisational management theory 17
organisations 20
organisers 117
organisers of demonstrations 110
Orgreave 108
Osmond 28, 35
out-smarting 13
Outing, Ch.Insp.Roger 227
outrage 66, 258
outreach 198
outsiders 55
over-reaction 115, 277
overcrowding 15, 94
Overtown, Miami 173
ownership 155, 222

P

pacification 250
Paki-bashing 26
Pakistan 27
Panel of Lay Visitors to Police Stations 56, 66
parental control 31, 32
parenting skills 8
Parry, Walt 176, 177
Parsons 12, 31
participant control 281
participant evaluation 224

Index

participation 14, 18, 19, 20, 82, 84, 142, 150, 155, 207, 223, 240, 243, 271, 281, 283, 291, 292
participation, equal 289
participative management 104
participative training 194
parties 18, 19, 244
partnership 91, 99, 193, 205, 227
patch 219
Pate, AM, Wycoff, MA, Skogan, WG & Sherman, LW 297
pathological explanations of behaviour 203, 251
pathological phenomenon 31
patience 120
patrol 30, 202, 250
Patterson, Jim 144
peace xii, 2, 36, 176, 181, 288, 292
peace camp 127
Peace Commission 66
peace keeping xii, 66, 80, 135
peace making 6, 176, 276
peace organisations 126
peace, positive 36
peaceful assembly 110
peaceful protest 292
peaceful settlement 275
peacemakers 126
Pearson 5, 14
Peel Centre 226
peer group pressure 8
peers 14
perceived intentionality 7
perceived threat 11
perceptions 220, 222, 245, 252, 254, 257, 276, 277, 280, 288
performance measures 138
permanent beat officers 99
permissiveness 32
Perry A. 208
personal commitment 260
personal leadership 98
personal problems 120
personal space 232
personality 230
personnel carriers 108
perspective 215
persuasion 253, 277
petition 196, 197
petrol bombs 62
phases (of disorder) 55, 58
Philadelphia 164, 246, 270
Philippines 20
Phillips, R & Leadbetter, D 254, 297
Phillips, SV & Cochrane, R 259, 297
Phizaclea 36
physical constraint 122
Pinkerton J. 195, 207, 208
Plainview, Texas 163
planning 111, 135, 233, 234, 256

planning, contingency 193
plastic bullets 57, 112
Platt 244, 245, 251, 253
Platt, AM 297
Platt, S 297
playing for time 136
pluralism 141
Plus Programme 94, 217, 266
polarization 31, 79, 117
police xii, xiii, 8, 10, 25, 29, 36, 40, 42, 53, 74, 90, 96, 97, 98, 99, 102, 107, 114, 116, 122, 123, 124, 126, 127, 128, 129, 142, 144, 145, 149, 151, 154, 163, 164, 165, 177, 178, 179, 180, 181, 183, 209, 213, 214, 222, 224, 227, 245, 280, 281, 288, 291, 292
  complaints 41
  failings 97
  image 78
  officers from outside areas 98
  priorities 106
  public support for 97
  senior officers 103
  specialist forces 115
  stereotyping of 94
police academy 163
police accountability 265
Police and Criminal Evidence Act (1984) 36, 96. 97, 103
police, attack upon 26, 91
police attitudes 94, 96
police authorities 113, 116, 292
police brutality 163
police commitment 265
police-community 30
police community awareness 221
police-community communication 164
police-community conflicts 90
police-community confrontation 42
police-community consultation 218, 264
police-community consultative groups 279
police-community cooperation xiv, 286
police-community disputes 278
Police-community forums 257
police-community liaison 17, 202, 269, 274
Police Community Liaison Officers 213, 224
police-community links 264
Police-community partnership 269
police-community relations xiv, 21, 29, 31, 37, 73, 93, 94, 98, 161, 165, 174, 218, 219, 220, 221, 222, 227, 271, 273
police community relations units 164
police-community relationships 181
Police-Community Workshops 217
police: complaints 182, 251, 267
Police Complaints Authority 81
police conduct 63
police confidence 251
police contact 88, 272
police culture 265

315

police defensiveness 265
police, departmental culture 268
police discipline 218
police, Dutch 119
police education 291
police efficiency 266
Police Federation 110
police forces 87, 89, 217, 218
Police Foundation 84
police goals 104
police harassment 32, 201
Police Home Beat Officers 224
police hostage situations 183
police image 267
police initiatives 265
police inspectors 220
police intervention 150, 213
police, Japanese 151, 264
police job specifications 291
police leadership 98
police management 266
Police Monitoring and Research Group 79
police morale 136
Police, Nord-Rhein Westfalen 118
police officers 224, 253, 291
  senior 95, 98
Police Open Days 97
police openness 265
police perspective 246, 268
police policy 242
police powers 109, 213
police practices 26
police prejudice 77, 78
police professionalism 265
police propaganda 109
police provocation 117
police: public alienation 36
police, public criticism of 172
police public information policy 268
police; public perception 217, 222
police racism 274
police recruitment 218, 267
police resources 99, 131
police response 90, 105, 172, 213, 249
police responsibility 193
police role 246
police sergeants 220
police shooting 40, 175, 250
police, social acceptance 265
police, social isolation 265
police specials 253
police strategy 102, 105
police-student relations 282
police supervisors 218
Police Support Groups 89
Police Support Unit 98
police tactics 25
police teams 184, 222
police trade union 90, 109, 123
police training 41, 116, 128, 193, 288, 291

Police Training Council 227, 228
police training schools 119, 128
police violence 246
police-youth conflict 191
policing 9, 29, 36, 58, 65, 73, 95, 98, 99,
    123, 128, 193, 217, 242, 268, 269, 270
  and disorders 101
  by consent 102, 110
  community 103, 104, 132
  consensus 9, 29, 80
  constructive 251
  contact 275
  contract 131
  improvements in 41
  neighbourhood 60, 74, 84, 88, 91, 99,
    132, 226 275
  normal 130, 133, 134, 136
  operational 95
  paramilitary style 108
  policy 98
  post-conflict 93
  post-riot" phase of 92
  practice 223
  preventive 132
  principles 81, 265, 291
  reactive 131
  riot 131, 137
  sector 219, 226
  policing skill 74, 95
  squad 131
  storefront 174
  strategy 129
  team 91, 132
  zonal 91, 132
Policy Studies Institute 58
policy-makers xiii
political activists 5, 289
political change 33
political exclusion 263
political leadership 28, 81
political motives 61
political philosophy 5
political sensitivities 284
politicians 67
poll tax protest 252
Pompa, Gil 161, 166
Portugal 112, 115, 122
position-taking 19
positions 241
positive thinking 234
post-crisis depression 233
post-crisis Intervention 263
post-crisis periods 233
post-war adjustment 8
posturing 279
Potapchuk, W 295
potential for conflict 166
Potter, J & Reicher, S 273, 297
Potts, LW 273, 297
poverty 13, 17, 34, 36, 41, 77

Index

Powell 14, 28, 29
power 9, 15, 33, 80, 152, 181, 289
   abuse of 4, 84
   balance of 289
power building 289, 290
power and control 234
power disparities 255
power imbalance 290
power relations 290
power sharing 84, 227, 291
power-striving 39
powerlessness 58, 263
pre-riot phase 251
precautions 54, 254
precipitating factors 241
precipitating incident 277
preconceptions 39, 229, 234, 242, 283
prejudice 19, 30, 212, 214, 241, 242, 282, 283
prejudice reduction 284, 292
preparedness 291
President's Commission on Law Enforcement and Administration 252, 297
press 178, 185, 195, 197
prevention 54, 91, 131, 132, 142, 146, 148, 263, 292
prevention of disorder 89, 257
preventive medicine 36
preventive strategy 105
preventive work 162
pride 284
Priestley P. 203, 208
primates 6
principles 81, 291
principles, civilised xiii
principles of conflict resolution 291
prisoners 8, 21
prisons 194
privatisation 35
privilege 204
probation officer 196
probation service 256, 257
probationers 95
problem-solving 8, 19, 120, 150, 191, 193, 195, 203, 246, 253, 254, 255, 278, 279, 280, 285, 288
problem-solving approach 88
problem-solving, creative 291
problem-solving orientation 281
problem-solving process 292
problem-solving techniques 234
problem-solving workshops 277, 280, 293
problems, definition of 204
problems, latent 290
problems, underlying 245
professional carers 229, 231
professional responsibility 226
professional workers 204, 232
professionalisation 149, 155

professionalism 105, 217, 226, 242, 265
Program for Conflict Management Alternatives 289
protest march 173
protest organisations 252
protestors 124, 240
Providence Human Relations Commission 163
Providence, Rhode Island 163
provocation 81, 83, 111, 117, 135, 241
provocative appearance 117
provocative technology 128
psychological blocks 276
psychological effects 119
psychological suitability 267
psychologists 280
psychosomatic illness 119
pub violence 6, 9
public See also: community; social;
public accountability 99
public attitude 94, 134
public behaviour 94
public conflicts 256, 277
public consultation 88
public disorder xii, xiii, 17, 39, 77, 91, 113, 118, 129, 130, 132, 138, 242, 292
public disorder crises 291
public disorder, stages of 91
public order 73, 102, 111, 114, 116, 119, 125, 129, 151, 162, 201, 218, 245, 286
Public Order Act 80, 109
public order crises 166
public order policing 108
Public Order Research Group 126
public order training 109
public outcry 112
public perceptions 217
public policy 148, 150, 151, 155
public relations 217
public resources 278
public safety 105, 106, 251
public scrutiny 65, 109
public service 218
public spending 34
public spirit 67
public support 265
public tranquillity 94
public-spiritedness 288
publicity 11, 67, 160, 197, 283, 289
publicity-seeking 258
Puerto Rican 165
Pugh, R 254, 297
punishment 14, 31, 36, 192
Punishment, Custody and the Community 195
Purdy, D 208
put-downs 19

Q

Quaker chapters 90

317

Quaker Council for European Affairs 89, 128
Quaker Peace Education Project 284
Quakers 122, 126, 275
quality of life 75, 271
Quisling 239

R

race 14, 28
race relations 29, 31, 218
Race Relations Acts 29
race relations and police training 219
race relations training 193
race riots 26, 88, 243
    American 252
race-related disorder 42
racial conflict 27, 169
racial disadvantage 25, 29, 30, 34, 263
racial discrimination 34, 64, 80, 177, 242, 263, 284
racial harassment 84, 192, 216
racial prejudice 81
racial tension 165, 166
racism 26, 28, 29, 34, 36, 60, 62, 83, 182, 204, 212, 257
    institutional 266
    working class 36
racist laws 94
Radio 111, 115
Railton Road 97
Range, Mrs. 178, 181
Rangel, Paul Jr. 175
rapprochement 283
Ratcliffe 28
rate support grant 35
rational argument 39
rational decision-making 241, 276
rational planning 261
rational response 39
rationality xii
Raven 5
reactions 10, 231
reactions, exploration of own 229
reactions, instinctive 193
reactions, positive 120
rebellion 33, 117
rebellious groups 292
rebelliousness 13
Reciprocal Training Scheme 226
reciprocity 291
recognition 188
recommendations 291
reconciliation 6, 14, 16, 90, 191, 192, 195, 203, 261, 283, 286
reconciliation service 210
recovery period 233
referral 153, 210, 213
reflection 213, 255
reflectiveness 8
reform 36, 193
refugees 171

refuges 66
Regan, Paul 215
regionalism 28
regulations 155
Reicher, S 273, 297
Reiner 78
reinforcement 7, 14, 265, 283
relationship, cooperative 280
relationship building 143, 193, 280
relationship, partial 273, 279
relationships 2, 6, 9, 14, 18, 19, 20, 74, 80, 92, 124, 142, 143, 147, 152, 153, 155, 166, 181, 192, 211, 239, 242, 244, 247, 250, 264, 272, 277, 282
relative deprivation 79
religion 14
remedial measures 97
reparation projects 16, 285
reporters 180
representation 82
representativeness 225
representatives 165, 245, 281
repression 7, 10, 34, 36, 117
reputation 185
resentment 171
resettlement programme 162
resistance 272
resistance, nonviolent 239
resolution 18, 142, 211, 290
relationship, partial 273, 279
resolution of crime 195
resolution, long-term 246
resources 151, 161 204, 205, 247, 255, 268, 283, 288, 292
respect 10, 142, 198, 212, 214, 222, 254, 258, 264, 280, 283, 288
respectability 78
response, systemic 182
responsibility xii, 20, 127, 138, 144, 155, 156, 166, 187, 191, 200, 204, 211, 215, 240, 247, 264, 273, 283, 291, 292
restorative justice 19
restraint 6, 40, 91, 105, 266, 291
retaliation 10
rewards 265
rhetoric 279
right to demonstrate 123
rights 39, 127, 204, 206, 234
riot xii, 1, 15, 25, 81, 82, 83, 91, 92, 99, 102, 105, 115, 130, 132, 133, 135, 139, 143, 163, 173, 245, 249, 250, 256, 263, 271 *See also*: Brixton; Handsworth, Birmingham; Notting Hill; Southall; St. Paul's; Tottenham; Toxteth. *See also*: policing, riot
riot shield 101
riot control 252
riot equipment 165
riot, phases of 133, 137
riot police 108

Index

riot police training school 113
riot, post-riot phase 138
riot protection equipment 136
riot sequence 134
riot, slow 93
riot squads 131, 124
riot: pre-riot stage 136
rioting 14, 93, 110, 112, 131
riots, types of 132
risk 146, 288
risk assessment 234, 254
risk-taking 15
Roach 88
robbery 31, 63
Robert Shaw primary school 197
Robins 11
Robinson, Superintendent John 107, 109
Robottom
Rock 14
rock concert 126
Roermond 109, 113, 124
role play 118, 120, 192, 212, 213, 232, 268
roles 214
Rose, D 27, 297
rubbish cases 142
Rubenstein, RE 5, 245, 277, 297
Ruckkriegel, W 253, 297
rumour 61, 94, 135, 143
rumour control centre 166
rumour-control mechanism 172
Rustin 82

S

Saarland 118
sabotage (of community programme) 281
Sadler, Sally 89, 244, 252, 256, 287, 288
Safe Neighbourhood Unit 226, 228
safety valve 125
Salem, RA 256, 277, 297
San Francisco 141, 149, 152, 153
San Francisco Community Board Program 141, 192
San Francisco Police Department 153
Sare, Gunther 109, 111
Sartre 5
Sawyer, Pat 193, 250, 254
scapegoats 34, 36
Scarman, Lord 9, 33, 34, 36, 37, 93, 95, 96, 217
Scarman Report 9, 65, 66, 73,103, 218, 219
Scheingold, SA 286, 297
school desegregation 162
school education 292
school officials 161
school security 161
school-leavers 35
schools 20, 67, 82, 192, 212, 283, 284
Scotland 112
Scotland Yard 54, 94, 110
Scots 27

Scraton 80
Scull 11
Sears 15
sectarianism 284
security 123, 179
Seifert, Deputy Police Chief 108, 123, 125
self control 8, 31, 119, 126, 233, 260
self-awareness 89, 280
self-confidence 19, 206
self-criticism xi
self-directed groupwork 203
self-discipline 31
self-esteem theories. *See* violence: theory of: interaction processes
self-help 264
self-policing 125, 161, 165
self-regulation 265
self-respect xii
self-serving actions 147
Selm 110
sensitivity 16, 95, 218
sensitivity training 280
sentencing 18, 32
service ethos 227
setbacks 98
settlement 143, 148, 278
sex-roles 12, 13
sexism 204
sexual identity 12
shame 15
shared goals 37
shared interests 244
Sheriff 197
Sherman, L & Berk, R 255, 297
shields 108, 115, 116, 118
Shonholtz, Raymond 20, 142, 191, 261, 264, 286
shooting 143, 286
shopkeepers 55, 59
shops 94
Short 9
short shield men 108
short-term advantage 290
short-term peacemaking 279
shuttle diplomacy 165, 166
siege mentality 82, 171, 271
Sikhs 26
simulations 268
simulator 174
single-parent families 35
situational features 7
skills 1, 16, 19, 35, 183, 185, 212, 235, 285, 286, 287, 288, 291
skills training 292
skinheads 26
Skogan, WG 146, 157, 297
Skolnick, JH 251, 297
slogans 123
slums 78, 79
Smelser, NJ 17, 241, 298

319

Smith, Rev Ervine 56
smokescreen 242
sniper shooting 286
social action groupwork 203, 205, 207
social animals 6
social anthropologists 6
social anthropology 17
social change 14, 15, 204, 289
social cohesion 78, 155
social conditions xii, 17
social conflicts 239, 292
social contract 269
social control 14, 80, 143, 147, 148, 150, 264, 292
social control mechanisms 257
social deprivation 125
social differentiation 15
social disadvantage 42, 192, 292
social disorder 32, 146, 263
social disruption 21
social exclusion 150
social expenditure 35
social identity 77, 84
social inequality 143
social injustice 80
social interaction 171
social isolation 265
social justice 62, 263, 289
social networks 150
social norms 7, 12, 14, 15, 149
social order 6
social policy 193, 243, 264
social problems 19, 279
social protest 83
Social reaction 1, 10. *See also* violence: theory of: sociological
social responsibility 288
social sensitivity 10
social services 149
social skills 19, 21, 83
social skills instruction 9
Social stresses 94
social unrest 42
social values 79, 149
social workers 191, 193
Social... See also: public ...; community...
socialisation 7, 265
society 16
Society of Black Lawyers 82
socio-economic decline 36
sociologists 6, 31
soldiers 8
solidarity 78, 147, 150, 218
Solomon 263
Solomos, J 295
Sorel 5
South African government 89
Southall 26, 32, 59
    riots 26
Southgate 26, 33

space 215, 216, 233
Spain 112, 115, 122
Special Events Coordinating Council 173
Special Events Planning Task Force 173
spokesperson 82, 123
Springfield, Massachusetts 165
squark-box 114
St. Paul's riots 27, 273
Stanford University 281
Statement of Common Purpose 81, 266
status 13
statutory provision 96
Stead, PJ 295
stench weapons 114
stereotypes 19, 124, 280, 282
stereotyping 83, 94, 122, 191, 214, 284
stewards 89, 106, 125, 126, 128, 252
stirrer 289
Stokes 29
Stone, Councillor 196
stone-throwing 108
Stonehenge 9, 249
stop and search 30, 81
Storch, RD 273, 298
Storr, 31, 235
Stratta, E 274, 298
Straus 8
Street, R 266, 298
street robbery 93
stress 89, 118, 120, 121, 139, 180, 183, 186, 188, 209, 229, 231, 265, 281
stress management 234, 254
stress, sources of 185
stressful situations 183
Strodtbeck 9
students 281
subconscious desires 241
subculture 13
suicide 14
summaries 176, 179, 180
support 199, 209, 233, 235, 277
support group 175
support systems 149, 188
suppression of conflict 8, 18, 289
surveillance 79
survival xii
"sus" law 30
suspicion 90, 143, 147, 257, 269
Sweden 115
Switzerland 111, 112, 123
symbolic location 78
synthesis xiv

T

T-groups 280
taboo 28
tactical objectives 280
Tadesse, M 271, 295
talking-shops 218
teachers 37, 284

320

Index

talking-shops 218
teachers 37, 284
solidarity 78
teaching, prosocial 8
team approach 188
team members 98
tear gas 112
Tebbitt 32
technical aids 89, 107, 111, 113, 117, 121, 161, 162
technology 111
Tedeschi 5
teenagers 30
television 11, 32
temporary settlement 245
Tenants' Association 60, 82
tension 12, 31, 36, 54, 56, 57, 63, 64, 66, 96, 127, 129, 130, 132, 133, 143, 163, 166, 186, 244, 256, 272, 288, 289
tension indicators 134
tension, reduction of 150
tensions, heightened 170, 171
terror 5
Thatcher 32
Thatcherism 34
theft 30
thinking, positive 234
third party 18, 19, 188, 209, 244, 246, 263, 290, 291
third party consultation 279
third party crisis intervention 256
third party dispute resolvers 185
third party initiatives 191, 275
THOMAS, CS 82, 296
THOMPSON, EP 254, 298
Thornton, Peter 110
Thorpe D. 203, 208
threat of disorder 255
threat of violence 241, 246, 258
threatening gestures 120
threats 1, 6, 10, 40, 244, 249, 276, 6, 40
Tilly 5
time 186, 214, 285
timing 233
Toch 8, 9, 14
Tocqueville, Alexis de 156
tolerance 7, 42, 119, 142, 159, 188, 243, 264
toleration 37, 80, 283
Tottenham 42, 65, 80, 83, 84, 112, 113, 219, 227
Tottenham riots 32
Tottenham Task Force 80
toughness 13
Tournier 6
Townsend 35
Toxteth 65, 256
Toxteth riots 9, 32. *See also* riots
trade unionists 30
Trade Unions 126

trade-off 37
trades union demonstrators 90
trainers 142, 290
training 16, 19, 20, 37, 40, 74, 82, 87, 89, 95, 96, 128, 141, 151, 176, 192, 209, 210, 213, 218, 219, 247, 254, 256, 261, 282, 284, 286, 287, 291, 293. See also: police training
training aims 221
training college 109
training, combined 268
training courses 109
training device 174
training, formal 265
training in conflict resolution skill 285
training, occupational 285
training, participative 194
training programme 95
training school 116
training, sensitivity 280
transforming power 287
translation services 163
tribalism 27
trigger 143, 163, 171, 231, 292
trigger event 250
triggering incident 134, 143, 165, 166, 169, 241, 243, 250
trouble 5, 9, 13, 16, 55, 60, 115, 200, 214, 255
trouble-makers 54, 123, 126, 289
trouble-shooting 191
truancy 18
truncheons 112, 115
long 108
trust 5, 53, 178, 179, 212, 214, 218, 241, 243, 247, 267, 290, 292
loss of 5
tunnel vision 37
Turner 15
Turner , JC & Brown, RJ 282, 298
Twain 21
Tyrrell, J 283, 298

U

Ulster University 284
ultimatum 240
Umbreit, MS 286, 298
Umweltgespräch 125
uncertainty 118, 183, 185, 209, 210, 258, 260
Uncle Toms 253
uncooperativeness 18
under-class 79
underlying causes 143
underlying issues 172, 214, 279
underlying problems 245
understanding 77, 81, 95, 116, 119, 120, 122, 127, 159, 177, 213, 218, 220, 224, 229, 242, 245, 277, 278, 282, 283, 287, 291

unemployed 26, 33, 79
unemployment 15, 25, 26, 29, 30, 32, 34, 35, 36, 37, 62, 64, 93, 94, 192, 210, 263
United States 12, 15, 20, 21, 126, 154
 Constitution 156
 Department of Justice 167
upset 231, 244
Urban Aid 35
urban decay 29
urban renewal 35
urban unrest 79. See also: riots
urbanisation 15
Ury 17
user-friendly 84

V

values 204, 205, 207
Van der Ven, Willem 108, 124
vandalism 36, 94, 200
ventilation of feelings 88, 245
Verhaltenstraining Zur Konflict-Bewältigung 119
vicious circle 36
Victim Offender Reconciliation Program 175
Victim Support 62
victimisation 147
victims 8, 21, 259, 286
video 231
Vietnam veterans 8
violence xii, xiii, 21, 31, 33, 36, 37, 39, 55, 56, 57, 58, 59, 61, 66, 67, 73, 89, 90, 96, 101, 102, 107, 111, 130, 141, 146, 152, 154, 155, 156, 165, 193, 214, 229, 231, 235, 241, 244, 252, 253, 256, 257, 258, 259, 263, 265, 286, 288
 causes of 17
 collective 25
 definition of 3
 enjoyment of, by police 59
 family 6
 intention 4
 normality of 4
 political 15
 public 6
 response to 3
 structural 33
 symbolic 16
 theory of 1, 3
  anomie 13
  biological 6
  consensus theory 31
  cultural theories 11
  frustration hypothesis 7
  instumental 5
  interaction processes 8
  self-esteem theories 9
  social learning theory 7
  social psychological 7
  social reaction 10
  sociological 10, 11
 against women 13
 containment of 268
 controlling 244
 domestic 194
 fear of 186
 institutionalised 264
 interpersonal 193
violent behaviour 21, 287
violent confrontation 252
violent disorder 80, 90
violent offenders 194
violent offending 12
Volkshogschool in Overcinge 122
Volpe, Maria 144, 254, 255, 298
voluntary associations 149, 287
volunteers 130, 142, 192, 209, 210, 213, 282
volunteers, trained 155, 156
vulnerability 232

W

Waddington 17, 240, 253, 255
Waddington, D, Jones, K, & Critcher, C 298
Waddington, PAJ 298
Wahrhaftig, P 167, 290, 295
Walker 30
Walsh, M 165, 167
war 15
war on crime 16
Ward, David 78, 191, 195, 196, 203, 205, 208, 251, 282, 286, 290
Warfield, Wallace 143, 166, 193, 246, 251, 252, 253
Washington 173
water cannon 111, 117, 121, 128
Watson 56
Watts 26, 161
 riots 15, 26
weapons 17, 36, 57, 164, 251
Weatheritt 84
Weist, KH 144
Welsh 27
West German police training 89
West Indian 64, 78
West Indies 27. See also Afro-Caribbean
West Liberty, Iowa 163
Wheeler, E. G. 235
white 26, 35
Whitehouse 11
Whitelaw, William 96, 112
wickedness 32, 62
Williams 13
Williams, Senator 160
Wilson and Kelling 147, 151
Wilson, JQ 12, 157
win-win solution 260
window-dressing 272
winner takes all 18
winners and losers 37
withdrawal 251
witnesses 186

322

Index

Wolfgang 8, 13
women, control of 12
women participants 225
womens' peace camp 114
Woodson, RL 286, 298
Woolman LT. 195, 208
working class 13
working class communities 77
working class culture 13
workshop design 221
workshops 127, 212, 214, 220, 222, 223,
    254, 280, 283, 284, 288
workshops, consultative 282
Wounded Knee 162
Wycoff, MA 297

Y

Yeo, Nigel v
Young 9
young people 35, 63, 65, 67, 106, 195, 225,
    272, 284
youth club 196, 271
youth club campaign 202
youth, detached 264
youth gangs 9
youth group 191
youth leaders 54
youth service 200
Youth Training Schemes 35
youth work 270
youth worker 111, 196, 201
Youth Workers 82
youth/police conflict 191
youths 63, 93, 111, 135, 137, 153, 179, 195,
    196, 272

323